Demythologizing Heidegger

THE INDIANA SERIES IN THE PHILOSOPHY OF RELIGION
Merold Westphal, *general editor*

Demythologizing Heidegger

JOHN D. CAPUTO

Indiana
University
Press
BLOOMINGTON • INDIANAPOLIS

The paper used in this publication meets the minimum requirements of American
National Standard for Information Sciences—Permanence of Paper for Printed
Library Materials, ANSI Z39.48-1984.

 ™

Manufactured in the United States of America

Library of Congress Cataloging-in-Publication Data

Caputo, John D.
    Demythologizing Heidegger / John D. Caputo.
        p.   cm. — (The Indiana series in the philosophy of religion)
    Includes bibliographical references and index.
    ISBN 0-253-31306-6 (hard). — ISBN 0-253-20838-6 (paper)
    1. Heidegger, Martin, 1889–1976. 2. Ontology—Political aspects—
History—20th century. 3. Philosophy and religion—History—20th
century. 4. Justice—Biblical teaching. 5. Philosophy, Ancient.
6. Heidegger, Martin, 1889–1976—Political and social views.
I. Title. II. Series.
B3279.H49C273   1993
193–dc20   93-461

1 2 3 4 5   97 96 95 94 93

In Memoriam
John G. Tich (1922–1993)
Colleague, Mentor, Friend

CONTENTS

ACKNOWLEDGMENTS   ix

ABBREVIATIONS   xi

Introduction
Demythologizing Heidegger   1

1. *Aletheia* and the Myth of Being   9

2. Heidegger's *Kampf*
The Difficulty of Life and the Hermeneutics of Facticity   39

3. *Sorge* and *Kardia*
The Hermeneutics of Facticity and the Categories of the Heart   60

4. Heidegger's Responsibility
The Myth of Being's Call   75

5. Heidegger's Revolution
The Politics of the Myth of Being   101

6. Heidegger's Essentialism
The Logic of the Mythologic of Being   118

7. Heidegger's Scandal
Thinking and the Essence of the Victim   131

8. Heidegger's Poets   148

9. Heidegger's Gods
From Demythologizing to Remythologizing   169

10. Hyperbolic Justice
Mythologizing Differently with Derrida and Levinas   186

11. Conclusion
Heidegger and the Jewgreeks   209

NOTES   215

INDEX   232

ACKNOWLEDGMENTS

Permission to use the following previously published materials is gratefully acknowledged:

Chapter 1: "Demythologizing Heidegger: *Aletheia* and the History of Being," *The Review of Metaphysics*, 41 (March 1988): 519–46. "Modernity and the End of Philosophy in *Being and Time,*" in *Hermeneutic Phenomenology: Lectures and Essays,* ed. Joseph Kockelmans (Washington: Center for Advanced Research in Phenomenology and University Press of America, 1988), pp. 81–90.

Chapter 2: "Heidegger's *Kampf:* The Difficulty of Life," *Graduate Faculty Philosophy Journal* 14–15 (1991): 61–83.

Chapter 3: "*Sorge* and *kardia:* The Hermeneutics of Factical Life and the Categories of the Heart," in *Re-interpreting Heidegger: Essays in His Early Thought,* eds. Theodore Kisiel and John van Buren (Albany: SUNY Press, forthcoming).

Chapter 5: "Heidegger's Revolution: An Introduction to *An Introduction to Metaphysics,*" in *Heidegger: The Texts of the Thirties,* ed. James Risser (Albany: SUNY Press, forthcoming).

Chapter 6: "Incarnation and Essentialism: A Reading of Heidegger," *Philosophy Today* 35 (1991): 32–42.

Chapter 7: "Heidegger's Scandal: Thinking and the Essence of the Victim," in *The Heidegger Case: On Philosophy and Politics,* eds. Tom Rockmore and Joseph Margolis (Philadelphia: Temple University Press, 1992). ©1992 Temple University.

Chapter 8: "Thinking, Poetry and Pain," *The Southern Journal of Philosophy,* 28 (Supplement) (1990): 155–82.

Chapter 9: "Heidegger and Theology," *The Cambridge Companion to Heidegger,* ed. Charles Guignon (New York: Cambridge University Press, 1992).

Chapter 10: "Hyperbolic Justice: Deconstruction, Myth and Politics," *Research in Phenomenology* 21 (1991): 3–20. Humanities Press International, Inc., Atlantic Highlands, NJ.

I wish to acknowledge the support of the National Endowment for the Humanities, Fellowship for College Teachers, 1991–92, which made it possible for me to complete this work. I also wish to acknowledge the support of Rev. Lawrence Gallen, O.S.A., Vice-President for Academic Affairs, Villanova University, for his generous subsidy of my work during the 1991–92 year.

ABBREVIATIONS

Works by Heidegger

BP   *The Basic Problems of Phenomenology,* trans. Albert Hofstadter (Bloomington: Indiana University Press, 1982).

BT   *Being and Time,* trans. Edward Robinson & John MacQuarrie (New York: Harper & Row, 1962).

BW   *Basic Writings,* ed. David Krell (New York: Harper & Row, 1977).

DT   *Discourse on Thinking,* trans. J. Anderson and E. Hans Freund (New York: Harper & Row, 1966).

EGT   *Early Greek Thinking,* trans. D. Krell (New York: Harper & Row, 1975).

G   *Gelassenheit* (Pfullingen: Neske, 1959).

GA 1 *Gesamtausgabe,* B. 1, *Frühe Schriften* (Frankfurt: Klostermann, 1978).

2   *Gesamtausgabe,* B. 2, *Sein und Zeit* (Frankfurt: Klostermann, 1977).

5   *Gesamtausgabe,* B. 5, *Holzwege* (Frankfurt: Klostermann, 1971).

9   *Gesamtausgabe,* Vol. 9, *Wegmarken* (Frankfurt: Klostermann, 1976).

13   *Gesamtausgabe,* Vol. 13, *Aus der Erfahrung des Denkens* (Frankfurt: Klostermann, 1984).

24   *Die Grundprobleme der Phänomenologie* (Frankfurt: Klostermann, 1975).

29/30 *Gesamtausgabe,* B. 29/30, *Grundbegriffe der Metaphysik: Welt—Endlichkeit—Einsamkeit* (Frankfurt: Klostermann, 1983).

40   *Gesamtausgabe,* B. 40, *Einführung in die Metaphysik* (Frankfurt: Klostermann, 1983).

45   *Gesamtausgabe,* B. 45, *Grundfragen der Philosophie: Ausgewählte "Probleme" der "Logik"* (Frankfurt: Klostermann, 1984).

51   *Gesamtausgabe,* B. 51, *Grundbegriffe* (Frankfurt: Klostermann, 1981).

53   *Gesamtausgabe,* B. 53, *Hölderlins Hymne "Der Ister"* (Frankfurt: Klostermann, 1984).

54   *Gesamtausgabe,* B. 54, *Parmenides* (Frankfurt: Klostermann, 1982).

56/57   *Gesamtausgabe, B. 56/57, Zur Bestimmung der Philosophie* (Frankfurt: Klostermann, 1987).

61   *Gesamtausgabe, B. 61, Phänomenologische Interpretationen zu Aristoteles: Einführung in die phänomenologische Forschung* (Frankfurt: Klostermann, 1985).

63   *Gesamtausgabe, B. 63, Hermeneutik: Ontologie der Faktizität* (Frankfurt: Klostermann, 1987).

65   *Gesamtausgabe, B. 65, Beiträge zur Philosophie (Vom Ereignis)* (Frankfurt: Klostermann, 1989).

ID   *Identity and Difference*, trans. Joan Stambaugh (New York: Harper & Row, 1969); a bilingual edition.

IM   *An Introduction to Metaphysics*, trans. Ralph Mannheim (New Haven: Yale University Press, 1959).

OWL   *On The Way to Language*, trans. P. Hertz (New York: Harper & Row, 1971).

P   *Parmenides*, trans. André Schuwer and Richard Rojcewicz (Bloomington: Indiana University Press, 1992).

PLT   *Poetry, Language, Thought*, trans. A. Hofstadter (New York: Harper & Row, 1971).

PR   *The Principle of Reason*, trans. Reginald Lilly (Bloomington: Indiana University Press, 1991).

PT   *The Piety of Thinking*, trans. J. Hart and J. Maraldo (Bloomington: Indiana University Press, 1976).

QCT   *The Question Concerning Technology and Other Essays*, trans. W. Lovitt (New York: Harper & Row, 1977).

SA   "The Self-Assertion of the German University" and "The Rectorate 1933/34: Facts and Thoughts," trans. Karsten Harries, *Review of Metaphysics*, 38 (March 1985).

SD   *Zur Sache des Denkens* (Tübingen: Niemeyer, 1969).

SdDU   *Die Selbstbehauptung der deutschen Universität. Das Rektorat 1933–34* (Frankfurt: Klostermann, 1983).

SG   *Der Satz vom Grund* (Pfullingen: Neske, 1956).

Spieg.   "Only a God Can Save Us: *Der Spiegel*'s Interview with Martin Heidegger," trans. M. Alter and J. Caputo, *Philosophy Today* (Winter 1976): 278–81.

SZ   *Sein und Zeit*, 10. Aufl (Tübingen: Niemeyer, 1971).

TB   *On Time and Being*, trans. J. Stambaugh (New York: Harper & Row, 1972).

TK   *Die Technik und die Kehre* (Pfullingen: Neske, 1962).

US   *Unterwegs zur Sprache* (Pfullingen: Neske, 1965).

VA   *Vorträge und Aufsätze* (Pfullingen: Neske, 1959).

VS   *Vier Seminare,* tr. (from French) C. Ochwadt (Frankfurt: Kloster-
         mann, 1977).

Works by Derrida

DPR   "The Principle of Reason: The University in the Eyes of its Pupils,"
         trans. C. Porter and E. Morris, *Diacritics* (Fall 1983): 3–20.

EO   *The Ear of the Other,* trans. Peggy Kamuf (New York: Schocken,
         1985).

FL   "Force of Law: The 'Mystical Foundation of Authority'," trans.
         Mary Quaintance, in "Deconstruction and the Possibility of Jus-
         tice," *Cardozo Law Review,* 11 (1990): 919–1045.

Glas   *Glas,* trans. John Leavey and Richard Rand (Lincoln: University
         of Nebraska Press, 1986).

OS   *Of Spirit: Heidegger and the Question,* trans. G. Bennington and
         R. Bowlby (Chicago: University of Chicago Press, 1989).

PF   "The Politics of Friendship," trans. G. Motzkin, *The Journal of
         Philosophy,* 85 (1988): 632–44.

Demythologizing Heidegger

Introduction

DEMYTHOLOGIZING HEIDEGGER

> There will be no unique name, even if it were
> the name of Being. And we must think this
> without *nostalgia*, that is, outside of the myth of
> a purely maternal or paternal language, a lost
> native country of thought. On the contrary, we
> must *affirm* this, in the sense in which Nietzsche
> puts affirmation into play, in a certain laughter
> and a certain step of the dance.
>
> Jacques Derrida

I have been moved in recent years to make a critical confrontation with Heidegger's thought, displacing the still too unguarded appreciation of Heidegger that characterized my earliest investigations.[1] This more critical confrontation has been provoked by both internal and external considerations.

I have been troubled, on purely internal, textual, and philosophical grounds, by the exaggerated and, as I say here, "mythic" significance that Heidegger attaches to the early Greeks, by what is called throughout the present study the "mythologizing" tendencies of Heidegger's thought. By this I mean the tendency of Heidegger to construct a fantastic portrait of the Greek sources of Western thought and culture—in the most classically German manner—and to represent these Greek sources as a single, surpassing, great "Origin" *(Ursprung)*, a primordial incipience or "Beginning" *(Anfang)* of the West. On such a scheme the Greeks do not represent merely the historical start of certain Western linguistic, scientific, and social traditions, nor even merely the most important historical source of these traditions. For Heidegger's "Greeks" are nothing merely "historical" *(geschichtlich)* at all, but something destining *(geschicklich)*, something steering the very destiny *(Geschick)* of the West, which leaves merely historical research behind. These Greeks represent an overarching, normative, claiming Origin to which "we"—and who "we" are is a critical issue here—are all bound more primordially than we can say and in reference to which everything later is to be compared, either as its falling away and oblivion or as the scene of its retrieval.

Such a view, I argued both in *Radical Hermeneutics* (1987) and in a separate study entitled "Demythologizing Heidegger" (1988),[2] is insupportable, both in itself and also on Heidegger's own terms, so long as one examines critically and closely just what *aletheia* means. For if *aletheia* is what Heidegger says it is, a process of concealment and multiple epochal movements, then *aletheia* could never take the form of a historically actual epoch and no age or moment in an age, not even a supposedly "founding" moment, could enjoy the kind of surpassing privilege Heidegger attaches to the early Greeks. The privileged status of the early Greeks forms the core of a vast, overarching, and—it is now plain—highly dangerous metanarrative, a sweeping myth about Being's fabulous movements through Western history. That metanarrative of Being, I argued, needs to be deconstructed down into a more radically pluralistic, disseminative notion of "events," or of the "happening" of Being and truth,[3] of the sort one finds in post-Heideggerian thinkers like Lyotard and Derrida.

I was, however, no less moved, jolted is the better word, by the publication of the studies first by Victor Farias (1987) and then, more importantly, by Hugo Ott (1988), in which the extent of the involvement of Heidegger with National Socialism was laid bare. Farias's research I found almost self-defeating because it took the form of a patently ridiculous frame-up of Heidegger, but Ott's study was, with some exceptions, a dispassionate, relentless, devastating documentation, solidly researched and founded upon incontrovertible archival evidence, of the full extent of Heidegger's political engagements. Whatever the faults of Farias, and they are considerable, the two studies together break the spell of the official story that Heidegger had been putting out since 1945, the massive cover-up of his actual political activity, Heidegger's Watergate (or "*Seins*-gate").[4]

These revelations cast Heidegger's later writings in a new light for me and compelled me to see that the "mythologizing" tendencies in Heidegger, of which I had been complaining on purely philosophical and textual grounds, and which I had until then conceived in an entirely apolitical sense, were in fact shot through with social, political, and ethical import that I had previously simply ignored. Lacoue-Labarthe's *La fiction du politique* (1987), in which the question of myth was also raised, and even more so Lyotard's *Heidegger et "les juifs"* (1988), where in the spirit of a certain Levinasianism the question of the oblivion of the "jews" in Heidegger's thought is raised, confirmed me in that view.[5] Texts that I had been reading for a quarter of a century suddenly and painfully took on a new and ominous significance, the results of which are to be found in the studies that follow under the themes of facticity, *Kampf (polemos)*, questioning, responsibility, *Wesen*, and the victim. With the writing of "Heidegger's Scandal"[6] for the Margolis and Rockmore collection, my thinking about Heidegger had undergone a basic shift.

At the same time that my thoughts had taken a new and more critical turn vis-à-vis Heidegger, I had for some time been more and more drawn to the flourishing discourse on justice astir in the writings of the French, in particular of Derrida, Levinas, and Lyotard. I was strongly attracted to the prophetic fervor of Levinas, to his biblical call for justice, to this remarkable phenomenon of a philosopher-cum-prophet, of a distinctly prophetic voice, raised up among the postmoderns. Levinas seemed to me a kind of modern-day (or postmodern-day) Amos, albeit of a rather more Parisian sort. I was likewise deeply attracted to the political pluralism and experimentalism of Lyotard and his more deconstructed, quasi-Aristotelianized, "pagan" notion of justice as multiplicity. Above all, I was influenced by the exquisite sensitivity of Derrida to the questions of judgment, singularity, law, and justice that character-izes all his works, but in particular the writings of recent years.

I was not, however, led to conclude that these French thinkers were given to the denunciation of myth, to a merciless demythologizing or antimytholo-gizing. On the contrary, I found what I call here a tendency to mythologize *differently,* to invoke *other* myths than the myth of Being. Thus instead of pure demythologizing I found a myth of biblical justice that is otherwise than Being (Levinas); a quasi-Kantian myth of the sublimity of unrepresentable justice, an idea without a concept (Lyotard); a deconstructionist myth of an undeconstructible, hyperbolic justice (Derrida). I concluded that it is not a question of getting beyond myth or of laying aside mythologizing altogether, which is no more possible than getting beyond or laying aside metaphysics, but rather of inventing new and more salutary myths, or of recovering other and older myths, myths to counter the destructive myths of violence, domina-tion, patriarchy, and hierarchy. The question of myth, like the question of metaphysics, obeys the dynamics of marginality, of being continuously "inside/ outside" or on the "borders." The issue, then, is not divided between mytholo-gizing and demythologizing—as if these always meant the same thing—but between dangerous myths and salutary myths; between privileging, elitist, and hierarchizing myths and myths that promote justice and multiplicity; between exclusionary and oppressive myths and liberating, empowering myths.[7]

The question of "demythologizing Heidegger" then comes down to the task of disrupting the myth of Being with the myth of Justice, of disturbing the power, glory, and prestige of Being with the poverty, invisibility, and humility of justice. It is not a question of deconstructing myth down into pure reason but of opposing one kind of mythic imagination with another, of opposing Heidegger's "phainesthetic" imagination with an ethical imagination, which imagines something invisible and unassuming that yet lays claims to us.

What I call here the myth of Being can be seen clearly to emerge at a distinct and fateful moment in Heidegger's path of thought *(Denkweg).* It was not a feature of the original project launched in the first Freiburg lectures (1919–1923), which eventually issued in *Being and Time* and which were, if anything, characterized more by a certain demythologizing than by a mythologizing tendency, as Bultmann certainly realized. (Here my work joins forces with the remarkable work being done on the early Freiburg period by van Buren and Kisiel, who together are showing the way into the pre–*Being and Time* pe-riod.)[8] The first Freiburg project, entitled a "hermeneutics of facticity," took the form of a two-pronged retrieval: on the one hand, of the factical lifeworld of the New Testament communities, which lay sedimented beneath the dogmatic ontotheology of the tradition; and, on the other hand, of the factical lifeworld of Aristotelian ethics, which lay sedimented beneath the metaphysics of *ousia*. The movements and rhythms of these "prephilosophical" sources— life before the long arm of philosophical conceptuality reaches it—were to be the sources from which philosophy itself would draw a new breath. These two sources, both biblical and Greek together, were taken to be a rich preconceptual soil that would nourish the work of philosophy, whose task it was to raise them up, by way of a "formal indication," to the level of ontological concepts. Heidegger was not interested in the theology of the second coming, for example, but in the ontology of the *kairos*, i.e., in the ontological structure of kairological time. The two sources, the Aristotelian and the Christian, are treated by Heidegger as "equiprimordial," to use the language of *Being and Time,* as different but coequal resources that will bring new life to philosophy, which has for too long been attached to the ghostly abstractions of a sedimented and inherited conceptuality. Heidegger thought the hermeneutic unfolding of either the Aristotelian world or the world of the New Testament, of either *polis* or *ekklesia,* would lead to the same result and uncover the same, universal factical structures, equally rich and equally originary.

It was only in the 1930s, in the period of Heidegger's active political engagement with National Socialism, that the twofold root of the tradition was pruned to a single root, to a single, simple incipience *(Anfang),* a Great Greek Beginning, from which everything Jewish and Christian, everything Roman, Latin, and Romance, was to be excluded as fallen, derivative, distortive, and inauthentic. It was in the now infamous rectorial address that the question of Being formulated in *Being and Time* became for the first time, publicly at least, an outright myth of Being structured around the inner spiritual relationship between Greeks and Germans. It cannot be forgotten that it was in the context of the National Socialist seizure of power that Heidegger narrowed down the beginnings of the West to a single "Origin"—*Anfang* and *Ursprung*—purely Greek, without Jewish or Christian contamination, and tied the future of the West to the German future, to the German capacity for thinking and questioning Being. The first form of the myth of Being is a political myth tied to a hellish ideology, fully equipped with robust and quite bellicose Greek gods and their German heirs, in which Heidegger undertook to produce a thought of Being that was *Judenrein,* thereby reproducing on the level of thinking what the Nazis were doing in the streets.[9]

Heidegger's thought was thereafter held captive by a sweeping metanarrative, a myth of monogenesis, a monomanic preoccupation with a single deep source, with an originary, unitary beginning, which he thought must be kept pure and uncontaminated, like a pure spring. But "[m]onogenealogy," as Derrida has recently said, "would always be a mystification. . . ."[10] The question of the "ontological difference" became the thought of the single, simple, unitary, all-gathering, uniquely One-fold.[11] Great poets and great thinkers were said to think all from the same site, gathered together in and by the same thought, saying the same thing. The very transcription of Greek words into Roman script became a scandal and a defilement. The accents of Aristotle and Kierkegaard faded away, first in favor of Nietzsche and Jünger, and then in favor of the "deeper" tones of Anaximander, Parmenides, and Heraclitus. All along, the whole project was steered by a certain Hölderlin, the poet of poetry, the German poet of Greek poetry, the Greco-German poet par excellence.[12]

The question of demythologizing Heidegger is the question of how deeply this myth cuts into the fabric of his thought, and how long and how far this myth persists after the cessation of his political activism and even after the end of the war. My own view is that the task of demythologizing Heidegger is both urgent and incessant and that it cannot be dismissed as a bit of ill will toward the man Heidegger or as merely a sanctimonious attempt to pass judgment on Heidegger's personal character. The responsibility to think these matters through cannot be evaded with the disclaimer that it is not our place to judge the man or to hold court over a man's conscience. For what lies before us is a philosophical task requiring philosophical judgment, not a personal or biographical issue,[13] *eine Sache des Denkens*, as Heidegger himself would say. The positions I defend below depend upon the analysis of texts and the soundness of my views, not upon settling the affair of Heidegger's biography. This is not a book about Heidegger's Nazism, but about Heidegger's thought. This is an incessant task, because what Heidegger regards as the inner truth of the spiritual relationship of Greek and German, which in 1933 is Heidegger's attempt both to elevate Nazi mythology to the level of metaphysics and to give a deeper, spiritual mooring to the revolution, is a "truth" that Heidegger never renounced. The myth is continuously transformed and reshaped, refined and redefined, but it is never renounced. Heidegger retreats and retrenches, revises and retrieves, but he never renounces it. The task of thinking, as I argue below, seems immune to *retractio*. The myth of Being shapes the way Heidegger thinks the question of Being after he has stepped down as rector in 1934, late into the war (GA 53, 106), and long after the war ended. It is defended proudly as late as 1966 (*Spieg.*, 282). As Pöggeler has written, "Was it not through a definite orientation of his thought that Heidegger fell—and not merely accidentally—into the proximity of National Socialism without ever truly emerging from this proximity?"[14]

If the myth of Being is tied up with National Socialist mythology, then demythologizing Heidegger is likewise an operation of denazification and of putting Heidegger's thought in the service of other, more honorable ends, ends that he himself would likely have abhorred, given his own disastrous judgment in political matters. At that point the death of the author is a necessity and the notion that the name of a thinker is the name of a matter to be thought is a blessing. I myself am convinced, as I argue in what follows, that this myth cuts deeply into Heidegger's thought. Just what remains of "Heidegger—*eine Sache des Denken*"[15]—once it is flushed out, just what sort of Heidegger remains, is for each one to decide. At the very least, a demythologized Heidegger is another Heidegger, a Heidegger who thinks against Heidegger.

The most dangerous and destructive elements of Heidegger's thought are rooted in this historically false and ideologically invidious tendency, which dominated the path of thought from the 1930s on, never ceasing to cast its spell over Heidegger's thought. By abandoning the project of the first Freiburg period, by leaving behind Kierkegaard and Luther—essential impulses of the early work (GA 63, 5–6)—and by treating Aristotle as a fading echo of the primordially early Greek, Heidegger left the question of Being in a state of utter mystification about ethico-political matters,[16] about the matter of our concrete responsibilities to one another. A deep "essentialization"[17] overtook the question of Being, an essentialization that displaced the hermeneutics of facticity, producing a profound mystification of responsible ethical and political life and a scandalous neutralization of concrete human grief and suffering. The *Kehre* turned out to be a significant turnabout on the questions of facticity and *Wesen*.

My proposal throughout this study is that the myth of Being proceeds from an act of massive exclusion of everything that is not Greek, not originary Greek, not pure and primordial Greek, and that the exclusion of biblical sources in particular is a fateful, even fatal failure.[18] This exclusion takes the form of a silencing and excision of what is called below the "jewgreek" elements in the tradition, for the tradition is a miscegenated and disseminated mix, both Greek and Jewish (and many other things as well, too many to count, classify, and register by name). Indeed, as I will argue, the later and more ominous developments in Heidegger's thought in the 1930s are already anticipated when, even in the early investigations into the New Testament lifeworld, Heidegger had already silenced and excised the thematics of *kardia* in favor of an ontology of the *Kampf* of faith. That encouraged the transition to the massive voluntarism of the early 1930s, which provided the ideological support for his hellish political activities and deplorable political judgments.

In formulating my confrontation with Heidegger in terms of Heidegger's exclusion of the "jewgreek" I use the expression Derrida has borrowed from James Joyce.[19] The "jewgreek" is the miscegenated state of one who is neither purely Greek nor purely Jewish, who is too philosophical to be a pure Jew and too biblical to be pure Greek, who is attached to both philosophers and prophets. That is the status that Derrida thinks befits Levinas himself, whose project it was not to supersede philosophy but rather to shock philosophy into place by way of exposing it to something other than philosophy. Just so, demythologizing Heidegger seeks to expose the myth of Being to the shock of a jewgreek myth of justice, to oppose a jewgreek myth and a jewgreek imagination to a pure Greek myth. Demythologizing Heidegger means disrupting this Greco-German myth of Greek purity, the myth of Heidegger's aboriginal and incipient *(anfänglich)* Greeks, Heidegger's private Greeks, who fueled the flames of his private National Socialism.

Over and against the Heideggerian myth of the purity of the beginning, jewgreek thinking embraces contamination, impurity, miscegenation, and dissemination, which are the categories or anticategories, the jewgreek existentialia of the myth of justice. Over and against the myth of a great incipient beginning, jewgreek thinking embraces the derivative, the non-originary, the secondary, and the repetitive. Over and against the myth of greatness, it embraces the small, the insignificant, the marginal, the low-down and no-account *me onta* (I Cor. 1:28), the ones of whom the world takes no account.[20] Over and against the time and place of the First Beginning it puts the time immemorial of justice and the placelessness and homelessness of the outcast. Over and against the show of shining *phainesthai* it puts the invisibility of what cannot manage to emerge into presence. By "jew" I mean above all what Lyotard calls *les juifs,* so that the expression "jewgreek" results from running together Derrida and Lyotard, Levinas and James Joyce, meaning everyone who is out, outside, silenced, deprived of an idiom or a home or both, who is either forbidden to use or has learned to despise his mother tongue, everyone who is Abrahamic, driven from native land, and, over and beyond Abraham, everyone who is Ishmaelic, for Ishmael was disowned by Abraham and Sarah in the name of protecting the purity of their legitimate line.[21] Jewgreek means Auschwitz, and every other name of ignominy and suffering, all the Auschwitzes, the victims of all the Nazisms, wherever they are found, in South Africa or the South Bronx, in El Salvador or Northern Ireland or on the West Bank.

Demythologizing Heidegger means to expose the purity of Heidegger's Greeks to the tension between the Jew and the Greek, to the impossibility of getting inside or outside the Greek or the Jew, of standing purely on one side or the other, of the philosophical or the biblical, of "myth" or "philosophy."

The fateful, fatal flaw in Heidegger's thought is his sustained, systematic exclusion of this jewgreek economy in order to construct a native land and a mother tongue for Being and thought. It allowed everything that is ominous and dangerous about the question of Being to break loose with a fury and it threatens to scuttle the most important insights acquired along the *Denkweg.*

None of this should obscure the fact that the task of "demythologizing Heidegger" is in fact a twofold operation. It is not only a negative work of exposing the insinuations of the myth of Being into the question of Being, of mercilessly suspecting everything, even what appears to be innocent. It is also at the same time the positive production of another Heidegger, another reading of Heidegger, of a Heidegger *demythologized,* of a Heidegger read against Heidegger. In this way, demythologizing and deconstructing, reading carefully and re-rereading, are positive and even remythologizing operations. That is why, contrary to many of Heidegger's critics, I will also point out the possibility of another Heidegger; of a critical as opposed to a memorializing conception of historical happening (chapter 1); of "another responsibility," over and above the responsibility of Germans to be good Greeks (chapter 4); of a question of Being that makes the privilege accorded to early Greeks and Germans tremble in questionability (chapter 5).

The present work is a companion to *Against Ethics*, which takes up where *Demythologizing Heidegger* leaves off by pursuing a conception of justice under the guiding hands of Lyotard, Levinas, and Derrida, by pursuing not a pure Greek but a "jewgreek" justice. While each book stands separately, the two books are profitably read together.[22]

Aletheia *and the Myth of Being*

I begin by locating Heidegger's mythologizing gesture, the fundamental operation that produces a mythologizing effect and that makes the question of Being
a question of myth. At the same time, and by way of the same demythologizing
analysis, I hope to show that it is also possible to release Heidegger from
Heidegger, to release the critical power in his delimitation of metaphysics from
its own mystifying, mythologizing tendencies. In this way it can be shown
that Heidegger's own best insights are obscured by his penchant for heroic
tales and privileged epochs, for first dawns and other beginnings; that what
Heidegger has to say about history and Being is best understood in critical,
not heroic terms; that historical thinking should serve primarily a critical and
strategic, not a hierarchizing and memorializing purpose; that it is necessary
to delimit the *mythos,* the *grand récit,* the sweeping metanarrative, in order
to get down to what Heidegger has uncovered. In this way, too, I offer a
justification for reading Heidegger today, even after the worst has broken
loose, an answer to those critics who doubt that reading Heidegger remains
a necessity.[1]

In order to identify the mythologizing operation I start with *Being and
Time,* where the mythology, in my view, is not yet in place, and then I turn
to *Grundfragen der Philosophie* (GA 45), a text from the late 1930s, where
the mythology of Being and the myth of the early Greeks saturate everything.

Modernity and the Greeks in *Being and Time*

It is certainly true, as Heidegger's critics have pointed out, that *Being and
Time*—in retrospect at least—can be seen to harbor in its ontological categories a politically conservative distrust of modernity, of liberal institutions, of
democratic confidence in ordinary people and in deliberative decision-making
procedures, of the Enlightenment ideals of cosmopolitan universalism and
egalitarianism, and, generally speaking, of life in the bourgeois world.[2] That
is true and it will prove to have an ominous import. But there is one point
on which this distrust of modernity is not in place, and this must not be
overlooked, both as a matter of the historical record and for my present
purposes. *Being and Time* contains no eschatological and antimodernist warn-

ings about the present time as an ominous end-time *(eschaton)* into which the Greco-European world has been driven, an extremity of decline defined by the unbroken sway of technique. It is important to see that *Being and Time* does not criticize the advent of modernity as the dead-end of metaphysics and that it does not look back with wistful memorialization upon the early Greeks.

On the contrary, Heidegger champions those advances of modernity that have made it possible now, more than ever before, to catch sight of the temporal meaning of Being. Were any epoch in the "history of ontology" to be privileged in *Being and Time,* it would be modern, Kantian and Neokantian, transcendental philosophy, certainly not Greek philosophy. However much he may have been opposed to Kant's Enlightenment cosmopolitanism in ethics and politics, Heidegger is very much in the debt of Kant's transcendental philosophy of time.[3] It is also important to remember that the Greeks whom he does hold in high regard in *Being and Time,* the ones who made the great breakthroughs, are Plato and Aristotle, not the early Greeks. Furthermore, it is important to see that the thrust of the argument of *Being and Time* is actually to discourage the mythologizing move, to discourage privileging any factical-historical interpretation *(Auslegung)* of Being, and to concentrate on the formal structure of the understanding of Being *(Seinsverständnis).* If anything, conceived as it was in collaboration with Bultmann's own project of demythologization, with raising concrete historical structures up to ontological formality, *Being and Time* actually encourages the opposite, *de*mythologizing tendency, which is part of what Heidegger meant by what he called in the first Freiburg period a "formal indication."[4]

Thus it is important to see that when, in the 1930s, Heidegger undertook to write a history of the declining fortunes of Being from the splendor of the early Greeks to the dark days of subjectivistic modernity, he was going against one of the basic tendencies of *Being and Time.* Heidegger's turnabout on modernity and his privileging of a mythic age of early Greeks are central and defining features of the turn *(Kehre)* in his thought; they were not features of *Being and Time* or of the work of the 1920s or the inevitable outcome of that work.[5]

I want to show in particular that in *Being and Time* what Heidegger means by the "meaning" of Being *cannot* have historical instantiation, because it is a transcendental theory *about* the history of metaphysics, not a theory which assumes a place *within* that history. In *Being and Time* Heidegger offers a transcendental account of the conditions of possibility of the meaning of Being, that is, of how one "meaning" of Being after another comes about. He does not propose the latest or best "meaning of Being." I will confine myself in this section to *Being and Time,* and then in subsequent sections show how the same argument ought to have held—but did not—in the later Heidegger as well.

In §6 of *Being and Time* Heidegger proposes the task of "the destruction of the history of ontology." The history of ontology is to be deconstructed down to its roots by showing that, regardless of the sorts of things that are said about Being overtly, every historical ontology is covertly committed to a temporal account of Being. Dasein has grown up in a tradition to which it has fallen prey so that the "primordial sources" of that tradition have been blocked off. Thus this tradition must be destroyed "down to" (*auf*: GA 2, 30/ BT, 44) its original experiences. The destruction is to be carried out backwards, beginning with Kant, because it was Heidegger's constant view throughout the Marburg years that it is only lately, in modern times, that the clue to the "meaning" of Being gets ferreted out. The existential analytic shows that the meaning of Being is to be determined in terms of time, that the temporality *(Zeitlichkeit)* of Dasein provides the clue to the temporality *(Temporalität)* of Being. The clearest case where that clue was followed up, however imperfectly, is Kant's doctrine of the imagination. But Kant's discovery operated unquestioningly within the traditional sense of Being (as what is present) and time (as the succession of nows). The work of Kant is the best effort yet, the closest metaphysics has yet come to putting its finger on the temporal meaning of Being. But Kant was waylayed by the weight of tradition, by the traditional ways of conceiving Being and time.

I wish to point out at once that the reference to "primordial sources" does not refer to a primal epoch with a privileged experience of Being which has subsequently been covered over by a history of ever-deepening oblivion. On the contrary, it is only *recently* that we have begun to awaken to the temporal sense of Being and hence have been in a position to see what is really going on in the tradition. Heidegger wants to read the history of ontology backwards because he takes his bearings from the modern problematic, from the transcendental determination of time, which is but a heartbeat away from the determination of Being in terms of time. The "historical destruction" is meant to loosen the grip which the tradition exerts upon us and which tends to block off a discovery which is breaking through in modernity. Heidegger wants to agitate and solicit that tradition which kept Kant "from working out the phenomenon of a 'transcendental determination of time' in its own structure and function" (GA 2, 32/BT, 45). In this "going back which destroys" *(destruierendes Rückgang)* into the history of ontology, the aim is to loosen the grip of ancient ideas on modern ones. Thus the first version of "destruction" or "deconstruction," far from being *post*-modern or *anti*-modern, is formulated precisely from the standpoint of the advantages of modernity, which has reached a transcendental determination of time.

Accordingly, Heidegger promises to go back from Kant to Descartes and to show how Descartes conceives the *cogito* in the most traditional manner, indeed, in medieval terms, as *substantia* and *ens creatum* or *ens finitum*. These "fateful prejudices" are tying the hands of later generations *(die Folgezeit)* (GA 2, 33/BT, 46). Nor does Heidegger think, at this point, that medieval metaphysics distorts Greek philosophy. On the contrary, the categories of Greek thought are "tailor-made" (GA 24, 168/BP, 118) for the Christian idea of creation. The two belong together in a metaphysics of making *(Herstellen)*, of form and matter, essence and existence, in which beings are conceived as products made in accord with ideal designs, as forms put into matter or made to exist outside the divine cause *(existentia* means *sistere extra causas)*.

But it is only when we get back to the Greeks that we get to the bottom of the traditional prejudices. Here is where the trouble starts. For it is with the Greeks that the decision is made for the first time—they are the beginning of the tradition—to take Being in terms of world-time, i.e., of both world and time. The Greek decision harbors a twofold prejudice: a cosmological prejudice and a presential prejudice. And this will explain why the subsequent tradition has, until recently (the advent of the transcendental turn), both (1) privileged the world over Dasein in a way that remains blind to the disclosive work of Dasein, and (2) privileged the time of things, i.e., of the presence of what is present, the presence of the present-at-hand, *ousia*. The result of this Greek decision is to block our access to time altogether. For (1) genuine time is primordially a phenomenon of Dasein itself, and things are in time because they are temporalized by Dasein, that is, given temporal determination by Dasein's own temporalizing understanding. And (2), insofar as things are taken to be "present" we tend to lose sight of their temporal qualities altogether and to treat them as stable, motionless, and timeless. The genuine concept of time requires the absential moment of futurity and having-been, which is preeminently characteristic of the temporality of Dasein—a Dasein that is clearly inspired by Kierkegaardian *Existenz*, i.e., Christian existence, a point I will pursue in later chapters.

Thus the Greeks made a fateful decision whose effects are still with us even today, and it is only today, in modernity, that we have begun to recover from it, for Kant has turned our attention (1) back to the subject, instead of naively taking the world for granted, and (2) back to the temporality of the subject, although unhappily he determined both the subject and time in the traditional way. The work of this destroying regress is carried out only when, going back to the Greeks, it puts its finger on this decisive move and catches the Greeks at that very point where they made this fateful slip. In uncovering the prejudices at work in Greek philosophy, we can free up the work of those who come lately, *wir Spätlinge* (GA 5, 326/EGT, 17),[6] who up to now had been working in the blind about time and the subject.

For this, Heidegger says, the word *ousia* can function at least as a clue. *Ousia* means the stable presence of things that are truly and enduringly present, not merely passing away. But *ousia* functions by means of a concealed time-clue: the present. Presence *(Anwesenheit)* is a function of the present *(Gegenwart)*. The stable presence and substantiality of things *(ousia, substantia)* are functions of the presential "now," which belongs to Dasein's temporalizing. The presence of things is conceived on the basis of a concealed temporal function. The temporality of Dasein—its experience of what is now—operates behind the back of the ancient ontology.

Hence the Greeks have an ambiguous status in this going back which destroys: as the beginning of all the trouble, they are important to its solution. It is with them that the attempt to get to the bottom of the confusion stops—for they are where it starts. *The destroying regress is then an exercise in troubleshooting.* It wants to know why Kant's attempt at a "transcendental determination of time" was waylayed, and it locates the trouble first in Descartes, then in Plato and Aristotle. It is in Plato and Aristotle that we see where the move to think of Being as presence was first made, to which everybody else thereafter just consented without question. This makes Plato and Aristotle very important, but in an ambiguous way. Something very important happened in and with them: they raised the question of Being for the first time. They let Being break out in all its wonder, and they did so in terms of time. But they themselves missed the temporal clues that were functioning behind their backs. Hence they got as far as the question of Being, but not as far as the *temporal meaning* of Being—which can only be flushed out in a hermeneutical reflection that focuses on how ontological theories come to be. The Greeks illustrate quite well—for us moderns—the crucial role that temporal clues play in the conception of Being, even though such clues remain implicit and in fact unknown to them. The Greeks operated within a temporal conception of Being but, because they failed to see the clues they were using, they defended a view of Being as timeless presence:

> Yet the Greeks managed to interpret Being in this way [in terms of time] without any explicit knowledge of the clues which function here, without any acquaintance with the fundamental ontological function of time or even any understanding of it, and without any insight into the reason why this function is possible. On the contrary, they take time itself as one entity among other entities, and try to grasp it in the structure of its Being, though that way of understanding Being which they have taken as their horizon is one which is itself naively and inexplicitly oriented towards time. (GA 2, 35/BT, 48)

The ambiguity of the Greeks is to determine Being and time in a way that is positively fateful for the rest of us. If we go back to them we can find out not only how the whole tradition managed to get off the ground in the first place but also what went wrong with the tradition subsequently, for what went wrong with the tradition went wrong first with the Greeks. Their importance lies in being both the source of the tradition and the source of the trouble—and it is for that reason that they are so instructive about the meaning of Being. They wrestled with the things themselves in a struggle among the giants (*gigantomachia peri tes ousias*, GA 2, 3/BT, 21)—the giants in question being Plato and Aristotle—which brought "Being" out of misty obscurity and into the light of thematic clarity, and they even thought Being in terms of time, *but* they did not appreciate the temporal clues they were using. The determination of Being in terms of time came about *in* them, but behind their backs, unwittingly, so that what they explicitly said suppressed the implicit time-clues they deployed. While they thematized Being, they did not thematize the temporal clues *in terms of which (woraufhin)* they thematized Being. They got to Being, but not to the *meaning* of Being.

Accordingly, it is only we modern ones, we latecomers, who can see what is going on in the history of ontology, which is why our destruction goes backwards, starting from the standpoint of Kant's discovery of the temporality of the subject, looking back into what blocked Kant's success. We read from the privilege of modernity's insight into the temporality of the subject, which is but one step removed from an insight into Being's "meaning."

But it is clear from the argument of *Being and Time* that there can be no moment *in* the history of ontology where what Heidegger means by the "meaning" of Being could ever have historical instantiation, other than at a certain point in time when a philosopher like Heidegger would reach a transcendental appreciation of how time functions. Plato and Aristotle produced an interpretation of Being *(Seinsauslegung)* that was not alert to the temporal clues *(fungierende Leitfaden)* that were functioning in it. They did not see that time performs a fundamental-ontological function, and that time is not just a being, or sphere of beings (temporal being vs. eternal being). It is all this talk of temporal "clues" "implicitly functioning" in "explicit" notions of Being which is important for my thesis. For such talk implies a movement of transcendental "delimitation" that gets beyond this or that idea of Being to the functioning ingredients in the idea, to the structural item or items which produce the particular historical sense of Being.

In other words, when Heidegger talks about the "meaning of Being" in *Being and Time* he intends this in a "functional" sense, not in a historical sense, and he certainly is not implying that the Greeks had it right and that it has been all decline and oblivion ever since. It is not his purpose to find the one true theory of Being that has been brought forth in the history of Being—whether among the Greeks or anywhere else—or to add it himself if it is missing. Rather, his aim is to put his finger on what is at work in *any* given theory of Being. He wants to show how ideas of Being are *constructed*—he wants to isolate their structural makeup—but not to come up with another idea of Being himself—and to deconstruct those that conceal their temporal clues. He does not want to get into the competition about Being, a competition which constitutes the history of ontology, but to deconstruct that history just to show how it was put together in the first place. One has to dismantle the sedimented, historically accumulated notions of Being, which now take on an air of authority and self-evidence, just to see where they were taking their clues—which Heidegger locates in time functions.

This means that Heidegger has a transcendental conception of "meaning" (as a condition of possibility), not the ordinary one, where meaning is something constituted and historically actual, as a close reading of *Being and Time* shows. For when Heidegger discusses "meaning" he does so in terms of a distinction between the "Being" of a thing and its "meaning." This is a distinction between what he calls the "primary projection" of a thing in its Being, and that "upon which" *(Woraufhin)* the projection is carried out, which is the hidden "function" which *organizes* the Being-structure *(Seinsverfassung)*. He writes:

> What does *"meaning"* signify? . . . meaning is that wherein the understandability [*Verstehbarkeit*] of something maintains itself [*hält sich*]—even that of something which does not come into view explicitly and thematically. "Meaning" signifies the "upon which" [*Woraufhin*] of a primary projection in terms of which something can be conceived in its possibility as that which it is. . . .
>
> To lay bare the "upon which" of a projection, amounts to disclosing that which makes possible what has been projected. . . .
>
> Taken strictly, "meaning" signifies the "upon which" of the primary projection of the understanding of Being. . . . All ontical experience of entities . . . is based upon projections of the Being of the corresponding entities—projections which in every case are more or less transparent. But in these projections there lies hidden the "upon which" of the projection, and on this, as it were, the understanding of Being nourishes itself [*nährt sich*]. (GA 2, 323–24/BT, 370–71)

Heidegger thus distinguishes the more or less overt projections of Being— entities are projected here, in science, in terms of *Vorhandensein*, and there, in everydayness, in terms of *Zuhandensein*—from the hidden, transcendental function that is at work in these projections, "sustaining" and "nourishing," that is, organizing them and making them possible. This hidden function is the *Woraufhin*, the implicit (transcendental) clue which explicit accounts of Being are always following without paying it any heed.

But such a theory of meaning puts a distance between *Being and Time* and any theory of Being that actually makes an appearance in the history of ontology, any particular historical account of Being (any "transcendent" as opposed to "transcendental" sense of Being). It puts Heidegger in the position of standing back from the fray in order to isolate the functional element that organizes, sustains, and nourishes any such projection of Being as does get put forward in the course of that history. The "history of ontology" discussed in *Being and Time* operates on the primary level—of the primary projections of Being. But *Being and Time* itself, as a treatise, operates on the fundamental-ontological level of the destruction of these projections; it aims at putting its finger on the implicit clues that are being followed in the history of ontology. That is, *Being and Time* operates on a transcendental or structural level, ferreting out the hidden functions in the actual historically constituted formations.

Perhaps one reason why Divison III, First Half ("Time and Being") was never written was that it has no work to do apart from the history of ontology—apart from feeling around for the temporal clues at work in the historical projections of Being which actually have been put forth from Plato to the present. *Being and Time* has no business getting *into,* or privileging some moment within, the history of ontology. It is rather a theory *of* the history of ontology. To find the "meaning" of Being is to locate the transcendental function that is performed, or the clue that is followed, every time some projection of Being appears on the scene (is constituted). The business of finding a "meaning" is an entirely functional one. This meaning never has and never can assume historical form in some theory of Being. The quest for the meaning of Being is a deconstructive one which dismantles historical theories in order to find out what makes them work. So the answer to Brentano's question about the manifold sense of Being[7] is that *there are only the manifold senses of Being*—unless you want to add to this the hermeneutic account of the functions by which they are constructed. But that is not one of the historical senses that Being has been given in the history of ontology.

The same point can be made about the later writings, as I will argue below. To think Being as *Ereignis* is to think that which grants the history of Being, that which sends the various epochal shapes and destinies of Being as presence. It is not to assimilate *Ereignis* into Being, or into the history of Being, or to make it the latest and best word about Being (SD, 22-23/TB, 21–22). The thought of the epochal dispensations cannot take on epochal form itself, cannot be clad in historical costume or have a historical form of life. Despite an intractable tendency to tell a story about the history of Being, what Heidegger has in fact accomplished is to "delimit" that history, to think its structural limits. Thus the real power of Heidegger's thought can be unfolded only when its mythological, storytelling tendencies are delimited.

What Heidegger has discovered is not a story that began in the early Greeks and culminated in modernity, but an essential delimitation of metaphysical thinking, which is *always* in place and which does not allow the privileging of any epoch, whether at the beginning (the later Heidegger) or the end (the tendency of *Being and Time*). The end of philosophy is, in the spirit of Kantian *krinein,* the pointing out of ends or limits, the delimitation of metaphysical thinking, and that plays no historical favorites. What Heidegger—at his best— thinks is the formal structure of the meaning of Being *(Being and Time)* or the sheer unfolding of *a-letheia,* the happening of the epochs as constrictions of the open expanse (the later Heidegger). But the "meaning" of Being, or that which "grants" *(gibt)* Being *(Ereignis),* can never take the form of an epochal structure *in* that history.

A Tale of Two Beginnings

Ten years later everything had changed. By the time Heidegger gave his 1937–38 lecture course *Grundfrage der Philosophie* (GA 45), the myth of Being was firmly in place. What had transpired in the intervening decade I will examine more closely below. For my present purposes I want only to identify the character of the transformation.

In *Being and Time* we were promised a story of the "destruction of the history of ontology." Beginning at the end, with Kant, it was to feel its way back through the tradition in a deconstructive gesture, looking for what had all along been blocking the discovery of the temporal meaning of Being, which had at last begun to emerge in Kant. By 1937 this story had been considerably recast. Modernity is not conceived as a breakthrough but as an *eschaton,* a dead end into which the West has run, and the task of thought is to make its way back into the primordial "Beginning" *(Anfang)* in order to recapture that fleeting moment which will make it possible for us today to begin anew, to make the present into an "authentic" end, which means a transition to another beginning (GA 45, 134). In the later writings the privilege that was accorded modernity in *Being and Time* is surrendered and the transcendental determination of time defended there is rejected. The very thing for which Kant was praised—"he was bringing the phenomenon of time back into the subject again" (GA 2, 32 24/BT 45)—becomes the reason he is criticized. The whole of modernity is looked upon not as a period of breakthrough and discovery of the contribution of the subject (and hence of Dasein), but as a subjectivizing of Being. Modernity is the age of the *Weltbild,* of the world as picture and representation, as an object for the thinking subject which sets itself up as the measure of all that is and is not (QCT, 115ff.) Heidegger's understanding of the history of ontology thus undergoes a profound upheaval. The end of the history of ontology is now the most extreme and radical oblivion of all, the *eschaton* (GA 5, 327/EGT, 17; cf. SD, 63/TB, 57), where the Western tradition has run into a deadly end, an end-state that threatens to destroy man, nature, and the gods, even if the bomb never goes off. Now the history of ontology, or of metaphysics, is read as a steady deteriorization or falling away *(Abfall)* from the primordial beginning *(Anfang)* (GA 45, 145).

Accordingly, the "destruction" of the history of ontology, which in *Being and Time* meant an exercise in troubleshooting, looking for what went wrong somewhere back in the tradition in order to repeat and redo it *(wieder-holen),* is reconceived as a work of recollective thought *(an-denken),* which tries to recover something that has dropped out of sight. Plato and Aristotle are still the source of the trouble, but that is because in them a primordial experience of Being was covered over. Hence Plato and Aristotle are not to be read backwards, from the standpoint of modernity, but forwards, as a falling away from the early Greeks, who now assume the place of historical privilege. Plato and Aristotle block off not what was to be discovered *later,* but what had been experienced in the primordial beginning which had *preceded* them.

Thus the word *Wiederholung,* which belongs originally to *Being and Time* (actually it belongs to Kierkegaard), where it meant troubleshooting, rooting out a critical error made at the beginning (Plato and Aristotle), is now transformed into *Andenken,* memorial thinking, i.e., thinking back into the originary event of the Western tradition (prior to Plato and Aristotle) and repeating the First Beginning. *Andenken* makes it possible to begin anew, with the same orginariness that characterized the First Beginning, and hence to effect "an other beginning."

Heidegger's 1937–38 lectures on the early Greek experience of Being and *aletheia* (GA 45) provide a more detailed picture of what Heidegger means by the two beginnings, what sort of privilege the early Greeks enjoyed, and what limitations, if any, they experienced. Heidegger is here telling the story of the history of truth. Truth means the truth of assertions when the assertion conforms to the state of affairs about which it speaks; truth is correctness *(Richtigkeit, adequatio, homoiosis).* This conception, which goes all the way back to the beginning of philosophy in Plato and Aristotle, is treated today as self-evident and self-grounding. No attempt is or can be made to verify it—we could hardly check every true assertion against it—but it is taken as a kind of eidetic insight into what truth must be (GA 45, §§20–24). Yet, Heidegger argues, *before* an assertion can be made about an entity the entity itself must be manifest, out in the open. Hence the correctness of assertions presupposes the openness of entities. The self-grounding definition of truth has a concealed ground in the openness of beings. How did this concealed ground get concealed? How did it drop out of view?

The trouble, as we have said, started with Plato and Aristotle. For when they formulated this "definition" of truth, they set off its limits, cut truth down to size for philosophy's purposes, and introduced a formula that could be handed down in a decontextualized form across the centuries. Their recourse to conceptualizing thinking cut this formulation off from its living context, from the Greek experience of Being as the open and manifest realm in which things appear and are manifest. If we look "back" at Plato and Aristotle they appear to be the first ones to have introduced a clear definition of truth as correctness, and everything before them looks fuzzy. But looked at in terms of their own predecessors, they can be seen as producing a "formulation" that presupposes a shared experience of the openness of beings. Hence, when Plato and Aristotle said *aletheia* is correctness, we today only hear the half of it. We hear the constriction of *aletheia* to correctness. We do not hear what the Greeks heard in a fully Greek way: that the correctness of assertions arises from and presupposes the manifestness and openness of entities themselves. The Greek view all along presupposes that truth is *homoiosis because* it is first and foremost openness. But only the shorthand, stenographic version was handed down, not the full experience (GA 45, §26).

Thus the "precision" which Plato and Aristotle lent was in fact a dangerous incision into the essence of truth, incising it precisely at its point of origin—in the Greek experience of *aletheia* as unconcealedness, in accordance with its etymology. Plato and Aristotle are transitional thinkers, effecting a transition from the rich, poetic, experiential thought of their predecessors to the leaner conceptualizations of philosophy. Hence we must read them in the light of their antecedents, of the early Greeks. The history of truth in the Greeks must be seen to stretch from Anaximander to Aristotle.

This is not to say, however, that the early Greeks themselves had formulated a notion of truth as unconcealment. That was not their task, their appointed destiny, their need *(Not)*. Their greatness lay in raising the question of the being *(das Seiende)* itself. Their vocation was to stay with the thought of the being itself, to persist with that thought, until they found the means to differentiate what is from what is not, as the present and enduring, the well-formed and delimited, which shows itself from itself *(physis)*. The being for them is what rises into well-formed and enduring appearance (GA 45, §§30–33). Their thinking arises from the sheer wonder *(thaumazein)* that the being emerges into appearance and perdures there (GA 45, §§36–39).

Now all of this takes place within the horizon *(Umkreis, Gesichtskreis:* GA 45, 147) of the open space of unconcealment. But it is the being itself, not its unconcealment, which is thematized. *Aletheia* as the realm of unconcealment is the concealed clue, the implicit horizon, the unconceived realm, *within which* the Greek experience of Being unfolds. It was not for them to raise the question of *aletheia* as such, but rather of *to on* "in" its *aletheia (on/aletheia)*. To have done otherwise would have skewed their destiny, subverted their task. Their vocation was to be the place where thinking, Being, and history itself are set into motion because there irrupts in them the question of the being in all its wonder. In the First Beginning *(Anfang)*, Being is the most question-worthy of all *(Fragwürdigste)*, even as today it has been flattened out into a self-evidence and taken without question *(Fraglosig)*. And while *aletheia* was the invisible element within which the early Greeks thought, palpably present on every page of their writings, it could never be spoken *as such* (GA 45, 147).

It belongs instead to us "latecomers" who live in the wake of the First Beginning, at the ending and unraveling of this Great Beginning, to make the end-state a transition to a new beginning. And the only way to do this is to do again what they did, to think again what they thought. We must recapture the wonder of the Beginning by experiencing again the wonder that the being is in its unconcealment. And for *us*—though not for them—that means to go back and see what was at work in their experience, to see the implicit clue which functioned in and enlivened the Beginning, which is the unspoken element of *aletheia*. *We* can think *aletheia* as such in a way that *they* could not.

Now the pieces of Heidegger's story are beginning to fall into place. Like every grand tale, it has a beginning, a middle, and an end—which, if it can become a genuine end, will effect a transition to another beginning. The early Greeks thought the being in its beingness as presence *(Anwesenheit)* within the element of *aletheia (on/aletheia)*. Plato and Aristotle tried to "sharpen" this with a "definition" of the link between thinking and the being which left the element of *aletheia* as unconcealment in the background. After that, oblivion set in with a fury and *aletheia* got Romanized and christened as *veritas*, and then modernized as *certitudo* and *Richtigkeit*. *We* today stand at the end of this long devolution and *so accordingly* we must go back prior to Plato and Aristotle and find out just what was happening in the early Greek experience which gave it its richness and fire, which made it the "hearth fire" (GA 45, 146) of the early Greek experience. That, we discover, is the implicit element of *aletheia*, within which they were thinking. For the early Greeks had the persistence to stay with the being as it rises into unconcealment and to *resist* the explanatory mode of thinking *(Erklären)* introduced by Plato and Aristotle that tries to dominate the being (GA 45, §38). Instead, they let the being be, in its presence, as it stands forth, unconcealed. And that is what we today must learn to do again, at the end of this tradition, at this dangerous moment of decision. So this is not a romantic story with a happy ending but a modern one that leaves us hanging in suspense.

But how is it possible for us to begin again if we are so driven by the technological will to manipulate and dominate beings, if the experience of beings in their simple unconcealment is so far removed from us, at an extreme remove *(eschaton)?* Just by realizing that *our* removal from Being is in fact *Being's* removal from us, its withdrawal from us, its forsaking of us *(Seinsverlassenheit)*. This extreme falling out from the early experience, this lack of a *need* to think about Being—because of all the ease, efficiency, and power that come from dominating beings—arises not from us but from Being. It is Being's own withdrawal that bears the best witness to Being today, in the age when Being has become nothing at all. It is a turning away *(Wendung)* on Being's part that constitutes the neediness *(Not-wendigkeit, Dürftigkeit)* by which we are beset today. If we today feel no need *(Not)* to ask the question of Being, that feeling is just the way we are tuned to Being. If the early Greeks were tuned to Being in wonder, the wonder is for us that we do not wonder. This experience that Being seems to have forsaken us *(Seinsverlassenheit)*, that we are left forsaken, is Being's own doing and *our way to Being*.[8] In the First Beginning the task was to raise the question of Being; at the end, the task is to make questionable what at the end of this long tradition has been flattened out into a triviality, a self-evidence, a tautology. Thinking in the technical age means to see in the technical epoch the epochal withdrawal of Being, the *Gestell* (GA 45, §40).

Were the early Greeks to have raised the question of *aletheia* they would have been deflected from their historical destiny. Their work was to think the being *in* its unconcealment *(on/aletheia)*, not *aletheia* as such (*aletheia* as *aletheia*). Inasmuch as *aletheia* provides the space of play within which early Greek thinking unfolds, to put that question as such would be to shatter that space and to disrupt that historical form of life (GA 45, 137–38). *Aletheia* functions like a hidden clue, not a manifest theme. *Aletheia* is what it is when it is not to be found, when it constitutes the silence of the opening whose sole function is letting-be. But that means that, as the horizon, "*aletheia must* in a certain way be overlooked" (GA 45, 147). *Aletheia* itself cannot appear; it can only be pointed out subsequently as the element within which a given historical form of life unfolds.

Why "A-letheia" is not a Greek Word

The necessary, structural withdrawal of *aletheia* as such explains why Heidegger would later be able to speak of the need to think "over and beyond" the early Greeks, to think *aletheia* in a way that is "no longer" Greek (cf. VS, 104). To think over and beyond the Greeks means to think *aletheia* as such, a structure that cannot occur *in* history, as a historical event, and not merely to think the being *in* its *aletheia,* which is what defines the event of early Greek experience. That is the point in Heidegger where there is a delimitation of the early Greeks, and it forms the precise point of entry for a deconstructive rereading of Heidegger. It is also just at this point that we can see the mythologizing operation take hold. For instead of seeing in *a-letheia* the essential delimitation of any historical manifestation of Being, Heidegger engages in a hypervalorization of *aletheia* as a Greek experience, an experience in which the German and the Greek are tied together in a fateful Being-historical way.

It is thus of the utmost importance to see the distinction Heidegger is making between the being in its *aletheia (on/aletheia)* and *aletheia* as such, for it holds the key to what I call here the Heideggerian mythology even as it tells us how to go about demythologizing Heidegger.

The special virtue of the early Greeks is that they did not "objectify" the being, i.e., turn it into an object for a subject, but rather they let it be what it is, as a self-showing rising into unconcealment *(on/aletheia):*

> The Greeks were the first to experience and think of *phainomena* as phenomena. But in that experience it is thoroughly alien to the Greeks to press present being into an opposing objectness; *phainesthai* means to them that a being assumes its radiance, and in that radiance it appears. Thus appearance is still the basic trait of the presence of all present beings, as they rise into unconcealment. (US, 132/ OWL, 38)

The Greeks experienced the phenomenality of the being, its radiant self-showing. But they left something out. For the experience of the phenomenality of the being presupposes the openness of the open, the open realm of the clearing of Being itself (which is what is meant by *aletheia* as such). Heidegger thus distinguishes two different steps in this regression: (1) from the correctness of assertions *(orthotes, rectitudo)* to the manifestness of the being (phenomenality; *on/aletheia*); (2) from the manifestness of the being to the openness of Being, to Being as the open, as *Seyn*, as *Lichtung, Ereignis* (*aletheia* as such).

Now the whole story—the great sweeping narrative—begins to take shape. For Plato and Aristotle, the definition of truth as the correctness of assertions is made with the openness of beings in the background (and fast dropping out of sight). In the early Greeks, on the other hand, the dominant tendency to define truth is resisted and the openness of beings (their phenomenality) is savored for what it is. But all of this remains within the *first* step, within the experience of the phenomenality of the being, of the being in its phenomenal unconcealment *(on/aletheia)*. Thus nowhere in Greece, in the history of truth from Anaximander to Aristotle, is the second step taken, to *aletheia* as such, as the open clearing. The open remains an implicit, unconceived, unformulated horizon. The Greeks got to phenomenality but they never named the clearing itself:

> This unconcealedness comes about in the unconcealment as a clearing; but this clearing itself, as *Ereignis*, remains unthought in every respect. To enter into thinking this unthought [*Ereignis*] means: to pursue more originally what the Greeks have thought, to see it in the source of its reality. To see it so is in its own way Greek, and yet in respect of what it sees is no longer, is never again, Greek. (US, 134–35/OWL, 39)

The experience of *aletheia* is thus both Greek and not Greek, and this two-sidedness is of decisive importance to the present study. For it presents Heidegger with the opportunity, at a critical juncture in his thought, not to enclose *aletheia within* a historical period. The opening of the open is both Greek and not Greek, that is, is "somehow" displayed within the historical limits of a definite era and yet is unable to be found or confined there.

There are accordingly two distinguishable senses of the word *aletheia* at work in Heidegger's story. In the first, let us call it the phenomenal sense, *aletheia* means the phenomenality of the being, its self-showing (what is present in its unconcealment, *on/aletheia*), prior to its reduction to an object of an assertion or, later on, to an object for a thinking subject. That is, according to Heidegger at least, a historical, Greek experience. In the second sense, let us call it here its more radical, structural, antehistorical sense, *aletheia* means the opening up of the realm of the unconcealed, the very granting of the presence of the present. It is useful, as a graphematic device, to introduce here the hyphenated form, *a-letheia*, to signify this sense of the word, for one wants to stress the emergence of the field of presence itself from a radical, intractable concealment.

In the first sense, *aletheia* means the unconcealment which adheres to the presence of what is present, the self-showing being, *phainesthai*. In the second sense, which is withheld from the Greeks, *a-letheia* means that granting which bestows presence in its phenomenality, that opening which, always out of sight, is that *within which* every epoch of presence takes place. In this sense, *a-letheia* means that a-lethic process which grants the epochs of presence. *A-letheia* means *aletheia*-as-such, the unthought element within which early Greek thought took place. In the first sense, *aletheia* means the epoch of presence as phenomenality. In the second sense, *a-letheia* means the granting of the epochs of presence, including the Greek epoch, even the early Greek epoch. More simply still, in the first case it means presence; in the second, that which grants presence.

To put it somewhat pointedly, we might say that in the first sense *aletheia* is a Greek word that describes the Greek epoch of presence as unconcealment (=phenomenality). But in the second sense, the hyphenated sense, it is no longer a Greek word and cannot be enclosed within Greek experience, for it is no longer a quality *of* their experience, no longer a feature *of* the Greek experience of presence, but rather that which grants (gives, bestows, lets be, opens up)[9] the Greek experience of presence as unconcealment/phenomenality. In short, *a-letheia* is no longer a Greek word. The hyphen breaks up its nominal unity, prevents it from belonging to a particular, epochal, historical language (just as does crossing out of *Sein,* or the attempt to respell *Sein* as *Seyn.*) Like Derrida's graphematic innovation, *différance, a-letheia* is not a historical word or concept but that which makes historical words and concepts possible.[10]

This distinction between the two senses of *aletheia* puts us in a position to understand the controversy about the etymology of *aletheia* and Heidegger's supposed retraction of his interpretation of Plato.[11] In the 1930s Heidegger developed the view that prior to Plato *aletheia* meant unconcealedness, whereas in Plato himself a transition begins in which *aletheia* as unconcealment comes to mean *orthotes* or correctness. But in 1969 Heidegger concedes that the use of *aletheia* in the sense of the correctness of statements can be found as far back as Homer:

> In the scope of this question, we must acknowledge the fact that *aletheia,* unconcealment in the sense of the opening of presence, was originally only experienced as *orthotes,* as the correctness of representations and statements. But then the assertion [in *Plato's Doctrine of Truth,* 1943] about the essential transformation of truth, that is, from unconcealment to correctness, is also untenable. (SD, 78/TB, 70)

To get this straight we have to distinguish three different issues. First, there is the etymological issue, as to whether *aletheia* contains an alpha-privative. That is a purely philological *(historisch)* issue, and on this point Heidegger is probably right, and he has nothing to retract here, although that debate is still going on. In any case, what Heidegger is after would not be affected one

way or the other by the outcome of the etymological debate. Second, there is
the question of linguistic usage (another issue for the science of philology),
that is, the question of how, regardless of its etymology, the word was actually
used. This is the level on which Heidegger's retraction is offered. He no longer
thinks that one should single out Plato as bearing the responsibility for using
the word *aletheia* in the sense of correctness. But this is so, not because Plato
did indeed take truth as unconcealment, but because Heidegger now thinks
that *no one* uses *aletheia* as unconcealment, whether in poetic, philosophical,
or everyday usage. That is, truth always is used in the sense of correctness,
before and after Plato.

Finally, there is the level of the matter for thought itself, which has nothing
to do with scientific philology. On this level, which is the only one Heidegger
is concerned with, Heidegger does not retract anything. He does not budge
an inch: as a matter for thought, truth as *orthotes, homoiosis,* derives from
aletheia, unconcealment. And so what he said in the 1930s remains in place—
but with one major exception. He no longer thinks it possible to translate
aletheia with "truth" (*"Wahrheit"*), for truth *always* means some form of correctness:

> Insofar as truth is understood in the traditional "natural" sense . . . *aletheia,*
> unconcealment in the sense of the opening, may not be equated with truth. Rather
> *aletheia,* unconcealment thought as the opening, first grants the possibility of
> truth. For truth itself, just as Being and thinking, can only be what it is in the
> element of the opening. (SD, 76/TB, 69)

> The natural concept of truth does not mean unconcealment, not in the philoso-
> phy of the Greeks either. (SD, 77/TB, 70)

As a "natural concept," as a word spoken in a historical language, a-*letheia*
(the open) is nowhere to be found. The most we can come up with is *aletheia*
as phenomenality, but even this is to be found only as background sense that
starts dropping out with Plato and Aristotle and that means correctness both
in ordinary usage and whenever it is thematized. If you *ask* the Greeks what
aletheia means they will always say correctness, but they will have unconcealment and phenomenality in the background. But what neither the Greeks nor
anyone else will say, what is nowhere to be found, in any natural language,
among any historical people, is a-*letheia,* the opening of presence:

> Instead we must say: *Aletheia,* as the opening of presence and presencing in
> thinking and saying, originally comes under the perspective of *homoiosis* and *and*
> *adequatio.* . . . (SD, 78/TB, 71)

"Truth" always means the relation of presence and thought which constitutes and defines a particular historical age, an epoch of presence, but a-*letheia*

names the a-lethic process which grants presence (Being) and truth. It is the opening itself, in which all Being (as presence) and all truth (as phenomenality, *veritas, certitudo, Richtigkeit*) are given and granted. *A-letheia* means the *Es gibt,* the very granting of the historical epochs. The history of the West is the story of the manifold determinations of Being and of truth, of so many accounts of the presence of what is present and of its presence to thought. That historical happening, which is the matter for thought, cannot be contained in, or show up in, some historical epoch because it itself is what contains a historical epoch. It gives the space *(Raum)* within which the plurality of entities belonging to that epoch play themselves out *(Spielraum).*

The disruptive hyphen names the open-ing of the open. The hyphen breaks up the nominal and natural unity of the word and prevents it from taking up residence within any natural, historical language. Like Derrida's *différance, a-letheia* is neither name nor concept and possesses no nominal unity. "The natural conception of truth does not mean unconcealment, not in the philosophy of the Greeks either" (SD, 77/TB, 70). "Natural" *(natürlich)* means historical—as when we speak in English of natural languages, by which we mean languages which exist in historical fact. And it means "natural" in the sense of Husserl's natural attitude, the level we inhabit prior to reflective thematization. Thus Heidegger is saying that no historical language thinks and says *a-letheia* as such. What any given historical language calls truth is something less than *a-letheia*—which grants presence and truth.

Thus it is necessary, structurally necessary, that the early Greeks failed to hear their own word *aletheia.* That follows from the very makeup of *a-letheia* itself. This failure does not arise from carelessness on their part but from the withdrawal of what grants from whatever is granted, even if what is granted is unconcealment as *phainesthai.* The failure arises because *lethe* belongs to the heart of *a-letheia* (SD, 78/TB, 71). *Lethe* means not only concealment but self-sheltering. The opening that grants the shining presence of what is present is itself concealed and sheltered. The matter for thought is not the shining presence of the present but the opening that grants the history of Being and truth, from the early Greek experience of Being, to the experience of Plato and Aristotle, and so on all the way up to the current epoch of the end-state, the deadly and decisive end, the *eschaton.*

The ambiguous privilege of the early Greeks is then nicely encapsulated by Heidegger when he says that we cannot get to the matter for thought unless

> we experience *aletheia* in a Greek manner as unconcealment and then, *above and beyond the Greek,* think it as the opening of self-concealing. (SD, 79/TB, 71) [emphasis mine]

Notice the two separate steps: (1) first, the Greek experience of *aletheia,* the return to the ancient beginnings and the Greek experience of *aletheia* as *phainesthai,* the shining gleam of appearances; (2) then, the movement beyond that historical, epochal determination of Being, that historical experience of Being and truth, that historical language called Greek, to *a-letheia,* the opening of the open, within which every historical epoch occurs and by which it is granted.

Now we can identify the historical "privilege" of the early Greeks: they are the privileged historical portal through which thinking passes in order to get to what is antehistorical, the very *Wesen* or coming to presence of history, which cannot be itself historical. How so? Because *a-letheia* as the open leaves its traces behind in the Greek experience of *aletheia* as *phainesthai.* The Greek *aletheia* is a trace of the originary, more than Greek *a-letheia.* But how is that possible? How can that *Wesen* of history, the process of letting history be, which can never be itself something historical, leave its tracks behind in some particular historical epoch? How can Heidegger make this claim stick, given the gulf between the historical experience of the phenomenality of Being in the Greeks (*aletheia* in the first sense) and the antehistoricality of *a-letheia* as the opening? How can any epoch of presence be more marked by the opening, bear more of a trace of the opening, than any other? How can anything made possible *by* the opening serve as a privileged clue *to* the opening?

Heidegger's answer comes in terms of a kind of phenomenology of horizonality. The history of the West is the history of successive epochs of Being and presence, and *a-letheia* is the element within which that history unfolds, the open space in which a clearing is made for the various epochs of presence— from Anaximander to the present. But *a-letheia,* in virtue of its very structure as *a-letheia,* remains out of sight, and is in a certain way always overlooked— even as it is implicitly at work, functioning. But the advantage the early Greeks had, according to Heidegger, is that this implicit clue was still functioning for them, that it was still a palpable, felt horizon, that everyone felt the power of its granting rather than just taking it for granted. That means that it must show up somehow, somehow leave a trace of itself, that aletheia *does* appear somewhere *inside* the very history which it is otherwise supposed to *grant,* viz. as something implicitly, prethematically experienced, but not thought as such. After all, it is one of the fundamental achievements of phenomenology to have shown how the unthematic, horizonal, functional clues at work in experience are not "given" or perceived, but co-given or ap-perceived along with what is thematic. There is no paradox in principle in saying that the early Greeks had a prethematic experience of *a-letheia* and that this implicit border became progressively obscured by the subsequent history of metaphysics, which was more taken by what the Greeks made thematic, the Being of beings, than with its implicit horizonal clues.

Now the story that Heidegger tells in his "history of Being" is beginning to look a lot like Husserl's story in "The Origin of Geometry," which both were telling just about the same time (1930s). Both stories turn on the notion of an originary experience that got impoverished in a proposition, cut off from its enlivening historical world, and then passed on in its dehydrated form to subsequent generations who lost its nourishing sense, and that produced the present crisis. Both stories invoke a notion of reactivation, or of "beginning again," doing again for ourselves and in our own way what was done in its own way at the time of the Creative Beginning *(Anfang)* or Primal Institution *(Urstiftung)*.

But the most telling comparison of all is that both stories have recourse to a kind of *a priori* history. Suppose we ask ourselves how Heidegger *knows* all this about the early Greeks. He denies that this is a factual, historical matter, a matter of ordinary historical research or "historical inspection" *(historische Betrachtung)*. As we have already seen, Heidegger is prepared to believe that, as a factual matter, *aletheia* may turn out not to contain an alpha-privative (which, philologically speaking, would reduce his rendering of the word to a pun). Furthermore, he is prepared to admit that no Greek ever in fact *used* the word *aletheia* in the sense of *a-letheia*. So then how does he know *what* is implicit and prethematic here? He could only have come upon this rendering of the early Greeks, which situates them at the beginning of quite a story, by way of *"geschichtliche Besinnung,"* a meditative-historical thinking, in tune with the matter of thought, that thinks in terms of the history of Being (GA 45, §13).

But such an issue-oriented *(sach-lich)* reading of the early Greeks amounts to a declaration about what the early Greeks *must have meant,* because the "very notion" of truth as correctness issues from a deeper notion of unconcealment. In other words, Heidegger here engages in what Husserl called an *a priori* sense-history, an *a priori* history of the genesis of sense, so that Heidegger's early Greeks are beginning to look a lot like Husserl's proto-geometers. But this *a priori* history is but the flip side of the genetic fallacy. In the genetic fallacy one tries to reduce the validity or meaning of something to the historical circumstances under which it arises; its *historisch* origin is taken to be the basis of its *sachlich* validity. Heidegger follows the opposite tack: because the very meaning of truth as correctness derives ontologically from truth as *aletheia,* there "must" be a historical correlate that instantiates this genesis. Because correctness arises from unconcealment as a matter for thought, that is how it "must have been" historically. Because truth as correctness depends for its condition of possibility upon unconcealment, that is what *aletheia* must have meant before it was historically formulated as correctness. Now if this history is not to be found by means of ordinary historical research *(historisch)*, it does yield itself up under a deep historical meditation *(geschichtliche Besinnung)*. And that is the very essence of a transcendental history.

Heidegger cannot resist assigning a historical correlate to this deep structure (the open). He cannot resist rooting around old words for the barely discernible traces of this ontogenesis, which "must" be there somewhere. He cannot resist giving the ontogenesis of *orthotes* from *aletheia* the form of a story—whatever the *historisch* case may be. If we can detect this ontogenesis in the word *aletheia* when we meditate upon it in a *sachlich* way (as *a-letheia*), then we *must* be able to hear it in the old, founding words, the words of elemental power at the Beginning and the First Dawn.

Now that is the heart of the mythological gesture that I find in Heidegger. It gives a historical instantiation to an antehistorical structure *(a-letheia)*, assigning it a definite time and place, giving it a proper name. This takes the form of a myth of origins, of a Great Beginning, of a great founding act back at the beginning of the tradition, which gives flesh and blood—mythic form—to a philosophical insight. In the Beginning was the *logos,* a great flash of early Greek fire, which vanished quick as a flash of lightning but left an afterglow that steadily diminished over the centuries, until it finally devolved into the present crisis of the Evening-land.

It is certainly not very difficult to find places where Heidegger sings a mythic anthem to the early Greek flash:

> There was a time when it was not technology alone that bore the name *techne.* Once that revealing that brings forth truth into the splendor of radiant appearing was also called *techne.*
>
> Once there was a time when the bringing forth of the true into the beautiful was called *techne.* And the *poiesis* of the fine arts was also called *techne.*
>
> In Greece, at the outset of the destining of the West, the arts soared to the supreme heights of the revealing granted them. They brought the presence of the gods, brought the dialogue of divine and human destinings, to radiance.
>
> When then was art—perhaps only for that brief but magnificent time? (TK, 34/QCT, 34)

The whole thing sounds a little like "Camelot," one brief, shining moment and all (which is a grand and enduring story, a point to which I will return at the end). But it is a rather tall story too and easy to debunk—if that is really required. One would not be inclined to sing such anthems to the Greeks if one were writing a history of power—of women, say, or of slaves. The Greek world was built around a set of exclusionary and hierarchical power relations, which placed male over female, free man over slave, Greek over non-Greek, of which the divided line provides the meta-physics, and the Pythagorean table of opposites the "early Greek experience." Do women and slaves also share in the clearing? Do the slaves who hauled the stones for the temple also participate in "setting the truth into the work"? How are the excluded present in the open? Heidegger would have gotten very different results if his perspective were the history of power instead of the poetics of truth. Or indeed if he had chosen to heed other temples besides the ones at Paestum, or other poets than Hölderlin, if, for example, he had actually listened to Trakl instead of making him say what he must have meant! Or if he had listened to James Joyce, e. e. cummings, or Mallarmé.[12]

To put it in the terms around which I have organized this study, Heidegger would have gotten very different results had he allowed the "jewgreek" considerations that I am pressing to intrude upon his exclusively "phainesthetic" considerations, to disrupt and shock *his* Greeks, his highly Heideggerianized Greeks, who think meditatively the rising up of *physis* as *phainesthai*.

In fact, Heidegger weaves a marvelous yarn about the early Greeks, which is guided by a litany of eminent Germans, a great Greco-German metanarrative: in addition to Hölderlin (whence the Fourfold and the two beginnings), the early Rhineland mystics, such as Meister Eckhart, mystical poets, such as Angelus Silesius *(Gelassenheit)*, and, let us not forget, Husserl and his phenomenological access to the *phainomenon,* the self-showing of what appears, which sets the scene for his conception of *phainesthai.* Heidegger chose to listen to Husserl with Greek and poetic ears, and to listen to the Greeks with ears tuned by a certain Hölderlin and Husserl. That was at one and the same time his genius and the fateful limit of his genius, his blindness and his insight.

Heidegger is exceptionally good at making the early Greek texts dance. He can bring them alive, and he has a feel for them which few can match. But it is possible to listen to other texts, to nourish, savor, and meditatively muse over many texts—including jewgreek texts such as the Hebrew and Christian scriptures, the Latin texts of the medieval masters, or even the texts of French *philosophes*—and to hear in them a deeper voice, to find in them a deeper structure.

Heidegger's view would be strengthened, not weakened, were it disentangled from this story, were it understood that this story is just a good story, were it understood that his thought is not dependent upon actually swallowing such a tall tale!

From Memorial to Critical History: Heidegger Demythologized

Now let there be no mistake: there is always room for a good story. We do our best teaching and learning through stories. That is why I do not think it is ever a question of advocating pure demythologizing. Demythologizing always eventuates in mythologizing differently, a point I will come back to in the concluding chapters of this study. That, too, is why we must come back to Heidegger's stories and the place they have within critical history. But before we do that we must be clear about this breach between critical and memorial history, clear about how austere a picture we are drawing of Heidegger. Hence we must ask ourselves what is left of Heidegger once we have been divested of the splendor of the early Greeks and the tale of the two beginnings. How are we to understand this more austere, more radicalized, demythologized Heidegger?

A-letheia is not truth and cannot be translated as truth, because it is that which grants the epochs of truth. It is not Being, because it is that which grants Being and presence. Demythologizing Heidegger drives us back to the extremity of the *Es gibt* that grants the epoch of presence, so that all "there is" is the springing up of the epochs, the epochal movements, the relentless un-folding of *a-letheia* (cf. SD, 20/TB, 19–20). There is no epoch of *(des)* the *Ereignis,* he says, for the epochs spring from *(aus)* the *Ereignis* (VS, 105).

On this reading, Heidegger's thought comes back full circle to its original point of departure. In *Vier Seminare* the seminar notes mark off three stages along the path of thought (VS, 73, 82–87). The first is the attempt to think the *meaning* of the Being of beings, to identify the "upon which" that organizes any projection of the Being of beings. That was given up because "meaning" is too closely tied to the structure of transcendental subjectivity. Then the effort shifted to locating the "truth" of Being. It is that middle period which we have been trying to demystify, as if the truth of Being implied that somehow, somewhere, some historical people actually thought and experienced Being "in its truth," as if Being actually *has* a singular "truth." Finally, the seminar says, there is the attempt to think the "place" of Being, its *Ortschaft,* the open space within which Being and time play themselves out, and here the guideword is neither meaning nor truth but *Ereignis.* In the final stage, the task of thought is to think the happening of the place of the epochs, that which grants the space and time of the epochs their play *(Zeit-Spiel-Raum).* Here there is no privileged meaning or truth of Being but only the unfolding of the many meanings and truths of Being across the epochs—none of which can be privileged, from Anaximander to the present.

I say that Heidegger has come full circle here, that there is but one Heidegger not three, not because I want to deny the developmental, shifting character of the "path of thought," but because I think this path traces out a circle that comes back to a kind of *Ur*-Heidegger, the Heidegger whose path of thought was set in motion by Brentano's book about the manifold sense of beings *(die mannigfache Bedeutung des Seienden).*[13] Heidegger began by asking about the multiple senses of Being and ended up conceding its multiplicity, acknowledging that all there is are the multiple senses, the manifold unfolding of the senses, meanings, or truths of Being. The truth of Being is the delimitation of truth and the proliferation of truths across the epochs. He began by trying to make a reduction *of* that multiplicity and ended by making a reduction *to* it. He began and ended with the "there is/it gives," the multiple sendings of Being and truth.

Thus the thinking which is turned toward the *Ereignis* has so radicalized the idea of history, has become itself so radical a thought, that it can no longer be cast as a history of Being in the narrative sense, of telling a story about great beginnings and dangerous turning points. It is by succumbing to this narrative impulse that Heidegger's "history of Being" becomes implicated in *Historie* and chronology and falls into privileging some historical epoch. But what this demythologized Heidegger has in fact accomplished is a description of every epoch in terms of a structurally necessary withdrawal, a moment of *lethe*, in which the open space itself, the opening up of the open within which a given epoch happens, withdraws from view in order that what is granted in that epoch may come to presence. That means that every epoch is equally epochal, inhabited by the structure of withdrawal, and no epoch can be privileged. On this accounting, "history" is "leveled," not in the sense that it is decimated, but in the sense that the hierarchizing of the epochs is undone and privileged historical spheres are robbed of their advantages. We get rid of dominating historical mountain peaks, not for a flat plain but for a populous range of competing peaks. The "danger" on this reading—if we may be granted an eschatological moment—arises from absolutizing *one* of the historical epochs, one of the periods of presence, to fill up the clearing with a particular and undisplaceable form of presence.

On this reading, *Wierderholung* as a theory of the historical "retrieval" of primordial beginnings is replaced by a more radical "repetition" conceived as the springing up of the different, the emergence of diversity, without hierarchical privilege. Heidegger has isolated the structural withdrawal of the open— *Ereignis, das "Es" das gibt, Austrag*, etc.—which makes possible the presence of the present that constitutes a given epochal sending. What he has isolated is "ontologically" primary—it is what is first in the order of the *Sache selbst*— but it is the most elusive of all in the order of "thinking" because of its very withdrawal.

Now the effect of this discovery is not to rush headlong into hierarchizing the epochs of presence from the radiant splendor of the early Greeks to the filthy smokestacks of the *Gestell*, but to see how the prestige of any *particular* epoch of presence has been compromised. Its effect is therefore to drive us from a memorializing to a critical conception of history. As something granted and given, as a partial sending of presence, no epoch has more than transient authority, no epoch sets the rule for another. The only rule the epochs recognize is the rule of justice, of *dike*, according to Heidegger's fabulous reading of Anaximander, where *dike* means to let the moments of presence while away. Injustice, *adikia*, results from the stiff-necked persistence of presence, which refuses to go under, to give way to another, to give its place to another. *A-dikia* is the refusal to make space for another. And that is what happens when the authority of an epoch asserts itself (GA 5, 357, 368/EGT, 45–46, 54).

It is not from sheer perversity that I want to bring Heidegger's reading of the early Greek epoch down a notch or two but from a concern with the matter of thought and a concern with the question of justice in a more ordinary sense, the sense which matters to concrete men and women in concrete historical time. The matter for thought is not the early Greek experience of presence—for that is to remain on the level of what is granted—but the granting itself, the open space of the clearing. And the thought of the clearing delimits the prestige of *any* epoch, something which from time to time shows up in Heidegger himself. In the 1930s, some three decades before Kuhn, Heidegger defended Aristotle's theory of falling bodies against Galileo, not because he thought that Aristotle is right and Galileo is wrong, but because he thinks it makes no sense to pass such a judgment, which conflates two different epochs of presence (GA 45, 51–53; QCT, 117–18). To do so is to put "correct assertions" from different (read: "incommensurable") "worlds" of unconcealment into meaningless combat with each other. Directly to compare Aristotle and Galileo on this point is as nonsensical as it would be to rank-order Aeschylus and Shakespeare. The competition among the various names of Being, the nominal unities of the various epochs of presence, is a lover's quarrel. We have neither the right nor the means to evaluate the epochs (SD, 62/TB, 56; SG, 136/PR, 79).

It is important to see that, more critically understood, Heidegger would not be construed as engaged in a search for the master name of Being. He would be engaged instead in underlining the historical contingency and dissolubility of all the master names for Being that have been forthcoming in the history of the West—*eidos, ousia, esse, res, Geist, Wille zur Macht,* etc.[14] To appreciate the contingency of the epochs of presence is to delimit the authority of all the names of Being and to preserve and shelter the mystery of what withdraws, of the clearing, which, while itself never named, is that which grants the names of presence. And that is what it means to keep the question of Being *open,* to let Being waver in questionability, tremble in irresolvability, according to the memorable demand of the first pages of *Being and Time.* It is to make that which has congealed into an easy self-evidence into an uneasy questionability, to transform that which has become a matter of unquestioning assent *(Fraglosigkeit)* into a matter of the deepest questionability *(Fragwürdigkeit).* We keep the question of Being open by letting the epochs of Being and presence rise and fall in the open space of the clearing.

In a "critical" theory of history, the names of Being have only a contingent authority (rather like the contingent necessity of which the scholastics spoke). An epoch of presence is nothing more than a temporary configuration or grid that has been thrown over beings, whose pretense to immutable validity must be kept in check. If history is possible only in virtue of the withdrawal, then the whole of history is the errancy in which the epochs are set adrift. "Error is the space in which history unfolds" (GA 5, 337/EGT, 26). The history of Being is the "forgetting" *(lethe)* of something that *never* was known. The epochs of presence are but temporary ways of filling the clearing with the brush strokes of presence, subject to the *dike* which finally commits it back to the flux.

"Awakening" from the "oblivion" of Being *(Seinsvergessenheit)*, on this account, is not a matter of returning to a primordial beginning in order to find there the secret to a New Dawn (GA 5, 327/EGT, 18). It is rather a raised awareness of the oblivion and its inextinguishability which keeps its distance from historical hierarchies of any sort. The awakening, Heidegger says, consists in a turn *toward* the oblivion, in awakening *from* the oblivion by awakening *to* the oblivion (SD, 31–32/TB, 29–30). It is thus a profoundly emancipatory thought, which puts us all on the alert for the powers that be, or presume to be, who give themselves airs of ahistorical necessity and immutable presence. It practices a Socratic vigilance about whatever purports to be "present." It is a critical alertness which holds the epochs of Being and presence in question.

This, I argue, makes for a more liberated view of Heidegger, one no longer caught in the double bind between two beginnings, too late for the gods and too early for Being (PLT, 4), waiting for a god to save us. For this demythologized Heidegger, *a-letheia* is not a Greek word. The hyphen breaks up its nominal unity, prevents it from belonging to any historical age or language. *A-letheia* is not the Greek or any other historical master name of Being, but rather the inconspicuous open space within which the history of the names of Being unfolds. *A-letheia* can never appear *in* that space—not at the beginning or the end—for it is the very opening up *of* that space, granting the epochs of presence their space of play.

That is why the best use of the history of presence is critical, not memorializing, that is, to play the epochs off each other, to let each be the corrective of the other, to put down the pretensions of one with the successes of the other, to use one to tell stories on the other, critical stories, in an effort not so much to fuse the horizons as to keep each in check, to humble the pretensions of any one in particular. Historical thinking is necessary but it is necessarily critical.

Remythologizing Heidegger

Only now is it possible to make room for Heidegger's stories—having first delimited them and situated them within a critical history. Demythologizing permits a certain *re*mythologizing.

The narrative impulse is not without a purpose. Heidegger could not have done without his stories. The promise of the "destruction of the history of ontology" gave *Being and Time* a punch which no mere "existentialist" treatise could have mustered up. His fabulous account of the early Greeks and of the lightning flash that lit up the early Greek countryside was a large part of the power of the later Heidegger, and I have my doubts as to whether the later Heidegger would have made half the impact had he not spun such a magnificent yarn. After all, not all stories are of equal merit and power. Great stories have power and impact. They have a "moral," make a point, impress upon us an otherwise lost lesson, and vividly embody a purely *sachlich* point.

We do our best teaching and learning through stories, and nobody has ever said that Heidegger was not a great teacher. Heidegger often tried to write poems, with uneven success, perhaps because his real talents lay elsewhere, perhaps because his real skills are narrative. He was extremely good at fiction, and I say this without sarcasm, because I do not situate this remark within a metaphysical opposition of truth and fiction, historical objectivity and fanciful artifacts, unprejudiced factual accounts and wishful thinking. I take it that such historical positivism has long been discredited. We have to do instead with (hi)stories which compete with one another for insight, depth, and persuasive power. Everything is an interpretation.

Heidegger has told a very powerful tale on contemporary technology, one with teeth in it. He very adroitly plays his poetic, Hölderlin-ish world of the early Greeks against the turbines and computers of modern "cybernetics" and the awful, grinding wheels of the *Gestell*. That is his most salutary and healing tale, his best tendency, one that becomes more and more urgent with each passing day in which the ecosystem is ground under heel—even if it does belong, in Heidegger himself, to an abominable politics and a regrettable geophilosophy.[15] Of course, he very conveniently forgets a long list of the very forgettable things about the early Greek world—from its infant mortality rate to the place it accorded (or better, denied) to women and slaves—but that is part of the rules of the game in good storytelling. We ought to have the good manners not to interrupt a master storyteller with such considerations.

His critique of technology is the most powerful part of his work, the part where everything he has to say comes to a head, where everything is, as he would put it, "gathered together" in the sense of *logos*. It is the tip of Heidegger's pen. Indeed, the confrontation with technology stands at the heart of the "reversal." This critique, almost entirely missing from *Being and Time*— as a matter of fact, *Being and Time* offered a quite positive phenomenological account of science (§69c)—appears for the first time only in the 1930s. Once again, Heidegger starts at the *end*, with what was coming from modernity, but this time with a radically *critical* point of view. Heidegger's reading of history begins with his own time, from his own time, about the needs of his time. Every great thinker regards his time as needy, as a turning point, a point of decision, an *eschaton* wavering between destruction and a new beginning, and wonders whether this darkest night of all is to be the dawn of a new day. Everybody looks back upon the past and sees it leading up to them and then tells a story about how they got there and where the way out is to be found. Thinking is essentially historical (and one can write the history of those who think otherwise). Thinking is essentially *geschichtlich*, that is, beginning with the present and worried about the future (GA 45, §13), an issue of "care," and not merely *historisch*, dispassionately rummaging through the archives of bygone days.

But the point of such storytelling is essentially *critical*. It is a way of de-limiting the pretensions of the present, of the powers that be, which take themselves to be present instead of having come to be, which lay claim to the master name, which set themselves up as master. Such historical thinking means to cut them down who give themselves airs of ahistorical importance and permanent presence, showing the earthly genealogy of everyone and everything that purports to have dropped from the sky. Heidegger is writing what Foucault calls a history of the present, a history anchored in a present crisis, telling a certain story about how we have gotten here and how we can get out, telling a story on the powers that be.

The essence of that story is to be found in the claim that technology issues from the withdrawal, that what comes to presence (*an-wesen*, verbally) in technology is withdrawal (QCT, 23–35). The *Gestell* is the way that presence currently has of filling up the clearing, that it is what is granted in and by the withdrawal of the clearing. Technology is that which issues from the invisibil-ity of the clearing; it is not what Being *is,* but the way it pretends to be, one more way of presencing but not the granting of presence itself. Technology is not the clearing, not the *Ereignis,* not the *Es gibt,* but rather something given, the presence that has descended upon us in our day. It is but one more master name with illusions of mastery.

Against this pretentiousness and this arrogance, which are indeed danger-ous, he tells the tale of another time, when things were better, more gentle, when thinking let beings be in their radiance and phenomenality. And that, it seems to me, is to say with all due flourish that there is indeed another possibil-ity for thought, a possibility scattered here and there, among Greeks and German mystics and poets, and even, *pace* Heidegger, outside Greece and Germany, perhaps even in North America, in Walt Whitman, say, or in the Australian bush. There is another relationship to the world in which we do not reduce ourselves to such a ravaging assault upon things. There is the possibility of letting things be, of being captured by the mystery by which the being emerges into Being, by the splendor of the simple (PLT, 7).

The thing *(die Sache!)* is not to be encumbered by the additional and unnec-essary burden of taking all this to be the singular privilege of a particular epoch, back at the Great Beginning, in the First Dawn, where once there was a spot known as Camelot. The phenomenality of the phenomena is as alive and well in the painting of the French Impressionists as in anything produced by the early Greeks. There is as much radiant splendor of the being in its Being, as much rising up into unconcealment, in Cézanne as there is in Anaxi-mander, and it makes no sense, on Heidegger's own terms, to rank-order them.[16]

The "other possibility" does not come first, before philosophy. It is not something aboriginal, primordial, at the dawn of the *Abend-land*. It is and always has been marginal, excluded, on the fringes, and it always took someone with an exorbitant turn of mind to take it up. Meister Eckhart, who gave Heidegger the word *Gelassenheit* (for which he gets a grudging acknowledgement in Heidegger's book of the same name), was a fringe figure in his day, suspect and eventually excluded by the Roman Curia, which twisted his arm into retracting some of his best lines. Thales has become famous for being out of step, extraordinary, and *he* lived in the Golden Dawn. We may assume that the early Greeks exhibited their fair share of pushing and shoving and everydayness and that Thales would have been just delighted if someone had taught him how to convert water into hydroelectrical energy, which is something he believed possible in principle anyway (without having the details at hand). It was ever thus.

Therefore, let us treat this account of the early Greeks as a good story, not a sheer fabrication, because it exploits certain things about the pretechnical world, but a story which at the same time is not tied to some historical, epochal correlate. Let us remember that all good storytelling requires a conveniently short memory. Memorial thinking is uncannily good at active forgetting, which is a big part of the way it works. Let us take it for what it is, a philosophical myth, and inch Heidegger a little closer to Plato the mythmaker—which he may not have liked. That, I think, will liberate the considerable power of Heidegger's thought from an enervating nostalgia and new dawn-ism, which strands us in a nostalgic longing for a lost world and a longing hope for a new dawn, trapped between the two beginnings, too late for the gods and too early for Being, feeling bad that we no longer speak Greek and afraid of being in bad faith if we buy a computer.

I am not opposed to hope itself, which is a highly emancipatory impulse. In the concluding chapters (10 and 11), I will defend the possibility of another hope, the hope of justice for the least among us. But Heidegger's hope is too enervating and Being-historical for me, too removed from the actual needs and the real destitution of those who have been deprived of hope.

I recommend a reading of Heidegger as offering a critical history which sets about the work of epochal delimitation, which robustly marks off the epochality and transiency of the diverse names of Being, which shows how every epoch is marked by withdrawal and granting, violence and letting-be, by possibilities for either, *mutatis mutandis*. Every epoch is possessed of its own grace and its own malice. Critical history takes aim at the hierarchy of epochs, levels the peaks and valleys in Being's own history, and claims, in accord with Difference itself *(Unter-Schied),* that the epochs, which wander about in errancy, are not better or worse but only different, that there are only the manifold senses of Being, the manifold ways in which the twofold unfolds, many Being's and many truths, playing themselves out in endless self-differentiation.

In critical history, the history of Being is the history of errancy. The matter for the thought, the springing up of the epochs in virtue of the withdrawal, is thereby released, let be. The history of the effects of the withdrawal is emancipated from the rule of nostalgia and hope, from every *telos* and *escha-ton*. Critical history releases the *Geschehen* in *Geschichte*, the *schicken* in *Geschick*. Thinking is released from the hermeneutic demand to decipher the one true message/meaning/truth and is admitted *(eingelassen)* into the place of the unfolding of the play, of the rising up and passing away of the epochs. There remain only the coming-to-be and the passing away of the epochal formations, the unfolding of the twofold, the issue of the *Aus-trag,* describable only and best as a *Spiel*. Here the only *arche* is a child-king who rules without why. It plays because it plays, Heidegger says, without ground and without why (SG, 186–88).

On this reading, Heidegger is construed as thinking the a-lethic process itself, the unfolding of the manifold epochs of presence, the manifold senses of Being and truth. This makes it a lover's quarrel, or a storyteller's preroga-tive, to take sides with one or the other of these historical configurations— with the Greeks or the Romans or the medievals, with the French or the Germans or the English, or even with *aletheia* itself in the age of the Greeks. What matters on this construal is the matter for thought, which is the mystery of what withdraws and shelters itself behind the epochs which it makes possi-ble. All there is *(Es gibt)* is the multiple truths and changing faces of presence, the multiple and polyvalent happenings of being and truth, so that the matter for thought is to be "located" in the a-lethic process itself, not in any of its effects.

Otherwise the result is a disaster, the very disaster against which Heidegger seemed to offer no resistance at all in the 1930s and which continued to affect his later writings even after his break with the Party. The myth of Being, the mythic thinking of a primordial Beginning situated wholly and exclusively in the early Greeks, and—this is the dangerous political payoff—of a *Volk* or a language which, in an equally mythical end-time, is alone suited to repeat that Beginning, to make possible an Other Beginning, was the most consummately dangerous tendency of Heidegger's thought. In the essays that follow I want to spell out in more detail the unfortunate consequences of Heidegger's mythic thinking, to unfold the dangerous and destructive implications of the mythic hypervalorization of the Greeks and of their experience of Being as *aletheia*. The danger and the destructiveness have to do with justice, with a blindness and insensitivity to the questions of justice, all of which is made possible by a monomanic infatuation, a mythic capitulation, to what is variously named *Es gibt, Ereignis, aletheia*.

The failure to guard against the mythicization of *aletheia* is the failure of all failures in Heidegger, the failure that provided the basis for his notorious politics. It makes nonsense of Rorty's claim that Heidegger's political engagements were entirely fortuitous, an unfortunate offshoot of bad political judgment, having nothing to do with the matter to be thought.[17]

At the end of this work, I will offer a study of another myth, not a (pure) Greek myth but a jewgreek one, a myth of justice, not a myth of Being but a myth that turns on what is otherwise than Being. It is a question of multiplying myths, of letting myth compete with myth, of letting myths of justice invade and disrupt myths of Being, of inventing feminist myths to disrupt masculinist ones, myths of peace to disarm myths of violence, of continuously inventing new myths, as many as we need, while watching vigilantly over the myths we embrace. We always need new mythologies to carry us over the gaps and failures of knowledge and nerve. It is never a question of thinking in absolutely demythologizing terms, but of opposing good myths to bad ones, salutary and emancipatory myths to totalizing and dangerous ones, of multiplying small myths and *petits récits* to offset the *grands récits* that threaten us all.

CHAPTER TWO

Heidegger's Kampf

THE DIFFICULTY OF LIFE AND THE
HERMENEUTICS OF FACTICITY

In the first chapter I set forth on a conceptual level the way in which the question of Being is transformed into a myth of Being. My concern there was strictly structural, aiming at the identification of the essential conceptual operation by which the myth of Being is constructed in Heidegger's thought. Now I want to shift my point of view to the genesis of the myth of Being along the path of thought, to follow its historical emergence in his work, and to identify the tendencies that allowed Heidegger's conception of history to follow a mytho-heroic rather than a critical course. This will also involve addressing the social and political implications of this development, from which I largely prescinded in the first chapter. I will go back to the beginning, to the earliest Freiburg lectures, now available to us with the publication of several important volumes of the *Gesamtausgabe* (chapters 2–3); move selectively through *Being and Time* (chapter 4); the writings of the 1930s during and immediately following the infamous rectorate (chapters 4–5); and then examine selected key texts appearing after the war (chapters 6–9). Throughout, my concern will be both to identify the destructive effect of the myth of Being on the question of Being and to sort it out from the possibility of another reading of Heidegger, of a Heidegger against Heidegger, of another Heidegger, a Heidegger demythologized.

One thing that emerges clearly from a reading of the first Freiburg lectures (1919–1923) is that Heidegger was from the start a revolutionary philosopher, bent on carrying out a radical renewal of existence and thought, on returning life to its deepest sources and resources. He always took it as his task to point the way toward a new order, was always aiming at some sort of "other beginning," of one kind or another. Heidegger was a "radical" who sought radical renewal, a radical whose radicality (to say the least) took various forms at various times, passing through any number of "turnings" (which are getting harder and harder to count).[1] The notorious call that Heidegger issued in the 1930s for radical "national" renewal, for an upheaval that would make the very foundations of national existence tremble, belongs to a fundamental trait of the Heideggerian project. Heidegger was a lifelong lover of revolutions, of turnings and overturnings, of destruction-and-retrieval, of new beginnings snatched from the midst of decline.

From the start—and it is with the start that I am concerned in this chapter—revolutionary renewal was conceived in terms of "difficulty" *(Schwierigkeit)* and "struggle" *(Kampf)*. Life, existence, history[2] can never be great if they let themselves be lulled to sleep by a love of ease and comfort. The richness and depth of life is a function of the battle that must ceaselessly be waged against the inherent tendency of our being to take the easy way out, to drift into decline and decay. I want to show here that it was just this philosophy of *Kampf,* already at work in the early Freiburg period, that dominated the thinking of the early 1930s when, assuming an ominous mytho-heroic form, it was enlisted in the service of a national revolutionary renewal. In *An Introduction to Metaphysics* Heidegger instructed the Germans on the saving power of hardness and on the danger that inheres in the desire for comfort. He warned them that the success of their revolution depended upon having the hardness to raise the question of Being from the ground up. The thing that will make this people great, he told them to their astonishment, is raising the question of Being.

Accordingly, it is a mistake on their part to want philosophy to make things easier when its real saving power is to make things harder. Without the difficulty imparted by radical philosophical questioning, the revolution will cave in to the love of the indifferent, of the masses, of the boundless "et cetera" of what is always the same. That is what is happening in Russia and the United States, where materialism and positivism have utterly extinguished philosophical questioning (GA 40, 49/IM, 46).

The last lines of the *Rectorial Address* still ring in our ears. This "moribund semblance of a culture" *(abgelebte Scheinkultur)* must be made to collapse under the pressure of "our historical-spiritual people"; the "greatness of this irruption" will be measured by the extent to which we grasp what Plato said, that everything great "stands in the storm" (Heidegger translates *"episphale"* as *"steht im Sturm"*) (SA, 480). After which Plato adds an old saying that must have pleased Heidegger greatly: "Fine things are hard [*kalepa ta kala*]" (*Republic,* 497 d).

This calamitous constellation of themes in the 1930s—greatness, hardness, history, spirit, nation, destiny—communicates in Heidegger with the question of Being, which dumbfounded his fellow Party members. Heidegger does not hesitate to mix Nazi rhetoric with the question of Being, National Socialism with Sophocles and Heraclitus. In *An Introduction to Metaphysics,* he speaks of the *"Kampf* for Being" (GA 40, 114/IM, 107), using this most Nazi of all words as a translation of Heraclitus's *polemos* (he is describing the difficulty that Being was making for Oedipus by giving him an eye too many). He wants to tell the Germans that engaging the question of Being is the great historic *polemos* that will effect their historic, destined greatness.

By the 1930s, the notion of *Kampf* had been assimilated into a myth of destiny and greatness and had lost the original sense it had in the early Freiburg period. For the discourse on *Kampf* and *Erleichterung* is not reducible to Nazi rhetoric but was originally a central part of the "hermeneutics of facticity" in the 1920s where it first emerged by way of Heidegger's revolutionary "destruction" of Aristotle and the New Testament. I want to show here how the politics of the question of Being, how the ontopolitics of the 1930s, emerges from a fateful, mythic transformation of the most exciting European philosophizing of the 1920s, from lectures on Aristotle and the New Testament—something of a "jewgreek" mix—which held the young Gadamer, Hannah Arendt, and countless others spellbound.

The University

In the famous lecture course of 1922 on Aristotle, Heidegger sharply critized the prevailing academic conception of philosophy as pure, detached, theoretical science. Those who desire undisturbed peace must understand that they will never enter into the radicality of philosophical thinking. Philosophy consorts with disturbance and unrest (*Unruhe,* GA 61, 93), he said. It makes trouble and causes a stir. Philosophy is *Kampf,* a battle. That is something we learn from Aristotle, who determined the Being of Life in terms of movement and agitatedness *(kinesis, Bewegtheit),* and from the New Testament,[3] which warns against the love of peace and security:

> But as to the times [*chronon*] and the seasons [*kairon*], brethren, you have no need to have anything written to you. For you yourselves know well that the day of the Lord will come like a thief in the night. When people say, "There is peace and security," then sudden destruction will come upon them as travail comes upon a woman with child, and there will be no escape. (1 Thess. 5:1–3)

The early New Testament communities lived with a sense of the uncertainty of things, of the radical contingency and unknowability of the coming "time" *(kairos),* the appointed hour, of the day of the Lord, and they stressed the need for care and constant vigilance. In the end-times we know neither the day nor the hour of the Lord's coming: "So then let us not sleep, as others do, but let us keep awake and be sober" (1 Thess. 5:6). It is not peace that will win the day but restlessness, not sleepy tranquillity but constant wakefulness. We should put on the "breastplate" *(thoraka)* of faith and a "helmet" *(perikephalaian)* of hope.

Taking his cues from a very different, nonmetaphysical Aristotle and from a wholly unphilosophical, very biblical and Hebraic sense of time and contingency—that is the "jewgreek constellation" I am addressing—the young Heidegger argued that philosophy too must be radically vigilant, marked by this restlessness which does not sleep. That is why Heidegger emphasizes that on this more radical conception of philosophy one should not speak of philoso*phy,* but of philosoph*izing.* Philoso*phy* is a fixed discipline, a sedate, formulaic, normalizing academic undertaking, an institutionalized activity with a sedimented discourse. But philosoph*izing* is a living act *(Vollzug),* something to be carried out, and it is to be judged in terms that befit genuine acting— in terms of its decisiveness, initiative, originality, and "radicality" (a favorite term of the young philosopher). Its aim is not to reproduce the most sedimented formulas of the classical texts but radically to appropriate these writings, disputing them "destructively" in order to make contact with and retrieve the founding experiences that gave rise to them at a time when philosophy and life were not disjoined.

Today, however, Heidegger points out, philosophy is to be found not in the life-situation of the *agora* but in the university. Hence any attempt to rethink what philosophy is, to think philosophically, is committed to rethinking the university. Thus as early as the first Freiburg period, long before the infamous rectorial address, Heidegger was already addresing the political enframing of the university (cf. GA 56/57, 205ff.). This is, he says, a hermeneutic requirement: to take up philosophizing in the context of its current situation. For better or for worse, philosophical activity is situated within institutional life. It was not always thus, and it may not be thus in the future, but we must begin where we are—that is what hermeneutics means—and today we philosophize in the university. Accordingly, the work of revolutionizing philosophy, of conceiving it more radically, involves us in a critique and a radicalization of the university.

Philoso*phy* is comfortable in the university. There it provides the opportunity for empty academic pugilism (GA 61, 67) and perpetuates a discourse that simply reproduces the prevailing order. But philosoph*izing* makes the very substance of our lives questionable. It arises from and returns to life (GA 61, 153). Philosophy moves within established frameworks and perpetuates the same debates; philosophizing undercuts these debates and makes these frameworks questionable. Nonetheless, philosophizing must find a home in the university. Heidegger does not side with Nietzsche or Schopenhauer—and we can add Kierkegaard—none of whom thought it was possible to think in the university, all of whom thought that philosophy can only function freely *outside* the university. Nietzsche, Heidegger says, did not know what he wanted; it is too easy to walk away from the university (GA 61, 66). Heidegger's aim is to revivify the university, to radicalize it. He wants neither academic business as usual nor a philosophizing that abandons the university, but a university that philosoph*izes,* philosophizing *in* the university.

Philosophizing, Heidegger says, is a dangerous profession. That was made plain in the very beginning by Plato, who has Socrates say in the *Apology* (28 e 4) that a man who has chosen to live philosophically takes a dangerous stand; he must hold his ground, stand and face the danger, like a soldier at his post, even at the risk of death (GA 61, 49–50). Philosophy does not proceed from the restfulness of absolute objectivity (GA 61, 162–67). The peace and tranquillity of scientific objectification, its love of security, is nothing less than a flight in the face of *(vor)* facticity (GA 61, 90). Philosophizing shuns all such weakness and comfort and embraces instead radical philosophical confrontation *(Auseinandersetzung)* (GA 61, 2). Philosophy is alive only in "polemics," which is not to be taken in the superficial sense of professorial debates. Philosophizing is *polemos*, confrontation, "destruction" of the tendency in its object to conceal itself (GA 61, 67).

The work of philosophy is not to manufacture conceptual ghosts, faint conceptual copies of life (GA 61, 80), he says (against his former teacher Heinrich Rickert). On the contrary, it is shot through from beginning to end with life. Philosophy is not *about* factical life, but it is *itself* a way of life, a *bios* in the original Greek sense—which, in the case of Socrates, also meant facing death—and it is the way of life that counters the tendency of life to settle comfortably in place.

Philosophy is what it is, and this is the source of its greatness, because it is radical questioning. Questioning is more rigorous than scientific exactness. The sciences have it easy, he says, because they do not have to be troubled by ultimate considerations. They can proceed with their daily work, operating within the secure confines of an already established tradition, while philosophy has to be there at the creation, founding and creating traditions, forging fundamental concepts (GA 61, 46). Philosophy is radical research (GA 61, 87), radical knowledge, knowledge that seeks out the principles behind all things (GA 61, 56–61.). This is not to say that philosophy lays hold of absolutes, which is but another way to take flight from facticity, but only of factical-historical principles whose actual content is always concretely to be determined by the way in which the principle is appropriated. Principles are formal indications, the result of formalizing and raising to the level of categorial formality the stuff of factical life.[4]

Because of its radicality philosophical questioning is, finally, methodologically atheistic (GA 61, 197). Questionability is not religious, but it may lead to a religious decision. When I philosophize, I am not religious, even if I happen to be a religious man. The art is to philosophize and still be religious. This is by no means the position adopted later in *An Introduction to Metaphysics* (GA 40, 9/IM, 7). There are no square circles here, just the age-old difficulty of squaring a life of faith with a life which questions all the way down, which operates, as he says, "from below," in a kind of radical phenomenology (GA 61, 195).

Heidegger does not have much to say about what such a university would look like. He merely takes pains to distance himself from contemporary discussions about "university reform." His radical renewal would cut far more deeply than any such "reform." These discussions about reform, he says, are "uncritical" and attempt to make the university fit the mold of a declining spirituality, which, with each passing year, sinks lower and lower (GA 61, 70). Discussions about reform fall prey to the allure of a "leader" *(Führer)*. This remark, which subsequent history has made so ironic, is conceivably at that point in time an allusion to Max Weber's "charismatic leader." If so, then Heidegger is probably complaining about liberal programs to democratize the university and to bring it in line with a modern, liberal, bureaucratic culture. That is perhaps what he means by a declining spiritual life. In the place of such spiritual decay, Heidegger asks for radical decisiveness, for confronting hard "either/or" choices: either being swayed by "untested" (= modern?) ideas or seizing radical (= traditional but sedimented?) ideas concretely and thereby winning our existence; either undertaking a genuine troubling about our factical life or letting everything go up in the smoke of mysticism and religiosity.

Instead of Nietzsche's flight from university philosophy, Heidegger puts his hope for renewal in a university that philosophizes and in particular in Freiburg, where Husserl's phenomenology gives us access to the structure of factical life (GA 61, 190–92). Factical life is always in flight from principles, from the ultimate Being and sense of things *(Seinssinn des Seienden)*. It is to reverse that situation, to counter that tendency, that the younger Heidegger calls upon philosophizing. We should not expect that a reversal of the tendency of factical life toward ease and comfort should come about without further ado, that it will come about in "blissful untroubledness and peacefulness" (GA 61, 72). We must instead be ready for toil and trouble, ready for the storm.

No one could have imagined just how stormy it would be.

The Categories of Factical Life

Everything in these early Freiburg lectures turns on the notion of "factical life," a concept taken from Dilthey which signifies concrete, historical existence. For Heidegger, factical life is determined in Aristotelian terms as something self-moving, a "being-moved" in itself, that whose movement proceeds from itself *(kinesis, Bewegtheit)*. Factical life does not simply lie about *(vorhanden)*, ready for inspection. It is elusive and on the move, continually withdrawing *(entziehen)*, re-moving itself from view. Philosophy has chosen for itself a moving target, something whose Being is movement itself, and that is what presents a difficulty to philosophy.

That is how Heidegger is first led to the notion of *Sorge* (care, trouble, worry, concern). Life, he says, is an unending concern with our daily bread *(sorgen um das 'tägliche Brot')* (GA 61, 90). The New Testament resonance is quite detectable here and is blended harmoniously with Heidegger's existential Aristotelianism. Factical life is troubled about its daily subsistence. According to Aristotle, every being in motion is marked by *privatio, carentia,* the lack of something that it needs, a lack which it is the aim of its movement to meet. Heidegger calls this state "need" or "want" *(Darbung,* which can also mean starvation). As a Being of care, factical life has needs and wants and it is constantly bestirred *(bewegt)* to meet these needs, living in continual instability, in *kinesis.* Life is unrest *(Unruhe:* GA 61, 93), according to Pascal (whose name often appears in these early lectures.)

Now it is just because factical life is disturbed by everyday concerns that it seeks to "secure" itself against want. It wants to be untroubled, safe and settled, which from the young Heidegger's point of view means that it wants to cover over its very being as needy, as *Darbung.* It wants to look whole, not in *privatio.* So the elusiveness of this being is just that it wants to cover itself up (GA 61, 120), to look like what it is not, to look as if it were without care, *sine cura,* se-cure—even though that very desire for security is itself a (deficient) mode of care.

The conception of factical life as a being that is delivered over to its daily concerns and difficulties is the horizon of Heidegger's thematics of the "difficult" and the "easy" in the early Freiburg period. The idea becomes explicit in Heidegger's enumeration of four "categories" of factical life (the first version of the later "existentialia"), among which are included what he calls the "light and easy" *(das Leichte).*

The first of these categories is called "proneness" or "inclination" *(Neigung),* which means that life is inclined in certain directions, not by something outside itself but by its own "weight," by the weight of its own being. Heidegger is possibly rewriting the Aristotelian notion of *hexis,* the habits by which factical life is regularized in certain patterns, set in its ways, and thus achieves a certain (false) security and "self-sufficiency." On this point, Heidegger appears to be following Kierkegaard, who criticized Aristotelian *hexis* and replaced it with the notion of "repetition." You can only have "bad" habits because "inclination" is inclined to fall. To hit the mark, on the other hand, is a matter of "primal decision," which must be continually "repeated."[5]

In the second category, factical life is given to the "abolishing of distance" *(Abstand-tilgung),* of the distance, that is, between itself and the world, between being-itself and the worldly projects and significances *(Bedeutsamkeiten)* in which it is immersed. Lacking the long look, factical life gets absorbed in worldly business. It does not take the measure of what matters and what does not, which is why it gets preoccupied with false distances, with the order of rank, with worldly advantage and success. Factical life thus is "hyperbolic," excessively caught up in worldly occupations, distracted and scattered about *(zersteut).* Life overshoots the mark in an Aristotelian excess *(hyperbole)*. The authentic care that life ought to have about itself, which requires a long look and true distance, is displaced by a plurality of worldly distances.

Life is too much *inclined into* the world to hold the world at a *distance*. Inclination is lulled into worldly security and covers over the insecurity of genuine choice. Factical life loses the chance to distance itself from its worldly acts. The world is "before me" *(vor mir)*, but by blocking off this "before" factical life prevents the "authentic coming-forth *(vor-kommen)* of life," the more radical and authentic appropriation of life (GA 61, 106). The upshot of this is that factical life is effectively shut off from itself, barred from access to its real care, which is what Heidegger calls "barring" or "bolting" *(Abriegelung)*, which is the third category. Life cuts itself off from itself, bars itself from itself, divests itself of its care and gives itself the look of something finished and settled, *sine cura*.

Thus the being that philosophy takes for its object is difficult indeed to seize upon, for it is a being that defends itself against itself *(es sich gegen sich wehrt)*, that constantly avoids itself. The excess is thus *also* a defect *(ellipsis)*, missing the mark—of the self—by coming up short, by failing to get as far as itself (GA 61, 107–108). Factical life misses the mark of life *both* by excess *and* by defect: by having too many worldly concerns, it does not have enough self-concern.

It is at this point that Heidegger adds a fourth category—"the easy" *(das Leichte)* (GA 61, 108–10)—directly by way of a text from the *Nicomachean Ethics* (II, 6, 1106 b 28):

> Again, missing [*Verfehlen*, failing] is manifold (for the bad belongs to the unlimited, as the Pythagoreans judge, but the good to the limited), whereas doing things right is of *one* kind. (Consequently one is easy and the other difficult. It is easy to miss the mark, but difficult to hit it.) Consequently, overshooting [*Ubershuss*, hyperbole, excess] and lagging behind [*Zurückbleiben*, ellipsis, defect] belong to badness but holding the mean belongs to virtue. [I have translated the German of the editors, who are using the vocabulary of the lecture course.]

The Being of factical life, its being-itself *(Selbstsein)*—which is what is doing service for *arete* in Heidegger's interpretation—is an elusive, moving target. While there is only one way to hit the mark, and that is hard, the arrow of factical life may miss its mark in a multitude of ways. Because it can be swept away by the excess of too many possibilities *(hyperbole)*, because it is too much inclined to be dispersed into its world, too easily drawn off by every passing wind, it always lags behind and falls short of its authentic self *(ellipsis)*. But to cut itself free from *(ent-scheiden)* the many and resolve upon the one— that would be hard.

Heidegger glosses this passage from the *Ethics* as follows:

Factical life always seeks to make things easy [*Erleichterung*]; inclination goes along with the drift [*Zug*], of itself, without adding anything on. Being-inclined corresponds to the pull, rushes towards it, "without further ado." The "further ado" would be what does not lie in the range of inclination. Even worldly difficulties are ways to make things easy. . . .

Life is caring, even to be sure in the inclination to make things easy, to flight. (GA 61, 108–109)

Life is "guilty" *(Schuld)*—it misses the mark—because it looks away from itself and transforms itself into a self-secure carelessness. Hyperbolically caught up in the multiple ways to be everything except itself, elliptically falling short of itself, factical life rushes headlong into the manifold *(pollachos)* and steadfastly eschews the one and only *(monachos)*, the *unum necessarium*. It goes on and on, endlessly tossing about, never making an end of it, taking every pain to avoid what Heidegger calls the "primal decision" *(Urentscheidung)*, which it must continually "repeat" *(wiederholen)* (GA 61, 109)—which is hard. Hard is the simple.

The being that easily misses the mark is characterized, Heidegger says in the awkward language of the course, by "relucence" and "prestruction." Relucence means that life basks in a reflected glow, is always illumined reflectively by the world to which it belongs, that life understands itself in terms of its worldly projects. Prestruction, a Latinate form of the German *Vor-bauen*, which literally means building beforehand and in ordinary German means "pre-cautionary," is a kind of fore-structuring. As a being of care and need, factical life takes precautions against the insecurity which everywhere besets it. Thus it builds a cultural world around itself *(Umwelt)*, which means that it is a kind of pre-forming (*Vor-Bildung*, GA 61, 128–29). Factical life structures its life in advance with stable objects and projects, surrounds itself with an *Umwelt* that assures life a secure passage. Prestruction promotes the illusion of self-sufficiency, thereby allowing factical life to lose sight of its fundamental insecurity (GA 61, 120).

Relucence and prestruction are categories of movement, ways that factical life keeps itself busy, astir, in motion. If "re-lucence" is a movement *back* (from the world to life), pre-struction is a movement *foreward* (from life to the world). Hence the "re-" and "prae-" refer to a kind of back and forth movement between life and the world and together make up the movement-structure of life lost in the world, in a ceaseless cycle of excess and defect. The movement that is thus exhibited Heidegger calls "ruinance" *(Ruinanz)*, which is what in *Being and Time* was called "falling," a more felicitous theological language borrowed from Kierkegaard. Heidegger means that the movement of life is a downward plunge *(Sturz)*, that life in its original decisiveness "goes to pieces," falls into ruin. The more the movement of care "mounts up" *(steigern)*, the higher its level of worldly concern (*Besorgnis: GA 61, 135*), the more steeply factical life falls or plunges forward into the world.

The world gnaws (*Nagen, Bohren: GA 61, 137*) at factical life, tormenting *(quälen)* it, gives it no rest, drives it to the point that life has no time for this, no time for that, that it must hurry on. Such time, which is not the time of objects but the time of *Ruinanz* (and of resistance to *Ruinanz*), Heidegger calls "kairclogical" time. *Kairos* is the "appointed" or "opportune" time, the time that has "come," that has been "fulfilled," as in Mark 1:15 *(peplerotai ho kairos)*. It is the time that Kierkegaard and Heidegger after him called the *Augenblick,* the moment of choice. The kairological is the sphere of decisions made or of decisions avoided. The fundamental movement of ruinance is to take time away, extinguishing the temporal and historical character of the kind of life which hits the mark, which cuts into the many and resolves upon the one in a primal decision (GA 61, 139–40).

Ruinance is seductive, because it leads us away from our true care, tranquilizing, because it lulls us into security, alienating, because it takes us away from ourselves, and nihilative, because it plunges us into nothing. One merely falls, one never comes to rest, one falls on nothing. The fall to nothing of ruinance is not an objective, observable property of an object, but a feature of a being whose Being is movement. Factical life keeps falling into nothing, keeps failing to hit the mark, keeps scattering itself in hyperbolic dissemination, keeps flinging itself into the "security" of lacking all care. Ruinance is not a "true"—in the sense of straight (as when a carpenter says a plumb line is true)—movement but a fall, a slanted incline. Factical life does not move forward, does not come forth *(vor-kommen)* and appear, which requires that it be upright, that it stand forth from itself in itself, but rather it falls, staggers, slips, plunges. So everything comes down to the difference between true and untrue movement, between a movement which hits its mark and one which is liable to fly off in any direction. Factical life ceases to "occur" and "come forth," not in the objectivistic sense that it ceases to be at all, but in the sense that it is not itself, that it does not press forward toward itself. It is "still there"—it is even quite busy and agitated—but it does not come forth, does not move forward. Its agitation is not true movement, true temporalizing.

The downward plunge of factical life is a headlong rush into security. Life turns away from its *questionability* in order to live with certainty, as if it had all the answers (GA 61, 152). Factical life constantly defends itself against itself, covers up and covers over its own groundlessness. That is why philosophy is always struggling against the very tendency of this being to cover itself up. Philosophy vigilantly pursues the questionability of factical life. Philosophical questioning, it turns out, is one very important way—actually it is the only way discussed in this lecture course—to counter ruinance:

One way of being-moved which counters ruinance [eine gegenruinante Beweg-theit] is that of philosophical activity, and this precisely inasmuch as it is carried out in the appropriate mode of access to questionability. (GA 61, 153)

Philosophizing must maintain itself as a radical questioning that answers questions in such a way as to keep them open, indeed to open up ever-new spheres of questionability. Questioning counters the falling tendency of life, disturbs its inclination to settle in place, makes trouble where life wants peace and security.

Now it is in this context—of radical philosophical questioning in a radicalized university—that Heidegger describes philosophy as a *Kampf.* Factical life is not just *vorhanden,* not simply a given, intuitable object which is immediately evident, but a resistant, self-concealing movement. Life is not presence *(ousia)* but movement *(kinesis).* Accordingly, life will not yield to an "intuition" effected in a neutralized theoretical attitude. On the contrary, philosophy must undertake an ongoing struggle *(Kampf)* with the tendency of factical life to cover up its own being as movement. Traditional philosophy—and Husserl culminates this tradition—thinks it can neutralize the disturbance within factical existence, calm its agitatedness, and proceed by means of untroubled intuition of pure givenness. But the young Heidegger sets out to exclude the Husserlian exclusion, block off the suspension or disconnection of factical life in order to put philosophy in the mode not of neutrality but of difficulty, to make existence tremble with the insecurity of radical questioning.

The ideal of knowledge and the optimism about givenness that are thus attained [in the traditional view of philosophy] are in principle and unrelentingly to be excluded [*auszuschalten*] from the attaining of an act of philosophical knowledge and its methodological securing. (GA 61, 153)

Philosophy today, safely and securely ensconced in professorial chairs, has paled away into disinterested speculation. Hence the genuine philosophical task is to disconnect, to put out of action—he uses Husserl's word *Ausschaltung* here—the ideal of philosophy as tranquil theory or pure intuition of simple and unencumbered givenness:

But this exclusion is not done with a methodological dictate, once and for all, but rather it is the *battle* [*Kampf*] which is always simultaneous with the act of philosophizing, [the battle of] philosophical interpretation *against its own factical ruinance.* (GA 61, 153)

Turning Husserl's own word against the master, Heidegger excludes what Husserl would include—the neutrality of the *epochē,* the tranquillity of pure intuition—and includes what the master would exclude—the facticity of life.

Philosophy is a "battle" against the lure of "intuition," of "immediate giv-enness," of pure scientificality. Insofar as it understands itself in terms of dispassionate objectivity, of absolute disinterest, science is part of the problem, not of the solution. By taking things at face value, philosophical objectivity sets itself up for a deception. Philosophy must take stock of the fact that the being which it has taken as its subject matter, as a being in movement, as the Being of movement, withdraws from sight, covers itself over, removes itself from view, indeed defends itself against philosophical questioning. In the place of Husserlian peace, of the calm correlation of noesis and noema, of intuition and presence, Heidegger puts the stormy battle between questioning and self-recessive life. The scene of intentionality is a *Kampf*.

Might it not be, Heidegger asks at the conclusion of the course, and this puts "pure" phenomenology to the test, that philosophy's "object" does not admit of "objectification"? Where is it written that the object of philosophy should have the character of an "untroubled purity and harmony"? Where is it written that its object could not rather have at its heart a fundamental "resistance" *(Widerständigkeit)* (GA 61, 155), a resistance that is unparalleled in its vehemence (GA 61, 178)? Might it not be, he says, that factical life would be something whose meaning is "broken" *(zerbrocken)* (GA 61, 155)? Philosophy is a battle *(Kampf)* because life is a battle. A being whose being is itself a battle thus demands a philosophizing that knows how to do battle.

The Hermeneutics of Jewgreek Facticity

In the early 1920s the philosophy of struggle and difficulty—Heidegger's *Kampf*-philosophy—was, as we have just seen, in part an Aristotelian concep-tion. The mark of *arete*—of *Selbstsein*, which is how *arete* functioned in the hermeneutics of facticity—is hard to hit. Being oneself requires practice and vigilance, conscience and practical judgment *(phronesis)*, all the skill and the know-how of a being whose being is being-moved. This was an Aristotelian-ism drawn from Aristotle's ethics rather than his metaphysics. Or better still, it arose from an Aristotle whose metaphysics has been deconstructed into his ethics, whose metaphysics of permanent presence *(ousia)* had been shaken down into the philosophy of household goods *(ousia)*.

The hermeneutics of facticity was, to no less an extent, a hermeneutics of the New Testament experience of life. This is the sense in which the hermeneu-tics of facticity has a "jewgreek" structure—for the horizon of the Christian scriptures, which were written in *koine* Greek, is the Hebrew scriptures. Spir-itually, intellectually, religiously, the Christian scriptures emerge from a Jewish world, which is why the best New Testament scholarship must understand again and again the Jewishness of Jesus.[6] It is upon a deeply Hebraic and religious—and not a Greco-philosophical—sense of time that the hermeneutics of facticity is drawing. Heidegger was particularly interested, in these early lectures, in the scriptural figure of life as a time of trial and trouble and of faith as a hard fight, a notion to which his attention was drawn by Luther and Kierkegaard. I have fought the good fight, Paul says, and I have kept the faith (2 Tim. 4:7). The battle in question is the battle waged by believers who understand that they still belong to the church "militant." The problem with Christians in this century where "everyone" is Christian, where there are "millions" of Christians, Johannes Climacus complained, is that Christianity has become triumphant and triumphalistic. Christians think that the battle is over, that they have "won," that they *are* Christian. It is as if "an army, drawn up to move in battle, were instead to march back to the city barracks in triumph."[7] Johannes Climacus, on the other hand, ever the seeker and the climber, acutely aware that he has yet to get as far as faith, as far as Abraham, makes no claim to *be* a Christian. Climacus confesses that he is not in the truth but in the untruth, and that for him to get into the truth, to receive the condition, would constitute a real movement, genuine motion.[8]

In philosophy, Constantine Constantius said, there is no real movement. From Plato to Hegel, philosophy has been looking for a way to smooth over the scandal of movement. Recollection *(anamnesis)* and inward memorializing *(Erinnerung),* having been scandalized by non-being, admit only of a kind of pseudomovement—from being to being, from already knowing to remembering—which always finds a way to draw *Wesen* from *Gewesen.*[9] Christianity faces up to the difficulty of real motion, of *metanoia,* of the hard battle, the good fight of faith. Christianity knows that non-being (sin) is real, that our being has been eaten into and eroded by non-being, and that making progress demands a real change. Any accounting for life on Christian terms means a parting of the way with philosophy's inveterate tendency to deny motion.

The hermeneutics of facticity emerged from an attempt to elucidate by way of a "formal indication" the ontological structure of both the Aristotelian *polis* and the New Testament communities as seen in the tradition of Augustine, Pascal, Luther, and Kierkegaard. The truly interesting thing here is how these two worlds, one Greek and one scriptural, were one, forging a single "jewgreek" unity, how each supported the tendency of the other, in the young Heidegger's mind. Far from seeing in scriptural experience the deep antagonist of Aristotle, which was certainly Luther's view, Heidegger thought that the hermeneutics of New Testament life opened up a new reading of Aristotle, one that shifted away from the Aristotle of medieval scholasticism toward a new and much more "factical" Aristotle. This new Aristotle would be read backwards, as it were, so that the *Physics* and *Metaphysics* would be read back down into the ethics. That, as I have claimed elsewhere, and as van Buren has now compellingly confirmed (*supra,* n. 3), is exactly what Kierkegaard had proposed. In the notes attendant to *Repetition,* Kierkegaard wrote:

... when Aristotle long ago said that the transition from possibility to actuality is a *kinesis* (motion, change), he was not speaking of logical possibility and actuality, but of freedom's, and therefore he rightly posits movement.[10]

Because life on earth is the hard work of earning eternity, the movement of time is "decisive," for in it one's eternal life is decided. Eternal life lies ahead (not behind) as the reward of one who sets his hands to the plow and does not look back, who resolves upon the one thing necessary. Philosophy on the other hand grinds the forward movement of life to a halt and makes life a movement in reverse, a movement that is no movement at all (unless of course you are willing to describe someone who is in full retreat as "on the move"!). The only exception among the philosophers to this denial of movement is to be found in Aristotle. Even then, *kinesis* is a category of freedom and novelty—of factical life—not (just) of physics and the regularity of physical movement. There is the hermeneutic key to reading Aristotle: to read the categories of the *Physics* and *Metaphysics* back down into the *Ethics*.

Thus the terms in which the philosophy of *Kampf* and difficulty first emerged were fundamentally jewgreek, set as they were by a reading of Aristotle in the light of the lifeworld of the New Testament, by an attempt to find a more Greek—more practical—Aristotle and a less Greek—less metaphysical—New Testament. There was nothing about it that would plunge it into extremist politics.

From Aristotle to Jünger: The Emergence of the Myth of Being

But sometime after his triumphant return to Freiburg in 1928 as Husserl's successor, Heidegger's revolutionary new beginning for philosophy took a new and ominous turn. The deeply Aristotelian tone became very Nietzschean. The voices of Paul and Pascal, of Luther and Kierkegaard, gave way to the wild-eyed rhetoric of Ernst Jünger. The paradigms of the Greek *oikos* and the New Testament *ekklesia* receded in favor of a great metaphysical *Volk*, of a German *Geist;* the church militant became a military German nation. The thematics of the hard work of repeating life forwards became a thematics of the saving power of "danger." The university radicalized by philosophizing became a fully politicized university. The Heidegger of the 1930s and his ominous "*Kampf*-philosophy" stepped on stage.

The first clear signs of this mutation are to be found in the lecture course that Heidegger gave in 1929–30 entitled *The Basic Concepts of Metaphysics: World—Finitude—Solitude* (GA 29/30), delivered at a time of worldwide economic depression and economic chaos in the world of the Weimar Republic.[11] The lectures contain an extended analysis of boredom. Boredom does not mean anything ontic—boredom with one's job, or one's spouse—but rather a "fundamental mood," a deep, profound boredom, one in which the world itself wavers in insignificance. In the middle of the course, in §38, Heidegger inserts a startling discussion of the "essential neediness" of contemporary life, one which, as Winfried Franzen points out, raises the question as to whether Heidegger has preserved his "ontological neutrality," i.e., whether he is keeping free of any specific ontico-existentiell ideal.[12] Is this ontology we are hearing or some kind of onto-politics? Is this the question of Being in all its radicality or the politics—*a* politics—of the question of Being?

In boredom, Heidegger says, one is left empty, with a void *(Leergelassenheit)*. The void is a lack or a need *(Not)*. Are we not today beset by many such needs? Heidegger offers us a not inconsiderable list: "contemporary social misery, the political confusion, the impotence of science, the hollowness of art, the groundlessness of philosophy, the debility of religion" (GA 29/30, 243) That is a sweeping condemnation of Weimar culture which leaves practically nothing standing, what would turn out to be a conservative denunciation of the chaos of the Weimar world. Heidegger wants nothing to do with the parties and associations designed to meet these needs, the determinate programs whose object it is to remedy these needs. Their only effect is to blunt the edge of neediness and to dull our senses about our true condition, our most profound void. Heidegger, we recall, was not interested in reform but in revolution.

So it is neither the particular needs that beset us, nor the particular remedies that have been devised to meet them that Heidegger pursues, but rather need itself, need as a whole *(Not im Ganzen)*. What is really needy about our condition is that we only experience particular needs and that we do not feel more deeply needy. It is the "absence of an essential oppression of our Dasein as a whole" (GA 29/30, 244) that constitutes our real need. We have too many programs and bureaucrats but no "administrator of the inner greatness of Dasein and its necessities." These bureaucrats are robbing us of our chance to be great, for the only way to be great is to confront an "inner terror" *(innerer Schrecken)*. The real distress is the absence of deep distress.

All of the hustle and bustle of these organizers, with all of their programs, serve to show only one thing: the deep void from which they are all taking flight. They are in love with peace and security, with "a generally complacent comfort in dangerlessness":

> This comfort in the ground of our existence, despite all the multiple needs, leads us to believe that we have no more need to be strong [*stark*] in the ground of our existence. We trouble ourselves about teaching skills. The present is full of pedagogical problems and questions. But by heaping up skills we will never replace power and might [*Kraft und Macht*]; if this does anything at all, it will only choke them off. (GA 29/30, 245)

The more programs, administrators, and associations we heap up, the more we induce in ourselves the illusion that we are meeting our needs, or at least doing our best to address them. We thus cut off access to a deeper void, and that loss of access is the true need from which we suffer. Now we can never become great and strong and powerful, never really hard and tough, unless we come to grips with the real terror of our lives. Terror makes us great.

Heidegger thus condemns the institutions of the Weimar state, of bourgeois democracy, on the grounds that they lack inner greatness and power, and this because they are concerned with making life comfortable, meeting our needs, curing our ills. They are making us soft. Presumably then we need something to make us hard.

In addition to being left with a feeling of emptiness, we also experience in boredom a sense of something being held back *(Hingehaltenheit)*. In the absence of a deeper need, something is addressing *(ansagen)* us which is refused a hearing *(versagen)*. But the ill which besets us is that we are so in love with comfort and convenience that we cannot experience this refusal. We would feel the sharp point of this refusal only if it pressed hard upon us. The result is that we are blocked off from that extreme point which makes Dasein be what it is, from that moment of resoluteness which constitutes Dasein (GA 29/30, 246). In boredom, Dasein is cut off from the most extreme demand of all: to be there.

Only by shouldering the hard work of existence can we truly take over our being-there. Dasein, being-there, is not supposed to be like a ride in a comfortable automobile, Heidegger says, not a way to sneak away from real danger:

> But because we are of the opinion that it is no longer necessary to be strong and to have to resist danger, we have all of us together snuck out of the danger zone of Dasein, and so relieve ourselves of the need to take over Dasein. (GA 29/30, 246–47)

The task of shouldering the weight of being comes down to a question of knowledge *(Wissen)*, a knowledge that brings us face to face with ourselves in the "moment in which it brings itself before itself as what is authentically binding" (GA 29/30, 247).

Now the "breadth of this void and the fine tip of this moment" (GA 29/30, 247) of choice are not a matter for objective science or verifiable assertions. We can "know" our neediness, know ourselves, only by breaking the ban, dismantling the obstacles we have erected against this most profound boredom and neediness. We must let ourselves be incised by the sharp tip of need instead of bending and blunting its tip with suddenly conceived programs, or burying it under an avalanche of depth psychology and psychoanalysis. We must let ourselves be instructed by what this fundamental mood of boredom gives us to understand instead of hastily blocking it off, covering it up. Hastening to meet our most superficial needs leaves us in the neediness of not knowing our deepest need (GA 29/30, 248).

So we must learn to question boredom, really to question it, and that means to have the courage to face what it discloses, to confront what truly besets us, and to bring it to that word which unfolds its truth and essential content.

Heidegger's discourse has become markedly more ominous here, more filled with the rhetoric of hardness, strength, power, courage, greatness. The rhetoric of difficulty has taken on an unmistakable political significance. Heidegger waves his hand dismissively at a whole range of determinate, deliberative social institutions and democratic structures and calls for a radical renewal, a deep resolve, a transformation of existence. It would be wrong to say that his discourse is devoid of particulars, because its whole point is to oppose particulars and to throw everything into the camp of some kind of inner spiritual transformation, one that is possible only by testing the mettle of Dasein against inner terror, by putting it to the test of the greatest difficulty. Hard is the great. We must let ourselves be *driven to an extreme* and not take intermediate preventive measures whose only effect would be to rob us of our anxiety, our boredom, of the disclosiveness produced by the extreme situation. A quick fix leaves a deep malaise to fester untreated.

In other words, the entire Aristotelian conception of a mean state *(mesotes)*, everything moderating, every sense of an Aristotelian mean has been jettisoned in the name of the extreme, of the excess of a heroic *metabole*. Aristotle has given way to Jünger.

So we need this neediness and danger. We need hardships if we are to be hardy. We need danger if we are to be great. We need neediness if we are not to be found wanting. The real danger is that we are making everything safe. It is the safe and the saving, all this safety and security, the lack of care and concern *(sine cura)*, that truly threatens us. The truly dangerous thing is safety.

A myth of danger and greatness has clearly taken hold of Heidegger, a myth whose motto is: in the safe, danger grows. This is the first and Jüngerian form of the Hölderlinian formula which guided the later—and reverse—myth to which Heidegger had recourse from 1936 on: in the danger, the saving grows. The Hölderlinian formula is an exact reversal, a flip of the line he had learned from Jünger and which had dominated his thought from after the publication of *Being and Time* to *An Introduction to Metaphysics*.[13] With the *Beiträge* (GA 65) Heidegger's revolution, his "renewal," took still another, and this time a poetic, form.

So it is possible to mark off at least three stages of the philosophy of difficulty: (1) the Aristotelian, or Pauline/Aristotelian (jewgreek), philosophy of the "hardness" of factical life as opposed to the paleness of philosophical conceptuality; the final upshot of this stage is *Being and Time*. (2) The philosophy of danger and hardness, the onset of the myth of greatness and hardness, in which Jünger's philosophy of pain and danger and the need for active nihilism has utterly transmuted the sense of "difficulty" that Heidegger first learned from *Nicomachean Ethics* and the New Testament. This militaristic, nationalistic ontopolitics provides the intellectual underpinnings of Heidegger's hellish political engagements and is expressed textually in the *Rectoratsrede* and in *An Introduction to Metaphysics*. (3) The final stage, set in motion with the *Beiträge,* in which Heidegger, in dialogue with Hölderlin, profoundly poetizes and transmutes the saving and the danger, this time into an epochal *Gefahr,* a sending of Being as *Gestell,* which can undergo a turning only if a god pulls it off for us. At this point Heidegger's thinking has been profoundly mythicized so that nothing is untouched by a deep-set mythopoetics of the destiny of Being, of the Danger and the Saving.

Three versions of the philosophy of difficulty: an existential, a mytho-heroic, and a mytho-poetic; an onto-hermeneutical, an onto-political, an onto-mytho-poetic; a pre-political, a political, a meta-political. Three economies of the difficulty of life: one that belongs to the economy of factical life, to *oikos* itself; one that was drafted into the army, into a military economy, where it became the stuff of which *Geist* and *Volk* are made; and finally one that doffs its steel helmet and takes up with shepherds along field-paths pursuing the errant ways of Being's epochal economy of sending and withdrawing in a deeply mythic view of history and Being.[14]

The Limits of Heidegger's Jewgreek Hermeneutics

The brilliance of afterthought is easy to come by. It is not hard to read backwards and to find signs of trouble right at the start, back in the early lectures on Aristotle and the New Testament, which sought to formulate the hermeneutics of jewgreek life. In retrospect, a good deal of what is contained in the lectures of the early 1920s was undoubtedly disturbing, full of bravado and phallic aggressiveness. Heidegger's reference to Socrates had a military quality to it and he had singled out a passage from the letter to the Thessalonians in which Paul speaks of the breastplate of faith and the helmet of hope. Indeed, as Kisiel has shown, Heidegger had a long-standing militaristic streak which led him to use military examples to illustrate phenomenological points, to exaggerate his own military experience, and to favor students like Löwith who had recently returned from the war.[15] Heidegger's first "turning," which shows up in the 1919 "Emergency War Semester" (held for returning war veterans), is immediately consequent upon his own war experience, which appears in retrospect to have a lot to do with the profound upheaval in his thought between 1916 and 1919. Kierkegaard said it would take an earthquake to shake some scholars out of their academic sleep, but the "force" of "factical life" seems to have been visited upon Heidegger by the sound of gunfire.

The university and the culture that were under fire were the democratic institutions—however imperfect—of the Weimar Republic, at that point swamped by economic chaos but never really supported by the intellectuals.[16]

The call for a radical decision sounded decisionistic in the absence of any determinate idea of what to do. Heidegger criticized mere "reform" because it was too piecemeal, too democratic, not radical enough. He disavowed any interest in a *Führer* solution, but the question could be raised as to whether all this sound and fury about a radical and primal decision, a deep and profound transformation of factical life, coupled with the military quality of it all, was not headed straightaway for just such a leader; whether, as Derrida points out about the 1935 *Einführung,* the *Ein-führung in die phenomenologische Forschung* of 1922 is not inextricably entangled in the *Führer*-philosophy of the 1930s (OS, 44).

I am interested here in another point, another—and as it turns out—fateful limitation in Heidegger's attempt to formulate the formal ontology of Aristotelian and Christian lifeworlds, what I shall call a missed opportunity. Heidegger's original strategy—to disrupt philosophy and the university by exposing it to philosophy's other—is brilliantly conceived. Heidegger wants to let philosophical conceptuality be disrupted by the concrete experience of life in the New Testament and by an Aristotle conceived in terms of the practical philosophy rather than the metaphysics. The disruption of philosophy so conceived was aimed at a renewal of philosophy, not at simply leaving philosophy behind. The whole notion of restoring life to its original difficulty, to all of the concreteness of facticity itself, taken in its original Aristotelian and Kierkegaardian sense, is, I think, an immensely salutary and suggestive move.

Far from contesting this beginning, I think it bears "repeating," giving it another try, this time in terms of what Heidegger curiously, fatefully left out. Heidegger managed to read the New Testament from one end to the other with his eye set on the categories of care and difficulty and never to have noticed the lepers and the lame, the blind and the beggars, the widows and the withered hands, the healings and the hungry crowds. While he was pointedly interested, as van Buren demonstrates (*supra,* n. 3), in Luther's *theologia crucis,* the theology of the crucified god, that always meant, for Heidegger, having the hardiness to take up one's cross, to fight the good fight. But Heidegger missed or ignored the thematics of the healing gestures that were addressed to all those who suffer. He left out the whole thematics of the ethics of mercy, of the cry for justice, the appeal that issues from flesh and pain, from afflicted flesh.

Pain is a "feeling," and Heidegger always took feelings to be a "merely psychological" category.[17] Feeling falls under the transcendental-phenomenological critique of psychologism, to the notion that it is a merely subjective state, that it does not "disclose" the world. Feeling is superseded by *Stimmung,* a richer and higher category for phenomenology which was always bent on the question of "world-disclosure" or "existential disclosure." Pain is too subjective a state, too world-shattering, driving the body inward, curling it up in agony and torment instead of projecting it ecstatically toward the world.

Pain for Heidegger was at most part of the difficulty of life, part of what I have to cope with, a test of whether I am hard enough, made of stern enough stuff. Pain is always my pain, part of my care, my *cura*. Heidegger never noticed that in the New Testament "care" also meant a deep responsiveness to those who suffer, like feeding hungry crowds, healing withered hands—even if that required a transgression of the law of the Sabbath—and even raising the dead.

Cura also meant healing, curing.

Heidegger was interested in the call of conscience, but he never heard the peal of pain that resounds throughout the New Testament. He never heard the call for mercy that issues from pain. He never heard the pain of the other, the pain that calls for healing, curing, *cura*. He heard that man was a being of need and concern for daily bread, a being of privation and *Darbung* (which also means hunger), but he seemed to miss the part about feeding the hungry, about ministering to the needy, about healing the leper. He heard the warning about a too hasty love of peace and security but he missed the part about comforting those who suffer and the peace that surpasses understanding.

So there was nothing in Heidegger's appropriation of the New Testament or of Aristotle to serve as a precaution against the reading that Ernst Jünger gave to pain in *Über den Schmerz* (1934). Jünger began by saying, "Tell me your relation to pain and I will tell you who you are" (something which Heidegger would translate—ludicrously, I would say, under the circumstances—into an observation about "translation").[18] There was nothing in this hermeneutics to resist Nietzsche's famous saying in *Ecce Homo*, what does not kill me makes me stronger.[19] In short, there was nothing in Heidegger's hermeneutics of factical life of the New Testament to insulate him against the contempt and scorn which Jünger and Nietzsche would heap upon New Testament ethics, its *ethos*, its form of life, its "world." Heidegger and Jünger had blocked off the ethics of mercy, of *cura* for the poor and the outcast, for those who are ground under by the power of this world, for those whom Lyotard calls *"les juifs"* in the generic sense, of whom the historical Jews are a case in point (in no small part as a result of the subsequent history of Christianity!).[20] Jünger and Nietzsche regarded this as an ethics of the rabble, an ethics of the worst, of those whom Nietzsche—quite rightly—thought smelled bad. They smell bad because they are made of flesh. Smelling bad is also a category of factical life, because it is a category of flesh.

There was nothing about Heidegger's appropriation of the New Testament categories to lead him to look upon the events of history from the point of view of the victims of history, the little ones who are ground under by history, instead of seeing it in the mythic terms of the march of the Great and the Primal through world time.

Heidegger's attempt to shock philosophy back into place, to quick-start it with a revolutionary jolt from the New Testament and Aristotle's ethics, ultimately exploded in his face. There was, as it turned out, nothing in it to stop it from running straight into *Kampf*-philosophy, a great myth of Being's struggle in and through a people chosen by Being's hand—even as there was originally nothing about it intrinsically to necessitate such a fateful turn. He had omitted the heart of the New Testament message, left the healing out of *cura,* left the mercy out of struggle and difficulty. Instead of a quick start, we got a fateful false start. Instead of an ethics of mercy, the most extreme valorization of mercilessness.

This amounted to an enormous missed opportunity for philosophy, which needed then as it needs now to ask what the "ontology" is which lies behind the ethics of mercy, what the hermeneutics of facticity would look like if it took into account the call that issues from *les juifs.* To a great extent that is what we got from Levinas, who was likewise interested in shocking phenomenology into a more radical mode by exposing it to its biblical "other" (the starting point of Heidegger and Levinas are interestingly akin), and from Derrida and Lyotard, who, under the influence of Levinas, suggest the possibility of a certain prophetic postmodernism. This is a point I will address below (Chapter 10).

The problem with the brilliant hermeneutics of facticity that Heidegger developed in those exciting lectures in the early 1920s was—to give it an ironic twist—that he never really got as far as care. When he listened to the fabulous tale of *cura* he didn't hear the whole story. He heard the myth of *cura* as a myth of *Kampf* but he never heard the myth of healing. The demythologizing of the myth of *Kampf* does not issue in having recourse to some sort of fictitious faculty of pure reason but in the imagination and invocation of other and more salutary myths, myths of healings and cures, myths of making the lame walk and the crippled straight, in short a myth of *cura* that has a heart.

CHAPTER THREE

Sorge *and* Kardia

THE HERMENEUTICS OF FACTICITY AND THE
CATEGORIES OF THE HEART

In the conclusion to the preceding chapter, I spoke of a certain missed opportunity, of the way Heidegger's philosophy of *Kampf* steered his conception of *cura,* thereby suppressing another and more radically biblical experience of *cura* and hence of factical life, one with a "heart." In the present chapter I wish to follow up that suggestion by sketching an alternate hermeneutics of facticity, a more radically jewgreek hermeneutics that issues in an other and quite different table of "categories," a table keyed not to the aggressiveness of resolute Dasein but to another kind of care. In this more jewgreek hermeneutics of facticity, *cura* does not mean *Kampf* but *kardia*.

One of the most striking features of Heidegger's program in the early Freiburg period was his call for philosophy to return to its prephilosophical beginnings, to the long neglected conditions of "factical life" *(faktisches Leben)* or, in the more transcendental tones of *Being and Time,* to "facticity" *(Faktizität)* (GA 2/BT, §6). Philosophy can do no better, the young philosopher argued, than to return to the most unphilosophical, theoretically impenetrable layer of factical pregivenness. Having sided too long with clear and distinct ideas, philosophy can get new life, he argued, only if it reattaches itself to the density of the beginning, from which it must always set out. In the beginning is the fact that cannot be turned into an essence, the facticity that cannot be transcended, muted, neutralized, or put in brackets.

Facticity was to be the means for radicalizing phenomenology (GA 61, 57–60, 195–97). Heidegger demonstrated the impossibility of getting beyond factical being-in-the-world, of gaining some transcendental high ground in which the facticity of human being could be neutralized. He showed the illusoriness of thinking that one could philosophize from this fantastic point, that one could adopt the view from nowhere. On the contrary, Heidegger said, it is always already too late. We can never get back past *(re-ducere)* our factical beginning. The density of the beginning is always already at work on us, behind our back. We are always already there.

The young philosopher hoped thereby to start a revolution, one that would transform and reinvigorate academic philosophy (and the academy itself) by turning philosophy into life itself taking categorial form (GA 61, 62–73). Kisiel has shown with meticulous care the birth of Heidegger's project in a transformation of the table of categories from the logico-grammatical categories of presence at hand *(ousia)*, the task of the habilitation dissertation on the Pseudo-Scotus, to the categories of factical life.[1] The whole idea behind the revolution the young Heidegger wanted to start, as I pointed out in the preceding chapter, was to think Aristotle's *Metaphysics* back down into his *Ethics,* to think the *ousia* of the *Metaphysics* back down into factical life, into *ousia* taken as *oikos,* everyday household life, house and hearth (a sense that is still alive in English usages like "a man of substance," in the sense of "a man of means").

Van Buren has shown that it is not too much to say that Heidegger first really learned that the question of Being needed to be raised anew from Luther's critique of Aristotelian metaphysics.[2] The prototype for the destruction of the history of ontology, van Buren has persuasively argued, is Luther's attempt to deconstruct medieval scholastic metaphysics in order to recover the authentic categories of biblical life. That whole Lutheran project also lay behind Kierkegaard's revolutionary rethinking of the categories of Christian "existence." It is this uniquely biblical and prephilosophical experience of life, the young Heidegger claimed, that makes the Greek philosophical notion of Being as presence tremble. Paul, Augustine and Pascal, Luther and Kierkegaard, first instructed Heidegger that Being does not reduce to the static presence *(stetige Anwesenheit)* of the Greeks, but is rather, in keeping with its temporal key, historical movement. It was here that Heidegger first learned that human being is adequately conceived not as *animal rationale* but as the temporality of a being faced with decision and expectation, uncertain of its future but resolved to act. Heidegger found in the New Testament stories a wholly different set of (pre)philosophical paradigms: not of neutrality and the *epochē,* not of the disinterested, objectifying thinking of Greek metaphysics, but rather of concerned struggle, of fear and trembling, of passion and resolve.

As we have indicated, Heidegger put this discovery to work not as a way of dismissing Aristotelian metaphysics (like Luther, who thought that Aristotle had been sent into the world as a punishment for our sins), but rather as a way of rereading and rewriting Aristotle. Heidegger submitted Aristotle to a hermeneutic violence that drew students to Freiburg from all over Germany and that, very much as he hoped, resulted in a fundamental reorientation of phenomenology. Indeed, he succeeded, perhaps beyond his expectations, in shaking philosophy in this century to its very foundations.

Home fresh from the war, the young philosopher was very much taken with Kierkegaard's sense that Christianity has not been brought into the world to comfort us in our old age and allow us to sleep at night. Christianity had to do with the terror of Abraham and the battle of the knight of faith. We ought not to believe ourselves prematurely enrolled in the church triumphant, Johannes Climacus said, while we are still paying our dues to the church militant.[3] Christian life is "repetition," Constantin Constantius said, by which he meant movement forward, putting your hands to the plow and not looking back, as opposed to the headlong retreat of Greek philosophy into an eternity left behind (anamnesis) and the pseudo-movement of Hegelian Aufhebung. As we have seen, Heidegger loved the rhetoric of vigor and robustness, of the "difficulty of life." We recall Johannes Climacus sitting in Fredericksberg Garden, puffing on a cigar, and conceiving it to be his life's work to make life difficult (whence Heidegger's reading of Nicomachean Ethics 1106b28; see GA 61, 108-110), inasmuch as the authors of the encyclopedias had already done enough to make life easy. Heidegger loved all this Christian militancy and Christian soldierism. Everywhere Heidegger looked, he saw a battle. Even his Socrates was a soldier (GA 61, 49–50).

Heidegger well understood the sense in which Christianity had come to bring not peace but the sword and to warn us against those who shout "peace and security" just when we need to be on the alert (1 Thess. 5:1–3).[4] But something important was missing from this hermeneia; a new "reduction" or exclusion was being enforced. Heidegger let the prephilosophical biblical paradigm shake the metaphysical understanding of human "existence" (factical life) as substantia, animal rationale, and even of Being itself as ousia, Anwesenheit. But he showed no interest in certain striking differences between the biblical narratives and Aristotle's metaphysical categories, a failure that I want to say was fateful and in one respect fatal. Heidegger thought that once Aristotelian metaphysical categories were deconstructed down into the factical categories embedded in the Ethics, and once the categories of scholastic metaphysics were deconstructed down into the factical experience of life in the New Testament, the results would be pretty much the same. Either way, the same table of factical categories would emerge and would serve as the basis of a universal ontological framework that was neither specifically Greek nor specifically Christian.

I want to show now that this jewgreek neutrality or universality cannot hold up, that there is a tension unnoticed by Heidegger that breaks it up. Heidegger seemed not to notice, or not to consider relevant, that, in comparison to the Aristotelian ethics in particular, the biblical narratives are not at all oriented to the phronimos, the prudent man (sic), the well-educated, moderate man of judgment, the aristocratic gentleman whom the younger aristocratic set should learn to emulate. Indeed it was of just these well-to-do, respectable gentlemen that the biblical experience of life was most suspicious. Instead of this mainstream prudent man, the biblical attention is directed to everyone who has been marginalized by the mainstream, to everyone who is out of power, out of money, out of luck, uneducated, and despised. Instead

of the uprightness of the man of good judgment, the biblical narratives turn
to those who are bent and laid low. Instead of the cultivation of health, these
narratives concern themselves with the infirm and the afflicted, with lepers
and cripples. MacIntyre is quite right to find a world of Aristotelian virtues
and vices in the novels of Jane Austen.[5] But the biblical world is not to be
found in the country estates and comfortable parsonages of the well-to-do,
but in the slums and alleyways where the "victims" of these wealthy Austeni-
ans dwell. Aristotle was surely right to say that a man ought not to seek honor
but that in virtue of which he deserves honor, viz., virtue. But the biblical
narratives were preoccupied not with honor but with dishonor, with all those
who were humiliated and dishonored, everyone whom the "world" had made
despicable, with all those who had never gotten as far as the debate between
true honor versus false, with all those who, as Paul said, "are not" *(ta me
onta)*, as far as the world is concerned.[6] Aristotle was on this point—and this
is not surprising—very Greek. He wanted his *phronimos* to shine with glory,
to glitter with all the *phainesthai* at his command, but he insisted that this be
earned glory, not a false shine. His was a hermeneutics of *aristos* and *arete,*
of excellence, of those who make themselves beautiful because they make
themselves men of good judgment and taste, of sense and sensibility. It was a
hermeneutics of the best and the brightest, the most beautiful and most honorable, the upper percentiles who would all get into the best schools and have
seminars with Allan Bloom. The biblical narratives, on the other hand, con-
sorted with outcasts and the rejects who drop out of school.

So the fabric and texture of factical life were decidedly different in the two
cases. On the one hand, a hermeneutics of excellence and *arete,* of putting
everything in order with the order of rank. On the other hand, a hermeneutics
not of glory but of humiliation, not of the strong and erect but of those who
have been laid low, not of the great but of the small, not of the straight but
of the crippled and bent, not of the beautiful but of the ugly, not of athletes
but of lepers, not of *eudaimonia* but of misery, not of prudence but of mercy,
not of the order of rank but of all those who drop to the bottom wherever a
logos and a *polemos* shake things down and distribute them into a hierarchy
(GA 40, 141/IM, 133).

The whole point of the biblical narratives seems to have been to put the
best and the brightest on the spot, to single out those who are not hungry,
not naked, not in prison and to ask them why not, to disturb and question
their autonomy and freedom with troubling analogies about camels squeezing
through a needle's eye. The biblical favor is not bestowed on the *aristos* or
archon—on the prudent man, on the rulers, or the wealthy, or the ones who
have the power—but on those who drop through the cracks, those who are
cast out and ground under, on the remnants and leftovers, the disenfranchised
and the different, on everyone an-archical, outside the *archē*. That deeply

offended Nietzsche's exceedingly Greek palate.[7] On this point even the young Heidegger is very Greek, still too Greek.

One point in the Aristotelian text that Heidegger seizes upon in particular is the notion that *phronesis* is precisely the ability to operate without hard and fast rules. Unlike the knowledge of unchangeables, *phronesis* is the know-how that knows how to cope with a changing market, a shifting scene, that has the wherewithal to operate in a world that is mutable through and through. That captured Heidegger's interest and the work he did with *phronesis* in those early days set the work of Arendt and Gadamer into motion and pretty much put hermeneutics in the twentieth century sense on the map. Heidegger quite rightly saw *phronesis* as the sort of knowing that is uniquely tailored to fit changeable being, the sort of knowing keyed to being as movement, not presence, and this was an insight of enormous moment for contemporary philosophy. But it is also the stuff of a significant contrast with the biblical narratives.

The biblical narratives were concerned with softening the bite of the Law, and so something like *phronesis* seems to come into play every time these stories put healing above the sabbath laws and more generally put human well-being ahead of keeping rules. But Heidegger made nothing of that point of comparison; it did not draw his interest. Furthermore, he never noticed the revealing difference between the Aristotelian and the biblical paradigms. The flexibility of *phronesis* is of a dominantly cognitive or noetic sort. *Phronesis* is a kind of *nous* that consists in having a sense for the mobility of loosely fitting principles, of what Aristotle called *schemata,* and hence a matter of a certain practical-cognitive adroitness in their application. The biblical sense of flexibility about the Law, on the other hand, was driven not by *nous* but by mercy, and was far less a cognitive matter than a deeply praxical one. *Phronesis* is a sense of what the individual situation demands, an *insight (nous)* on the part of practical understanding into the idiosyncrasies of the particular, whereas mercy is a giving way on the part of what the biblical narratives call the *heart (kardia),* which is not so much "insight" as a certain giving in to the needs of the other.[8] Mercy is a tenderness of heart that takes the demands of the one who is afflicted to override and trump the Law, to lift the Law from the backs of the ones who need help, especially when they are afflicted by the Law itself. It is not so much insight and practical *nous* as a kind of melting or succumbing to the needs of the other. This biblical flavor also shows up in Thomas Aquinas's version of Aristotelianism, when Thomas argues that it is *caritas,* not *prudentia,* which constitutes the form of the virtues, that without which the virtues are hollow rule-keeping.[9] It is possible to compare and contrast and even temporarily to confuse *phronesis* and *techne,* but it would never be possible to confuse mercy with *techne.* The biblical "cardia-logy" (or even "hetero-logy") could never look like a "technology."

The biblical stories proceed from a different conception of factical life, one that was enamored neither with rules, as in modernity, because they favored a kind of radical mercifulness over rule-keeping, nor with "excellence" *(arete)*, because their heart was with the outcast, with the worst not the best. Heidegger fixes on the first point and misses or ignores or just is not interested in the second point. His implicit ontology of the biblical lifeworld was guided chiefly by his interest in *phronesis* and *techne* as kinds of practical knowing, and in knowing as a kind of unconcealing. However many clues he took from the biblical discourses, his interest remained on this point at bottom very Greek. His concerns turn entirely on the phenomenological question of the "constitution" of the "world," with how "it worlds," with *techne* and *phronesis* as kinds of practical knowing, knowing how, which, as it were, light up the public space. He was not at all interested in the notion of those whom the world cast out, the shadows who inhabit the margins and crevices of the world. In Heidegger's "everyday world" there are no beggars, lepers, hospitals, homeless people, sickness, children, meals, animals. In general, there is very little room in the early Freiburg lectures for the category of what Merleau-Ponty would call "flesh." Yet the "kingdom of God" *(basileia theou)* is a kingdom of flesh, of banquets and of hunger, of cripples made whole, dead men made to live again, a realm of bodies in pleasure and pain, of flesh and blood. In Heidegger's factical lifeworld there are, however, plenty of tables, chairs, houses, tools, and instruments of all sorts, including even automobile turning signals—"table, jug, plow, saw, house, garden, field, village, path" (GA 63, 90)—all beings of concernful "care" *(Sorge)*. Heidegger heard the *Sorge* in *"sorgen um das 'tägliche Brot'"* (GA 61, 90) but he underplayed the *Brot,* the sphere of bread and flesh.

Heidegger thematized the materials of factical life—not of upper-crust Austenian or Aristotelian factical life, which was much too comfortable and bourgeois a scene for Heidegger (cf. GA 61, 187–88), and so not factical enough. Most of the wrinkles of facticity have been smoothed out for the Austenian set. When Heidegger thought of facticity he thought of struggle and work, and so he incorporated Kierkegaard's attack upon the comfortable bourgeoisie of "Christendom" into his story. Now let there be no mistake about this: It was a startling and revolutionary proposal on Heidegger's part to say that such workaday "things" were the fitting subject matter of philosophy's venerable and ageless pursuit of the *Ding an sich.* My complaint here is only that his conception of "factical life" is not factical or perhaps praxical enough. *Faktizität*—which is after all a Latinism coming off *facere, factus sum:* making, made—is too strongly oriented to this artisan world, too much taken with the paradigm of practical goods and the unique sort of cognitivity it requires. It ignores the scenes of *praxis* and afflicted flesh, the *praxis* of afflicted flesh, which are essential to the biblical lifeworld.

Heidegger had at least a partial glimpse of this category. In an interesting

passage in the early lectures, when Heidegger is describing the world of everydayness, he writes:

> In *the* room stands *the* table (not "a" table alongside many others in other
> rooms and houses) at which one sits *in order to* write, eat, sew, play. . . . Its
> standing there in the room means: it plays a role for such and such a use; this or
> that is impractical, unsuited for it. . . . Here and there it shows lines—the boys
> made themselves busy at the table; these lines are not just occasional interruptions
> of its coloring, but rather: the boys have been here, and still are. This side is not
> the easterly side, the small side is not so many cm. shorter than the other, but
> rather this is the side at which my wife sits if she wishes to read; earlier we had
> this or that discussion at the table; here a decision was made with a *friend;* there
> a certain *work* written; that *holiday* celebrated. (GA 63, 90)

There is an interesting quality in this account of the world of everyday things.
For while his eye is on the table, he sets out the concatenation of the table
with other elements: the boys, his wife, a friend, i.e., with the elements of the
other. That is an opening to be pursued. The kitchen table still bears the
marks of *"die Buben,"* the scalawags who marked it up. The table points to
the presence of the boys, who are still there. Had Heidegger followed this up,
had he pushed it harder, he might have brought the world of utensility closer
to the sense of factical life that I am here pursuing and that I think is systematically excluded or even suppressed.

What he needed was a still more radical account of the factical world, a
still more concrete facticity rooted in the *praxis* and flesh of life, in the griefs
and joys of everyday life and concrete being-in-the-world. For the factical
world is a world of family meals around the kitchen table, or of friends one
has welcomed into one's home, and Heidegger captures that in this passage,
although he tends to mute it in *Being and Time.* That is an opening, but only
privatively. For factical life is no less the world of those who have no food, a
world quite literally of *Darbung* (GA 61, 90), of *steresis, privatio,* of the
hungry and homeless and of children abandoned by their parents. The world
of everydayness is the familiar piece of clothing of someone close, the sort of
thing that grieves the heart when it is come upon after their death; and Heidegger catches sight of that. But it is also the grief of those who go unclothed,
who dress in rags, who leave nothing behind when they die, who vanish
without a trace, without provoking a memory, perhaps even without a name.
The world of everydayness is the broken pair of skies in the cellar—"that is
my youth," he says quite acutely (GA 63, 91). But it is also the world of the
lame and the crippled. "This book was a gift from so and so"—but it is also
the world of those who cannot read. The factical world is the world of living
bodies surrounded by the sphere of utensility, but it is also the world in which
those bodies have been shattered, shamed, disabled. Now it is always the
latter, the *steresis,* the privation and the deprivation, that is the special focus

of the biblical narratives, the preferential option it exercises. Biblical factical life is a world not of able-bodied being-in-the world actualizing its potentiality for Being, but of disabled beings whose potencies have been cut short.

Heidegger's revolutionary impulse lay in seeing that these matters, hitherto considered altogether beneath the dignity of philosophy, were in fact the very prephilosophical materials from which philosophy itself is forged, to which philosophy seeks to give "ontological-categorial" form. But his impulse was aborted or narrowed by a certain philosophical prejudice in favor of the cognitive-aletheiological features of the world that has the effect of neutralizing the flesh. His impulse was cut short by a new and more subtle *epochē* that enforced a new and different neutralization of factical life. In Husserl, the philosopher carried out a reflective disengagement from and neutralization of factical life that turned being into permanent presence and philosophy into an impossibly pure *theoria*. For Heidegger, the philosopher is situated from the start in the prereflective, pregiven world of factical being-in-the-world. But Heidegger in turn enforces a whole new layer of reductions. Fundamental ontology shuts down, excludes, or neutralizes the whole dimension of being dis-abled (instead of having a *Seinkönnen*), of being cast out of the world (instead of being projected into it), of suffering and enervating grief (instead of moodful tuning), of illiteracy or aphasia (instead of *Rede* and *Gerede*). The full measure of facticity is suppressed by the ontology of everydayness and the world of work and care. Heidegger had quietly closed down the operations of the flesh, the whole "economy" or "world" of bodily diminishment, distress, and vulnerability, in short the "world" of those whom the world casts out, those who are despised by the world and "world-poor" in a more literal sense than Heidegger gives to this word. "It worlds" (GA 56/57, 73) but it also "de-worlds" one into poverty and destitution. That is the "world" that in biblical terms was called the "kingdom."

These are matters that go to the heart of what Aristotle called *steresis* *(privatio)* and that Heidegger translated, almost ironically, as *"Darbung,"* neediness and literally "starvation." Yet no one in the hermeneutics of facticity is starving—or ill, disabled, diseased, suffering, in need of help and succor;[10] and no one ministers to the needy. It is a world of able-bodied artisans and equipment, of a busily engaged but thoughtless bourgeoisie, and above all of able-bodied knights of anticipatory resoluteness. Everyone seems to go skiing on the weekends. Nowhere is anyone laid low. Sometimes the equipment breaks, but bodies do not break. There is an implicit ontology of the body, to be sure, in Heidegger's hermeneutics of facticity, but it is very much an agent-body, not a patient; it does not suffer. There is no flesh, no real feeling. On the contrary, *Gefühle*, feelings in their most concrete and factical sense— pleasures and pains, feeling ill and feeling well—are explicitly barred from the scene of "ontology (the hermeneutics of facticity)."

Heidegger's conception of "factical life" fails to address the range of life, the totality of the "interest" we take in life, of *"inter-esse,"* which means being radically inserted in the midst of the rush of existence. "Facticity" needs to include the movements of pleasure and pain, the exclusion and neutraliza- tion of which simply reenacts, this time on an existential-phenomenological level, the transcendental reduction, i.e., the attempt to purify, decontaminate, and disengage thinking. The "world" is not only the disclosive features of being-in-the-world but the shattering of the world; not only utensility but palpability; not only resoluteness but the dissoluteness of shattered lives. The world includes the gaunt faces of real *Darbung,* of those whose bodies are being "eaten away." The thought of being eaten, of having one's body con- sumed by a parasite or a disease, is an *Angst* not provided for in the hermeneu- tics of anticipatory resoluteness. Such consumptiveness is always implicit in the grim metaphorics used to describe the archi-diseases, the diseases that over the centuries have done emblematic service for the ultimate vulnerability of our bodies—leprosy, the plague, cancer, and nowadays AIDS.[11] The relentless consumption of the body by a virus for which there is no cure: that surely is *Darbung* and surely part of "the difficulty of life." Eating—the haleness of people gathered around a plentiful table in friendship, the "hearty appetites," the hunger of those in good health—and being eaten away belong to the same economy. That economy is an essential part of the revolutionary "other" in the prephilosophical materials supplied by the biblical "world." Heidegger just did not hear or see or show any interest in any of it. The biblical materials projected a "world" of banquets and beggars, lepers and cures, bodies wrapped in death cloths and bodies emerging from tombs. But Heidegger assimilated all of that into Greek terms, into *energeia, phronesis,* and *techne,* silencing the terms of mercy and *kardia,* which were the most distinctively non- or prephilosophical categories of the biblical narratives, the categories most likely to scandalize philosophy, to shock it, to radicalize it—since that was Heidegger's whole idea.

Heidegger made no room for *kardia,* flesh, disablement, affliction. He had an implicit phenomenology of the body as a tool-user, as a being of a certain spatiality, and as subject to death, which was organized around the concept of *Sorge.* But he missed or neutralized the unique quality of the body as "flesh," as "vulnerability," the body in need, the body of the suffering, the bodies of those who lay claim to those who are well-off. Being well-off and being laid low go to the core of factical life, of a throwness in the sense of being thrown out, which would be a different kind of ek-sisting, which ante- dates and is older than my freedom. But *kardia* and the flesh fell before a new *epochē* that was driven by a very Greek, phenomenological-aletheiological re- duction.

Heidegger's view of "feeling" in the early Freiburg lectures is very telling and entirely consistent with his later views. In the discussion of "kairological" time, Heidegger speaks of something that "torments" factical life, gnaws at it, bothers it—something matters to factical life inasmuch as much factical life is full of care and concern. "Torment" (*Qual,* GA 61, 137–38) of course belongs to the sphere of flesh and affliction, which were thematized by the biblical narratives. But then Heidegger adds:

> It is not sufficient, i.e., in terms of interpretative categories it is on the wrong track, if one wants to characterize these (formal) characters as "feelings." "Feeling" is a psychological category, whose categorial structure is confused, at least is not definite enough to amount to anything in the present interpretation. (GA 61, 138)

The reason for this is familiar, and it represents a constant view of Heidegger's, from these early Freiburg lectures to his last writings. Feelings are purely private, subjective states, without the power to "disclose" the world. Against the reductionism of the empiricists, which reduced feeling to private mental states, Heidegger actually gave unprecedented importance to the affective sphere. He did this by interpreting feelings in terms of *"Stimmung,"* a very rich German word that means mood and has a strongly intentionalist quality. Literally *Stimmung* means "tuning," the way factical life is tuned to the world, its at-tuning, and hence its being-toward the world. To have a feeling in this sense is to be responding to the world in a certain way, a way that was ultimately determined in *Being and Time* as "finding oneself" *(sich befinden)* in the world into which one has been thrown (GA 2/BT, §29). That in turn means that mood "discloses" the world as that which is always already there. The most important of these moods is anxiety, whose central ontological role in disclosing the Being of Dasein in *Being and Time* and in disclosing Being itself in *What is Metaphysics?* is quite rightly famous. Far from being private states, moods disclose the Being of Dasein, the Being of the world, and meaning of Being itself and hence enjoy the highest phenomenological prestige, far outstripping anything merely psychological.

That I take to be an impressive demolishing of the empiricist notion of private mental states on the basis of a brilliant phenomenological interpretation. I have no desire to detract from the importance and originality of this analysis, which represents in my view a major superseding of the mind/body dualism that has confounded philosophy since the seventeenth and eighteenth centuries, indeed since Plato himself. But I am interested in the new set of eliminative and reductionist tendencies that this highly phenomenological-disclosive view itself sets in motion. The success of Heidegger's analysis turns on his ability to redescribe feelings as disclosive-intentionalist structures and to take moods as their paradigm. But not all feelings are moods. There is a considerable importance to be attached to feelings just insofar as they are not disclosive, indeed insofar as they remain, to use the most classical vocabulary, quite "inside" the "psychological" sphere. There is a considerable difference between a "feeling" like "anxiety" on the one hand, which has a strongly intentionalist value—its whole import is to be a certain kind of apprehensiveness, an apprehension of I know not what—and a "feeling" like "pain," where the disclosive value is not the only value. Pain is pain precisely when it is "blinding," not disclosive. Pain tends to cut the world off from us, to turn us in upon ourselves. A being in pain folds in upon itself, "curls up" in pain, contracts upon itself in an "inner agony," in worldlessness, in the loss of one's world. Pain closes us in on ourselves, closes down our worldly life, and hence is not primarily a dis-closive event.[12]

This is not to say that pain is without its disclosive value, for pain discloses in the mode of a symptom (GA 2/BT, §7a), and this is so true that the most insidious diseases cause no pain until it is too late. But the symptomatic view of pain, in terms of the function it performs, tends to disengage from the pain and to look on at it *(anschauen)*. It requires another party, like a physician, to "diagnose" it. The disclosiveness of pain is not its only feature. As a lived state, pain does not primarily indicate something else; it "is" what is. For pain is an event of the "flesh," of a being *in* pain, who suffers, who is humiliated and laid low, and who calls for help or relief. Pain on its *nondisclosive* side, inhabited from within, the suffering of an individual *in* pain, is precisely an event of the "flesh" and hence the precisely factical datum in which Heidegger is not interested. That is the side of pain which is overridden by the phenomenology of disclosiveness, which consigns pain to something "psychological."

Pain belongs to another register of events—to that of suffering and of ministering to suffering—than the "disclosiveness" by which everything is monitored in the "hermeneutics of facticity." Even as he radicalized phenomenology Heidegger perpetuated its prejudices. He turned the phenomenology of intentionality, which still took the thetic propositional mode as paradigmatic, back to its prethematic base in concernful factical life. Later on, he continued the same radicalization of phenomenology by pushing back even further to the event of *aletheia*. But this radicalization remained within the horizons of phenomenology's valorization of manifestness and truth, of *phainesthai* and *aletheia,* and left the issue of the flesh, of pleasure and pain, and of *kardia,* which is sensitivity to afflicted flesh, on the shelf, bracketed as onticopsychological cases of the structure of the disclosiveness of *Befindlichkeit,* outside the pale of "fundamental ontology" or the "thought of Being."

To that extent, the early lectures fail to stay with the facticity of life, with its situatedness and concreteness, with all of its prethematic immediacy. The significance of pain lies not in its ability to disclose the world but in its power to close the subject down, to shut it in on itself, to deprive it of worldly life, to reduce it to "ruins" in a far more radical and literal sense of *Ruinanz* than the lectures allow (GA 61, 131ff.). Again—and this is the far side of the same point—the pain of the "other" has the capacity to draw the subject out of itself, to draw it into an "ek-sistence" of a different sort, in a uniquely powerful way. Pleasures and pains go right to the core of the existing individual, to the concrete case of life that is ever mine, which is this body, here and now, at this time and place. Pleasures and pains concretize us, draw us back down into the most immediate situatedness of our lives, and constitute in a unique way all the intensity and "feel," all the flavor and quality of our embodied, living being-in-the-world.

Pleasures and pains establish a new register of events, with a table of categories of their own, which is simply missing from Heidegger's aggressive, able-bodied ontology. The significance of pleasures and pains lies not in their world-disclosiveness but in the way they close factical life in upon itself and deprive it of a world. The "subjectivity" of "feelings" is an objection to them only if one is enforcing a transcendental-ontological reduction. In fact, feelings explain how the "subject" in one important sense is constituted. Postmodernist critics have done considerable damage to the modernist notion of subjective agency, individual autonomy, reflective transparency, and prelinguistic interiority. They have in effect finished the job of demolishing the Cartesian subject first launched in *Being and Time.* But the result of this critique is to bring to the fore another subject, the subject as patient, as subject to grief and misfortune, power and oppression. What I mean by "my" life, by "I" myself, in the most elemental sense, is the incommunicability of "my" pain, "my" pleasures, the pleasures and pains, the feelings, that define my factical life. What I mean by the subjectivity of the "other" is the one in pleasure or pain, the one whose face is twisted with torment or streaked with a smile. That is the sphere and the subject matter of the categories of *kardia*.

Heidegger tended to take two closely related views on the question of feelings and in particular of pain. On the one hand, he devalued them as purely psychological because they do not have ontological significance, i.e., do not disclose the world. That, as I have argued, is a transcendentalist prejudice that fails to see that their ontological significance goes in a different direction, not in disclosing the world but in constituting a whole new register of events keyed to *praxis* and suffering.

In the second place, because Heidegger regarded feelings as purely subjective states, as defining a purely interior sphere or mental state, he tended to treat them as something to be mastered. This is connected with all the military bravado in these early lectures—a militarism that rears a very ugly head in the following decade. As we have seen in the previous chapter, Heidegger valorizes struggle and strife, hard work and strenuousness, and a taste for the difficult. He is contemptuous of the love of comfort, of bourgeois ease, of making things easy. He wants factical life to gather itself together, to press ahead in a primal decision, to stand its post in the battle of life and not to blink in the face of difficulty. He wants to be hard, not soft; hard on the self, pushing the self to the limit, and hard on the other, no coddling of others, no robbing them of their anxiety, taking away their shot to stand on their own. Pain is always my pain, a psychologico-empirical state, something to be overcome, a test of my strength. There is no room in this ontology of factical life for the pain of the other as exercising a claim over me, as mattering to me, as calling and soliciting me. In short, there is no room for the categories of *kardia*. The pain of other will make others hard and strong (so long as it does not kill them).[13] Van Buren has shown that in the early Freiburg days Heidegger was very much taken with Luther's *theologia crucis*, with Christian life as a matter of taking up one's cross, putting one's shoulder to the heavy weight of life.[14] But Heidegger omitted the entire framework of mercy and *kardia*, of lifting the burden of the other.

Heidegger was drawn to the idea of the Christian soldier but he was deaf to the solicitousness about the flesh in the biblical narratives, in jewgreek stories about healing the crippled, making the blind to see, feeding the hungry crowds, even raising the dead. The fortunes of the flesh, its well-being as well as its debilities, are at the center of these stories but they do not so much as register on Heidegger's attempt to bring the factical life of the biblical narratives to ontological-categorial determination. He has no category of the flesh and no category of the claims of the flesh of the other on my flesh. He takes the biblical narratives off in the direction of Aristotelian *phronesis* and *techne*, of Kierkegaardian resoluteness and temporality, but he leaves the healings behind. He was very responsive to the *Sorge*, the care for one's being-in-the-world, but he entirely missed the *cura*, the healings, the caring for the flesh of the other, the *kardia*. For *cura* also means healing the flesh of the other, tending to the other's pain and afflicted flesh. To put this as ironically as possible, the author of *Being and Time* never really thought *cura* all the way through.

Conclusion

This omission, I said above, was fateful and, in an important respect, fatal. Eventually it caught up with him. Sometime around 1928 or 1929, shortly after he returned to Freiburg from Marburg as Husserl's successor, the whole thing took an ugly turn. What started out as a vigorous effort to return philosophy and the university to concrete life ended up in the 1930s as a kind of *Kampfsphilosophie*, a philosophical celebration of danger that easily accommodated his notorious politics and the unhappy story of Heidegger's Nazi engagement, as we have seen in the previous chapter.

Even after 1936, when he gave up his political ambitions and took still another "turn"—this one keyed not to Aristotle and Kierkegaard (1919–23) or to Nietzsche and Jünger (1928–29), but to the poetry of Hölderlin—and after the war, when the pain and torment of millions were plain to see, Heidegger still had learned little about pain, flesh, and *kardia*. I do not share the view of many Heidegger commentators who think that by 1936 or at the latest by 1945 Heidegger had learned his lesson. His baffling silence about the Holocaust, the scandalous comparison of the gas chambers to modern agriculture, the mythologizing of pain into the "rift" between Being and beings in the commentaries on Trakl, the notion that real homelessness is not a lack of housing (in postwar Europe!) but failure to think the essence of dwelling, that real killing (said in 1943!) is not the loss of human life but murderousness toward Being—these are all scandalously insensitive to real "factical" pain and concrete human suffering. Beyond insensitivity, they represent what I will argue below is a kind of "essentializing" tendency in Heidegger that transcends the concrete and suffering subjects of actual history. It is still essentialism whether one chooses to think in terms of a verbally understood *Wesen* (Greco-German) or a nominatively understood *essentia* (Latin and Romance), because the result is the same, viz., the loss of facticity, of the concretely existing and situated subject of real historical events. Such essentialism does not merely depart from or move beyond the original project of the first Freiburg period, to return philosophy to the concreteness of "factical life." It flatly contradicts it. Such essentialism represents a new, higher, and still more abstract and austere reduction.[15]

Heidegger had dropped all reference to the idea of "factical life" and "facticity" after the 1920s. He turned more and more toward the search for the Origin *(Ursprung)* and Essential Being *(Wesen)*—of truth, of poetry and art, of technology, of thinking, of human being, of Being itself. He made it plain that "onto-theo-logic"—the fateful joining of Christian theology and Greek metaphysics—only served to block off the Origin. His was to be a task of thinking back beyond metaphysics and beyond the fateful Latin-Christian distortion of early Greek experience to the "First Beginning," a mythical Great Greek Origin (now monomanically conceived so as to *exclude* the biblical origin, and a lot of other origins, too). Such thinking would be at the same time a thinking forward, back to the Future, back to what is coming, a kind of second coming, or "Other Beginning," to Being's possible turn back toward us. What has all along slumbered in the essence of Being *(Gewesen)* may—if thinking prepares a space for it—come again toward us: *Wesen* is *Gewesen* and *Anwesen*. Such a task was hardly to be described as a "hermeneutics of facticity"—it was nothing of the kind, nothing so meager—but as the "thought of Being" *(Seinsdenken)*, the thinking of essential Being *(wesentliches Denken)*. Factical life had given way to essential thinking, to thinking Being's own history *(seinsgeschichtliches Denken)*.

Such a project is aboriginally Greek, for the Origin is Greek. The idea behind *wesentliches Denken* was to be as Greek as possible, maybe even more Greek than the Greeks themselves. The idea was to keep thinking purely in the element of what is Greek and not to let it be contaminated by what is not Greek, e.g., by what was Jewish or Christian, Latin or French. Of course it goes without saying that Greek is not contaminated by German, because German is Greek, spiritually, essentially. German and Greek: in essence the same.

At that point the project of the deconstructive retrieval of early Christian experience, which was a centerpiece of the early Freiburg lectures on the hermeneutics of facticity, and of the correlative retrieval of Aristotle's ethics, had been entirely renounced. (Heidegger even made the attempt to expunge it from the record, from the official intellectual biography, the one given out in brief strokes for public consumption. At one point he and his literary executors even planned to exclude these lectures from the *Gesamtausgabe*.) In its place the myth of Being, the myth of the pure Greek Beginning, had taken firm hold.

The repudiation of the hermeneutics of facticity, along with the hyperessentialism that characterizes the later writings, constitutes the most ominous side of Heidegger's thinking, the most wildly and dangerous mythologizing side which turns the question of Being into a fantastic myth. The mythical call of Being drowns out the "call of the other," the call of the most concretely situated and factical being of all, which is also the call of justice, the site from which justice is called for.

If one asks, from a Levinasian perspective, what has become of the biblical call of the "widow, the orphan, and the stranger" in Heidegger's later writings, the answer is that it was never there, that it was omitted from the earliest Freiburg period on, that it was excised from his hermeneutics of the factical life of the New Testament right from the start, in favor of the machismo of Christian soldiering. That omission was from my point of view both fateful and fatal. Its fatal effects were delayed for ten years. They were first felt in the political disasters of the 1930s, and then in the scandalous omission of human grief from the "History of Being" in all of the writings after 1936, an omission that led him into a scandalous silence and then into obscenely tasteless pronouncements about essential homelessness or essential destruction, as opposed to real, factical homelessness, destruction, and suffering.[16]

One can only imagine how a new Johannes de Silentio would react to this new speculative leap into *Seinsgeschichte*, to this gigantic metanarrative about the march of Being through History that leaves factical life in the dust. "The present author is by no means a *Seinsdenker*," Johannes would say. "He has no such prodigious head for the History of Being, and he has no information for the reader about the scheduled arrival of the Other Beginning. As for himself, he is stuck in between the two beginnings, hardly able to move an inch. He is still trying to cope with the difficulties of factical life and it will be some time, he fears, before he can turn his life's task over to recovering the Great Greek Origin."[17]

Johannes de Silentio, where are you when we need you?

CHAPTER FOUR

Heidegger's Responsibility

THE MYTH OF BEING'S CALL

The myth of Being is essentially a myth of "responsibility," of the essential necessity to answer a "call," of having a "vocation" and of responding to it. The myth of Being valorizes necessity, not chance; vocation, not opportunity; responding to fate, not getting lucky.[1] In the 1930s, the "call of conscience," first worked out in *Being and Time* in Aristotelian and especially Kierkegaardian tones, was transformed into an ominous myth of the "destiny" of a "people" *(Volk)*, whose Great Beginning summons it to a future greatness. As such, the myth of Being is no less a myth of "greatness" itself. In this and the following chapter I want to present the worst consequences of Heidegger's mythologizing tendencies, first, by tracing the point of departure of the philosophy of vocation and responsibility in *Being and Time,* and then by turning to the disastrous form that the call of conscience assumed in 1933. I will conclude by sketching the possibility of "another responsibility," a demythologized responsibility—for I do not want to reject the idea of responsibility itself—one that Heidegger himself neglected, even as he himself opened it up.

The Vocation of Dasein

In *Being and Time,* conscience is a "voice" *(Stimme)* that calls, a call *(Ruf)* that "appeals" *(an-rufen),* that "calls upon" and "summons" Dasein to action *(auf-rufen).* Conscience is ontologically a voice, not merely metaphorically, because it has the formal structure of "discourse" *(Rede),* which is a mode of "disclosure" in which something gets uncovered, passed on, said. When we "hear" the voice of conscience we are given to understand something. As something "factical," thrown in among others, Dasein is always listening to someone or another; it always has its ear out for what is going on. But for the most part, it listens in on what "they" say and so it silences its "own" inner promptings. "Conscience" is the call that calls Dasein back to itself, that fetches it back *(zurückgeholt).* That, Heidegger says, tends to come as a bit of a shock *(Stoss)* even as it seems to come from afar (GA 2, 359/BT, 316).

What does conscience say? What is Dasein given to understand? Nothing—

literally. The call does not provide any ontic direction, but leaves us with a deeply unsettling, ontically indefinite sense that we have not seized upon the possibility which is *uniquely ours* to seize. It leaves us with a deep, unsettling, indefinite "sense of responsibility." Its distinctive mode of discourse is silence: we are visited by a voice that says nothing, stirred by a call that grows silent when once we lend it an ear. The call, Heidegger says, is "indefinite" *(unbestimmt)*. This is a *Stimme* whose voice is *unbestimmt*, untuned, indeterminate. Dasein has a vocation *(Bestimmung)* but it is *unbestimmt*, a vocation that is not (yet) much more than an evocation, that simply warns against every avocation, every sidelong call, a call that calls from the very heart of Dasein but has nothing definite to say.

How can we determine *(bestimmen)* this vocation *(Bestimmung)*? How can we respond and be responsible if we do not know what to do? Heidegger appreciates the urgency of that question but, urgent as it is, he regards it as belonging outside the text. The existential analytic cannot help. For how the call gets its ontico-existentiell specificity, its determination, is a matter for each existing individual to determine, not for an existential ontology. But while Heidegger wants to exclude this question from the ontological analytic, he keeps coming back to it. He tells us that it is not the business of the existential analytic, that it is a matter to be worked out outside the text of *Being and Time*. Yet the question is, does he not, in the end, say too much?

The call seems to come from afar, to sweep over and overtake Dasein in the midst of its everyday bustle. The self that is visited by conscience is familiar, but the call has an unfamiliar, uncanny *(un-heimlich)* character; it is more an "it" than an "I," more alien than familiar. It calls—from afar: that is the barest phenomenality of the phenomenon of conscience, before it is painted over by theology as the voice of God, or by biology as a genetic code (GA 2, 366/BT, 320). This distant, indefinite, reticent, uncanny voice proves itself to be nothing other than the voice of anxious Dasein itself addressing itself, of Dasein as a pure possibility-to-be. What stirs in the stir that conscience provokes is the deep structure of Dasein, its own Being as a Being of possibility, as *Seinskönnen*. It is this potentiality-to-be that wants to be heard, that refuses to be silent (GA 2, 368/BT, 322).

The provocation that anxious Dasein produces is incessant. The sense of responsibility, of the need to respond, is inescapable. This is a guilt that is not meant to be erased, a debt that is not supposed to be paid off (the way the Christian is always "in sin"). Authentic Dasein never has a "good" conscience. Dasein can never say it has paid off its debts and does not owe anything. For the very Being of Dasein is to live under this guilt/responsibility. The opposite of *schuldig*, then, is not "innocence," but "irresponsibility." One either assumes one's *Schuldigsein* or one does not; one either takes it up or takes flight. Taking flight is not innocence but irresponsibility, a refusal to hear and heed the call that overtakes us. Dasein is always responsible for its own being in the world, always carries the burden of being-one's-self on its shoulders, a fact that is felicitously captured in the etymological link between the German *schuldig* and English "shoulder," which derives from the Middle English *schuldern,* meaning to assume a weight or burden, to shoulder a responsibility.

There is also a metaphorics of "weight" in *Being and Time,* by means of which inauthenticity is described as "dis-burdening," lifting the weight of responsibility, the weight of Being. Inauthenticity suffers from the unbearable lightness of Being, the alienation that comes of having failed to assume the weight of responsibility, the weight of guilt. Authentic existence is heavy even as inauthentic Dasein is an ontological lightweight.

Dasein's responsibility for itself is a strictly ontological notion and so it must be rigorously "formalized" so that its everyday sense of being responsible for some wrong that has befallen others is removed. The *ontological* guilt/responsibility of Dasein is not that it has caused harm to others but that it is responsible for its own Being and it cannot shift this burden to someone else.

Heidegger can reject the criticism that the existential analytic is an essay on selfishness because, concerning itself with resoluteness, it deals with the purely formal condition of possibility of both selfishness and unselfishness. Without this "ontological responsibility" Dasein would and could never assume any responsibility to other persons. People who spend themselves without reserve in the service of others are people who want to have a moral conscience, who are roused, who let themselves be aroused, by the plight of others. They have made a searching, sometimes even a searing personal decision. The existential analytic wants to cut beneath the altruism/egoism debate and to treat both as possibilities only for a being whose Being is being-responsible in the first place.

Heidegger says that the strictly formal element in guilt/responsibility is the idea of "not": to be guilty or responsible always means that Dasein is *not* something, and that it and it alone is responsible for this "not" (GA 2, 376/BT, 328–29). This "not," however, is not something we *do* not, but something we *are* not. This "not" is the very Being of Dasein as being-responsible (being guilty). The "not" of guilt/responsibility is structural and ontological, so that Dasein never *is* its own self, never meets and discharges its responsibilities in such a way as to put them behind it. It never lifts the burden of responsibility from its shoulders; that illusion is indeed of the essence of inauthenticity (irresponsibility/innocence). The operative distinction is rather between the one who takes flight from this responsibility, who conceals it in the rush of everyday existence, and the one who takes his stand in it, confronts it, who assumes or shoulders his responsibility. Dasein does not incur guilt from something it does or fails to do (which Heidegger calls "factical indebtedness") (GA 2, 385/BT, 337), but rather is guilty from the very fact that it is "there" at all.

Heidegger says that the issue or task for Dasein is to "*be* 'guilty' *authentically*—'guilty' in the way in which it is" (GA 2, 381/BT, 333), a good deal of the sense of which is captured by substituting "responsible" for "guilty." Understanding the appeal or call of conscience amounts to hearing it, heeding it, letting oneself be called forth to the possibility that is disclosed in it, "becoming free" for it instead of taking flight from it (GA 2, 381/BT, 334). Hearing the appeal does not make one innocent, but frees one for one's guilt/ responsibility. Authentic Dasein achieves the condition of *wanting to have a conscience (Gewissen-haben-wollen*, GA 2, 382/BT, 334), instead of not wanting to, instead of taking flight from the burden which conscience lays upon Dasein. The opposite of guilt in *Being and Time* is the unbearable lightness of irresponsibility, unshouldered Being, unguilty *(un-schuldig)*.

At the end of the analysis of conscience, Heidegger asks again: Upon what does authentic Dasein resolve? How does the *unbestimmte Stimmung* get its *Bestimmung?* But this time he points out that resolute action will not consist in some *ab initio* originality but in a certain original seizing upon the situation in which Dasein finds itself put and which can be disclosed in a unique light by conscience itself (GA 2, 395–98/BT, 345–47).

The reason that a definite determination of Dasein's vocation cannot, in principle, show up in a universal existential ontology is that part of what Heidegger means by Dasein is "mineness" *(Jemeinigkeit)* and "ownness" *(Eigentlichkeit)*. This being is its *own,* and while we can, in a formal ontology, point this formal feature out, we cannot give it content. Dasein alone can hear its own call and follow its own conscience. "Authentic" (responsible) Dasein is not simply pushed about by the prevailing currents of everyday existence, but takes a stand "of its own," makes a choice "on its own," reflecting its "own" initiative. But the troubling thing about the way the notion of ownness functions in *Being and Time* is that there seems to be a "one and only one" quality attaching to it, an absolutely unique quality which attaches to my potentiality-for-Being, which Heidegger describes as my "ownmost" *(Eigenst),* nonrelational *(unbezüglich)* possibility, which is "not to be outstripped" *(un-überholbar)*, certain *(gewiss)*, and unable to be determined *(unbestimmt)* in general terms (GA 2, 349–53/BT, 307–11). The idea seems to me tied up with a metaphysics of "vocation," which enters into a dangerous liason with the myth of Being.

The effect of this idea of the singularity of one's "ownmost" and "authentic" possibility is to reintroduce in a surreptitious way the idea of "essence"— the idea that had been displaced by assigning the primacy to *Existenz* in §9— by claiming that there are lingering essential possibilities in history and in individual lives. Something is "calling" these individuals, or these histories, to their fulfillment, to authenticity, to essential actualization. Heidegger claims that "I" have some (essential) being that is uniquely my own, not a universal or generic essence, to be sure, but a singular essence or essence of singularity, a *haecceitas*. There *is* some sort of self for me to actualize, some sort of essential possibility awaiting my resolute choice. I have a "fate," not in the sense of something *necessitated* and *deterministic,* which is clearly denied in *Being and Time,* but in the sense of a "calling," a "vocation," rather in the way a religious thinker speaks of "the will of God for me." I am defined by my "responsibility" to be myself, to find my truth, to my own self to be true. I have an appointed essence, and my historical existence, my existential historicality, is to find it, to resolve upon it, to actualize it.

This becomes plain as soon as we examine the place of "chance" in *Being and Time.* The opposite of having a vocation is to admit that our lives are steered by chance. That is *exactly* what Heidegger resists, here in *Being and Time,* and as far as I can tell always and throughout his life. He does not want to hand Dasein over to chance, but to have it answer a call; he does not want Dasein to submit to the force of circumstantiality, but to have a true vocation. The whole point of the "moment of truth" and of the "disclosiveness" of the call of conscience is that, in this moment, what is outwardly a set of circumstances into which one has been put is transformed into an essential possibility. In virtue of its responsiveness to the call in a factical situation, Dasein finds its ownmost-possibility-to-be, its "vocation."

But the economy of "vocation" is deeply at odds with the economy of "facticity," which is an economy of change, fortuitousness, good fortune and misfortune, bad luck and serendipity, everything that we mean when we say in English, "that happens." From the standpoint of facticity, all that is "called for" in a given situation is to make the best of it, to do what we can, to see if we can introduce a little variation into the existing situation, to try to be imaginative, to take our chances and to see "what happens." With the slightest change of fortune Dasein would have been located in different circumstances and the best course of action would have been entirely different. Heidegger would have done well to drop the whole idea of Dasein's true vocation, its ownmost destiny; he would have done better to have pushed instead the idea of trying to introduce variation where it finds an oppressive uniformity, and to let it go at that. His failure to do so leads to trouble, both philosophically and politically.

This difficulty is intensified when we consider that what sharpens the call of conscience and narrows the moment of vision to the uniqueness of its ownmost vocation, is being-toward-death. Resoluteness is *vor-laufend;* it passes under the eyes of death, meets death face to face, not of course by actually dying, but by confronting it, letting one's line of vision run right into death, "projecting upon" it, letting its mortal possibility bleed into our very action at the "moment" in which we take action. The anticipation of death fires the steel of resoluteness, burning out the impurities of everydayness and the "they," stripping Dasein down to ownmost essence, its essential *haecceitas.*

This is heavy, hard talk. It is the formalization of the *theologia crucis* in *Being and Time,* what has become of the Christian formula *memento mori,* but here functioning outside of its religious context. The whole thing takes on an ominous tone in the discussion of "historicality" in §74, which begins by insisting still one more time that the existential analytic should not be expected to determine what resolute Dasein is specifically to resolve. "In the existential analysis we cannot, in principle, discuss what Dasein *factically* resolves in any particular case." Still, he adds, it can ask "whence, *in general,* Dasein can draw those possibilities upon which it factically projects itself" (GA 2, 506/BT, 434). The existential analytic cannot say what in particular an individual is to do, but it can mark off where it will find the general range of choices available to it. This general determination is supplied by an analysis of "historicizing" *(Geschehen),* which, Heidegger says, has both an individual and a collective dimension.

Passing under the eyes of death gives resoluteness its urgency, but it does not tell Dasein what to do.[2] What Dasein factically resolves upon is a function of the historical situation into which it is thrown. But this thrownness is now described as a "heritage" *(Erbe)* that Dasein takes over *(übernimmt),* as an inherited tradition that it hands itself down *(Sichüberliefern)* (GA 2, 507/BT, 435). What we might have been inclined to take—from the standpoint of the economy of facticity—as a kind of "brute" givenness or fortuitous circumstance, the sheer "that it is" of the chance situation in which I find myself "thrown," is now redescribed as a treasure of inherited possibilities and goods that are handed over to us ("everything 'good' is a heritage," *alles 'Güte' Erbschaft ist).* This remarkable transformation is the issue of resoluteness itself. In a text that is worth full citation, Heidegger writes:

> The more authentically Dasein resolves—and this means that in anticipating death it understands itself unambiguously in terms of its ownmost distinctive possibility—the more unequivocally does it choose and find the possibility of its existence, and the less does it do so by accident. Only by the anticipation of death is every accidental and 'provisional' possibility driven out. Only Being-free *for* death, gives Dasein its goal outright and pushes existence into its finitude. Once one has grasped the finitude of one's existence, it snatches one back from the endless multiplicities which offer themselves as closest to one—those of comfortableness, shirking and taking things lightly [*Leichtnehmens!*]—and brings Dasein into the simplicity of its *fate* [*Schicksal*]. This is how we designate Dasein's primordial historicizing, which lies in authentic resoluteness and in which Dasein *hands* itself "down" to itself, free for death, in a possibility which it has inherited and yet chosen. (GA 2, 507/BT, 435)

Instead of happening upon the nearest thing available, resolute Dasein seizes upon the one thing necessary. Resoluteness transforms chance into fate, multiple possibilities into singleness of purpose, easy drift into hard choice, accidental happening into what has all along been sent *(schicken)* its way to do. Fate implies neither necessity nor chance, but freedom, where freedom means to seize upon one's essential possibility, to find one's essence, to forge one's fate for oneself (cf. SG, 109/PR, 62).

Moreover, the whole analysis of Dasein's individual "fate" *(Schicksal)* is also deployed on the level of Dasein's collective "destiny" *(Geschick)*. It is often objected that Heidegger's account of resoluteness and authentic temporality is so individualistic that it makes no room for "others." In fact, however, historicality does indeed have a collective or communitarian sense, a national and a social sense, but of the most unfortunate kind. Because Dasein is also *Mit-sein,* its historicizing is also a co-historicizing *(Mit-geschehen);* and as individual Dasein gives itself a fate, collective Dasein gives itself a destiny. "This [destiny, *Geschick*] is how we designate the historicizing of the community, of a people *(Volk)*" (GA 2, 508/BT, 436). *Geschick* is not the sum total or product of individual fates but rather a holistic form of its own, a possibility that belongs to the totality as such. The collective prefix *"Ge-"* in *Geschick* refers to what it is sent a whole people or community to do and to the collective resoluteness that seizes upon a holistic possibility.

The whole that is gathered together into the simplicity of a *Geschick* is not "mankind," or the "West," or "Europe," but (our) community, (our) people *(Volk).* This is a bald and gratuitous move. Why should the collective *Geschick*—even granting that there *is* such a thing—be the *Geschick* of a people? Why not of a continent or an age? Why not *Menschheit* instead of *Volk?* What lies behind this is Heidegger's personal antagonism to Enlightenment universalism and his affection for a community of strife, of antagonists, of national antagonists and antagonistic nationalisms.

Indeed, what is *a* "people"? Is it defined by race, blood, and ethnicity? By the unity of a single language? Or by legal citizenship in a state? One can hardly imagine that it is a multilingual, multicultural conglomerate of immigrants of the sort one finds in the United States. Who is *this Volk,* the one referred to in *Being and Time?* Is it merely the existential-formal structure of *Volklichkeit,* or does Heidegger have something *existentiell* in mind? Does the unity of the *Volk* allow, even demand, the maintenance of its purity? What if someone not of this *Volk* were to apply for residency, or to gain a measure of importance in the social system of the *Volk?*

What is a *Volk?* In the late 1930s, in the *Beiträge,* Heidegger gives us a pertinent answer: "The essence of the *Volk* is its 'voice' *(Stimme)*" (GA 65, 319). A people is defined by the call that calls across the generations, that binds the people to a single calling, gives them a vocation. So a people is a cultural, linguistic, historical unity that is defined by its assigned destiny, its voice/calling *(Stimme, Bestimmung).* But, Heidegger is quick to add, this is no argument for the common people, for populism. Such a voice is not to be found among the uncultured common men, for the uncultured (unformed) are the ill-cultured, misformed *(Verbildet).* "The *voice* of the people speaks rarely and only in a few, and the question is whether it has *yet* come to sound forth."

It is not only a question of hearing but of who has the ears to hear the voice of the people.

Whose people does Heidegger have in mind? Whose collective and collected vocation is this? Is this Germany's? Once again, the existential analytic must practice perfect discretion about existentiell matters. This people is each and every one's own people, in each case ours, a kind of *Je-unserig-keit*. Heidegger has in mind a multiplicity of unitary peoples in strife who maintain their national vitality by an ongoing *Kampf*, a struggle and contest, both *ab intra*, within their own national community, and also *ad extra*, with other national communities, in a kind of antagonism of nationalisms, the highly destructive tendency that has characterized European nationalism both before and after the cold war. That is why Heidegger says that the power *(Macht)* of this collective possibility, of "our destiny," can only emerge from "struggle" *(Kampf)* and "communication" *(Mitteilung)*, from a kind of communication-through-struggle, which is the sort of theory of community that emerges from his *Kampfsphilosophie*.[3] The power of this people's vocation will emerge from its struggle. This struggle is the collectivist counterpart to the individual's anticipation of death. In collective confrontation with death, "we" nurture a hardness for the "struggle"; we resist taking the "easy" way out, as a people, collected together in a common fate. For that is the only way to seize "our destiny." Hence the "full historicizing" of Dasein—the most complete account of what it is that Dasein resolves upon that *Being and Time* permits itself— is a matter of the "fateful destiny of Dasein in and with its 'generation'" (GA 2, 508/BT, 436). Enough said.

That is how the *Unbestimmtheit* of the voice acquires determination, how it becomes the vocation *(Bestimmung)* of Dasein, how this quiet and uncanny call finds its own voice *(Stimme)*. The vocation of Dasein arises as a response to a call that issues from out of the abyss, that calls Dasein into the abyss, where, lingering for a while in the cold comfortlessness of death, Dasein finds its calling, its vocation, its essence, its self.

The Vocation of the German University

In 1933 the not quite perfect discretion observed in *Being and Time* about every ontic instantiation of its ontological categories was publicly, intentionally, and even with a certain amount of fanfare laid aside.[4] Speaking as the new rector of Freiburg University, Heidegger delivered his own "address to the German nation," a rectorial address, and in it everything ominous about the authentic historicizing of Dasein in and with its people was unleashed.

The rectorial address marks the first published appearance of the myth of Being, the first time the spiritual destiny of the Germans as the heirs of Hellas is announced in terms of the question of Being, thus raising Nazi ideology to the level of spirit and metaphysics, which Heidegger later described as an attempt to refine Nazism. The myth of Being arises from Heidegger's attempt to give the Nazi political program of 1933, which he warmly embraced, a higher, spiritual form, to back it up with Being itself, not with value-theory. It is here that we see the appearance of Heidegger's search for a new mythology, displacing the Jewish and Christian one, a pure Greek, as opposed to a jew-greek, mythology. It is this mythology—originally deeply tied to Nazi ideology—that persists in one form or another throughout Heidegger's work. Right up to the end Heidegger is still peddling the spiritual primacy of the poetry of Hölderlin and of the German language itself in virtue of its inner spiritual kinship with the early Greeks (*Spieg*, 282) in the destiny of the "West" (instead of Germany). Right up to the end, Heidegger is systematically erasing the traces of the jewgreek. The question of demythologizing Heidegger is ongoing and incessant and can never be left off, because the myth of Being was never renounced by Heidegger himself. Furthermore, because the myth of Being is tied originally to Nazi myth, the question of denazifying the question of Being can likewise never be left off.

That Heidegger's political activities in 1933 are bound up with certain features—but certainly not every feature—of *Being and Time*, and in particular with the sections of the book that we have singled out for particular attention, we have on no less authority than Heidegger himself—at least according to Karl Löwith, reporting a meeting he had with Heidegger in Rome in 1936. In reply to a suggestion from Löwith that Heidegger's political engagement "lay in the essence of his philosophy," Löwith claims that "Heidegger agreed with me without reservation, and added that his concept of 'historicity' [*Geschichtlichkeit*] was the basis of his political 'engagement' [*Einsatz*]."[5] What came to a head in 1933, indeed what broke out with a fury, was the whole idea of "responding" to the "essential destiny" of "our people," this time openly identified as the Germans. The idea of vocation had come home to roost with a fury.

The address is keyed to the notion of historical responsibility. The new rector calls the students and faculty to their historical calling and vocation, which is to will the essence of the German university. Although the call is issued by the rector it is not Heidegger who is calling. Rather, something calls through Heidegger "from afar"—from Greece—to the Germans—for the Germans have a responsibility for the West[6]—calling their nation and university back to itself and thereby forward to its future. German destiny has a special relationship to the Greek Beginning of the West, and it can be met only "if we again place ourselves under the power of the *beginning* of our spiritual-historical Dasein" (SdDU, 11/SA, 471). In the beginning lies the future, what we are being called *to* calls to us from afar, from our distant beginning. The German university can respond to its historic charge only by going back to that great irruption (*Aufbruch*) in which the Greeks broke open the question of what is as a totality (*das Seiende im Ganzen*), the irruption that opened up all the sciences. The Germans—those Germans, Heidegger and his people, his generation—have a kind of deep reciprocity with the Greeks. When Greeks call, Germans answer. A Greek calls from a distant mountain but the echo comes back in German. German responsibility, the responsibility of the German university, is to answer the Greek address, to respond, in kind, i.e., in German, to what calls in Greek. The address that Heidegger is giving here, the rectorial address, calls to the Germans to be responsible to the Greeks, because Germans are responsible for the West, because Greeks and Germans communicate with each other in an inner way. There is a special line of communication between Greeks and Germans, what Derrida would call an onto-hermeneutical postal service running messages about the truth of Being back and forth between Freiburg and *magna graecia*.[7]

Heidegger's topic is the university. He does not address the disorientation of a university in which the sciences no longer understand their roots in metaphysics, which was the concern of his inaugural address, *What is Metaphysics?*, delivered on the occasion of his return from Marburg to Freiburg to assume Husserl's chair (BW, 91–112). Nor does he speak to the "idea" of "the" university, a topic to which an incoming philosopher/rector might have been strongly drawn. Rather, Heidegger's topic is the *German* university— the university of "our people"—and its "spiritual mission." For the German university has a vocation. The university belongs in the center of "our" nation, which is itself in the center of Europe, which is itself the center of the West, caught in the pincers of the endless *et cetera* of the United States and Russia. Like Fichte before him, Heidegger calls upon the Germans to stand up to their mission, to be ready for the call that calls to them through the rector, but not from the rector, calling them to service, to their fate and destined mission.

Now is the moment of historic truth *(Augenblick)*, the moment when the Germans have the chance to transform the university and the nation in the blink of an eye, from top to bottom, not with piecemeal reforms and compromises arbitrated through "established procedures," but with the radicality of a revolutionary irruption *(Aufbruch)* which will break up this "moribund pseudo-culture" (SdDU, 19/SA, 480) and sweep clean the university and the nation. Now is the moment of supreme responsibility, the time for the supreme response to that distant call which calls to the German nation from across the epochs. Let this response begin here, Heidegger is urging, here in the university, in this university in Freiburg, and let it thereby give direction *(Führung)* to the response of the entire nation, to the collective response and resolve of the people, of a whole "generation."

The mission *(Auftrag)* of the German university, the call that sweeps over it, issues not from the rector but from the essence *(Wesen)* of the German university. Every university has a charter or a mission statement, but German universities are unique in this regard. They have received a commission from their essence, their German essence. We are beginning to see now a commingling of the ontic and the ontological—which *Being and Time* never really did manage to keep apart—of a rather surprising kind. "Germany" evidently has an "essence" and somehow enters into the realm of Being and *Wesen*, and this gives direction both to the nation and to the university. This *Wesen* does not show up only in German universities, but also in the German language— in German poets and philosophers—which is singularly necessary for Being's well-being, since Being singles the German language out for its self-disclosure while ignoring most other European countries and language groups, not to mention non-European ones.[8]

Here, for the first time, we find Heidegger favorably invoking the idea of "essence" *(Wesen)*, a notion that was supposed to be displaced in *Being and Time* and, in its one central occurrence in the text, was placed in scare quotes (GA 2, 56/BT, 67).[9] The rectorial address marks the beginning of a growing essentialism in Heidegger's thought that will finally displace the notion of facticity to the point that "essentializing thinking" *(wesentliches Denken)* will eventually represent the utter confounding of what was once called the "hermeneutics of facticity." Heidegger does not renounce this essentialism after the war but continues to refine it and raise it to the level of a higher "verbal" notion.[10]

The German university can be led into its destined end, can fulfill its historic mission, only if those who lead it (and hence those who follow the leaders) are themselves led by this essence.[11] It is in the subordination of students and teachers alike to this *Wesen* that I find what seems to me to have been the first paradigm for Heidegger of "overcoming subjectivism" or "humanism" in favor of responding or conforming to a higher power. The displacing of subjectivism by way of responding to a call from on high first occurs here.[12] In the rectorial address, this is described as a matter of submitting *(fügen)* to a distant command *(ferne Verfugung,* SdDU, 13/SA, 473). Both the leader *(Führer)* and the led *(Geführten)* must be guided by the essence of the university:

> Do we know about this spiritual mission? Whether we do or not, the question must be faced: *are* we . . . truly and jointly rooted in the essence of the German university? Does this essence have genuine strength to stamp [*Prägekraft*] our Dasein? (SdDU, 9/SA, 470)

Do we—do they, do those Germans—know our (their) essence? Do we (they) know what calls for a response? Are we (they) responding to what calls to us (them) from out of the essence of the German university?

But has the university not been determined from of old in terms of self-governance and academic autonomy? Is that not its oldest, most hard-won heritage? To be sure, but autonomy can only mean following the lead *(nomos, Führung)* of one's ownmost essence *(autos)*, being "what we ought to be"

(SdDU, 9/SA, 470). If authenticity carried with it some suggestion in *Being and Time* of Kantian autonomy, the notion has been deeply transformed in 1933 to mean submitting to a law of essence. Autonomy means to place oneself under the law of one's own essence (SdDU, 15/SA, 475). The self-assertion of the university is its common will, its collective resolution to become what it always already is, to resolve upon its ownmost potentiality for Being *(eigenstes Seinkönnen),* its sense of responsibility for itself. But that will not come by chance (nothing does; chance only leads to nothing). It requires knowledge and reflection *(Wissen, Selbstbesinnung),* not just the superficial knowledge that comes of studying the history of the university, but a deep, essential knowledge, a knowledge of its essence, which is where the determination of its "mission" is rooted.

The Germans cannot fulfill their mission unless they know who they are, and not just know it, but will it, assert it. Only if the German university asserts its identity, wills its essence, can it be faithful to its own and unique mission. Contrary to *Being and Time* (GA 2, 56/BT, 67), the existence of the German university lies in its "essence," depends on it. The rectorial address embraces essentialism, which it gives an ontohistorical significance. Together, teachers and students, leaders and led, must will this essence with a common will *(gemeine Wille),* collectively seize upon the possibility that is sent their way at this moment of truth and historic opportunity. For the university must be, through science, the guardian and leader of "the spiritual fate [*Schicksal*] of the German people [*Volkes*]" (SdDU, 10/SA, 471).

When the Germans will the essence of the German university, then "science and German destiny" come together in an "essential will to power" *(Wesenswillen zur Macht).* But that is possible only under two conditions: first, if the Germans expose *(aussetzen)* science to its deepest necessity *(Notwendigkeit),* push it to the extreme, drive it to the extremity of extreme need; and second, if they expose themselves or push themselves to the limit, if they stand up under this German fate "in its most extreme need" *(äusserste Not).* The Germans have to push both science and themselves to their limit, drive them into their most extreme condition, into a state of need and distress. The way to necessity, to what it is all along "necessary" for the Germans to do, i.e., what is inscribed in their essence and commissioned to do, their destiny (we see how *Wesen* and *Notwendigkeit* communicate), is rooted in need *(Not).* They will not make any progress on the way to fulfilling the mission of the university unless they are extremists, unless they push themselves to the brink, unless they bring both science and themselves to the point of extreme distress *(Not),* just the way Dasein must resolve under the eyes of death, of its most extreme need, if it is to find its ownmost potentiality for Being. The way to necessity is through need and distress; need *(Not)* is the turn which necessity *(Notwendigkeit)* must take if it is to find itself, discover its essence.

We see then multiple lines of communication in this text: between need and necessity; between necessity and essence *(Wesen)*, between *Wesen* and destiny. The destiny (or vocation) of the German nation (university, language) is the necessity inscribed in its (their) essence, in the essence of the German; it determines what the German nation has been sent to do, its unique, ownmost possibility, determination, vocation. The way to necessity/destiny is need and distress: from *Not* to *Notwendigkeit*.

So the question for the rectorial address is, how can the Germans press science to its end, push it into its most extreme condition? How can they will the essence of science? By going back to the Greeks, who alone know the path from need to necessity. From the Greeks the Germans learn this guiding thought, which will teach them how to drive knowing, to drive themselves, to an extreme, that knowing *(Wissen, techne)* is weaker than necessity *(Notwendigkeit, anankes)*, which are the words that Aeschylus has Prometheus speak (SdDU, 11/SA, 472). Necessity is the overpowering weight of fate *(Ubermacht des Schicksals)*, for which, for all its defiance, knowing is no match, against which knowing must finally fail. So there is a kind of struggle between knowing and necessity, an uneven contest which knowing always loses. That is because knowing struggles with the power of concealment *(Macht der Verborgenheit)*, wresting unconcealment from concealment, pitches itself, quite literally, against the powers of darkness. Still, the loss that knowing suffers is not merely a loss, but a creative impotence *(schöpferische Unkraft)*. For in spending itself in struggle against concealment, in doing its best to hold out against fate's necessary concealment *(standhalten, ausharren,* SdDU, 12/SA, 473), in giving its all, knowing is driven to its extreme and pushed to the summit of its strength, of its *energeia,* its being-at-work. Knowing is tested, stretched, hardened, made to suffer *in extremis;* it finds the way of need and distress *(Not).*

We can see that for these prototypical Greeks knowing was no academic, armchair affair but rather the highest, hardest, most demanding praxis, and precisely "the innermost center of all that binds Dasein to people and state." This is a locution that bears notice: *des ganzen volklich-staatlichen Daseins* (SdDU, 12/SA, 473). It fleshes out in concrete and existentiell terms what the ontological category of "historicality" in *Being and Time* meant for Heidegger in 1933: the bond of Dasein not only to its people but also to its state, to a people/state, *Volk-Staat.* We might have been inclined to believe, on the basis of *Being and Time* (at least prior to the discussion of historicality), that anticipatory being-towards-death, which strips Dasein down to its naked individuality, left Dasein in a permanently atomized, individualized, apolitical condition. But that is not the case, for there is a kind of repetition of individual being-toward-death on the collective level, a common struggle with death, with the extremities, which welds a whole people together, forges them into *Volk* and *Staat,* into a *Volk-Staat.*

Now however far back this Great Greek Beginning lies behind them, how-

ever much it has been covered over and distorted by Christianity (SdDU, 12/
SA, 473), it still stands before them as the task that has been posed for the
Germans, as their *Auftrag*. In this Great Greek Beginning lies a great German
future. The reciprocity of *back* and *to,* of being called back to our factical
situation and of being called forth toward our authentic self, which in *Being
and Time* preserved a strictly existential-ontological neutrality (or at least
tried to), here gets filled in with proper names: the call calls Germans back to
their Greek beginning and forth to their German future.

It calls, Heidegger says, like a "distant command that bids" *(ferne Verfü-
gung)* them to repeat it *(wiederholen),* to catch up to it *(einholen),* to submit
resolutely to it *(entschloss fügen)* (SdDU, 13/SA, 473). Short of this death-
defying, heroic conception of science, of Promethean defiance, science will be
nothing more for the Germans than an "accident," not a necessity, a fated
mission, a destined commission inscribed in their *Wesen*. Science cannot be
their essential destiny if it is safe and comfortable, if it is *gefahrlos*—lacking
danger. How can the Germans be great, be what they ought to be, without
danger? Need *(Not),* and therefore necessity *(Notwendigkeit),* needs danger.
They will never be a match for their great German being and destiny unless
they live dangerously; science will never be a path for them from need to
necessity, to destiny, unless it is dangerous business.

The Germans can—they should, they must, they will, they already have!—
repeat on their part the great Greek irruption. They must match Greek spiritual power with the power of the German spirit. Now if the greatness of the
Greek inauguration of philosophy lay in "wonder," the greatness of the German echo will lie in "questioning" (cf. GA 45, §§36–39). Questioning, says
Heidegger, is "unguarded exposure" *(ungedecktes Aussetzsein)* before what
conceals itself, "unguarded holding of one's ground" *(ungedecktes Standhalten)* before the all-encompassing, unencompassable totality of what is, before
an uncertain abyss, a dark dominion of concealment (SdDU, 14/SA, 474). The
"questionability of Being" is a dark and dangerous abyss, the danger of the
abyss, of groundlessness, and "questioning" throws away the security of the
ground and leaps into the abyss. To raise the question of Being is to live dangerously.

Indeed, it is the superior power of the questionability of Being that will
forge a new state, that will drive the people to work and struggle, and that
will allow the university to transcend careerism and a preoccupation with
professional preparation.

Such questioning, as a kind of heroic, knowing resolve, as an all-out, death-
defying assault on Being's self-concealment, will create a "spiritual world,"
for a spiritual world is one forged by exposure to "the innermost and most
extreme danger" (SdDU, 14/SA, 474). So we see now a connection between
"spirit" and "danger": the measure of spirit is the danger to which it exposes
itself. The spiritlessness of modern Germans is their bourgeois love of safety

and comfort; they are not ready for anxiety. The aim of the revolution is to change all that. The Germans lack spirit, but the German spirit is the greatest of all: become what you are. Questioning will strengthen the German spirit, which is, however, no less "tied to the powers of earth and blood" (SdDU, 14/SA, 475). Questioning will transform these effete intellectuals who populate the university; it will give these armchair, chalkdust philosophers the chance to see the real danger of their posts. A university professor's post is not supposed to be a soft job behind the lines; the calling of the professor, his profession and vocation, is nothing safe and comfortable. It is rather the most dangerous, frontline "post" (*äussersten Posten der Gefahr*, SdDU, 14/SA, 475), and his orders are to make a frontal assault on the concealment and uncertainty of Being.

Thus strengthened by questioning, the German people will not drift aimlessly, or just let things happen by chance, but will march straight and erect toward their destiny, in tune with the "law presiding over the march that our [his] people has begun into its future history" (SdDU, 14/SA, 475). But this is a somewhat odd march, because in it the followers, the students, are already in line; they are already of a new mind (*neuen Mutes*). "The German student body is on the march" (SdDU, 14/SA, 475). The students have already heard the call and have already begun to march to its tune (*Stimme/Stimmung*). They already know their own vocation (*Bestimmung*); a ready and willing student body is looking for ready leaders, looking for professors ready to take the lead. That will be Heidegger's role: to radicalize, to revolutionize, the teaching faculty. For Heidegger and the students, they together, have already heard the call and already speak in tune (*gestimmtes Sagen*). (Does that put the faculty in the middle, pressing them with revolutionary pincers?)

The students, then, are very responsive, very responsible, the most sensitive responders of all, the ones with the best ears for what calls back and forth to the German *Wesen*. The professors, on the other hand, appear unresponsive, hard of hearing; they seem to be the irresponsible ones in the university, the German university. They do not appear to be responding well to the new mind; they appear to be caught up with concerns over academic freedom and established procedures.

In the end, all these Germans must become *one*. The three services—the labor service, the armed service, and the knowledge service—must become one. Within the university, the various colleges and departments must unite and override their differences; and the faculty and the students must become one (by letting the Rector-*Führer* ride herd on the faculty from above and letting the students battle them from below). This is a lot of unity for someone interested in the "ontological difference" and in the "not" between Being and beings. For Heidegger, once you posit the "not" between Being and beings, that brings beings into a unity, gathers them up and collects them together, sending them off in just one direction, with one *Schicksal, Geschick,* and

Auftrag, commissioned in the same army, marching to the tune of the same Greek drum, giving them all *Stimmung* and *Bestimmung.* Being able to raise the question of beings as a totality *(das Seiende im Ganzen)* seems to produce a deep national totality *(Ganzheit);* establishing the ontological *difference* seems to produce a sizable *totalitarian* result.

Such unity is bought only by battle *(Kampf),* for a community is a unity of battling elements, held together by the law of Heraclitean strife. Battle makes us strong. Danger gives us spirit. Struggle, difficulty, hardness, having a sense of distress *(Not)* are the only way to meet one destined purpose, and they are a lot better than sitting around hoping it will fall into our laps or happen by accident, a point that has been made by the noted author of *Vom Krieg,* Karl von Clausewitz. Leading implies resistance, and in the back and forth of leading and resisting we will get one, unified, tensed whole, a community defined by its strife, not by its deliberative and adjudicative procedures. As a battle community, the university will lead a kind of soldierly existence—maybe even have battle games, for after all, these same students who serve in the knowledge service will also serve in the armed service—leading simple, spare, frugal lives, welding two wills into one will.[13]

Do the Germans will to be strong, to live dangerously? "Do we, or do we not, will the essence of the German university?" Are they going to change this place from the ground up, or are they just going to tinker (democratically) with this and that, altering this procedure or that? Well, that question will not even arise if and when "the spiritual power of the West fails, when its joints crack, and when this moribund semblance of a culture caves in and drags all that remains strong into confusion" (SdDU, 19/SA, 479–80).

So let there be no doubt: "But we do will" *(Aber wir wollen)* "that our people" *(unser Volk)* "fulfill its historical mission" *(geschichtlichen Auftrag).* It all comes down to responsibility and hearing the call. Still, even if the faculty do not cooperate, the matter is already decided: "For the young and the youngest power of the people"—the students—". . . has by now decided the matter." They must decide; they will decide; they have already decided. They will be and they are what they have already been. *Wesen* is all.

The address closes by invoking once more the special communication of the Greek with the German. It all comes down to whether "the splendor and the greatness of this irruption [*dieses Aufbruch*]," the National Socialist revolution, the new mind, the radicalization and Nazification of Freiburg University, will be a match for the great Greek irruption, of which it is to be the retrieval, to which it is to be the response, the echo, the answer. Can the German university match the greatness of the storm with which the Greeks launched a Promethean assault upon what is as a whole? That is the responsibility of the German university at this moment of revolutionary opportunity.

Another Responsibility

Given the persistence of the myth of Being in Heidegger's thought, and given its deep alliance with Heidegger's National Socialism, the task of demythologizing Heidegger is all the more pressing and unavoidable. For even after he resigned the rectorship in 1934, Heidegger did not repudiate his National Socialist dream but transmuted it and turned it over more explicitly to the never-renounced "inner truth" (GA 40, 208/IM, 199) of the movement. Heidegger never abandoned the ideal of a revolutionary renewal—a point to which I will return in the next chapter—as opposed to a piecemeal tinkering with one thing or another, and he never renounced the idea that this other beginning depended upon the unique power of German thinking and poetizing to recover the primordial power of early Greek Beginning. Instead, he redescribed and rethought the coming of the "new mind" and the "new order" of National Socialism as an "Other Beginning." To be sure, the "Other Beginning" was removed from the realm of human willing and political action and made dependent upon powers that run deeper than any political leader or party (even as he and the Party leaders began to fall out). That is because the Other Beginning does not depend upon political leaders or even on philosophers and poets but upon the deeper *Wesen* and truth of Being, upon Being's deep essence. Continuing to identify this essential depth and greatness with the German language and people, and with the *Geschick* that linked Greek to German, Heidegger held the history of the West to be largely a Greco-Germanic affair. Throughout the war he remained vehemently anti-American and anti-Russian and an enthusiastic supporter of the German cause, and he thought that the United States was out to annihilate Europe and, by that fact, the aboriginal Beginning.[14]

Heidegger put a distance between himself and the Party leaders but not the essential truth of the movement as he understood it. The sort of disagreement Heidegger had with the Party is made clear in *An Introduction to Metaphysics*, which I will examine in the next chapter, and also in the *Beiträge:*[15]

> But if *Ereignis* constitutes the coming to presence of the essence of Being, then how near is the danger that the appropriation [*Er-eignung*] is and must be rejected because man has become incapable of becoming Da-sein inasmuch as the unleashed madness of the colossal has overpowered him under the guise of the "great." (GA 65, 8)

Authentic, inner, true greatness, which is the greatness of the Great Greek Beginning, is not to be confused with great rallies, great marches, great assemblies, great noise, he contended. Heidegger identified the inner truth and greatness of the "national" in National Socialism with the link of this nation, this people, with the Greeks, of whom it is the historic destiny and responsibility of the Germans to be the heirs. Heidegger was greatly disillusioned to learn that this view was not shared by the vast majority of Party regulars and that they were not about to hoist him on their shoulders for proclaiming it. Apart from his own ineptness as an administrator, this was the source of his breach with the Party leadership. But the breach with the Party was not, as he would later portray it, a breach with the "movement" or with the "essence" of the German. It put him at odds with the "impossible people" (SA, 484) who really ran the Party, but it did not prevent him from remaining an ardent supporter of the national cause during the war. Nor did it diminish his hyper-Germanism and hyperspiritualized nationalism, which persisted until the end of his life.

After the war, this breach ceased to be a matter of concrete politics and political movements.[16] He withdrew into a kind of Being-historical meta-politics in which the history of the West is described in terms of the languages and lands that Being favors, of the progressive drift away from the Great Greek Beginning, and of the need for a renewal that still had to be German.

The task of "demythologizing Heidegger" is twofold. On the one hand, it means to hold Heidegger's text to the fire of the myth of Being, not to let it twist free, relentlessly to show the persistence of the myth even in texts that might otherwise be regarded as innocent. On the other hand, it consists in showing a Heidegger *demythologized,* another Heidegger, a Heidegger against Heidegger.

That opportunity presents itself here, in the question of responsibility, which is an idea no one wants to renounce. In particular, it presents itself in *Der Satz vom Grund (The Principle of Reason),* a text written by Heidegger nearly a quarter of a century after the rectorial address, a decade after the thousand-year reign of the Third Reich had ended, and one of the last lecture courses he gave at Freiburg before his retirement. The brilliant lectures of *Der Satz vom Grund* are a virtuoso performance by the sixty-six-year-old philosopher, and I have examined them more closely elsewhere.[17] A vintage piece of "late" Heidegger, the text is organized around the extraordinarily polyphonic motif of the *"Satz,"* which is at once a principle *(Grundsatz),* a saying and decree *(Spruch),* a claim *(Anspruch),* but also a leap and a musical "movement" (SG, 151/PR, 89). Heidegger wants to know what is saying and playing, claiming and declaiming, leaping and even sleeping in Leibniz's "principle of sufficient reason." Something calls to us from afar, from beyond Leibniz, for Leibniz's principle—"every being must have a reason"—is not really Leibniz's, even if, historiographically, it appears for the first time in his writings (what about Spinoza?). Leibniz is at best the lute on which Being plucks (SG, 118/PR, 68). He is less the speaker than the addressee, less the player than the played. Everything in *The Principle of Reason* is aimed at fathoming the power in this polyphonic *tour de force,* at hearing what is playing in this *Satz* and in learning to join in this music (SG, 188/PR, 113).

Der Satz vom Grund, like all the later writings, is marked by the myth of the Great Greek Beginning and the hope of the Other Beginning, which will bear an essential relationship to German mysticism, poetry, and thought. But there is also another twist in this text, another move brought out quite well by Derrida (DPR), one to which I am particularly drawn. It reveals an other side to Heidegger, a more postmodern, deconstructionist, demythologized side that, I hope to show, also opens up certain ethico-political possibilities. These possibilities, which I enthusiastically endorse and to which Heidegger himself would have been radically opposed, belong to what Allan Bloom calls, in a grumpy but accurate complaint, the Nietzscheanized left.[18]

The key to the possibility of "another responsibility" is the new attitude taken by Heidegger toward power and greatness. The power that finds a voice in Leibniz's principle of sufficient reason ("nothing is without a sufficient reason for being"), which Leibniz called the *principium grande,* the principle of great power *(grossmächtiges Prinzip),* is the power that rules over modernity, that holds us all in its sway, by which we are driven hither and yon.

> This is the power with which the *principium magnum, grande et nobilissimum* holds sway. For its wielding power [*Machten*] calls the tune [*durchstimmt*] and determines [*bestimmt*] what we are able to call the spirit of modernity, the spirit of its supposed completion, the spirit of the atomic age. (SG, 80/PR, 43)

Every time this principle calls, modern mankind responds. All thought and all being in modernity, even God himself, remain within its sphere of influence. Still, Heidegger says, however much we submit to the power of this voice, we are, in a deeper sense, oblivious of it.

How is that possible? Because while we are highly *responsive to* this principle, we are not being responsible about all this responding, not taking *responsibility for* our unquestioning response. We do not realize that we are being driven about by an imperious command that does not negotiate or compromise. This other responsibility is so different from the sense of responsibility in the 1930s that the best parallel to it is actually an anti-military parallel. Heidegger is worried that we just keep taking orders, that we do not question the authority from which they arise, that we are too quick to respond, too ready to march, too willing to charge when the trumpet sounds, too ready to dance to the tune of its triumphal music. We should worry more about where the call is coming from and what it wants us to do. No blind obedience to our orders *(Auftrag)* here; now we have to take responsibility *for* what we are responding *to.* We need another kind of responsibility.

So there are two kinds of responsibility (and more than that, no doubt),[19] one which is too quick on the draw, a kind of instant response, which obeys upon hearing; and then another responsibility, which wants to listen more discerningly, to hear and overhear what is really calling, one which assumes responsibility for what calls for a response, a more responsible responsibility as opposed to the irresponsible responding that just obeys. Now this unquestioning response, this irresponsible responding, produces an effect that is *unheimlich,* Heidegger says. It threatens everything *heimisch,* the home of man upon the earth, threatens to turn the university, indeed the entire earth, into grist for the mill of scientific rationality, to grind them up in the *Satz vom Grund.* The more we attempt, in keeping with the principle of ground, to subdue the earth to human needs, the more the ground is pulled from under us and the more we lose our true ground and basis, our *Bodenständigkeit,* our capacity "to build and dwell in the realm of the essential" *(Wesenhaften)* (SG, 60/PR, 30–31). Heidegger undoubtedly has in mind the earth of the *Schwarzwald.* But he does not say that his point is restricted to a strictly German earth; he does not, thankfully, refer to "earth and blood" and he does not say anything about "our people." In fact, lots of people, many peoples, can resonate with this complaint. People from Montana and Colorado, for example, from the land of the boundless et cetera, whose mountains are actually a tad taller (some would even say more majestic) than those of the *Schwarzwald,* can hear what Heidegger is saying. Heidegger has struck a global nerve with this complaint.[20]

It is as though we are the victims of a game *(Spiel):* the more we seek to ground, the more ground we lose; the more we submit to grounding, the more the ground withdraws from under us. Who or what is playing with us? Is this a game perpetrated by the hidden power of the principle of great power? (SG, 60–61/PR, 31) This could be a very dangerous game and we might end up being the losers (SG, 186–88/PR, 112–13). What is the power wielding all this power *(das Machtende)* in the principle of great power *(grossmächtendes Prinzip)?* (SG, 53/PR, 26) Who or what is toying with our lives and planet? This is definitely a more global, planetary Heidegger, a de-Germanized, Greenpeace Heidegger: a Heidegger who is speaking to everybody under the sun.

To see and hear this much, that beyond the loud proclamation of the command to render reasons there lies a more gentle region where Being and ground play together, is to make a leap into another kind of thinking and responding. The effect of this leap *(Satz)* from the principle of reason *(Satz vom Grund)* to the music *(Satz)* in which Being and ground play together, to the saying about Being *(Satz vom Sein),* is freedom:

> The destiny [*Geschick*] of Being is, as address [*Zuspruch*] and claim [*Anspruch*], the decree [*Spruch*] out of which all human speaking speaks. In Latin, decree is *fatum.* But *fatum,* as the decree of Being in the sense of the self-withdrawing destiny, is nothing fatalistic, and this for the simple reason that it can never be

anything of the sort. Why not? Because Being, inasmuch as it sends itself, brings forth the open space [*Freie*] of the space of play of time [*Zeit-Spiel-Raum*] and thereby frees humans into the open space of their ever-destined essential possibilities. (SG, 158/PR, 94)

The sphere of freedom is described by Heidegger as an open space, a place of free play, where thinking is no longer subject to the authority of the principle, where the demand to render reasons has lost its force. In this free and open region *(das Freie)* thinking is released *from* the grip of the metaphysical principle, released *to* the free play of Being as it rises up and gathers itself together in the splendor of its emergence, to Being as *physis* and *logos.*

Heidegger thinks the spell of metaphysics is broken by a leap into the realm of that which, having antedated metaphysics, also lies ahead of us as our destiny, an aboriginally early Greek realm, a realm to which we can think forth *(vordenken)* only by recalling *(andenken).* That is the mythic shape he gives to his story. That is his great metanarrative about the deep sleep of Being, of the demise of Being as the original unity of *physis, logos,* and *einai* into the *Satz vom Grund.*

Now let us make a distinction here. Insofar as this is a good yarn, a powerful tale with a punch to it, insofar as we do not attribute any more to it than that, insofar as we just regard this as one more story with a point to it, then demythologizing Heidegger turns out to be a matter of turning the history of Being into one more tall tale, turning a *grand récit* into a *petit récit,* taking it with an intentional suspension of disbelief. Then it is one more way of delimiting the technological destruction of the earth, a kind of Greenpeace myth of a salutary kind.

But insofar as this tall tale is given historical instantiation, insofar as Heidegger or anybody else thinks that the only way to break the grip of metaphysical principles is to open up thinking to a premetaphysical epoch, where thinking once was free of the tyranny of metaphysical principles, insofar as one attributes to such a freedom a historical coefficient in the age of the early Greeks, then one embraces Heidegger's worst and most metaphysical side, the outright mythologizing of his project, as we have shown in the opening chapter, a Greco-Germanic mythologizing, which, apart from its exclusionary, delusionary, and romanticizing tendencies, is simply dangerous.

Let me sketch here the outlines of a Heidegger demythologized. "Our languages speak historically," he says (SG, 161/PR, 96). That means that the historical occurrence of language is always in accord with this or that historical age. Greek, Latin, and modern vernaculars like German and—*pace* Heidegger—French, English, and all the rest are not only linguistico-grammatical structures but historical ones as well, divergent ways that Being has been understood historically. Greek and Latin are not only languages but also a time and a place, epochs of Being.

Humans speak only inasmuch as they respond historically to language. But this responding is the genuine way in which humans belong in the clearing of Being. The multiplicity of meanings of a word does not really stem from the fact that in speaking and writing we humans at times mean different things with one word. The multiplicity of meanings is always something historical. It originates from the fact that, in the speaking of language ever according to the destiny of the Being of beings, we ourselves are always meant, i.e., addressed differently. (SG, 161/PR, 96)

We human speakers do not so much mean as we are meant; we do not so much speak as we are addressed, and this always by the ever-varying historico-linguistic epochs or constellations of meaning in which we find ourselves ensconced by our historical circumstances. There is, there always was, a historical plurality of discourses—and that is all, "only" (*nur:* SG, 188/PR, 113) that.

With this thoroughgoing historicizing of discourse, this recognition of the plurality of historico-linguistic standpoints, the possibility opens up of "delimiting" the authority and prestige of anything that speaks with great power, of anything that purports to be a *principium grande.* The ground is pulled out from under any such principle, its historical groundlessness—i.e., contingency—is exposed, exposing thus the historical abyss, the abyssal historicality, that lies beneath the powers that be. But of course that also goes—*pace* Heidegger—for any supposed Great Greek Beginning, or for any great Greco-German poet, or great spiritual language, which on this accounting are but one more linguistico-historical event after the other, each with their own strong points and weak points, depending upon the story you happen to be telling. The important shift here is that, at this point, quite to the contrary of the tendency of the 1930s and its myth of greatness, and even to the dominant tendencies of his later writings, "thinking" has become an exercise in suspicion of greatness, at least of that greatness that makes a great show of its power. The greatness of the question of Being turns around into questioning greatness.

The leap of thought lands in an abyss, in historical groundlessness. The ringing authority of the principle of reason is so much sounding brass. But the leap of thought is also a leap of freedom, for it lands in the "opening" (*Freie*) of historical coming-to-presence (*An-wesen*), of open-ended historical-linguistic pluralism. There is a plurality of epochal sendings, of languages of Being, of ways that Being takes shape. Being—let us say a historical form of life—holds its ground for a while, and then is forced to give way by the pressure of historical change, by the irresistible power of becoming. On this demythologized accounting the historical tradition is a translation without an original. There are only translations and transitions. No translation is a betrayal, because there is no homeland, no native land or native language of Being.[21] There never was—*pace* Heidegger—anything incipient, original; nobody was there at the beginning because there never was a single, clear beginning.

There is—*Es gibt*—this multiplicity of tongues, this plurality of ways to be, the incessant ebb and flow of historical constellations. Only this. There is/*Es gibt* the play of the epochs, and that is all. There is because there is. It plays without why. Because. That is the austere note on which Heidegger concludes the text of *The Principle of Reason:*

> The destiny of Being: a child, playing a board game; the kingdom—i.e., the *archē*, the grounding which institutes and overpowers, the Being of beings—belongs to a child. The destiny of Being: a child who plays.
>
> Why does the great child perceived by Heraclitus in the *aion* play the worldgame? It plays because it plays.
>
> The "because" sinks into play. The play is without "why." It plays for the while that it plays. There remains only play: the highest and the deepest. (SG, 188/PR, 113)

The princely power of the principle of reason amounts to no more than a child at play: that is Heidegger's ultimate reduction of the prestige of metaphysics, his delimitation of the authority of the metaphysical principles. The great power of the *Satz vom Grund* is not the paternal power of the law, the law of paternal power, but a child playing a board game of Being, a game of ground and abyss, *fort und da*. The voice that sounds in this authoritative saying is the song of a child's tune. The kingdom over which the *Satz vom Grund* rules is the plaything of a child; the epochs of Being are so many rolls of dice, i.e., so many historical combinations, so many linguistic configurations, so many epochal constellations.

This "other responsibility" is the responsibility to wonder about all this hearing and hearkening to what metaphysics demands, to this resounding call to power, to this prodigious will to power. This other responsibility is not another principle of responsibility but a responsibility for principles, a responsibility for responsibility, a responsibility to hear what lies outside the range of metaphysical power, a responsibility *for* those of us—all of us—who have been swept up in the power of the principle of great power.

The result, or one possible result, of this demythologizing is a world that, with the exception of its ecologism, Heidegger—the man—would abhor. It is a multilingual, multicultural, miscegenated, polymorphic, pluralistic world without national-ethnic unity, without the unity of a single language or a deep monolinguistic tradition. It is a world of gay rights and feminists, of radically democratic, anti-hierarchical, anti-elitist structures, with a pragmatic view of truth and principles, and in which children would be educated not in a classical Gymnasium but in free public institutions with schools in which Andy Warhol would get as big a hearing as Sophocles and Aeschylus, schools filled with computers and the latest technological advances, schools that make a particular effort to reach the disadvantaged.

Heidegger would rather be dead.

Unfortunately, the sharp bite of this very powerful text, which opens up just such possibilities, is blunted by its mythology. The rigor *(Strengheit)* of the *Es gibt* is softened by the myth of origins, by the story of the aboriginal tongue, of Being's chosen people and favored language, by the Greco-Germanic hermeneutics, by the *grand récit* of how *logos* devolved down into *Grund* as *ratio.* Heidegger wanted always to hear beyond the sayings of metaphysics *(über-hören)* in order to overcome *(über-winden)* metaphysics by overhearing another voice, another, aboriginal Greek voice. In the most classical metaphysical style, the very style Heidegger himself taught us to make questionable, he reaches beyond the multiplicity for the overarching *archē,* the gathering unity.

But on my demythologized reading, there is no other voice; there is nothing to hear. One hears only the echo of the shifting, withdrawing ground, of ground giving way to ground. There is only "there is" and hence the confession, the concession, of the multiple senses of Being, or the multiple languages of being, of the multiplicity of "there is," of the irreducible manifoldness, which Heidegger always "betrays"—a bad metaphor which suggests a native land—which he always tries to trump and supersede. Hence in this text, after saying "There remains only play" (SG, 188/PR, 113), Heidegger hastens to add this comfort and this assurance: "But this 'only' [*nur*] is all, the one, unique." So this "only" is not only an "only" but the aboriginally unique and only one. It is rescued from being the "only" of the naked, bare, comfortless "there is," of the "only this and nothing more." It is not the only of the many but the only of the one. That I treat as a moment of retreat, of a "shrinking back" of the same sort he attributed to Kant, whose discovery of the radicality of the imagination Kant himself found too unnerving. What I called *radical* hermeneutics wants to hold Heidegger's hand to the fire of his own *Es gibt* and of its high and dangerous play, hold him to the "only" with no "buts," and so to deconstruct this Greco-Germanic ontohermeneutics.

But if there is no higher or deeper voice, no original, aboriginal command or decree, no categorical imperative, no favored language of Being to address us, what then is this "other responsibility"? What is there to be responsible to? What can responding mean if no one or nothing is calling, over and beyond the plurality of particular calls from epoch to epoch?

Such a responsibility is, to begin with, the responsibility to remain alert to every claim and call that threatens to overpower us, to every principle that lays claim to authority, that puts on princely airs. Let us apply this to Heidegger's most infamous moment: it is the responsibility to listen long and hard to everything that lays claim to being the destined call, the true vocation—of Dasein, of the German university, of "our people." This is the responsibility to keep an ear tuned to hollow notes and sounding brass, especially the brass of marching bands. It is the responsibility to question lockstep responsiveness to what calls us all to order, to question what announces itself as the long awaited new order. So it is what Derrida would call a responsibility *for* all these principles that demand a response; a responsible vigilance, a vigilance about responding. It is not so much a principle of responsibility but a taking responsibility for principles.

But what is this a responsibility *to?* In one sense, nothing at all: Nothing, the abyss, the echo that comes back when we tap against a hollow surface, the hollow ring, the ring of the void, of empty space. This is not so shocking; it is after all a lot like *Being and Time,* which said that the call of conscience says nothing: no thing, it gives no specific ontic directions. One hears only the echoes of the ground giving way, of historical and linguistic shifts.

But in another sense, this is everything, just what we need. This kind of responsibility is very freeing and is actually getting us nearer to a certain ethical or political responsibility of the sort I sketched above. Even Heidegger himself, cultural conservative and antipostmodernist that he is, intimates as much. For Heidegger gives us two examples of the freedom that comes of making metaphysical principles tremble. First, this sense of the groundlessness beneath the *Satz vom Grund* frees the "earth," which is being subjected again and again to the principle of sufficient and efficient reason, which is being ground under by the *Satz vom Grund,* attacked, assaulted, exploited. That is something all of us, from the Rockies to the rain forests, can resonate with. He also said it could free the "university," which has built itself on this high and mighty principle which threatens to turn the university into a machine for producing functionaries for the prevailing system, forces it to give a reason for its being to the state and to the market forces, forces it to show that it serves a useful purpose, including—maybe even above all—a national purpose. Those are Heidegger's examples in 1956 and they are very good ones.

But we can expand this; we can push Heidegger beyond Heidegger, overhear in Heidegger what Heidegger himself does not hear. This responsibility that makes itself responsible for all this responding, that awakens to the abyss beneath every ground, is a matter of being responsive to the "other" of every principle; it tunes its ear to the excluded of every community, to the plurality of ways to be, to the different, to the Babelian multiplication of tongues, to what is on the margin of every center, to the sheer multiplicity of the there is/*Es gibt*. The upshot of this Heidegger, this Heidegger against Heidegger, is a profoundly pluralistic, decentered openness to the other. It is what we can call, what Derrida and Levinas and Gadamer, each in different ways, would call, openness to the other, to the call of the other, of the different that is silenced by the call of the same. It cultivates a sense of responsibility to everything that has been declared abnormal, unnatural, irrational, heretical. It makes itself responsible for questioning everything that purports to speak with the voice of the law, nature, normality, reason, orthodoxy; of everything that takes itself to be authorized to speak in the name of the nation, of truth, of God. That requires an ear—for a hollow ring.

(It is not that the voice of God is nowhere to be heard, but only that this voice is always and already couched in human terms, and that the task of differentiating the human and the divine is subject to a permanent and ineradicable undecidability.)

The "other" responsibility toward which this analysis has all along been straining is responsibility to the "other," to the "call of the other."

With this bit of postmodern hermeneutics we have ourselves made a leap—beyond Heidegger but by way of Heidegger—into a certain region of responsibility. Here a space opens up for another application of Heidegger's thought and for the makings of another responsibility, for another myth of responsibility, for mythologizing differently. Let us freely admit that this is an idea that owes a debt of responsibility to what Heidegger says—and to what he does not say, for these are matters about which he was himself stone-deaf and disconcertingly unresponsive. This amounts to a *Satz* he just would not make.

CHAPTER FIVE

Heidegger's Revolution

THE POLITICS OF THE MYTH OF BEING

The myth of Being was a profoundly revolutionary myth, a myth of revolution itself, a tale of a fabulous turnaround in Being's own fortunes. It was conceived in and as a moment of the revolution, as the revolutionary thought par excellence, the alpha and omega of the revolution. It was the goal for which the revolution should strive and the driving force behind it.

In 1933, as the one person who understood all this, and the one person capable of raising the question of Being, and thus of raising the revolution to the level of the question of Being, Heidegger was convinced that he could be *the* philosopher of the revolution, the one man who could provide the new *Reich* with a truly philosophical voice, with genuine spiritual leadership. By showing the Party the origin of the "movement" in the primordial Greek Beginning he would make plain to all the spiritual authority of National Socialism as the true future and destiny of Germany, of Europe, of the West. That was the dream, the myth, that held him captive. Such a philosophical vocation was not to be assumed lightly. It did not belong to just anybody, but only to a National Socialist thinker—to one who was of a "new mind"—who could at the same time think radically, metaphysically, historically. This was Heidegger's vocation.[1]

By the time of the 1935 lecture course, *An Introduction to Metaphysics,* it was quite clear to Heidegger that the Party was inclined to pass up the opportunity to have the greatest German philosopher since Nietzsche as its intellectual leader.[2] The ideological control of the Party had fallen into lesser hands, to smaller minds, to contemptible, thoughtless, "impossible" people (SA, 484). Party members were baffled by the connection that Heidegger was making between the meaning of the revolution and the question of Being. They were troubled by all his talk about the Nothing, which seemed to them so much nihilism. They were worried about Heidegger's call for a radical questioning that would expose everyone and everything to the insecurity of the abyss, which did not seem to them an effective way to run a revolution. As deeply as Heidegger was committed to the *Führer* and to the new order, they really were not comfortable with him and they did not understand the way he spoke. Besides, he had made quite a mess of things as rector at Freiburg the one time he did have real administrative authority. The best way that Heidegger could serve the movement, they had concluded, was to stay at his post as a professor, where they could count on his loyalty to the national revolution—even though they were not sure what the revolution meant to him—and to let them run the revolution and the Party.

The Myth of Questioning

That is why Heidegger makes no attempt in *An Introduction to Metaphysics* to conceal his disdain—born no doubt of considerable disappointment—for these party ideologues and apparatchiks for the direction in which they were (mis)leading, seducing *(verführen)* the movement and maybe even the *Führer* himself.[3] In Heidegger's mind, the movement was being taken over by its least worthy, its most spiritually benighted elements, by people who do not understand that the greatness of Germany's future must be linked with the Great Greek Beginning. They mindlessly identify the greatness of the movement with Max Schmeling instead of with Sophocles;[4] they mistake the truly gathering power of the *logos* with mass rallies (GA 40, 41/IM, 38); they confuse the aboriginal power of historical destiny with the superficiality of subjectivistic "values." These party hacks do not think; they do not know how to question. The philosophical works that these people are peddling—and this is the phrase that (rightly) stuck in the young Habermas's throat—"have nothing whatever to do with the inner truth and greatness of the movement [Party?[5]]" (GA 40, 208/IM, 199). For this inner truth and greatness is spiritual, metaphysical, historical; it has to do with the need to think, to question, to philosophize in a true and great manner. That is what Heidegger was offering them and that is what they, at their peril, were refusing.

The ideologues who had gained control of the Party do not understand that the success of the revolution is tied to philosophy. If the nation is to be renewed from the ground up this can only proceed from a *Grund-frage,* from questioning into the ground, from a radical and fundamental questioning that would make the ground tremble. A revolutionary renewal of the nation must be keyed to radical, revolutionary thinking. The power of the revolution must be keyed to the "hidden power" (GA 40, 3/IM, 1) of the question of Being. Great nations ask great questions; nations of the highest rank ask the question which is first in rank. A radical revolution requires that we let the very ground tremble by letting the "why" pull the ground out from under beings as a whole and then by letting this why "recoil" upon ourselves so that we too tremble and waver in insecurity, we who ask this question. The power of the nation is a function of the "power of the spirit" *(Kraft des Geistes)* to raise the most "originary" *(ürsprünglich)* of questions, to put the "why" to things, to make the "leap" *(Sprung)* which thrusts away, leaps away *(Absprung)* from all the safety and security of life (GA 40, 7–8/IM, 5–6). Security is the death of philosophy—whether this security comes from faith or from somewhere else. Philosophy occurs only where there is daring *(Wagen:* GA 40, 10/IM, 8).

Philosophy is radical questioning and questioning is not something that can be housed safely in a university that is reduced to career training and producing state functionaries.[6] If you try to master philosophical questioning like a skill and put it to work for you, then what you do will not be philosophy. If you try to make philosophy catch up to the times and be timely, you will destroy it. If you try to use it, you will find it is useless. The worst thing the Party can do is to try to use philosophy like a tool for its own purposes, to treat it in a purely utilitarian fashion.

Heidegger is by no means suggesting that the question of Being cannot serve the national purpose, that it has nothing to do with the great destiny of the people, but only that the party hacks have gotten the thing backwards. That is why he adds: "But what is useless can still be a force *(Macht),* and perhaps the only real one" (GA 40, 10/IM, 8). If you try to use philosophy to produce an echo *(Wiederklang)* of the times, you will miss the genuine "harmony" *(Einklang)* of philosophy with what is really happening in the history of a people, indeed you will miss its capacity to ring in advance *(Vorklang),* to announce in advance a great breakthrough, ·to produce something new, to create new spaces for the spirit. Put in Derridean terms, philosophy is *glas,* a tolling that tolls in advance, that calls up something new, that announces a new order, which is at the heart of the etymological link between *glas* and *classicus:* philosophy announces, indeed it creates an order of rank. The question that is first in the order of rank (GA 40, 4/IM, 2) will bring forth a new order of the highest rank, a new *classicus* that will repeat the classical Greek order.

When we give ourselves over to radical questioning, i.e., to philosophy, the inherently revolutionary power of philosophy will give something to us and hence to the revolution. Great philosophy, as radical questioning, is inherently revolutionary, for it creates a new space, a revolutionarily new and other beginning. We must not attempt to use philosophy for the revolution, but we must let the revolutionary power of philosophy use us:

> It is absolutely right and in order to say that "You can't do [start] *[anfangen]* anything with philosophy." It is only wrong to suppose that this is the last word on philosophy. For the rejoinder imposes itself: granted that *we* cannot do anything with philosophy, might not philosophy, if we let ourselves be engaged with it, do something with us? (GA 40, 14/IM, 12)

We must not apply philosophy to the times, but let philosophical questioning open up a new space of time *(Zeitspielraum),* a new age, a new order, "another beginning" (GA 40, 42/IM, 39).

But philosophy will do this for us only if we recognize its unique nature, for philosophy is one of the few truly "autonomous" and truly creative possibilities that have been granted to human Dasein (a possibility which is also now a necessity) (GA 40, 11/IM, 9). Philosophy will effect renewal only if we give it its head, if we let it loose in radical questioning, if we admit ourselves into it. But it is an appreciation of the uniqueness of philosophical questioning, and above all of the question of Being, that is lacking in those elements in the Party who have now gained power. Their misunderstandings—there are two of them—of philosophy could not be more perverse.

(1) Because philosophy goes to the very ground and essence *(Grund)* of things, these people expect philosophy to provide a grounding *(Grundlegung)* for a historical people, something upon which we can build up the culture *(die Kultur aufbauen)*. And they complain when it does not; e.g., now they are complaining that metaphysics did nothing to prepare for the revolution! (Would that were so!) But that is to expect too much of philosophy, Heidegger says. It is to mistake philosophy for a tool you can use to build something. It is to misunderstand the uniqueness of philosophy: philosophy belongs to a special creative few who, by giving themselves over to radical questioning, will produce a profound transformation, who will change things all around *(Umsetzung)*, who will create a new space which the many can later on comfortably fill up as if it had been there all along as a matter of course. But this creative work cannot be expected to produce direct and immediate results, and furthermore it will not happen by an *Aufbauen* but rather by opening up a kind of knowledge that will "light a fire under, that will threaten, that will necessitate all questioning and valuing" (GA 40, 12/IM, 10).

Now all that sounded to the Party a lot more like an *Abbauen* of the culture than an *Aufbauen*. We can see why the Party was worried about this. Heidegger's idea of getting the movement underway was to threaten and question everything, a notion which did not, evidently, capture the Party's fancy. The people who were running the Party expected philosophy to give everybody a foundation *(Grundlegung)* and Heidegger was offering them a destruction *(Abbauen)*, and they could not see how that would help at all. That was the gist of their differences. They were not divided from Heidegger by their shared devotion to the success of the revolution but by their differing conception of the role that philosophy, especially Heidegger's philosophy, was to play in the revolution's success. Heidegger was telling them that the revolution would succeed only if they entrusted themselves to the groundlessness of radical questioning, to the truly revolutionary power of philosophy to make revolutionaries out of those who gave themselves over to it. But it was beyond the party members how throwing themselves into an abyss was going to bring about the new order. Such a conception of philosophy seemed to them a lot more likely to endanger the revolution than to secure it. The totalitarian designs of the Party would clearly not tolerate the kind of questioning that Heidegger had in mind.

One of the more interesting results of the work of Farias and Ott is the account they give of the perception of Heidegger within the Party and the Party's reasons for keeping him out of power. Although not a Nazi report itself, the response of the faculty at Munich to a Nazi minister's proposal of Heidegger for a chair there is typical. The Munich faculty was wary of a tendency in Heidegger's philosophy to "dissolve into an aporetic of endless questioning"; it suspected him of skepticism and worried that this endless questioning of Being would lead to paralysis.[7] Farias thinks that the party hierarchy regarded him as a very radical revolutionary, "a rebel against compromise with the need to respect the rhythm of political development," a threat to the Party's attempt to consolidate power.[8] Ernst Krieck and his circle considered his question of Being to be nihilistic, not only because Heidegger talked about the Nothing, but because of the restlessness of a questioning that never came to an end. They thought Heidegger's influence was subversive. One of the most interesting critiques comes from one Walter Jaensch, whose philosopher brother Erich was an early and strident opponent of Heidegger. Farias writes:[9]

> [W.] Jaensch emphasized the danger of Heidegger's "revolutionary ardor." Heidegger had joined National Socialism simply because of his innate penchant for revolution, period. "Well-informed sources say that he fears the day when revolution among us would cease. It is certain that this 'pure revolutionary' would then no longer be on our side, but would be a turncoat."

The radicality of Heidegger's thought, of the question of Being, its capacity to recoil on whatever or whoever tried to enlist it in their service, its capacity to pull the ground out from under things, made the Party more than a little nervous about Heidegger.

It is in this light that we should view Heidegger's formulation of the charge of nihilism made against his thought:

> Moreover, he who takes the nothing seriously is allying himself with nothingness. He is patently promoting the spirit of negation and serving the cause of disintegration [*Zerstörung*]. . . . What disregards the fundamental law of thought and also destroys the will to build [*Aufbauenwillen*] and faith is pure nihilism. (GA 40, 26/IM, 23)

At the end of the lectures he warns his students that without the question of Being the Germans will stagger around:

> We stagger even when we assure one another that we are no longer staggering, even when, as in recent years, people do their best to show that this inquiry about

Being brings only confusion, that its effect is destructive [*zerstörend*], that it is nihilism. [One must be very naive to suppose that this misinterpretation of the question of Being, renewed since the appearance of existentialism, is new.][10] (GA 40, 211–12/IM, 202–203)

In other words, the Nazis raised the same sort of objection against Heidegger that most people raise against "deconstruction" and "postmodernism" today, that this thinking is nihilistic, that it could never eventuate in building anything but only in tearing things down. It is demoralizing and debilitating, negative and nihilistic. It might have been useful in unbuilding and deconstructing the Weimar state, but it was of questionable worth for building the Third Reich. Heidegger looked so radical and revolutionary to them that they were worried that he would not be content with a National Socialist revolution.

That was what Heidegger was up against in trying to assert his right to be the philosopher of the new Reich. He would try to show them the revolutionary potential of the question of Being in *An Introduction to Metaphysics*. He would show them that asking the question of Being was the great gift of the German spirit and that it went to the heart of the greatness of the German nation. That went to the essence of the myth of Being and constituted its point of convergence with Nazi mythology. He would warn them that failing to measure up to this question, his question, would only reproduce the failure that occurred in the nineteenth century when Germany failed to measure up to the greatness of German Idealist thinking.

(2) In the second misunderstanding of philosophy, it is conceded that we ought not to expect philosophy to supply a *Grundlegung* or an *Aufbauen* of the culture, which would be to demand too much; but it is expected that philosophy "could still contribute to the facilitation of its construction" (*Erleichterung ihres Aufbaues*: GA 40, 12–13/IM, 10).[11] Philosophy draws a world map that marks off the various regions of beings and that should provide a very useful orientation for us when we set out on our various purposes. Philosophy can also put the house of the sciences in order by reflecting on their foundations and presuppositions, thereby relieving science of a lot of work. Philosophy, in short, can make things easier.

But the truth is, Heidegger says, that "philosophy by its very nature never makes thing easier, but only more difficult [*schwerer*]." With this point, we come back to the issue of the *Kampsphilosophie* discussed above (chapter 2). That philosophy makes things more difficult results only partly from the philosophers' well-known penchant for saying even the simplest things in a difficult and forbidding language. The real explanation for this, Heidegger says, is that "making difficulty for historical Dasein [*Erschwerung des geschichtlichen Daseins*] and hence fundamentally for Being pure and simple is really the genuine meaning of philosophical activity." "Making things difficult," Heidegger continues, "gives the weight [*Gewicht*] (the Being) back to things, to beings." To take things lightly, to make life easy *(Erleichterung)*, is to rob things of their weight, to expose them and oneself to the unbearable lightness of Being, to let things float away in ontological weightlessness. (Were it not for the fact that the Nazis invaded his country, I would wager that Milan Kundera must have kept *An Introduction to Metaphysics* on his shelf.)[12] "Making things difficult," Heidegger adds, "is one of the essential, fundamental conditions for the origin of everything great. . . ." By greatness, Heidegger hastens to add, he means "before all else the destiny [*Schicksal*] of a historical people [*geschichtlichen Volkes*] and of its works" (GA 40, 9/IM, 11). The party leaders do not see the tie between greatness and difficulty, and between difficulty and questioning. (And not only the party leaders but most philosophy professors who take their job to consist in presenting a certain amount of material clearly so as to facilitate understanding.)

This amounts to a perversion, a perverse reversal of philosophy from intensifying the difficulty *(Erschwerung)* to making things easier *(Erleichterung)*. But this is a perversion of a deeper truth. Philosophy may have nothing to do with facilitating the "culture business"—it is not the sort of thing to get a leading role in the works of popular culture or to make the rounds of the talk shows—but it does make possible a truly "historical existence." It makes historical existence *great* and it does this because greatness and difficulty go hand in hand. Philosophy is a kind of primordial historicizing just because it is primordial troublemaking. Philosophical questioning gives historical existence depth and weight by making both Dasein and *Sein* itself more difficult.

What sort of difficulty does philosophy produce? What does Heidegger mean? What is the horizon within which we are to think difficulty? This much at least is clear. Philosophy is ground-breaking, path-making, originary; it creates historical openings where previously there was only closure, habituation, and stagnation. It is driven by a deep energy that can energize an entire people *(Volk)*. It is driven by a relentless questioning, a merciless will to know that cuts through the banalities of culture to the deep structure, the *Wesen*, of that people's historical destiny. Above all else, difficulty means questioning, the difficulty of really asking questions rather than just repeating formulas. Without the ground-breaking work of philosophy a people will drift aimlessly, frivolously, consumed by consumerism, overrun by the rule of the masses, the indifferent, by the measureless et cetera of the always the same—just as in America and Russia (GA 40, 49/IM, 46), where they have no philosophy— and in Weimar Germany, where they caved in to the easy life, where life really was a cabaret. Without the hardness and comfortlessness of philosophy, a historical people will lack all aim, indeed will remain only a soft, comfort-seeking culture and never become historical, never acquire a destiny. Without the ground-breaking work of philosophy, the Party itself will be misled into mistaking the essence of the revolution and confusing the inner truth and greatness of a historical-epochal movement with the banalities of mass rallies and prize fighters.

So Heidegger will set the Party straight about the true meaning of the revolution, which is now in danger of being perverted by the manifest spiritual shortcomings of these ideologues. He will show them that the revolution has nothing to do with Max Schmeling and everything to do with Sophocles; that it has nothing to do with the "crude scribblers" who speak in Nietzsche's name but with the profound void of Being (GA 40, 39–40/IM, 36), which is the meaning of the nihilism spoken of by Nietzsche. He will warn them that by its degradation of spirit into calculative intelligence, National Socialism is putting itself in league with Russian Marxism and American positivism. Hence he warns them of a triple threat:

> The spirit falsified into intelligence thus falls to the level of a tool in the service of others, a tool the manipulation of which can be taught and learned. Whether this use of intelligence relates to the regulation and domination of the material conditions of production (as in Marxism) or in general to the intelligent ordering and explanation of everything that is present and already posited at any time (as in positivism), or whether it is applied to the organization and regulation of a nation's vital resources and race [*Lebensmasse und Rasse eines Volkes*]—in any case the spirit as intelligence becomes the impotent superstructure for something else, which, because it is without spirit or even opposed to spirit, is taken for actual reality. (GA 40, 51/IM, 47)

The biological racism of these ideologues misses the truly spiritual character of the movement. Heidegger does not condemn the cultivation of the body and the sword but he demands that these practices be ordered by a spiritual principle:

> For all true power and beauty of the body, all the sureness and boldness of the sword, all authenticity and inventiveness of the understanding, are grounded in the spirit. . . . It [the spirit] is the sustaining, dominating [principle]. . . . (GA 40, 51/IM, 47)

Volk means something spiritual, something linguistic, and something "metaphysical" (in the language of 1935); it is not to be crudely reduced to something physical and biological.[13]

Heidegger wants to show them that the revolution is all about "another beginning," by which is meant not a simple imitation of the First Beginning, but a "retrieval" *(Wiederholung)*, beginning again *more originarily*, "with all of the strangeness, darkness, and insecurity that attend a true beginning" (GA 40, 42/IM, 39). He takes it upon himself to show them that the struggle—the *Kampf*—in which the Party is engaged is not related to boxing matches but to Heraclitus's *polemos*, which he translates as *Kampf* (and later as *Ausei-*

nandersetzung), for *polemos* is the father of all things. In *An Introduction to Metaphysics,* Heidegger tries to refute the charge of nihilism by demonstrating that it is only by entering into the aboriginal struggle with Being—what he called the *Kampf um das Sein* (GA 40, 114/IM, 107)—that the German nation could live up to its destiny and the revolution could be true to itself. The question of Being, far from being a vacuous abstraction or a nihilistic wallowing in the void, will alone raise the people and the Party to the heights of their power, of their spirit, and will save the nation and the movement from their own worst tendencies.

Polemos is not war in the human sense, nor a strife between gods and men, but rather that aboriginal struggle *(Kampf)* that first sets out the differences between things and sets up the order of rank among gods and men, men and slaves (GA 40, 66/IM, 62). No leveled-off mass man here, no standardization of the spirit here (GA 40, 50ff./IM, 46ff.), not in Heraclitus, for struggle and strife create the differential order of rank:

> Because Being as logos is basic gathering, not mass and turmoil in which everything has as much or as little value as everything else, rank and domination are implicit in Being. If Being is to disclose itself, it must itself have and maintain a rank. That is why Heraclitus spoke of the many as dogs and donkeys. This attitude was an essential part of Greek Dasein. Nowadays a little too much fuss is sometimes made over the polis. If one is going to concern oneself with the polis, this aspect should not be forgotten. (GA 40, 141/IM, 133)

The best *polis* maintains an order of rank and does not disperse into democratic diffusion and turmoil. Struggle *(Kampf)* is the *logos* which collects things together, snatching them away from the dissemination of democracy and ordering them hierarchically. Being and the true are for the strong because Being and the true are hidden and superior:

> What has the higher rank is the stronger. Therefore Being, the *logos* as gathering and harmony, is not easily accessible and not accessible to all in the same form; unlike the harmony that is mere compromise, destruction of tension, flattening, it is hidden. . . .
> The true is not for every man but only for the strong. (GA 40, 141/IM, 133)

This aboriginal struggle *(polemos)* which brings forth beings (the beings that contend with one another) is then carried on and sustained by the great creators, the poets, the thinkers and statesmen. Their role, in Heidegger's view, is to throw up certain temporary blocks or barriers which contain for a fleeting moment the enormous power of the overwhelming. Their poetry, their deeds, their thought, in short their works, capture this enormous power of *physis,* if only for a fragile moment, thereby establishing something new, a new order of things, which then soon enough, all too soon, is simply passed along to the "many," who use it, look at it, copy it. The great world epiphany that irrupted with the struggle between the world-creators and Being, the greatness of which can only last for a short time, all too soon degenerates into the peace and tranquillity of mere visibility. The Being of things is all too soon gone out of them. As soon as this great *Kampf* ceases, as soon as men cease to surpass themselves and grow stronger, as soon as the creators vanish, then the decline *(Verfall)* has set in (GA 40, 68/IM, 63). What does not grow stronger, dies.

We can see what Walter Jaensch and Heidegger's other Nazi critics were worried about. It belongs to the very "logic" of the "great" that it is a time of irruption and struggle, which can last for only a short time, after which it seems, by an inevitable momentum, to suffer a decline that lies "in the very essence of the beginning itself":

> Since it is a beginning, the beginning must in a sense leave itself behind. . . . A beginning can never directly preserve its full momentum; the only possible way to preserve its force is to repeat, to draw once again [*wieder-holen*] more deeply than ever from its source. And it is only by a thoughtful repetition that we can deal appropriately with the beginning and the breakdown of the truth. (GA 40, 199–200/IM, 191)

Once things stabilize they fall in decline and require still another revolutionary struggle and retrieval. Now that is not a bad way to foment a revolution, some Nazis thought, but it is no way to consolidate it. Heidegger was not advocating an anarchical view, because his attitude was uncompromisingly hierarchical: these renewals came from the top down, from the creators, while the dogs and donkeys stayed on a leash. But his view did seem to imply permanent struggle *(Kampf)*, ceaseless repetition and renewal, an endless succession of revolutions. That is why Jaensch feared that Heidegger would soon enough turn on the Nazi revolution once it had succeeded. The question of Being issued in a politics that was always oriented toward a *new* order, but it seems unable to accommodate itself to the thought of the stable continuance of such an order once it was brought about. Presumably, on this accounting, even if the later Heidegger's "other beginning" were actually effected, it would soon enough go into decline and we would be back to waiting for still another beginning and still another god to save us from this now eclipsed beginning. There always seems to be still an "other" beginning waiting in the wings.

In any case, one sees Heidegger's revolutionary program: the National Socialist revolution must be the repetition of that Great Greek Beginning in which the great tragedians, statesmen, and artists grappled with Being itself in the forging of the First Beginning. The *Kampf* in which this great revolution is engaged stands or falls on the basis of its capacity to repeat its original Greek model, the Heraclitean *polemos,* which is its progenitor, its father.

In the final lectures of the course Heidegger offers a striking interpretation of the choral song from *Antigone,* which gives remarkable voice to his views. *Kampf* must be thought in terms of "the poetic stamping of the *Kampf* between Being and appearance" that is provided by Sophocles (GA 40, 115/IM, 108), not in terms of the boxing career of Max Schmeling. The Greeks were engaged in a great battle between Being and appearance, in wresting Being from beings, bringing beings from concealment to unconcealment—in their temples, their tragedies, and their Olympic contests (GA 40, 113/IM, 105–106). Sophocles's Oedipus embodies Greek Dasein because he is driven by a fundamental "passion for the disclosure of Being, that is, the struggle for Being itself" (*Kampf um das Sein selbst:* GA 40, 114/IM, 107), a drive against which he himself heroically shatters—which is his greatness. Oedipus had an eye too many, Hölderlin said, which is "the fundamental condition of all great questioning and knowing and also their only metaphysical ground," Heidegger adds.

The passion of Oedipus is what knowledge meant in the great age of Greece. It had nothing to do with placid professors disinterestedly seeking objective science. Knowing was a matter for philosophers, not for school teachers (GA 40, 129/IM, 121). It meant war, struggle, *polemos* with the power of Being. Nothing shows this more clearly than the choral song from *Antigone.* Sophocles determines the Being of Greek Dasein in terms of *deinon. Deinon* means on the one hand the terrible *(das Furchbare),* the overwhelming power *(überwaltigendes Walten)* of what fills us with terror; it means Being as terrifying *physis.* On the other hand *deinon* names man as the most violent one, the wielder of power *(to deinataton, das Gewalt-tätige),* the one who enters into mortal combat with the overwhelming. *Deinon* as a whole names the *Kampf* between Being and man.

But Heidegger wants to translate *deinon* as *unheimlich,* uncanny, unfamiliar, not-at-home, not in order to attenuate the sense of power, but to accentuate it. The most uncanny one *(Unheimlichste)* means the one who has been cast out from everything homelike and familiar, from everything "safe and unendangered" *(ungefährdeten:* GA 40, 160/IM, 151). The strange and uncanny one forsakes safety for the sake of danger, leaves the safety of home in order to embrace the danger of the battle for Being. We see here the earlier, even mirrorlike reversal of the later Hölderlinian formula: where the danger is, the saving grows. Here Heidegger takes exactly the opposite tack, one inspired not by Hölderlin but by Ernst Jünger: it is the safety of the home that is dangerous, and only real danger will save us, i.e., will make us strong and great.

The violence of the most violent one is his violent knowledge *(Wissen)*—which is how Heidegger translates *techne*—by means of which he can do battle with Being, with *physis:* breaking out upon stormy seas, breaking into the earth with plows, snaring animals into his nets (all of which is just what

Heidegger later on meant by the *Gestell*). Still, this is not a course the violent one has chosen for himself, but one into which he has been cast by the overwhelming; it is the fate that has been enjoined upon him by *dike*. Nor is he finally successful, for the violent one in the end must shatter in death against the overwhelming. There is no mastery of death (GA 40, 167/IM, 158). But this is clearly not to be construed by Heidegger as a lesson in *Gelassenheit* but rather as a call to heroism. In the heroic shattering against the overwhelming, the uncanny one asserts his order of rank, the superior power of his knowledge, which, if it must crash against Being, shows the uncanny one to be first and highest and strongest among beings and peoples. In this succumbing to Being, Greek Dasein asserts its preeminence among beings. In their loss is their victory.

For it is in doing battle with Being that the violent and uncanny one shows his true power *(machanoen, techne)*, the power that has been entrusted to him to bring Being into the work of art, to subdue the overwhelming power of Being as *physis* just long enough to let it shine there (GA 40, 168/IM, 159) before it overwhelms and destroys us. The greatness of the violent one does not consist in his power to subdue *physis*, for that is beyond man, but in having the heart and the courage *(tolma)* to dare to enter into this mortal— and ultimately losing—*Kampf* with Being and its succession of victories and defeats:

> Thus the *deinon* as the overpowering [*dike*] and the *deinon* as the violent [*techne*] confront one another.... In this confrontation *techne* bursts forth against *dike*, which in turn, as the Enjoining [*Fug*], the commanding order, disposes [*verfügt*] of all *techne*.... The knower sails into the very middle of the dominant order; he tears it open and violently carries Being into the being; yet he can never master the overpowering.... Every violent curbing of the powerful is either victory or defeat. Both, each in its different way, fling him out of home and . . . unfold the dangerousness of achieved or lost being. . . . This violent one stands at all times in venture [*tolma*]. In venturing to master Being, he must risk the assault of non-being, *me kalon*. . . . (GA 40, 169–70/IM, 160–61)

Disaster is not something that befalls humans if they slip up; it is built right into the conflict between humans and Being:

> Violence against the preponderant power of Being *must* shatter against Being if Being rules in its essence as *physis*, as emergent power. (GA 40, 171/IM, 162)

It is necessary *(notwendig)* for man to be "thrown" into such a needy condition, such a state of affliction *(Not)*, because man is needed and used by Being itself as *physis* for the display of its overwhelming power. So it is only when human Dasein pushes itself to the most extreme condition of need and affliction that *physis* as such comes to appear *and* that man himself is brought to the full power of his own essence.

Now we can finally locate what Sophocles means by "the most uncanny one": "to be posited [by the overwhelming] as the breach in which the Overwhelming bursts into appearance, in order that this breach should itself shatter against Being" (GA 40, 172/IM, 163). Man is forced beyond himself and toward Being and this precisely in order to bring Being into the work—into city and temple, statue and poem. Precisely in this shattering against the overwhelming, man himself achieves his greatest eminence. The violent one despises all help, all compromise, all petty satisfactions and security, because he has surrendered himself up to Being to serve as that breach in which Being itself will shine with power and glory.

Here, then, is the message that Heidegger bears from Sophocles to the National Socialists: the greatness of National Socialist works, of their cities and armies, of their universities, their buildings, and their artworks, can never be realized unless they see that such works are the setting-into-work of the overwhelming itself, that such works bring Being itself to a stand, give it a place, and unless the National Socialists see that the Being of man is to-be-posited, set up by Being itself for this work of setting into work. This has nothing to do with "culture" or "values" but with how *history* happens as the issue of Being itself. The Greeks did not decide to turn out culture for the next few millennia of the West to savor in their museums and consume in their museum giftshops, but to inaugurate history by responding with violence to the violence of Being (GA 40, 172–73/IM, 164). The danger is that the Germans will take the side of the chorus itself, which expresses, in the song's final lines, the opinion of the lowest and most common elements of the city, who want nothing to do with such exceptionality, with such unhomeliness, and who prefer the undisturbed peace and tranquillity, the safety, of lives without violence.

Demythologizing Questioning

The National Socialists, evidently, were not at all sure about this. It was not at all clear to them how much good Heraclitus and Sophocles could do for the revolution, or what difference it would make whether you backed up National Socialist claims with value-theory or with the overwhelming power of *physis*. One gets an insight into the Party's judgment on Heidegger from a dossier kept on Heidegger by the Party and uncovered by Jacques Le Rider in the archives of Quai d'Orsay. In response to a 1938 questionnaire on authors whose works were being taught in Germany, a Freiburg party bureaucrat says of Heidegger that he is politically reliable and even important because he was such a famous academic. But he also thinks that Heidegger is rather a puzzle, that he does not have his "feet on the ground," seems "cut off from the world," and that his thought is a little too "individualistic."[14] The document shows us that four years after his resignation from the rectorate Heidegger was still a member in good standing in the Party—he in fact never renounced his party membership—but that the Party was largely baffled by his person and even more so by his thought. The Nazis thought that Heidegger served a purpose in his post at Freiburg, that they could rely on his political loyalty, but they did not have the slightest inclination to let either Heidegger personally or his thought be a guiding force in the new Reich.

Part of my argument is that the National Socialists were right to keep their distance from Heidegger. I do not mean that they were right to question his "tactical abilities" as an administrator, as the Quai d'Orsay dossier says, although they certainly were. Nor do I mean that they had reason to be wary of his political sympathies, for they did not, although that is how Heidegger tried to make it out after the war. Everything that we have learned about Heidegger the man from Farias and Ott, and from the publication of the *Gesamtausgabe* war lectures, confirms that Heidegger was a loyal supporter of the Third Reich right up to the end of the war.

But it seems to me that they were quite right to be troubled about all this talk about the questionability of Being, the groundless abyss beneath whatever we call a ground, the Nothing that "nothings," that withdraws and leaves us empty. They were right about his thought, more so than he himself was, although they barely understood a word he said. They had their doubts that the issues Heidegger was raising would be of any use at all in consolidating the revolution. Insisting upon the radical questionability of everything, making everything tremble, was not a bad way to rouse the revolutionary spirit, but it was no way to establish the new order. It was a very useful way to make trouble for the powers that be, the prevailing structures. But it was no way to consolidate one's gains, for one of the characteristics of the question of Being was what Heidegger called its "recoil" upon itself, so that whatever emerged from the question would itself be put into question and nothing would be left standing, not if you let the question loose, not if you let it provoke the trembling and insecurity of which it was capable.

On this point, the party members had a better sense of the political impact of Heidegger's question than did Heidegger. For if Heidegger had turned this question loose *on* National Socialism, instead of putting it into the service *of* National Socialism, what would have been left standing? Heidegger tried to persuade the Party that the greatness of German Dasein lay in its philosophical resources, and that the greatness of philosophy lay in its power of revolutionary questioning, but the Nazis were worried that such an irruptive force could just as easily become questioning *of* the revolution. Heidegger tried to persuade them that a revolution from the ground up required a questioning of the ground, but they could not see why this questioning could not be turned against the grounds of the National Socialist revolution itself. Heidegger wanted the revolution to be fired by revolutionary questioning; they were worried that this might result in questioning the revolution.

And they were right. For the very idea of a recoil is built right into the question of Being, a self-questioning, which is why I have been maintaining that the possibility of demythologizing Heidegger is built right into Heidegger, that the work of demythologizing Heidegger issues in a Heidegger demythologized, is a case of bringing Heidegger to bear against Heidegger.

Consider the questions that could have issued from such an irruption, from letting the power of Heidegger's questioning turn on Heidegger's politics. Would not such a politics begin to "waver and oscillate" in instability? Would not Heidegger's words recoil on his National Socialism, that every being is "half being, half nonbeing, which is also why *we can belong wholly to nothing, not even to ourselves*" (GA 40, 31/IM, 28)—and if not to anything, then not to National Socialism either? Suppose we let the little appendage—the *und nicht vielmehr Nichts*, "and not rather nothing" (GA 40, 24ff./IM, 22ff.)— recoil upon everything that made up Heidegger's National Socialism.

Why should we think in terms of the great *and not rather of the small?* Why should we be preoccupied with great beginnings and great things—and not rather with the little things that are all around us, each of which *is* and contains all the wonder of the *is rather than not?* And does not Heidegger do this *too?* Even in this text, are not some of the most powerful passages dedicated precisely to the piece of chalk, the high school, the mountain range, the early Romanesque door (GA 40, 38/IM, 35)?

And if we break the grip of the great, then what power would the myth of the Great Greek Beginning have over us? Or the idea that beginnings are great instead of small? Or that the Greeks are to be thought in terms of greatness? Or that the Greeks are *the* beginning? Are not Jews and Christians part of the beginning? And why stop with Greeks? Did the Greeks drop from the sky? Why not Egyptians and Mesopotamians?[15] Why is not Sanskrit Being's primeval tongue? And why must everything since the Greeks be the loss of greatness? And if the myth of the Great Greek Beginning is questioned, then what remains of its metaphysico-political counterpart, the myth of the Great German Future? And if that is questioned, then must we not question a party—or a movement, it makes no difference—that is so single-mindedly dedicated to such a future?

But if the Greek Beginning begins to waver, then what are we to think of repetition/retrieval *(Wiederholung)?* What would there be to repeat? Perhaps nothing at all, perhaps there is no beginning, nothing distinctly first which then gets repeated again and again. Perhaps the very idea of a "Beginning" is a myth? Perhaps there is a repetition that does not have anything to repeat? Why must repetition be the repetition of a distinct and Great Beginning *rather than not?* Why not a repetition that repeats *forward* instead of *backward?* Could there not be a repetition that produces what it repeats? That produces as it repeats? And might that not all start by chance, so that a month ago we had no idea we would be involved in this repetition, that we would by now have something going, that we would be on the move?

Again: Why should we think in terms of essential destiny—and not rather of a certain uncontrolled historical proliferation and chance? Why is there destiny *rather than not*? Is not the whole idea of destiny not entirely ill fated, mythic, and dangerous? Why not think in terms of the opportunities that present themselves from time to time, little breaks and chances here and there, unforseen Kierkegaardian "moments,"[16] little openings and possibilities instead of vast historical epochal clearings? But if we make the notion of destiny tremble, then should we not tremble at the thought of the Party of destiny, or the people of destiny?

Again: Why should we think that Being has a *Wesen* at all *rather than not*? Have we broken the grip of essentialism simply because we have shifted it from the nominative, essentialistic sense of *essentia* to the supposedly more primordial Greco-Germanic verbal sense of *An-wesen*, of coming to be and passing away? Have we made *Wesen* tremble simply because we have lifted it up a notch from the nominative to the verbal and put it in process?[17] Why must we think in terms of *Wesen* and the *Wesentliches* at all, *and not rather* of the accidental? What is the Being of *Wesen* and *Un-wesen*? And why must we devalorize everything accidental, inessential, outside, excluded, trivialized, everything small and insignificant, which may turn out in the end—who knows?—to be very important? Why is it necessary, as Heidegger thinks in *Being and Time* (§74), to drive out everything accidental and to convert it into what is historically necessary and essential? Why not learn to live with the accidental, to operate among the changeable and variable? Is that not the art of politics?

Again: Why must there be *the* history of Being *and not rather* many such histories, a whole host of them, a proliferation of histories, which tell us many stories, so many that they are impossible to monitor and to organize into a grand narrative of Being's singular upsurge and decline? The notion that this is not man's history, not a story controlled by a human agency, but a history that is visited upon man is itself a disruption of the most sedimented conceptions of history. And that is part of the power of Heidegger's thought. But why not many such histories? And why a history of Being rather than of something that is Otherwise Than Being, as Heidegger's most famous antagonist, Emmanuel Levinas, has put it? Is Justice, as Levinas describes it, Otherwise Than Being? If we must think in myths, if there is no such place as the outside of myth, if that utopia is but another myth, then is not justice the substance of another, more salutary myth, the subject matter of mythologizing differently?

But if we remain faithful even to the notion of Being, what is it about Being that weds it to "our people," that makes it the specific energy and power of

any people? Why does Being not belong to any and every people? To all and
to none (GA 40, 38/IM, 34)? Why should there be people, *Völker*, national
unities at all, *rather than not?* Why not many peoples and peoples who have
been miscegenated beyond identifiable recognition, whose identities are being
gradually blurred? Heidegger thought in terms of the saving power of "our
people." He thought that the greatness of the German people could save us
from the endless et cetera of Russian and American people. But what does
thinking about Russian, German, and American give us? Stalinism, Nazism,
Hiroshima and Viet Nam and the Gulf War. Dead bodies, dead people. Must
we not be always inside and outside our people? American and not American?
We are always already American (or French, or something), but we need to
see how profoundly dangerous that is. Not evil, but dangerous.

Now we are back to danger. Heidegger, who always loved danger, had an
eye too few for the real danger. He was oblivious of the danger of stirring up
the sentiments of greatness, of people, of destiny, of the love of violence and
danger. He did not see the danger in danger; he thought it was saving. The
danger was that he was not making these ideas questionable, that he did not
let the question of Being recoil upon them, exposing them to the little appendage "and not rather," the little "not" that makes them tremble. Heidegger
thought the question of Being belonged in the service of "people," "greatness,"
and "destiny." He did not have the courage or the power—although he was
very interested in courage and power—to turn the question of Being on the
great destiny of his people, to throw them into question and confusion, which
is just what the Nazis feared. It was to their perverse credit that the Nazis
sensed quite vividly that Heidegger's questioning could break loose in just
such a disruptive volley of questions as we have just sampled as would throw
National Socialism itself into question. But Heidegger himself never saw that,
at least not as regards this hellish movement's "inner truth and greatness."

I would say, to use a military figure, that Heidegger betrayed the question
of Being, that he handed it over to the enemy, enlisted it in the service *(Dienst)*
of a people, that he conscripted and confined it to one people and one language
(or two: Are Greek and German one or two?). He did the same thing to Greek
tragedy; he made Sophocles wear a steel helmet, and later on even Antigone
herself (GA 53, §17). Let us say that our task today, like the allied armies
descending on Freiburg (from which, Ott tells us, Heidegger beat a hasty
retreat),[18] is to liberate the question of Being, to liberate Heraclitus and Aristotle, Aeschylus and Sophocles, from their German captors. Let us make the
Germanness of Heidegger tremble, make it waver in insecurity, in order to
liberate Heidegger from Heidegger, to turn Heidegger against Heidegger, and
this by means of Heidegger himself. Let us make Heidegger truly the name,
not of a man, but of a matter to be thought.

CHAPTER SIX

Heidegger's Essentialism

THE LOGIC OF THE MYTHOLOGIC OF BEING

From Facticity to *Wesen*

When the war ended and we were visited with a new wave of Heideggerian texts, a constellation of writings called today, by a certain simplification, the "later" Heidegger, everything had changed. The massive voluntarism of the early and mid-1930s—which had not appeared in any major publication and was known only to those who witnessed Heidegger's rectorate and heard his lectures—was completely superseded by a new and provocative discourse on *Gelassenheit,* which first took shape in the *Beiträge* (GA 65). The concerns of the 1920s with the hermeneutics of factical life had completely vanished. From facticity, Heidegger's interests turned more and more toward the search for the Essential Being *(Wesen)*[1] and Origin *(Ursprung)* of truth, of poetry and art, of technology, of language and thinking, of human being, of Being itself. The myth of a deep Essential Being, both structurally primordial and historically Greek, was firmly in place. The task of thought was not to cope with the contingencies of changeable, factical life but to break through to what is originary *(ursprünglich),* incipient *(anfänglich),* and essential *(wesentlich).* Such a task was hardly to be described as a "hermeneutics of facticity"—it was nothing of the kind, nothing so meager—but as the "thought of Being" *(Seinsdenken),* the thinking of Essential Being *(Wesen, wesentliches Denken).* The hermeneutics of factical life had given way to essential thinking, to thinking Being's own history *(Seinsgeschichtliches Denken).*

The idea behind such *wesentliches Denken* is to be as Greek as possible, to be hyper-Greek, even more Greek than the Greeks themselves. Far from attempting to raise up the structure of factical life in the New Testament communities or in the Aristotelian *polis* to ontological formality, the whole idea of essential thinking is to keep thinking purely in the mythic element of what is early Greek and not to let it be contaminated by what is not primordially Greek, e.g., by what was Jewish or Christian, Latin or French, theological or ontological. This is a matter of purity, not of blood but of tongue, not of biological purity but of linguistic-spiritual purity. Greek is not, however, contaminated by German, because German is in essence the same as Greek, connected to Greek by an inner spiritual bond. The French themselves testified to this, for they themselves confessed that when they try to think, they can only do so in German, being sure that they cannot make it in their own language.[2] Thinking thus is aboriginally Greek, but it can only be conducted today, in the time of need, while Being waits for an open space and a new god, in German, which is where the saving God will undoubtedly arrive. The myth of Being and the coming God was no less a myth of the greatness of the German language, in which language itself speaks *(die Sprache spricht)*, and the greatness of German poetry, for the key in which all great poetry is played is set by Hölderlin.

The myth of Origin, a myth of primal Greek purity, of what is purely Greek, or purely hyper-Greek, and hence of what is Greco-German, held sway in the "later" Heidegger every bit as powerfully as it had in the mid-1930s. It was indeed the permanent legacy of the politics of the 1930s; it was the politics of the 1930s turned over to its inner and essential truth. The path of thought was marked by a repeated *repetitio (Wiederholung)*, but never by *retractio*.

The writings that appeared after the war were marked by a heavily coded discourse organized around the notion of Essential Being *(Wesen)*, by a recurrent logic of a deep, primordial, originary truth, which proved to be the logic of mytho-logic. Here I wish to examine a brief but symptomatic passage from *A Letter on Humanism,* Heidegger's landmark 1947 statement addressed to the language-poor French after the war, the opening statement in which the later Heidegger stepped on stage, in which the "essentializing" logic of the later thinking, of this *wesentliches Denken,* is clearly marked. The passage makes evident a certain recurrent formula or law in Heidegger's later writings, a certain semantic regularity that operates upon these texts, the heavy coding that organizes and pervades all the writings published after the war. I will call this formula the law of "essentialization"—of *Verwesentlichung,* if you can say that in German—because of its systematic valorization of *Wesen* over that of which it is the essence. One might also call it the "logic of essence" *(Wesen),* which is to say the same thing. The effect of this discourse is ultimately to displace what was once called the hermeneutics of facticity, which survives in the later writings in a diminished form. Still, the logic of facticity, however weakened, manages to offer a certain opposition to the dominant logic of essentialization and, although greatly attenuated, makes it impossible for Heidegger to complete the operation of essentialization, to impose the law of essence as mercilessly as he would like.

The law of essentialization is the logic of Heidegger's mythologizing thinking, the logic of the mythologic of Being, providing it with a kind of epistemic or meta-epistemic authority.

The rigor *(Strengheit)* of the essentializing mythologic is, as Derrida shows, always to avoid "contamination," to keep the aboriginal *Wesen* pure, even and precisely when that *Wesen* admits of *Un-wesen*.[3] The aboriginal *Wesen*, the whole complex of *An- und Ab-wesen*, resists contamination by whatever is not essential *(wesentlich)*, not Greek. In the remarks that follow I want to show how this law affects what Heidegger has to say about *Lebe-wesen*, living being, and above all about the living body, the animal organism, which must be kept pure of anything nonessential. I am particularly interested in how this essentializing discourse in turn is related to Heidegger's view of pain and human suffering, a matter that will concern me in this and the following two chapters. The worst effect of Heidegger's later writings is the mystification they produce about these matters. The reading that I am undertaking here will never be far from Derrida's *De L'esprit*, because it was Derrida who first showed that Heidegger's treatment of the animal is deeply emblematic and symptomatic of his entire text, that it is not an accident, but obeys a deep textual law (OS, 47ff.) I will concentrate my reading on a few sentences from *A Letter on Humanism*.[4]

Wesen and Lebewesen

"Metaphysics does indeed represent beings in their Being, and so it thinks the Being of beings" (GA 9, 322/BW, 202).[5] To be sure—*zwar*, Heidegger concedes this—metaphysics thinks the Being of beings. It is indeed capable of projecting beings in or on their Being: it sets them forth *(vor-stellen)*, sets them up *(auf-stellen)*, puts them on display, on exhibit *(Aufstellung)*. Metaphysics is constantly setting *(stellen)* beings out in one order or another, one historical, epochal order after another, and so it is no surprise that metaphysical positing *(vorstellen)* should end up making the final push, the *Ge-stell*, the collective *(Ge-)* mobilization *(stellen)* of every being as raw material for an unleashed will to power. This has been going on a long time now, ever since the whole thing got underway in Plato. *In* Plato—this was not anything Plato did but something that got done in Plato—beings are set forth in their Being as *eidos*, given the look of availability for sight, of visibility, the look of look itself. Being sets up an order for beings, an arrangement into which things can fit themselves, giving them one look or another—as *eidos, ousia, esse, Subjekt, Vernunft, Wille zur Macht*—in one thinker or another, such as Plato, Aristotle, or Aquinas; Descartes, Kant, Hegel, or Nietzsche (this is a selective reading list: there are never Anglo-Saxon names on it, and at most one French name).

The Being of beings is—we can say this in English if we play with the German—a "frame-up" (for a *Gestell* is a frame). It frames things out, puts them in a frame, gives them a look which they might well consider an injustice if they could have their say, enframes them in some ontological order or another, so that henceforth beings are bound from the ground up to some ontological *ordo*.

"But it does not think Being itself, does not think the difference of both"

(GA 9, 322/BW, 202–203).[6] But metaphysics does not think Being as such. That means that metaphysics does not "think" at all, but only sets things up, pushes things around. It does not think Being as such *or*—this amounts to the same thing—it does not think the difference between Being and beings. Metaphysics does not see that every time it lines beings up in some order-of-Being or another, it has "contracted" Being to some historical-categorial frame or another, confined it within some ontic or entitative order. For an order-of-Being *(ordo essendi)* is nothing other than a certain mode of Being, a certain *kind* of Being and not Being, not Being *itself*, not Being in its removal from any ordering category, in its difference from any categorial order.

I interrupt this reading momentarily and ask: What would that be like? What would it mean to think Being *itself*, Being in its removal or *difference* from any mode of Being? Would not anything we say about Being inevitably be entitative, ontic, based upon a transference from some order of beings? How could it avoid bearing the traces of some ontico-historical setting? Would it not have to take the form of some natural, empirical language, be phrased under certain linguistic constraints? Is Being not always "contaminated" by something ontic, something entitative? How would it ever be possible to get so far removed from beings as to attain Being in its uncontaminated purity? Would that not be as unlikely, as impossible, as the pure *epochē* for which Heidegger criticized Husserl on the grounds that the purity of transcendental consciousness was always already contaminated by the facticity of Dasein? Is not Heidegger here repeating, reproducing, the same Husserlian and transcendental gesture? Does not the "facticity" of Dasein—which was brought to bear against transcendental phenomenology—likewise impede the purity of Being's transcendence, of Being's removal from beings? In general, does not the logic of facticity always already subvert the logic of purification and non-contamination? Is not the "principle" of facticity, the principle that says that we can never get to pure principles, pure beginnings, is that not a principle of contamination and is that not *also* Heidegger's principle? Is it not one of Heidegger's most famous teachings, against Husserl, that things (both Being and human being) are always already contaminated? Is not Being always already contaminated?[7]

"Metaphysics does not ask about the truth of Being itself" (GA 9, 322/BW, 203).[8] Metaphysics does not think Being itself, or Being in its difference from beings, or now—this is a third formulation—Being in its "truth." The truth of Being is Being that has not been constricted to any mode, narrowed to any category, confined to any region, enclosed within any frame. It is the sheer, clear open-endedness of Being's "clearing," the openness of the Open itself. The truth of Being is Being's open space, the open range within which every regional, categorial mode of Being occurs.

I interrupt again to point out again the mythologizing: Is not the *truth* of Being also a *mode*, a limitation of Being? Is not the truth of Being delimitable from its goodness or its beauty? Is not the truth of Being a *region* too? Is it not, after all, a very Greek category—*aletheia*—and does it not then have an ontico-historical regionality? Is *Greek* truth to be identified with truth "itself" (if it has an "itself"), with the "difference" between truth itself and particular truths, with the very "truth of truth"? Indeed, is the whole discourse on "Being" not itself a constraining, regional "category"? It is not a Hebrew category, for example, and if we tried to think in Hebrew would we not hit upon something which is "otherwise than Being" and hence of a different order? "Being" *(einai)* and this *"aletheia"* are characteristic concerns of Athens, not Jerusalem. They are Athenian regionalizations, which may seem like foolishness over in Jerusalem. How can that be identified with the "Open" itself, if it has an "itself"? Are we to say there is no Open in Jerusalem—or that things are open differently?

"Nor does it therefore ask in what way the essence of man belongs to the truth of Being" (GA 9, 322/BW, 203).[9] Now Heidegger turns to the question of human being: metaphysics never troubles itself with how the essence of human being belongs to the truth of Being. Instead, it is enough for metaphysics to determine the essence of human being in terms of *animal rationale,* the *zoon logon echon:* the living thing equipped with reason. But such a definition treats human being as a particular kind of entity, situates it within the opening that Being opens, within Being's clearing. Such a view of human being comes too late to catch the Being of human being's relation to Being. For "reason" *(Vernunft)* has already taken in *(vernehmen)* the Being of beings, already taken up Being in one or another of its categorial modes, is dependent upon Being's being already cleared, open, "there."

But above all else—*vor allem anderen*—metaphysics does not ask whether the "essence of human being, incipiently and most decisively, lies in the essence of animality" (GA 9, 323/BW, 203). Here the logic of *Wesen* begins to set in. Can human being simply be inserted within the class of beings called animal, within some animal phylum, no matter how generously it may be supplemented with "reason" or even "spirit"? Is that not to think too little *(zu gering)* of human being?

A Derridean interruption: What is wrong with animals? Why is Heidegger not happy to be an animal? What is so little, so small—*gering*—about being alive, a living thing, a living being, a *Lebewesen?* Some animals are quite large, even very magnificent, not little at all, and is it not a matter of great concern that so many animals are daily disappearing from the earth? What is Heidegger resisting? Why does animality diminish human being? Why is that so rather than not? Why is it never questioned?

The *Wesen* of human being is to be the open place for Being "itself"—in its difference from beings, which is also its truth—which is cleared beforehand, which is "there" before "animal" ever arrives on the scene. Human being is not so much a being as a relationship to Being's truth, within which categories such as animal and rational come to pass. "Animality" closes down, narrows, enframes human being within a biological genus, an animal frame.

Now we begin to see the effects of the operation of *Verwesentlichung*. In the same way that Being is removed from beings, purified of them, so in a parallel operation that produces an exactly analogous effect, human being, the *Wesen* of human being, is removed from animals, is *not* any animal, is purified of its animality, and is raised up into its true, authentic, genuine excellence. The excellence of human being is not that it is an excellent animal, but that it excels anything animal, indeed it excels any being whatsoever, because it has, or it is *(west)*, in the essence of its Being, a relationship to Being. Human being's relatives and neighbors are not to be found in the forest but with Being. Humankind is a friend of Being, is of Being's kind, but not a kin of animals. Dasein is no Saint Francis.

(But are there no animals in the Black Forest?)

The empirical species *anthropos,* the upright, hairless, talking biped may indeed be correctly represented as a zoological being, as a rational animal. But there is more to human being than anything zoological or even anthropological, and that is man's *Wesen,* the *Wesen* that is happening *in* man and that cannot be represented. This *Wesen* is not something that human being is *(ist),* but something that comes to presence *(west)* in human being and draws it outside itself, something that happens to human being, that comes over it, that takes it over, that holds it outside of itself, beyond itself, in ecstatic openness to Being. For to think the Being of human being it is necessary to think beyond representation, to think something beyond, outside, over and above the human. Human being ek-sists—its *Wesen* lies in ek-sistence—it stands out ecstatically in the clearing of Being's truth. The ex-cellence and excess of ek-sistence over the rational animal exactly parallels the excess of (the truth of) Being over beings (in their Being).

So we are led by the logic of essence to a strange result, an old mystical result, the oddity of which launches the conversation on a country path: the *Wesen* of human being is nothing human (DT, 58).

Here is the code, the logic, the semantic regularity that I set out to identify under the law of essentialization. This statement is reproduced, structurally, again and again in Heidegger's texts:

—The essence of technology is nothing technological (QCT, 44);

—the essence of language is not found in human speaking (PLT, 189ff.);

—the essence of dwelling has nothing to do with having four walls and a roof over your head (PLT, 161);

—the essence of destruction has nothing to do with nuclear annihilation (PLT, 166);

—the essence of pain has nothing to do with feeling.

(I will come back to the last formulation later.)

We have here, I propose, a deeply Heideggerian law, a deepset Heideggerian formula, a recurring logic. The discourse on *Wesen,* on the order of essence, is, as Derrida says, deeply marked by the desire for noncontamination. The *Wesen* is—it must be, that is what "is" means—uncontaminated by anything entitative or nonessential. Being is—it must be—uncontaminated by beings; just so, human being is uncontaminated by animality, anthropology, psychology. That is the *Wesen* of each, of Being and of human being, and it is in their *Wesen* that they are joined to each other. To "think" properly, to learn to think Being as opposed to beings, to think the Being of human being, is to learn this code, to encode Being and human being in the terms of *Wesen.* To think is to decontaminate.

Ek-sistence is not contaminated by animality, is not a special kind of animal, for the very attribution of "animality" to "man" has *already* been made possible by Ek-sistence; such an attribution occurs in a space that has already been cleared by (in) Ek-sistence. Ek-sistence gets there, to the clearing—it is already (in) the clearing—before rational or animal, which are metaphysical determinations dependent upon the clearing.

But if the clearing effected in and with Ek-sistence is not an animal affair, does it not involve a human body? Indeed, but with this proviso: "The human body is something essentially other than an animal organism" (GA 9, 324/ BW, 204).[10] The human body belongs to a different order of essence than does an animal organism. So Heidegger wants to decontaminate the body, to sterilize and immunize it, to purify it of anything organic, biological, nonessential, entitative. He wants to put it beyond the reach of *Lebensphilosophie* and biologism, to think the *Wesen* of the *Lebe-Wesen* and to transcend the *Leben.* But then does Heidegger mean to deny that ours is a body with organs, with liver or lungs? Of course not. (Then, does Dasein have a heart, *kardia?*)[11] That is all "correct," an accurate representation *(Vorstellung)* of the "objective" body, of the body as scientific object. But the *Wesen* of the human body lies outside the organic, in the role it plays in providing a clearing or opening for Being.

This is a very eye-opening approach to take to the body. It promises to set this whole discourse out on a new footing, give it heart, new air to breathe, give it a whole new life. What would this be like, a body conceived as an opening for the clearing? This could be a revolutionary approach: the body not as object but as the space of a clearing.

But then Heidegger's discourse suffers a relapse: in a most classical gesture, he proceeds to situate human being between the gods ("Thou has made him a little less than the angels") and (other) animals, in an uneasy, "abyssal" (GA 9, 326/BW, 206)[12] distance and kinship with animal bodies, which is why the essence of divinity might seem even closer to us than that of animals, whose relation to us is scarcely able to be thought. That is to reproduce the oldest and most classical operation of the great chain of Being.

Heidegger is clearly uneasy about this animal body of Dasein's. It is hard to place, to put *(stellen)*. He does not want human being or the human body framed out in terms of *Lebe-wesen*, living being, thought in the framework of life, but rather of Being, or Being's truth. This has been a constant in his thought ever since the Marburg period when, taking a transcendental turn, he dropped the expression "factical life" and replaced it, in *Being and Time,* with "existence" and "Dasein." That was the first time that Heidegger read (the) "life" out of Dasein. His continuing critique of biologism has been a constant ever since *Being and Time* and it was a crucial point of difference with Nazi racial ideology. Human being is not first and foremost a form of organic life but a relationship to Being, a place where Being comes into its truth, a place where "world" and "language" also take place. Animals, on the other hand—if they had a hand, which they do not, but only grasping mechanisms—which are certainly organic living things, are lacking in world, language, truth (and hands); they are world-poor.[13]

The suggestion that we think the human body as a place of truth is extremely interesting but it ends up reproducing the most classical gestures of metaphysics. It reinforces on the level of the thought of Being the most conventional metaphysical hierarchy, the *ordo essendi:* of divinities, human beings, and animals—so that one gets the same reading of human being, one is led to the same results, whether one thinks only in terms of the Being of beings, as in metaphysics, or of the truth of Being. Furthermore, Heidegger reproduces what Foucault calls the classical "transcendental/empirical" couplet, this time in terms of "thinking/representing" or "ek-sistence" and the "rational animal," the place of Being's clearing versus the empirical species that appears within that clearing. Essential thinking ends up reproducing everything that we mean by "transcendental," by uncontaminated transcendental purity.

In other words, essentializing thinking reproduces the whole logic of traditional essentialism, but on a higher level. Whatever transformations Heidegger has effected in the notion of essence, however often he puts this word "essence" between quotation marks, essentializing thinking remains a version of "essentialism." To be sure, Heidegger raises the discourse on essence from *essentia* to *Wesen,* from the Latino-Romance to the Greco-Germanic, from the nominative to the verbal, from inert whatness to a mobile coming to be and passing away. But he reproduces all the essentials of essentialism by clinging to the distinction between the pure *inside* of human being—where there is truth, clearing, Being, language, world—and the impure, contaminated *outside*— where there are only organic functions and environment, brute stupidity, mute silence, in a word (or two), "(mere) life." Inside and outside are separated by an abyss. Human being and ape have an unearthly, uncanny resemblance to each other, which seems to frighten Heidegger, to scare him almost as much as the photographs of the earth that were sent back to the earth from the moon (*Spieg.*, 277). Thinker and ape stare at each other across an abyss, perhaps on adjacent *Schwarzwald* peaks: Heidegger on one mountaintop and, across the valley, one of those famous Black Forest apes to which Derrida refers staring back at Heidegger.[14] Heidegger is unnerved by it all (we have no report on the feelings of the ape.) In any case, life is on the outside, life has been read out; no (more) *Lebensphilosophie* in *Seinsdenken*. The thought of Being drives out the philosophy of life.

Heidegger's treatment of the animal shows his hand. It verges on a Cartesianism which treats animals as little more than machines. For there never was such an abyss between human and animal. That is an assumption borrowed from the most classical anthropocentrism of Western metaphysics, the most classical privileging of humankind, that gives preeminence to human thought, to *nous* or *logos*, a preeminence which Heidegger's whole critique of "subjectivism" has otherwise undermined.

Heidegger excludes the animal body, the living body from the dignity, the greatness of the clearing. Even as he fleetingly opened up the very possibility of thinking the body as a place of clearing, a place of and for the Open. In *Gelassenheit* Heidegger identified the belonging of thought to Being as *Vergegnis*, and the belonging of things to Being as *Be-dingnis* (G, 55–56/DT, 76–77), but he has no word or thought for the belonging of animals—of the *Lebe-wesen*—to Being. Can we here, on his behalf and in analogous movement, speak of *Be-lebnis*, of the way that life is overtaken by Being and opens up a living clearing?

For the animal's body is not *for the animal* a scientific object—presuming that animals, like most of us, lack a knowledge of advanced physiology—but a living body, an agent body, marked—*mutatis mutandis*—with mobility, spatiality, agency, and all the other features of the body subject analyzed by Merleau-Ponty. Animal bodies open up a world of bodily life, of bodily interaction with the natural world, with one another, and with us, all of which (these various "worlds") have "lived" rather than "objectivistic" properties. The living body is a place of "spacing," of *différance*, which opens up a living space, the spacing of body with natural world, of body with body, of animal with animal.

Heidegger said: "The human body is something essentially other than an animal organism." But if "organism" means the body object, the object of representational (*vorstellend*) thinking, then animal bodies also are something essentially different than "animal organisms." In other words, the operative distinction is not between human being and animal, as Heidegger tries to make out, but between lived body and objectified body, and that is a distinction that we would want to preserve on behalf of animals too, on behalf of any *Lebe-wesen*. We "understand" such things about animals quite instinctively, we gain entry to their bodily space, whenever animals are treated like objects, when, for example, their bodies are brutalized for our needs, when cows are treated with hormones which grossly increase their productivity of milk but cause them great pain, when they are herded into stalls barely large enough to hold them and which prevent them from moving about, when they are mercilessly slaughtered for their hides. That is a kind of *Mit-sein,* a kind of *Mit-leben-sein,* a way to be "with" animals that Heidegger misses with unfailing regularity, but in which the openness of their world, the spacing of their living is regularly co-disclosed.

We understand all this best and quite instantly when we cause animals pain, when they are in pain, whether or not we cause it. We understand—this is part of our *Verstehen*—the difference between the lives animals lead when they are nearly tortured to death by us for our purposes and when they are left in the "wild," in the "open," to lead lives undisturbed by human purposes. The wild, the open spaces, constitutes an altogether different "world" for them, which is "cleared" or "opened" for them in a way quite different from a zoo or a stall. Does this not have for them the structure of "truth"—in the sense of manifestness, of an open space, and so also an ek-static structure? We do not suspect animals of having "propositional truth"—*vor-stellen,* objectification, distantiation—but we can easily take them to live in a sphere of manifestness. It is not a little interesting that the artificial intelligence industry is able to build computers that perform higher logical functions like mathematics which are vastly superior to human abilities, but they find it far more difficult to build robots that can perform the most ordinary bodily acts, acts that we share with animals, like moving adroitly through a crowded room. The living body opens a living space that artificial intelligence finds exceedingly elusive.

The "essence" of the animal, the *Wesen* of *Lebe-wesen,* lies in a (certain) ek-sistence, which is why animals are often admired by philosophers like Nietzsche and by poets like Trakl and Rilke. Heidegger regarded that valorizing of the animal as inverted metaphysics and he rejected it expressly. Heidegger wants no part in Rilke's attempt to describe the prereflective immersion of plant and animal life "in the world" and the difficulty that reflective representing human consciousness has recovering that primal immersion. He regards Rilke's description of this world as an "Open" as a thoroughly metaphysical concept of the Open, operating under the shadow of Nietzsche's inversion of metaphysics, which is quite removed from "the essentially more primal lightening of Being" (PLT, 108).[15] He resists contamination to the end. He wants to keep his Open pure: no animals allowed. He will not permit the body a role in the clearing.

I am not suggesting that we give up the Heideggerian innovation, that human being can be thought in terms of the clearing or space it makes for Being, for world, for the realms and regimes of "truth" or manifestness, for the plurality of cultures. I just want to multiply, complicate, and contaminate this pure Greco-Germanic space. In the spirit of Derrida, I want to contest the sharp distinctions that define a sphere of uncontaminated purity that belongs to the deep structure of Heidegger's discourse.

Heidegger wants to make a pure cut between the truth of Being and metaphysics, to sever them and insist on a clean, sharp difference. I want to say that the truth or manifestness of Being is always a function of, always tied to and bound up with, the facticity of the beings *in* which it comes to pass, that the truth of Being is *always and already* the Being of beings, that *the truth of Being is that there is no truth of Being.* The truth of the Dionysian, Nietzschean, Derridean woman is that there is no truth. Being and truth, the multiple houses of Being, are always already Greek or German, Roman or French, Hebrew or Christian, always tied to a time or a place. By an analogous operation, the *Wesen* of human being is always and already contaminated by the empirical species man, the empirical, anthropological, psychological being, the animal being of human being. "Human being occurs essentially in such a way that it is the 'there' [*das "Da"*] of Being, the lighting of Being," Heidegger writes (GA 9, 325/BW, 205). To be sure, but the Being of the there is not a *tabula rasa,* not a wholly neutral place, but is always already factically constituted. It cannot—and this is just a familiar part of an orthodox Heideggerian logic of facticity—escape the constraints of its own facticity. That would be a fundamental misunderstanding.

But such a factical being is a body, often enough, too often, a body in pain.[16] My reference to the animal in pain is not a passing comment. Bodies and pain are singularly intertwined, interwoven. Bodies suffer pain and pain awakens us to the life of the bodily other. Bodies and pain open up a certain world or open space. Bodies enter into the ontological makeup of the "there." Bodies play a role in the way Being gives itself. The being of human being as a *Lebe-Wesen* has everything to do with the *Wesen des Menschen.* Human being on this accounting is drawn into an unnerving kinship with animals, with other *Lebewesen,* so that the essence of divinity recedes and the "beast" draws uncomfortably close.

Bodies—living beings—create spaces, open up clearings, create distances between themselves and one another, between themselves and things. The distance and differences among things are a function of a feeling, desiring, acting body. Bodies attract and repel one another, they are inviting or hostile. The truth of Being has a bodily look.

In the end, the argument that I am mounting in this reading of Heidegger eventually leads to the question of obligation—and hence of justice. Bodies in pain create the space of obligation. The body in pain calls out for help, addresses us, lays claim to us. The body in pain constitutes a curved space: it comes to us from on high—claiming our response—because it has itself been laid low. Famines, food shortages, lack of housing, violence create political spaces and call for individual and collective response. Such space cannot be related to a secondary, derivative place, to a contaminated, nonessential, enti-tative occurrence *within* the clearing that has already been opened, cleared by some Greco-Germanic primordiality that somehow or another got there first, ahead of obligation, before justice. Levinas's rejoinder to this is for me deci-sive: ethics—I would rather say obligation or justice—is first philosophy; obli-gation is already there at the beginning. It is not anticipated, preceded, made possible by some more primordial *aletheia,* some Greco-German *a priori,* thank you very much. Obligation happens at the start, as soon as there is being there, as soon as there are bodies, which is very early on. As soon as there is a clearing there are bodies and obligation; as soon as there are bodies and obligation, there is a clearing.

But bodies and pains are just what has been read out from the *Wesen* of human being, just what is excluded by the logic of essentialization, locked out by essential thinking, made derivative, downstream, secondary, founded, nonessential. For the only "pain" that thinking admits is essential pain, the pain that is "truly pain." Of true pain Heidegger says:

> Its essential being [*Wesen*] remains closed to every thinking [*Meinen*] that repre-sents pain in terms of feeling [*Empfindung*]. (OWL, 181)

and again:

> We should not represent pain anthropologically as feeling [*Empfindung*] that makes us feel afflicted [*wehleidig*]. We should not think of the intimacy [of pain] psychologically as the sort in which sentimentality [*Empfindsamkeit*] makes a nest for itself. (PLT, 205)

Pain without feeling? That can only mean—if it is coded in terms of *wesen-tliches Denken*—the tear, the difference, the rift between Being and beings, a tear in Being, not in flesh. The body that is not an animal organism is a body without feeling, that *feels* no pain (which is the only pain worth mentioning) and that feels no life (which is the only life worth mentioning). The only pain recognized by thinking is the pain that has been decontaminated of the interweaving of pleasure and pain. But a body that is vulnerable to pleasure and pain is the only body worth mentioning. The *Wesen* of pain, or of the living body, for Heidegger is uncontaminated by feeling and pain, uncontami-nated by everything that we mean by a body. It remains pure and untouched by everything empirical, anthropological, psychological. Heidegger keeps missing the mark of human being, of the place of human being, because he does not know how to situate the human body. Dasein has had the life read out of it and has become evidently a disincarnate, ghostly spectre, a bit of *Geist, de l'esprit.*

That is what accounts for a good deal of Heidegger's habit of saying the most shocking and insensitive—which means unfeeling—things about living things: that real destructiveness is not found in the universal incineration of all life, human and otherwise, but the loss of a Schwarzwaldian *Ding;* that real homelessness is not a matter of children freezing on winter streets but a loss of the sense of *Wohnen;* that agricultural technology and gas chambers are "essentially the same" *(im Wesen dasselbe).* The real scandal of this last remark is not removed by explaining the sense of *Wesen* which motivates it and up to a point explains it. Rather, the very explanation draws the notion of *Wesen* into the scandal. For it belongs to the essence of Heideggerian *Wesen* to neutralize the distinction between life and death, to raise itself up to a point of such transcendental purity that it can no longer tell the difference between agriculture and murder.

That is the point to which Heidegger is driven by the logic of *Wesen,* and that I take to be a *reductio ad absurdum* and an obscenity more ominous than "contamination"—which is after all nothing more than the inevitable companion of incarnation and the ineluctable condition of "factical life," which is after all a highly miscegenated jewgreek matter, not at all pure Greek.

It is to this scandalous point to which Heidegger is driven by the essentializing mythologic of Being that I turn now.

CHAPTER SEVEN

Heidegger's Scandal

THINKING AND THE ESSENCE OF THE VICTIM

I turn here and in the next chapter to what I regard as the worst consequences of Heidegger's essentializing, mythologizing thinking, i.e., the utter mystification it perpetrates about the concrete fortunes of actual human beings, the welfare of whom is displaced in the later writings by a tremendous *grand récit* about Being's fabulous itinerary. This is Heidegger's worst side, verging at times on obscenity, the side that requires the most merciless critique, the most subtle deconstruction, the most rigorous demythologization.

Heidegger is led by the inordinate valorizing of the *Wesen* of Being and truth (and of history, technology, art, dwelling, etc.) into the most radical insensitivity toward the exigencies of "factical life." The transformation of the question of Being from a hermeneutics of facticity to an "essential thinking," from facticity to *Wesen*, is accompanied by an ominous, unearthly indifference to concrete historical life. The redescription of *essentia* as *Wesen*, the movement from nominative to the verbal sense of essence (which itself is constructed from *esse, essens*), explains but does not remove, indeed it even intensifies the insensitivity of essential thinking to the needs of life. That would be problem enough for any thinking, but in a thinking conducted in the aftermath of the Holocaust, "after Auschwitz," as Adorno puts it, in the midst of unspeakable misery, for a thinking that once aligned itself enthusiastically with the forces that produced this very misery, it approaches obscenity. If St. Augustine was a philosopher of conversion, as Maritain once pointed out, a philosopher whose entire *corpus* reflects his religious conversion,[1] Heidegger's *Denkweg* seems constitutionally incapable of conversion and *retractio*. His thinking undergoes the most "astonishingly protracted"[2] backpedaling and revisioning of its National Socialism, without ever finally extricating itself from its "proximity."[3]

Indeed, it is not merely a question of insensitivity toward victims. It is more importantly a question of the axiomatics of a discourse that nullifies and silences the suffering of victims, consigning it to a principled oblivion that approaches rather exactly what Lyotard means by a *differend*—an injury deprived of the idiom in which to register its pain.[4] Essential thinking, I will argue, bears a scandalous analogy to the gesture of the revisionist historians who erase the Holocaust by treating it as an unverifiable rumor.

I speak of a "thinking" (Denken), not the thinker (Denker).[5] I have not been appointed to pass judgment on Heidegger the man or anyone else. My concern here is with die Sache des Denkens, not die Sache Heidegger; with essential thinking, not with Heidegger's biography.

The reference to Augustine does not come from out of the blue but refers to an exchange reported to have taken place between Heidegger and Bultmann and recorded by Fisher-Barnicol. When Bultmann suggested after the war that, like St. Augustine, Heidegger write his Retractiones, not waiting like the Saint until the end of his life, but now and for love of the truth of his thought, Heidegger's face froze over and he left Bultmann without saying a word.[6] Indeed, even after his death what Heidegger left behind for us was no Retractiones but the 1966 Der Spiegel interview, which, far from being a posthumous retractio, only perpetuated the cover-up, the protracted backpedaling. The comparison with Augustine is telling and the silence is indeed scandalous. One could have been mistaken about the Party's intentions in 1933, but after 1945 it was no longer possible to mistake who the Nazis were and what they had done. It would have been dangerous to speak out during the war—and who among us can be sure about how we would have dealt with Nazi terror were we faced with it ourselves—but after the war nothing prevented one from speaking. One waits for the word of thinking, "a hope, today, of a thinking man's coming word in the heart," as Celan said in "Todtnauberg."[7]

Indeed, when the silence is broken, when a word comes, the scandal worsens. For the fact of the matter is that, a few years after the war, Heidegger did advert to the Holocaust in a now notorious passage from an unpublished lecture, "Das Gestell" ("The Enframing"), that was part of the 1949 lecture series held at Bremen upon which "The Question Concerning Technology" was based:

> Agriculture is now a motorized food industry—in essence, the same as the manu-
> facturing of corpses in gas chambers and the extermination camps, the same as the
> blockading and starving of nations, the same as the manufacture of atom bombs.[8]

The comment is at first more baffling than anything else. Is something very "deep" intended here? Or does it betray a shocking insensitivity to mass murder? Is it "damning beyond commentary," as Thomas Sheehan says, who brought it to the attention of American readers?[9] What does it even mean? Of what was Heidegger thinking when he compared modern methods of farming with the Holocaust? In what possible sense are tractors and farm equipment, which make it possible to feed thousands of hungry people in underdeveloped nations, to be compared with the gas chambers in which millions were ruthlessly murdered? Is the remark a work of thought or an obscene comparison? Philippe Lacoue-Labarthe, in a sensitive and penetrating study of Heidegger's politics, grants that there is a grain of truth in the comment but he regards it nonetheless as "scandalously inadequate."[10] The scandal of the silence is compounded by the scandal of the occasional discourse.

What does it mean to say that such incommensurables—motorization and murder, technology and the victim—are essentially the same? What does "essence" mean here? What is the essence of essence *(Wesen)*? What is the essence of the "victim"—an unheard-of question, a question never asked by Heidegger himself—if the mass production of victims can be essentially the same as motorized agriculture?

I undertake here a close reading of this passage in connection with two other equally unsettling texts from the postwar period in an effort both to understand this text, which is clearly the first order of business, and then to insert the question of the meaning of the "victim" within the question of the meaning of Being—to observe the fate of victims in the myth of Being.

One might suppose that this is an offhand comment, strange and atypical. Actually, the opposite is the case. Heidegger says things of this sort with disturbing regularity. The passage obeys the deepest laws of Heideggerian discourse, whose outlines I have traced in the preceding chapter. It is heavily coded, almost formulaic, a profoundly typical gesture on his part, belonging integrally to what I called in the preceding chapter the logic of essentialization, the logic of the mytho-logic. The passage is written from the standpoint of "thinking" *(Denken)*. Thinking is always a scandal and a stumbling block, not only to common sense, which is satisfied with the banalities of what "they" say on television and in the newspapers, but also to scientific reason, for science does not think. The thinker means to offer a deeper reflection *(Besinnung)*, to cut beneath the superficiality of everyday observation, to say something more "essential" *(wesentlich)* ["in essence, the same . . ." *(im Wesen das Selbe)*]. Journalism and political science, which are concerned with concrete events, with entitative goods and evils, literally give no thought to what is coming to pass in essence, in the *Wesen* of things. *Wesen* is to be understood verbally: as that coming to presence which governs the appearance of everything present *(Anwesendes)*, which puts its stamp upon everything that is.

The thinker is engaged in a meditation on the "essence" of technology, not on this or that technical thing, this or that piece of technological equipment. This remark has a parenthetical quality, like an aside. The thinker pauses for a moment to swing back over the concrete and entitative, to show with a passing glance how the meditation upon the *Wesen* can throw light on the *Anwesendes,* on what is all around us, all over us, today. The task of thought is to uncover what is really and authentically happening in the technological world, which thinking determines as the age of the "enframing" *(Gestell)*.

Something deeper is going on in the mechanization of agriculture than first meets the eye. Motorized farming, making a technological industry out of it—complete with an "agricultural science" that actually passes itself off as university or college education today—is not neutral. It is not a mere technological means that can be used for good—to provide food for the hungry—or for ill (to exploit underdeveloped nations, to poison the earth with pesticides). What is coming to pass in the phenomenon of modern agriculture runs so deep that it is comparable to the most momentous events. For the same thing—"in essence the same"—is going on elsewhere: in the Russian blockade of Berlin and in the American manufacture and deployment of the atom bomb over Japan. (It was 1949, the same year as the former and four years after the latter.) The tractors of modern agriculture belong together with the two notorious "pincers" (Zange)—Russia and the United States—described in the famous prewar lecture course An Introduction to Metaphysics. Russia and America "are both, metaphysically speaking [i.e., in essence], the same; the same dreary frenzy of unleashed technology and of the groundless organization of normal man" (GA 40, 41/IM, 37). Tractors and pincers, bombs and blockades, airlifts and air raids—in essence, the same.

But the difference now, after the war, is that Germany—the homeland itself, "our people" (GA 40, 41/IM, 38)—lying in the middle of the middle land (Europe), has itself been swept up in the same groundlessness and unleashed technology that Heidegger warned against in 1935. The gas chambers of the Holocaust—which are neither Russian nor American—are in essence the same as pincers. The revolution has failed. Everything that Heidegger hoped for has been ruined. Far from serving as the antidote to global technology, far from asserting its metaphysico-spiritual greatness, far from assuming its destiny in the history of Being, Germany capitulated, and this defeat is of greater consequence for the history of Being than Germany's capitulation to the allies. Germany succumbed to the same massive technologization that it was its historic mission to offset and resist. The Third Reich, the much longed for—and mythic—"Other Beginning," has served only to scar Hölderlin's "skies" with aircraft; to erode his "earth" with tractors and fertilizers; to drive his gods to flight; and finally—this is the horizon of the remark—to replace his "mortals" with the mechanical production of corpses in gas chambers. The inner truth of the movement—that means its vocation as the eschatological agent, as the vehicle of the German repetition of the Greek Beginning, as the occasion of the new dawn of the West, now in the end-time (eschaton) (GA 5, 327–28/EGT, 18–19)—has been destroyed. The Party, its ideologues and political hacks, devoid of thought and of a thoughtful poetic guide, have plundered the "world" of the "Fourfold" and tragically betrayed the "movement." Russia, the United States, the Third Reich: in essence, the same.

There is, moreover, a semantic rhythm in the passage, a rhetorical play of opposites, that we must not miss. What specifically is coming to presence (west, an-west) in the agricultural industry? What "is" there, really, authenti-

cally? Nothing less than the rape of soil and field *(Acker)* by automized equipment, a violent assault upon an earth that was once tended by the loving hand
of the farmer *(Bauer)*. Where once farmers waited upon the heavenly gifts of
rain and sun, now vast irrigation systems and fertilizers push the soil beyond
its natural yield, maximizing crop production and multiplying the food *(Er-
nährung)* supplies. Now all that is in essence the same as what takes place in
the death camps and gas chambers, even though the one produces life and
the other produces death. For there holds sway in both the same essence of
technology, the rule of the *Gestell,* the darkening *(Verdüsterung)* of the earth
(GA 40, 41/IM, 38). The same *Wesen* comes to presence in the filthy smokestacks of modern food-processing factories and in the smokestacks of Auschwitz. Tractors and gas chambers, artifically fertilized crops and mechanically
produced corpses: in essence the same. How so? Because whether what is
produced is nourishment or a corpse, a nourished body or a dead body, life
or death, Being is nonetheless understood as raw material *(Bestand)* and the
same rule of the *Gestell* holds sway. For coming-to-presence *(Wesen)* is not
measured by life or death but by the stamp that Being bears at any given
moment in its history.

The same essence prevails, too, in the blockade of a city: a massive military
technology surrounds a city, squeezes it to near death with its lethal pincers,
and produces starvation *(Aushungerung)*. The production of food and starvation; nourished bodies and starving bodies: in essence, the same, the same
fury of unleashed technology. What happens when the tending of the field
(Ackerbau) becomes a motorized industry is the same, in essence, as technologically enforced hunger.

Finally, the same will that sets upon earth and field with unrelenting harsh-
ness in modern industrial agriculture is the same will that is unleashed in the
production—and let us add the detonation—of the bomb. The earth is destroyed not merely in fact (August 1945) but in essence. Automized farm
equipment and nuclear bombs; nourished bodies and incinerated bodies: in
essence, the same.

The massive power of the *Gestell* levels, abolishes, transcends the distinction
between nourishment and starvation, life and mass death.

But one could object—the ethicist, the political scientist, the journalist, people of common sense, the hungry people in the underdeveloped nations, the
people being sent to the gas chambers—they might all object that there is a
vast difference between using technology for good and using it for evil, for
preserving life and for killing people. That is a literally thought-less objection,
arising from the bankruptcy of metaphysics, which assumes that the essence
of technology is neutral. The *Wesen* of technology is nothing technological,
nothing we use, nothing we can master, but something which needs and uses
the essence of man.

The thinker is by no means unaware that thinking is a scandal and a stumbling block to science and common sense (G, 27/DT, 55–56). Indeed, one senses that he takes a certain delight in this scandal, a pleasure in the order of rank that has always separated thinkers from Thracian maids and made a mystery out of Heraclitus to the curious tourists who were out to catch a glimpse of a thinker at work. In itself, there is nothing inherently scandalous about the fact that thinking should throw those who do not think into confusion. That is an old gesture on the part of thinkers, a structural feature of thinking (which is never loath to assume the mantle of something extraordinary and great).

Still, we ask, is it possible for thinking to raise itself to so sublime a point that it neutralizes the distinction between life and death, between feeding people and murdering them?[11] We are still troubled by this discourse on essence, still scandalized. Is this because we do not hear what is calling in the thinker's words, because we do not hear that more essential call to which the thinker himself responds? Have we failed to hear the thinker? Or has the thinker failed to hear everything that calls, failed to respond to everything that addresses him, failed in his responsibility?

Let us proceed slowly. Let us turn to two other passages—in fact there are many others—that obey the same formula, the same logic of essence.

(1) In an address to an architectural society, in the midst of the postwar housing shortage, Heidegger remarks:

> On all sides we hear talk about the housing shortage [Wohnungsnot], and with good reason. Nor is there just talk, there is action too. We try to fill the need by providing houses. . . . However hard and bitter, however hampering and threatening the lack of houses remains, the *real need* [eigentliche Not] *of dwelling* does not lie merely in a lack of houses. The real need of dwelling is indeed older than the world wars with their destruction, older also than the increase of the earth's population and the condition of the industrial workers. The real plight of dwelling lies in this, that mortals ever search anew for the nature of dwelling, that they *must ever learn to dwell*. What if man's homelessness [Heimatlosigkeit] consisted in this, that man still does not even think of the *real* plight as *the* plight? Yet as soon as he *gives thought* to his homelessness, it is a misery no longer. (VA, 162/ PLT, 161)

The passage is governed by the axiomatics of authenticity, of what is genuinely and really (eigentlich) needy, the "real plight" (in Hofstadter's translation), as opposed to what is not the authentic need, what is less than a real plight, what is "merely" (erst) a lack (Mangel, Fehlen). A more primordial neediness (Not) cuts deeper than mere lack, which is derivative, secondary, not so needy, somehow inauthentic, not a real plight. Those who are really needy, who have needs of a more profound sort, they are *not* (Heidegger makes a liberal use of italics to emphasize his point here) those who have been victimized by world wars (Heidegger uses the plural; there have been two of them, so far) and their destructiveness. Homes have been destroyed; people roam the streets by day, sleeping without shelter by night. Indeed, we do not require a world war to bring this about. In every major city the homeless seek out the cavernous hollows of urban subway systems, huddle against the sides of buildings for protection against the wind. The sprawl of poverty, laborers crammed into substandard housing, these are phenomena of war and peace.

The misery such people endure is, to be sure, "hard and bitter," "hampering and threatening," but it is not authentic need, not *eigentlich*. Such people are not really needy. Let us say that they are in pain, that they suffer, but that their pain is not essential enough, not old enough, not primordial enough—since it is merely "anthropological" (PLT, 205). The valorization of authenticity communicates with the valorization of *Wesen*. The authentic need for dwelling consists in this, that mortals must seek the essence of dwelling, must search for what is really and truly coming to presence in dwelling. The authentic need is the need to *(müssen)* learn the essence of dwelling. Indeed, this need is of an even finer and more subtle essentiality than this, and this in keeping with the dynamics of "oblivion," of the forgottenness of the forgottenness. For the really real need (to learn to think), the authentic neediness of this need, is that men do not yet grasp that this is *the* need, that there is one need above all, that all needs are gathered together in(to) the site of one need, the really essential need, the essence of real need.

The need for dwelling is not merely that we do not know the essence of dwelling but that we do not know that we do not know, that we do not know that this is necessary, what is needed most of all. What we really lack is thought, not shelter; what we really need to provide for is thinking, not housing. But then, *as soon as (sobald)* one gives thought to this essential neediness *(Notwendigkeit)*, the lack of *Heimat*, as soon as one begins to *think* on what is truly coming to presence in homelessness, this essential homelessness is over and all its misery *(Elend)* is ended. The thinker can put an end to this misery, or can at least prepare for ending it, by lending the weight of thought to the essence of dwelling. The lack of dwelling units *(Wohnungsmangel)* threatens to blind us to the deeper need of *Heimat (Heimatlosigkeit)*, which is the dwelling that is built by thinking. The house that we really lack is the house of Being, the home we really need is to make our home in a thoughtful poetic language in which we can ponder the essence of dwelling and of the true *Heimat*.

Finally, there is one last connection to be made, one more link in the axiomatics that links *Eigentlichkeit* with *Wesen*, and that is the valorization of the "call"—which returns to the question of the responsibility (which we discussed in chapter 4) of responding to the call. For from this essential homelessness, this lack of thinking on the essence of dwelling, there issues the address, the summons *(Zuspruch)* that *calls (ruft)* to us, that calls us into dwelling. In responding to this call, mortals can bring dwelling into the fullness of its essence, and they can do this by building out of authentic dwelling and thinking for the sake of dwelling, so that dwelling is tied to thinking and thinking to dwelling. For real building, essential authentic building, is really *(eigentlich)* dwelling, which is what calls to us in the old word *buan* (VA, 147/ PLT, 161). Hence the building that understands itself as and in terms of dwelling unfolds into the building that builds buildings. So the *fullness* of dwelling will *also* include actual buildings, places where people will come in off the streets and into shelters. Answering the call of homelessness will bring the essence of dwelling into its full complement. Dwelling in its proper essence— as thinking the essence of the home and the homeland—is to be supplemented by the inauthentic, improper actuality of actual housing units that will fill the need for shelter. The authentic neediness of thinking the essence of dwelling calls mortals into dwelling and also, as a supplement, unfolds into actually building houses. To the thought of authentic dwelling, which meets the need for the *Heimat*, there comes the afterthought of filling the lack of actual dwelling places, the inauthentic, mere lack of a place to sleep and live. The concrete work of building houses that will bring people in out of the cold is, from the point of view of thought, an afterthought. It must come after thought, not chronologically but essentially; it must be led into its essence by the essence of thought, which must itself follow after *(nach-denken)* the essential direction given to thought by the essence of dwelling.

But what if—at the risk of thought-lessness, or perhaps of venturing upon another kind of thinking—one were simply to question this order of essence, the before and after of *Wesen*? What if one were to say that what essentially calls to us in homelessness is not the essence of dwelling but the cries of those who suffer from the lack of shelter? What if the call were really the cry of grief? What if the call were the appeal for help of those who suffer? What if the summons by which we are summarily called were the summons for aid by the victim? What if responding to the appeal of the victim constituted "another responsibility,"[12] over and above, or perhaps otherwise than responding to the call of being? What if this were indeed the oldest responsibility of all? What if the poor were the oldest of all, those who are always around? What if the pain of those who cry out in homeless nights were older, more authentic, more primordial, more essential than the call to think the essence of dwelling? What if the "neighbor" were not the nearby *Bauer* in the Black Forest, a stone's throw down the road, but the homeless ones who roam city streets? What if the neighbor were *not* the one whose home is nearby, but the one who has no home at all? Would that be to reinstate a biblical as opposed to a Hellenic horizon in this discourse, to shift the discourse on the home from a Greco-German *Heimat* to a biblical neighbor (PF, 644)? What if the neighbor were to be thought not in terms of nearness but of otherness, of that other one who needs shelter? What if the entire discourse on dwelling, *ethos,* building, and *Heimat,* together with the Greco-Germanic rhetoric of the Four-fold were displaced and everything were reorganized around the call of those who suffer? What if the homeless were no longer an afterthought who must *also* be provided for in order to serve the needs of the essence of dwelling, in order to bring it into its fullness, but rather thinking would become thoughtful concern for the other, responsiveness to the call of the other?

What if one were to question the hierarchical impulse that leads one to distinguish the more essential essence of what is coming to presence in dwelling from the concrete need for shelter? We see the profoundly disturbing analogy of this passage with the passage on the Holocaust: thinking can distinguish the essence of homelessness and hunger in such a way that the authentic and essential thing would not be that people are actually homeless or hungry. Even if we understand *Wesen* verbally, as what is coming to presence, is there not something profoundly Platonic in thought's step back from the lack of housing to the essence of dwelling? For *Wesen* understood verbally—even written in Middle High German—wants to be uncontaminated by that of which it is the *Wesen.* The essence of technology is nothing technological; the essence of language is nothing linguistic; the essence of starvation has nothing to do with being hungry; the essence of homelessness has nothing to do with being out in the cold. Is this not to repeat a most classical philosophical gesture, to submit to the oldest philosophical desire of all, the desire for the pure and uncontaminated, not to mention the safe and secure?

What if, in short, the entire axiomatics of *"Wesen"* and *"Eigentlichkeit"* were to be displaced, so that one could no longer be drawn into devalorizing world wars and their victims as inauthentic, nonessential, and into hierarchizing thinking and suffering? What if the entire problematic of responsiveness and responsibility were to include the victim?

(2) In his essay "The Thing" Heidegger remarks upon the prospect of a nuclear conflagration which could extinguish all human life:

> Man stares at what the explosion of the atom bomb could bring with it. He does not see that what has long since taken place and has already happened expels from itself as its last emission the atom bomb and its explosion—not to mention the single nuclear bomb, whose triggering, thought through to its utmost potential, might be enough to snuff out all life on earth. (VA, 165/PLT, 166).

In a parallel passage, he remarks:

> ... [M]an finds himself in a perilous situation. Why? Just because a third world war might break out unexpectedly and bring about the complete annihilation of humanity and the destruction of the earth? No. In this dawning atomic age a far greater danger threatens—precisely when the danger of a third world war has

been removed. A strange assertion! Strange indeed, but only as long as we do not meditate. (G, 27/DT, 56).

The thinker is menaced by a more radical threat, is endangered by a more radical explosiveness, let us say by a more essential bomb, capable of an emission *(hinauswerfen)* of such primordiality that the explosion *(Explosion)* of the atom bomb would be but its last ejection. Indeed, the point is even stronger: even a nuclear bomb, or a wholesale exchange of nuclear bombs between nuclear megapowers, which would put an end to "all life on earth," which would annihilate every living being, human and nonhuman, is a derivative threat compared to this more primordial destructiveness. There is a prospect that is more dangerous and uncanny—*unheimlicher*—than the mere fact that everything could be blown apart *(Auseinanderplatzen von allem)*. There is something that would bring about more homelessness, more not-being-at-home *(un-heimlich)* than the destruction of cities and towns and of their inhabitants. What is truly unsettling, dis-placing *(ent-setzen)*, the thing that is really terrifying *(das Entsetzende)*, is not the prospect of the destruction of human life on the planet, of annihilating its places and its settlers. Furthermore, this truly terrifying thing has already happened and has actually been around for quite some time. This more essential explosive has already been set off; things have already been destroyed, even though the nuclear holocaust has not yet happened. What then is the truly terrifying?

> The terrifying is that which sets everything that is outside [*heraussetzt*] of its own essence [*Wesen*]. What is this dis-placing [*Entsetzende*]? It shows itself and conceals itself in the *way* in which everything presences [*anwest*], namely, in the fact that despite all conquest of distances the nearness of things remains absent. (VA, 165/PLT, 166)

The truly terrifying explosion, the more essential destruction is that which dis-places a thing from its *Wesen,* its essential nature, its ownmost coming to presence. The essential destruction occurs in the Being of a thing, not in its entitative actuality; it is a disaster that befalls Being, not beings. The destructiveness of this more essential destruction is aimed not directly at man but at "things" *(Dinge),* in the distinctively Heideggerian sense. The *Wesen* of things is their nearness, and it is nearness which has been decimated by technological proximity and speed. Things have ceased to have true nearness and farness, have sunk into the indifference of that which, being a great distance away, can be brought close in the flash of a technological instant. Thereby, things have ceased to be things, have sunk into indifferent nothingness.

Something profoundly disruptive has occurred on the level of the Being of things that has already destroyed them, already cast them out of *(herauswerfen)* their Being. Beings have been brought close to us technologically; enormous distances are spanned in seconds. Satellite technology can make events occurring on the other side of the globe present in a flash; supersonic jets cross the great oceans in a few hours. Yet, far from bringing things "near," this massive technological removal of distance has actually abolished nearness, for nearness is precisely what withdraws in the midst of such technological frenzy. Nearness is the nearing of earth and heavens, mortals and gods, in the handmade jug, or the old bridge at Heidelberg, and it can be experienced only in the quiet meditativeness which renounces haste.

Thus the real destruction of the thing, the one that abolishes its most essential Being and *Wesen*, occurs when the scientific determination of things prevails and compels our assent. The thingliness of the jug is to serve as the place which gathers together the fruit of earth and sun in mortal offering to the gods above. But all that is destroyed when pouring this libation becomes instead the displacement of air by a liquid; at that moment science has succeeded in reducing the jug-thing to a non-entity *(Nichtige)*. Science, or rather the dominion of scientific representation, the rule of science over what comes to presence, what is called the *Wesen*, which is at work in science and technology, that is the truly explosive-destructive thing, the more essential dis-placing. The gathering of earth and sky, mortals and gods, that holds sway in the thing—for "gathering" is what the Old High German *thing* means—is scattered to the four winds, and that more essential annihilation occurs even if the bomb never goes off:

> Science's knowledge, which is compelling within its own sphere, the sphere of objects, already had annihilated things long before the atom bomb exploded. The bomb's explosion is only the grossest of all gross confirmations of the long-since accomplished annihilation of the thing. (VA, 168/PLT, 170)

When things have been annihilated in their thingness, the mushroom clouds of the bomb cannot be far behind. So whether or not the bomb goes off is not essential, does not penetrate to the essence of what comes to presence in the present age of technological proximities and reduced distances. What is essential is the loss of genuine nearness, authentic and true nearness, following which the actual physical annihilation of planetary life would be a "gross" confirmation, an unrefined, external, physical destruction that would be but a follow-up, another afterthought, a less subtle counterpart to a more inward, profound, essential, authentic, ontological destruction.

But what if we were simply to resist this hierarchizing of inward and outward destruction and run the risk of a certain thought-lessness? (Or is this instead perhaps another kind of thinking?) For where are we in truth to locate the distorted, the displaced, the terrifying? Where the thinker does, in that which sets the thing outside the *Wesen* upon which thought would meditate? Or rather precisely in the prospect of the nuclear omnicide, the loss of all, the universal incineration, *holos-caustos,* the holocaust to end all holocausts, the war to end all wars? Or, to aim the question at Heidegger himself: Is there not something deeply unsettling in a thinking which is anesthethized before unspeakable suffering, deaf to the cries of the victim?

Having taken into account Heidegger's critique of biologism, must we not now begin to reconsider the implications of the prioritizing of Being *(physis)* over life *(bios)* and of Heidegger's denigration of the formula that describes man as the *zoos,* the living thing, endowed with *logos,* with speech and thought?[13] For does not this subordination of life in the order of *Wesen,* of what comes to presence, imply the unsettling valorization of things, "compliant and modest" *(ring und gering)* in number, as measured against the all too many mass of living beings with which Heidegger ends this essay (VA, 181/ PLT, 182)? Is there not rather an incommensurability, a lack of common measure, which forestalls this hierarchy, which allows us at once to be "vigilant" (VA, 180/PLT, 181) about the "thing" even while we are not less vigilant about the life of living beings, the shelter and the nourishment they require, and the threat to life on earth? Has not the time come to rethink the relationship between the Being of the thing and the Being of living things, between what once was called the ontological and the ontic?

It is now possible, I believe, to understand Heidegger's troubling assertion about the Holocaust, his association of modern agricultural technology with the gas chambers and extermination camps. The statement is governed by the rigor of "thinking" and it is made possible by the axiomatics of "*Wesen,*" authenticity, and nearness. It is possible to understand what Heidegger is saying, but I do not believe it is possible to remove the scandal. The remark becomes intelligible once one sees that it is the issue of "thought," but it does not become less problematic. On the contrary, I think the remark serves rather to draw thinking into its problematicity. I should like now to offer an explanation of just what is so problematic about "thinking."

I would say that Heidegger's path of thought has been governed from the very start by what I would call here a certain "phainesthetics." His thinking has always turned on the experience of Being as *phainesthai,* as the self-showing of the *phainomenon,* as that which shows itself from itself as it is in itself, first discussed in the opening pages of *Being and Time* (§7a). Being means the appearing *(Erscheinen)* of what appears, the shining gleam *(Scheinen)* of beauty *(Schönheit).* His thought has been guided by an axiomatics of the beauty and simple splendor of what shines forth and radiates. *Axiom:* that means neither the assumptions needed in an axiomatic system nor the "values" of modern axiology but that which overtakes and over-whelms the thinker, that whose shining aspect we are bound to hold in regard (SG, 34–35/PR, 15–16). Being is primal presencing, the interplay of presence and absence, rising up and passing away while lingering for a while, the gentle play of the four together. Phainesthetics: that means Being is such as the poet (which poet?) experiences and thinking is such that it must be conducted in the closest cooperation with the poetic experience of the Fourfold.

What calls to us above all in Heidegger's thought, what calls thinking into thought, what calls human speaking into language, is that address which calls upon the help of thought to bring the essence of what shows itself into its self-presentation. The task of thinking and speaking is to be responsive to this primordial call, to let it come to presence *(west)*, to let it come toward *(an)* and overtake us. Thus when Heidegger undertakes essential thinking *(wesentliches Denken)*, to think on things in terms of what is coming to presence in them *(wesen* in the verbal sense), what he means is something phainesthetic. Presencing *(wesen)*, coming to presence, coming toward us and concerning us *(Anwesen)*, means above all self-showing, shining with a primordial, gleaming radiance.

Shining with an early Greek glow: like a gleaming Greek temple, its white marble flesh glistening in the sun, towering toward a brilliant blue sky, the open and the free *(das Freie)*, proudly overlooking the rich blue Mediterranean waters below. Everything blue and white, shining and glimmering. The place is filled with gods—and mortals too, lifting gifts of bread and wine, the fruit of earth and sun and soil, in humble gratitude for the giving of what gives, for what is given here, for a now forgotten but aboriginally unforgettable gift.

But, as Lyotard has argued, there is a singular forgetting in all this recalling, a failure to hear the silent anaesthetics of the sublime in all the bombast of this Greco-German phainesthetic. To take as its task to think the forgotten, to think what is primordially forgotten, that, says Lyotard, is "the 'moment' in Heidegger's thought where it approaches, indeed, touches, the thought of the 'jews.'" But it is also the moment to which Heidegger's thought never rises, for in Heidegger the thought of Being's shining beauty remains profoundly insensitive to the sublime, to the other who calls to us from the silence of destitution and shocks our freedom.[14] It is precisely this other kind of oblivion, this oblivion of the other, that stirs within these strangely skewed and scan-dalizing accounts of the truly authentic danger, of the real loss of home, of the truly unsettling and terrifying—and above all of the gas chambers. For nowhere in the call of Being is the cry of the *victim* to be heard, nowhere the plea for mercy, the summons for help. The silent peal of Being is deaf to the appeal of suffering. The assault upon the earth which turns the soil into an object of agricultural engineering is more primordial than the ravages of hun-ger, than ravaged bodies. The matter to be thought is not hunger and starva-tion but whether one works the land with hand and oxen instead of with motorized equipment. Hungry and undernourished bodies do not figure in the account, do not come to presence; hunger is *(west)* not, it simply is *(ist)*.

That valorization is possible only on phainesthetic grounds, on the constriction of experience to "world and thing," on reducing everything that is to the call of Being, to shining glow and gleaming beauty. It is a world in which a wholly *other* kind of responsiveness and responsibility has been silenced, a responsibility to those who live and die, to those who are embodied, who suffer or are in pain, who grow old and infirm, above all, to innocent victims. The thinker leaves no room at all for the victim in the history of Being's self-showing.

This is a Greek world, or rather a world of phantasmatic Greeks invented by Germans, a Germanico-Greek world of the innocence of becoming, of the lack of all guilt, where *dike* and *adikia* have to do strictly with the play of presence and absence.[15] Nothing or no one is guilty; there are no victims in the epochal play, no dead bodies, no spilled blood, no incinerated flesh, no death camps; or at least, they are not essential, not what is really happening. The dark night of the oblivion, of the withdrawal of Being—that does not mean the rule of injustice and murder no more than the primordial call of Being has anything to do with justice. Justice has been "naturalized," not in the sense of naturalism or materialism, but rethought in terms of *physis*, of emerging into presence. The only *ethos* that is permitted is a more essential, originary *ethos*, an early Greek poetic *ethos*, which dictates a more poetic mode of dwelling on the earth. There is no call of conscience, no response that says guilty,[16] and so there are no victims. There is/it gives only the epochal shifts that have fallen into an escalating history of oblivion from *eidos* to Technik. Now, in the end-time *(eschaton)*, Hölderlinian skies are marred by industrial smoke. The tranquillity of hillside farms has been disturbed by the roar of motorized equipment that drowns out the tinkle of the cowbells. It gives/there is everything, all beings—except victims.

The victim never comes to presence, never makes an appearance on the scene of the history of Being. There are no victims in the First Beginning, in the great early Greek epoch before metaphysics, no women, no slaves, no non-Greeks who figure at all in that glorious first start where all is still well with *Wesen*, understood verbally. Neither do the victims figure in the end-time of the history of metaphysics, when they are gassed to death by motorized equipment. For that is not the matter of concern *(die Sache)*; they are not the task for thought.

That is why the gas chamber is the same as the tractor, as motorized farm equipment. The victim is invisible in the history of Being, is not a matter of concern, is not what is at issue. The victim does not come toward us and concern us *(an-wesen, an-gehen)* in the history of Being, does not call to *(an-rufen)* us. The victim has no voice in the call of Being, cannot speak, cannot be heard. The victim is thus a *differend*, in Lyotard's sense. Victims have been robbed of their voice, do not have the means to register a protest on their own behalf about the damage that has been done to them.[17] Victims do not make their appearance on the register of Being. Their cry has no say *(Sage, sagen)*; they are not an appearance, do not reach the level of *Wesen*, cannot show themselves from themselves. What is a matter of concern is the manner of their death—gas chambers, a motorized technological means—not the matter itself, the *Sache selbst* of murder.

Let us cite another, even more scandalous saying about gas chambers, attributed to Faurrison and mentioned by Lyotard:[18]

"I have analyzed thousands of documents. I have tirelessly pursued specialists and historians with my questions. I have tried in vain to find a single deportee capable of proving to me that he had really seen, with his own eyes, a gas chamber."

Faurrison wants to doubt that the gas chambers existed. Heidegger does not doubt their existence but wants to think through to their essence *(Wesen)*. The gas chamber certainly exists, but it merely is *(ist)*. The important issue is not that it exists but how it comes to presence *(west)*. So when we want to talk about what really is, what is really essential, when we make the step back to the difference *(Unter-schied)*, then there is no difference between tractors and gas chambers. Now it is part of the idea of victim "not to be able to prove that one has been done a wrong." It is impossible for the wrong to make an appearance. That is what Faurrison has done, for he demands that the victims of the gas chambers testify to the wrong that has been done to them. He requires a resurrection for proof.

But the thinker has made the appearance of the victim almost as difficult. The victim does not have to prove that he or she is *(ist)*, but that he or she is *(west)*, i.e., attains the level of *Wesen* and so matters a little. Victims must show that they are essential, that they belong to the essence of what is calling us to think and speak and act. (Or rather that they are a matter of concern, for this whole axiomatics of essence and authenticity is at the root of the trouble, the source of Heidegger's thoughtlessness.) But that is what the victim cannot do. The victim is a matter of indifference for the matter of thought, a matter of phainesthetic indifference. It makes no difference to the history of Being, of *phainesthai*, whether there are or are not victims. In the history which runs from shining Greek temples to industrial pollution, there is no place for victims.

Die Sache des Denkens: that means *phainesthai* and shining appearance, rising up out of sheltering concealment, coming into presence and lingering for a while, *An- und Ab-wesen, Wesen*. Thinking: that means a responsiveness to that which calls for thought, calls upon us and asks to be thought. What then of the appeal of the victim, the silent peal of the starving and homeless, or the still deadlier silence of the murdered? Do they not call for thought? Or for poetizing?

Would it not be possible to think and poetize differently, otherwise than Heidegger and otherwise than with Heideggerian indifference? Do we not need to interrupt this vast hymn to *phainesthai* and phainesthetic glory with the sharp tones of another song, to complicate Heideggerian *Dichtung* with another lament, not for the lost splendor of the shining Fourfold, but for the orphan and for the outcast, for *les juifs*?

Is it not possible to poetize differently, to sing the song of another *mythos*? Can one not imagine another poetizing, another idiom for poetizing, another poetic voice?[19]

> Take away the bombast of these temple hymns and invocations of Being's glory. Take away from me the noise of your Greco-German songs.
>
> I despise your bombast and your feasts and I take no delight in the gathering of your all-gathering *logos*.
>
> I will not look upon the rising up of your mighty temples, their stone-hard columns thrusting proudly into the sky.
>
> I will not accept the offerings of such poets or of the priests of such piety, this piety that prays without regard to all that is holy, to all that is laid low.
>
> To the melody of these Greco-German harps I will not listen.
>
> But let justice sweep over the land like flowing water, lifting up those who have been laid low.
>
> "But let justice roll down like waters, and righteousness like an ever-flowing stream."

When the time is ripe, when the appointed hour strikes, when the *kairos* comes to pass, then, the prophet Amos says, there will be darkness over the land, not light. Then will everything turn on being able to tell the difference between murder and its opposite. Is not the *kairos*—the very structure that set the "hermeneutics of facticity" into motion—the moment in which one sees clearly the difference between justice and injustice, between murder and agriculture, instead of amalgamating them in phainesthetic indifference, instead of consigning this difference to the most intractable oblivion?

It is not a matter of amplifying what Heidegger calls thinking so that thinking *also* includes the call of the victim. It is not a matter, as I once suggested, of needing to extend Heideggerian *Gelassenheit* to other people instead of restricting it to jugs and bridges.[20] The matter for thought *(die Sache des Denkens)* and the task for thought *(die Aufgabe des Denkens)* must be more profoundly disrupted by an otherness to which they are systematically made deaf in Heideggerian discourse.

It is not a question of opening thinking to the victim but, as I now think, of effecting a leap into something otherwise than thinking, otherwise than what Heidegger calls thinking. Because there is nothing the victim can do to gain a voice in the call of Being, it is necessary to open oneself to other calls, to respond to the call of what is more profoundly other, to the call of what is otherwise than Being.

It is not possible to ask about the *Wesen* of victims, their coming to presence, for it is just in virtue of *Wesen* that victims vanish from view. We are thus left with one final, fatal Heideggerian reversal, with a *Kehre* that leaves us aghast, that the *Wesen* of the victim is a victim of *Wesen*—understood verbally.[21]

CHAPTER EIGHT

Heidegger's Poets

It was Heidegger's constant contention from his first work on Hölderlin in the 1930s that the insularity of philosophy and even of thinking *(Denken)* itself must be shattered by holding them in constant exposure to the otherness of poetry *(Dichtung)*, to the thickness and density *(dicht)* of poetizing *(Dichten)*.[1] But it is a matter of no small irony and no little importance that Heidegger's thought of *Wesen*, his essential and essentializing thinking, has had the effect precisely of insulating *Denken* from *Dichten*, of holding poetry's most disturbing and menacing effects in check, in just such a way as to allow Heidegger's mythologizing tendencies to go unchecked. Heidegger consistently transforms the tragic site of his poets with unfortunate and sometimes just plain tasteless results. In a recent and quite remarkable study of Heidegger's poets, Veronique Foti says that her study of Heidegger and the poets[2]

> . . . traces its own genesis to what was at first an inchoate but persistently troubling awareness of a deflection in Heidegger's readings of his chosen poets, which occludes transgression, excess, or loss and constrains the poetry to fit the exigencies of an *essential* if always "polemical" (or differential) unification. . . . Heidegger's deflections and conflations have the fundamental character of an aesthetization of the political (conjoined with a mythical recasting of history); as Lacoue-Labarthe has insisted, such aesthetization constitutes the key aspect of his involvement with National Socialism.

After subtle analyses of Heidegger's interpretation of Mörike, Trakl, Rilke, and Hölderlin, Foti focuses her work on Heidegger's silence about Paul Celan, his refusal to enter a dialogue with Celan:[3]

> What makes this refusal important is not only that Celan writes out of the experience of the Holocaust but also that he both situates his poetry in relation to Hölderlin and criticizes and repudiates the aesthetization of the political, whereas Heidegger develops his own aesthetization in dialogue with Hölderlin.

My own interests here lie in establishing the effects of Heidegger's mytho-essentializing of the poetry of Trakl, in which the "deflection," to use Foti's excellent formulation, of the tragic site is plainly to be observed. Heidegger's

mythologizing of Trakl takes the form of a massive allegorization in which
the suffering that finds an idiom in the poetry is transported to a mythic site
(Erörterung), to a kind of never-never land of essential thinking. The poetic
experience of pain and suffering is systematically allegorized into an event in
Being itself, the alternative being, on Heidegger's scheme, to treat it as "merely
anthropological." It is thus impossible, in the terms enforced by *wesentliches
Denken*—either *Wesen* or anthropologism—for pain and suffering to establish
their own idiom, to speak on their own terms, to issue a call or appeal that
could be registered or allowed to matter as a matter of *Wesen*. While poetry
has always been regarded as an important and indispensable idiom for suffering, Heidegger's poet cannot, in principle, respond to the call of suffering—
which is the very gesture of the silencing of the "victim"—or poetize from
out of the experience *(aus der Erharfung)* of factical pain. Poetry, like thinking
itself, is a matter of hearing the call of the other beginning in the resonances
of the First Beginning. Thinking's dialogue with poetry, like thinking itself, is
essentially a mythologizing tuned to a myth of *Wesen*.

Heidegger's Trakl: Spirit and Pain

"Pain is truly pain [*wahrhaft Schmerz*]," Heidegger writes in "Language in
the Poem," "when it serves the flame of the spirit" (US, 65/OWL, 180). There
is thus a true pain, the very truth of pain, which, by the whole power of
Heidegger's logic, is the "essence" *(Wesen)* of pain, and which, according to
the demands of essential thought *(wesentliches Denken)*, cannot be painful;
there is no "body in pain," to use Elaine Scarry's expression. For the *Wesen*
of pain cannot be contaminated by that of which it is the essence. This deeper,
more profound pain, Heidegger says, is to be coordinated with the "flame of
the spirit." True pain belongs to the spirit. But this "spirit" is not to be thought
of as the opposite of the bodily—although there is no question of bodily
pain—but as flame. What then is the "flame of the spirit"? If no one is actually
burned, if there is nothing searing or caustic (not to say holocaustic) about it,
would this not be a completely spiritual flame, an immaterial burning? That
is just what Heidegger has set out to deny. Everything depends upon seeing
that this flaming spirit belongs neither to a Platonic pneumatology nor to a
Christian spirituality, that it is neither a Greco-ontological nor a Christo-
theological spirit. This is not a spiritual pain and also not a spiritual spirit,
but something more essential, more ghostly *(geistlich)* than either Christianity
or Platonism can think.

It would be insensitive to think that pain has anything to do with feeling
or sensation *(Empfindung)*:[4]

> Its essential Being [*Wesen*] remains closed to every thinking [*Meinen*] that repre-
> sents pain in terms of sensitivity [*Empfindung*]. (US, 62/OWL, 181)

And again:

> We should not represent pain anthropologically as feeling [*Empfindung*] that makes us feel afflicted [*wehleidig*]. We should not think of the intimacy [of pain] psychologically as the sort in which sentimentality [*Empfindsamkeit*] makes a nest for itself. (US, 27/PLT, 205)

In the earlier of the two Trakl essays, in which Heidegger is commenting on "A Winter Evening," Heidegger offers an explanation of this more essential pain. The first stanza of the poem summons up "things"—house, table, window, bell, snow—in which the Fourfold *(Geviert)* gathers itself together. The first two lines of the second stanza invoke mortals—"wanderers"—who also belong to the *Geviert*. With the reference to the "tree of grace" in the last two lines of this stanza the poet thinks the "worldling" of the "world" in all its shining splendor. Hence the effect of the first two stanzas is to name at once the way things bear world and the way world grants things (US, 22–25/PLT, 200–202).

Thus it falls to the third stanza to name the "between" *(inter)* that holds world and thing apart even as it bears them both toward one another in their "intimacy" *(Innigkeit)*. The between is the dif-ference *(dia-phora, Aus-trag, Unter-Schied)*. By anyone's accounting the oddest line in a poem otherwise marked by the simplicity of its language occurs in this stanza:

Pain has turned the threshold to stone.
    [*Schmerz versteinerte die Schwelle.*]

The only line in the past tense, it contains a startling, typically Traklian, symbolist image—of pain turning a threshold into stone. For Heidegger, the threshold, as the "between" that divides the outside from the inside, is *(ist)* the *Austrag*, which bears together as it bears apart, which endures in stony hardness. But the threshold has been made hard by pain. How so? Is this because the threshold must provide a hard, stony barrier to keep the cold, naked pain without, on the outside, in still petrification, so as to shelter the warmth of grace within (cf. the alternate version of the poem US, 17/PLT, 195)? Or because pain cuts so deeply, so sharply into flesh that it can turn wood or even flesh into stone?

Those suggestions are not "false"; to be sure, they may even be "correct," but they are not "essential." "But what is pain?" Heidegger asks, to which he answers: "Pain rends. It is the rift." Pain tears, rips, rends apart, leaves us in shreds, in tatters—almost:

> Pain indeed tears asunder; it separates, yet so that at the same time it draws everything to itself, gathers it to itself. . . . Pain is the joining agent [*Fügende*] in the rending that divides and gathers. Pain is the joining of the rift. . . . Pain joins

the rift of the difference. Pain is the difference [*Unter-Schied*] itself. (US, 27/ PLT, 204)

Pain "is" *(est)* the rending that joins, the *Austrag* that bears together what it bears apart. Pain is the intimacy of the between which bears world and thing toward each other. Pain is not to be borne, but rather pain bears, is a bearing *(Tragen)* that sustains or holds world and thing together, holds things in world, lets world issue in thing.

Heidegger has carefully altered the poetic *mise-en-scène*. He decenters the poetic scene, shifting the focus toward the threshold and away from its ostensible center, the table with the bread and wine placed upon it. The effect of this is to shift the scene from the gift of bread and wine to the giver, from the bread and wine, which restore the travelers weary with pain, to the threshold of light, which he takes to be *Austrag, Unter-Schied*.

The bread and wine, which thus gather together the Four, have become Hellenized, Hölderlinian bread and wine, no longer Jewish or Christian, no longer reminiscent of the meal that Christ shared with the disciples. Heidegger seals the poem off from Christian bread and wine, which are inextricably tied to cut flesh and spilled blood. The changed staging shifts the poem away from flesh and blood toward the shining of the *Ding*, toward light, lighting, clearing, thinking's clearing, which is the Fouring *(Vierung)*. The Fourfold comes to presence in and through the rift of difference, which is the more essential pain *(wesentlicher Schmerz, wahrer Schmerz)*. Heidegger's thoughtful "situating" *(Erörterung)* of Trakl's poem, to which I will return below, is thus a certain clearing up and purifying *(erläuteren)* of it, a decontaminating of the poem that purifies it of its Christian contamination and of the stain of blood.

Everything in the poem is organized around the pain. For it is pain that "institutes" this scene by dividing outside from inside, darkness from light, cold from warmth, hunger from nourishment, wandering from rest. Pain drives the traveler within and motivates the whole movement of the poem, setting the wanderer on his path, setting up the distinction between inside and outside. Pain is the differential spacing. That is a very powerful restaging, but we must recall that pain here has nothing to do with feeling or sensation. This pain is the rift between Being and beings, world and thing, and that is what sets up, makes possible, the appearance of bread and wine. The poetic experience of pain is not the experience of suffering, but of the *Unter-Schied*. The scene is instituted by a pain that is taken to mean the bearing in and bearing out upon one another of world and thing, not by physical or mental pain. Heidegger insightfully says that crossing the threshold of pain institutes or founds the scene, that it opens up this space. But this *Unter-Schied* does not mean the transition between weariness and rest, or between the hardships of travel and the warmth of hospitality, but rather the difference between world and thing.

In virtue of true, essential pain, world and thing come to shine *(scheinen)*. The world in all its gleaming beauty *(Schönheit)* appears, in keeping with all the elemental power of that deep Greek word *phainesthai*. This is not a matter of modern "aesthetics" but of a deeper, more essential *phainesthai* that inaugurates what I have called a "phainesthetics" of a different and more essential order. But the *aesthesis* of this phainesthetics lacks a deeper *pathos,* as Lyotard objects, which deprives the pain of its poetic idiom.[5]

But would that painless pain not constitute a spiritual pain after all, a pain without feeling? Has not the spirit returned in the end?[6] The whole force of Heidegger's analysis is bent on resisting that objection.

"Pain is truly pain when it serves the flame of the spirit." Listen to the rest of this text:

> Trakl's last poem is called "Grodek." It has been much praised as a war poem. But it is infinitely more, because it is something other. Its final lines (193) are:
>
>> Today a great pain feeds the hot flame of the spirit,
>> The grandsons yet unborn.
>
> These "grandsons" are not the unbegotten sons of the sons killed in battle, the progeny of the decaying generation. If that were all, merely an end to the procreation of earlier generations, our poet would have to rejoice over such an end. But he grieves, though with a "prouder" grief that flamingly contemplates *(anschaut)* the peace of the unborn. (US, 65/OWL, 184)

There is a great deal to assimilate here and to do so would draw us into a reading of a very dense text, something that we can only partially undertake here. But let us pull a few threads.

Trakl's poem "Grodek" would not be a great poem if it were only about war, about some historical *(historisch)*, political event, some episode in history—say World War I, or the battle of Grodek, where many soldiers were killed—that could be studied historiographically. There are many war poets, but only a few great poets, and only great poetry is a matter for thought, is worthy of thought. Great poets are concerned with a more profound eventuality that belongs not to mere *Geschichte* but to *Seinsgeschichte*. So this celebration of "Grodek" as a war poem is merely what "they" say *(man rühmt)*, a common opinion. But for thinking, it is "infinitely more," because thinking is itself infinitely greater than common opinion. "Grodek" infinitely exceeds any war poem because it addresses something "other" *(anderes, allos*—whence the "alle-gorizing"), not a (factical) war, but something more essential, the matter for thought. Accordingly, "Grodek" is infinitely more than a poem about killing young men.

That enables us to think more essentially what the poet in this passage is poetizing as the unborn, "the grandsons yet unborn" *(die ungebornen Enkel)*. Trakl's references to "dying warriors" *(sterbende Krieger),* the "wild lament of their broken mouths," and "spilt blood" *(das vergossene Blut)* are apt to mislead the thoughtless. They *(man)* think the poem laments the sons unborn of the fallen sons, a striking image which prolongs the pain by referring the death of the sons back to the life of their parents, the survivors. By living on, the mourning parents' loss is doubled—"O prouder mourning" *(O stolzere Trauer)*—as the loss of slain sons becomes also the loss of grandsons forever unborn. But that is not essential.

Were the poet describing "only" the death of soldiers and the loss of the unborn children, were that all *(Wäre es nur an dem)* that was at stake, he "would have to rejoice over such an end" *(müsste jubeln)*. For that would mean the end of the decaying generation, of the lower kind, who, being unable to procreate their decaying type, would happily be going under.[7] According to Heidegger, the poet does not rejoice but mourns, but with a prouder *(stolzere)* mourning, which means a more essential mourning. Prouder and more essential than what? Prouder than parents grieving over dead sons and unborn grandsons. Prouder than that. For Trakl is a great poet. (Maybe even, on Heidegger's accounting, the poet means prouder than mourning. Maybe thinking is more essential than mourning and must be decontaminated of the pain and sting of mourning. Thinking knows how to recall. But does it know how to mourn?)

What then does the poet mourn? Who then are the grandsons referred to by the great, grieving, prouder, more essential poet? They are called "grandsons" because they are not sons, Heidegger explains, and this signifies a discontinuity, a skipped generation, a leap *(Sprung)*, a primordial leap *(Ursprung)*, by which something new emerges. "Between them"—the unborn—"and this generation"—the decaying generation *(das verwesende Geschlecht)*, the ones who have lost their *Wesen*—"lives another generation" (US, 65/OWL, 184). That discontinuity is necessitated because of an "origin different in essence" *(andere Wesensherkunft)* of the coming, unborn generation, an origin that is "out of the earliness of the unborn" (US, 66/OWL, 184). The poet lives in the *Zwischen-zeit*, the in-between time, the interim, between the decaying generation and the unborn generation, too late for the (Greek) gods, too early for Being. "Unborn" means too early, not yet born, coming, on the way—but not forever lost. The earliest is the oldest of the old. So this is a mourning turned toward the *not yet born*, the coming dawn, the Other Beginning. The poem is transported by Heidegger's *Erörterung* to the mythic sphere of Being's movements back and forth between *Wesen* and *Verwesen*.

We are now in a position to offer a reading of pain and of the flame of the spirit. The poet has written:

A great pain feeds the hot flame of the spirit,
The grandsons yet unborn.

Die heisse Flamme des Geistes nährt heute ein gewaltiger Schmerz,
Die ungebornen Enkel.

Heidegger comments:

> The "great pain" is the beholding vision whose flames envelop everything and which looks ahead into the still-withdrawing earliness of yonder dead one toward whom the "spirits" [*Geister*] of early victims have died. (US, 66/OWL, 184)

The pain is a "vision" that consumes everything *(das überflammende Anschauen)*. It sees what is coming; it looks ahead *(vorblickt)* to that "early morning" *(Frühe)* for which it is too early, for which it mourns. In this more essential pain inflammation is really illumination. Searing is seeing, *Anschauen*. The fire that is burning here, which this pain feeds, makes light, makes a clearing. The flame of the spirit lights the way from darkness to light, from the vesperal decline of the old decaying generation to the matinal brightness of the coming day.

That is how I would all too hastily summarize an astonishingly dense text (US, 59–65/OWL, 179–84), a text that has also drawn Derrida's attention (OS, 97–98, chs. 9–10). Here Heidegger establishes that the fire of the spirit is a fire that lights and lets shine *(erglänzen lässt)*, a burning that flickers up and down, between concealment and unconcealment, in which the rage of evil is held in check and gathered together by the fire's more gentle side. Derrida is right to insist on the Schellingian echoes of these formulas about the spirituality of evil. But I am pursuing a further point, that spirit has become light *(Erscheinen, Lichten)*, a matter of phainesthetics, and hence that the spirituality of evil represents a certain evaporization of evil, that it does not produce ash except in some more essential sense, whereas Schelling himself had the merit to be talking about actual or factical evil. The flame of the spirit is neither a material nor an immaterial thing, because it belongs to an entirely different order, that of *Erscheinen (Leuchten, Anschauen, Schauen)*, which for Heidegger is the order of *Wesen* and of *wesentliches Denken*. Trakl's entire discourse is transported to the order of shining appearance and essential seeing.

That explains why Trakl can write of stony pain:

> So painful good, so truthful is what lives;
> And softly touches you an ancient stone.
> Truly! I shall forever be with you:
> O mouth! that trembles through the silvery willow.

On Heidegger's accounting: the stone is impenetrable and of ancient origin, an appearance of an earlier dawn that once glowed silently. The first dawn was entrusted to the stone, which keeps it safe over the epochs, keeps it safe for another coming, another advent (US, 63/OWL, 182). The petrified pain is thus the long enduring, long concealed essence of truth. (Recall that the mention of the stone in "A Winter Evening" is the only line of the poem in the past tense.) Whence everything disturbed, hemmed in, everything dismal and diseased *(Unheil und Heillos)*, every distress of disintegration—all of that is only the appearance *(Anschein)* in which truth conceals itself. "Pain is the grace of essential being in everything that comes to presence" *(die Gunst des Wesenhaften alles Wesenden)* (US, 64/OWL, 183). Its *gegenwendiges Wesen*, its essence, which twists and turns against itself, is ruled by a higher simplicity, in virtue of which all becoming takes its origin out of an early dawn that is at the same time the advent of another coming. Pain's harmony is harmony with the holiness of the blue, with its deep recess and coming dawn, with the movement between *Heil* and *Unheil*, which is the movement between *Geviert* and *Gestell*, Fouring and the loss of the Four.

So pain's *gegenwendiges Wesen* is the history of truth, of lighting and illuminating, of concealing and harboring. Evil is not a matter of matter, but of concealment, of *Unheil*, of the unholy darkening of the earth, of time of the metaphysical animal, the time of the declining type (which means the *Gestell*). But such concealment is in adverse, inverse relation to un-concealment, which holds the former always in check. Concealment is the *gegenwendig* side of the lighting, illuminating, clearing that is cut by the rift of pain, of the path that is cleared by pain's flaming luminosity. Pain is—again, this is the same result as the earlier essay—the cut between concealment and unconcealment, that is, it opens up the space between world and thing or closes in on itself in stony self-concealment, harboring an old, aboriginally old *(uralt)* secret.

Pain is the fire that illumines our way by marking out the path that the sun traces as it runs its course through the solar year. Pain's flame is solar light:

And thus the poet must call "spiritual" the twilight, the night, and the years— these above all and these alone. The twilight makes the blue of night to rise, inflames it. Night flames as the shining mirror of the starry pond. The year inflames by starting the sun's course on its way, its risings and its settings. (US, 66/OWL, 184)

But is this not the oldest, most Platonic, the most metaphysical image that the West knows—the sun of seeing, the fire that lights? Is this not the oldest spirit of the West? Not so, says Heidegger, for what "comes-to-presence" *(west)* in this spirit and indeed makes it "pure spirit" *(lauter Geist)* is "apartness" *(Abgeschiedenheit)*.

But what is apartness? In "The Springtime of the Soul" Trakl wrote "Something strange on the earth is the soul" *(Es ist die Seele ein Fremdes auf Erden)*. The impersonal and neuter constructions, *"es ist" "ein Fremdes,"* suggest the alienation of the strange one, its *Ent-fremdung*. This tormented mind/heart/ soul *(Seele)*, it is a strange and alienated thing. *Es ist*/it is: adrift, unhappy, strange, alone, cut off. It wanders in exile in the realm of *Es ist*, is carried away from the happy conviviality of men and women, parents and children.

The line occurs in the stanza following the poet's invocation of his tormenting and incestuous relationship with his/one's sister, just after the line "Hour of grief, of the silent gaze of the sun" *(Stunde der Trauer, schweigender Anblick der Sonne)*, which refers to the noontime hour of the encounter with the sister, of the grief and torment of incest, found in the preceding paragraph. *Es ist*/it is a dark, incestuous, death-dealing passion, in league with grief and self-destruction:

> O my sister, when I found you by the lonely clearing
> In the wood, at noon, in a great silence of all animals,
> You were white under the wild oak, and the silver thornbush blossomed.
> A mighty dying and the singing flame in the heart.

Es ist/it is an impossible/necessary desire. The consummation of the desire sends the poet/brother reeling, expelled from all civilized custom and law. *Es ist*/it is an outcast, outlaw, alienated, wandering, mad, unborn, half-born, early dead thing. A dark bell tolls down in the village, peacefully accompanying the funeral; myrtle blooms over the white eyelids of the dead brother.

Just like poor Kaspar Hauser. In "Kaspar Hauser Song" Trakl makes use of a story that had made quite a sensation by way of Jacob Wassermann's novel *Kaspar Hauser*.[8] Chained from his earliest years to the floor of a windowless basement cell, then set free to wander, alone and helpless, Kaspar could barely speak, had never seen the sun, trees, or flowers, or a snowfall. Eventually murdered as mysteriously as he had been originally abducted, Kaspar had come into the world only to have his throat slit:

> Saw snow falling through bare branches
> And in the dusking hall his murderer's shadow.
>
> Silver it fell, the head of the yet unborn.

One captures a great deal of the strange one's apartness in the image of Kaspar, who never was quite born, who never quite made it into language and into humankind, who before he could make his way back into the human *Geschlecht* was cut down—with a cut that drew blood. Kaspar was *unterwegs zur Sprache* in a way that Heidegger does not imagine. The poet seems to take Kaspar as an image of innocence, of a primal Eden, a "crystal childhood," whose arrival among mankind and in language is his destruction. To be born is to be condemned to lose the crystal childhood, to rush headlong into the decay and deformation of mankind, the scene of evil, murder, and forbidden desire. In this aberrant and unholy economy, early death, dying before being fully born among men and amalgamated with mankind, is the best and most profitable way out. The kinship between Kaspar and the poetic standpoint— the standing apart—adopted in the poetry seems particularly vivid.

> *Es ist die Seele ein Fremdes auf Erden.*

But essential poetizing is too great a matter to be concerned with Kaspar or with incest. It is not interested in sisters, not in Trakl's sister, not in Poly- neices's sister.[9] For these women do not truly come-to-presence, do not enter into the essential being of *Abgeschiedenheit*. For "[a]partness is pure spirit":

It is the radiance [*Scheinen*] of the blue reposing in the spirit's depth and flaming in greater stillness, the blue that kindles a stiller childhood into the gold of the primal beginning. (US, 66/OWL, 185)

Apartness is *Erscheinen,* the radiant shine of *phainesthai,* a sky-blue radiance that is transformed from twilight to dusk. It is a gathering power:

That power carries mortal nature back to its stiller childhood and shelters that childhood as the kind, not yet born to term, whose stamp marks future genera- tions. The gathering power of apartness holds the unborn generation beyond all that is spent and saves it for a coming rebirth of mankind out of earliness. (US, 66–67/OWL, 185)

The lever that operates Heidegger's essentializing reading of Trakl is plainly visible here. Heidegger's *Erörterung* effects a wholesale relocation or transpor- tation *(ent-örterung)* of the poetic scene into a mythic space. The apart one is resituated as one set apart, "one of the select" *(Erlesenen)* (US, 68/OWL, 188). His madness *(Wahnsinn, ohne Sinn)* is merely his lack of the common, vulgar mind, of the thoughtless ones. His is the solitude of one who finds his way alone and who refuses the dead ends of common mankind, following the light of the flame of the spirit. The apartness *(Abgeschiedenheit)* of the one set apart is, essentially speaking, not the half mad, tormented, incestuous, outcast stranger of Trakl, but rather one resonating with the authenticity *(Eigentlichkeit)* of authentic Dasein in *Being and Time.*
The path of apartness spells the end of evil:

The gathering power, spirit of gentleness, stills also the spirit of evil. That spirit's revolt rises to its utmost malice when it breaks out even from the discord of the sexes and breaks into the realm of brother and sister. (US, 67/OWL, 185)

This is Heidegger's only reference to incest. The flaming spirit that is neither Christian nor Platonic seems also to be a very immaculate *Geschlecht* (which also means sex and family), without sexual contamination, a very pure *Seins- geschickliches Geschlecht.* In any case, the duality of sexual conflict, and the perversity of incest, all evil generally, will all be ironed out in the coming dawn:

But in the stiller onefold simplicity of childhood is hidden also the brotherly and sisterly twofoldness *(geschwisterliche Zwiefalt)* of mankind which collects

itself together there. In apartness, the spirit of evil is neither destroyed and denied
nor set free and affirmed. Evil is transformed. . . . Apartness is the gathering
through which human nature is sheltered once again in its stiller childhood, and
that childhood in turn is sheltered in the earliness of another beginning. (US, 67/
OWL, 185) [trans. modified]

In short, the flame of the spirit is set afire by the radiant shining of the new
dawn *(Frühe)*, the morning blue of a new day, a new kind, a new *genus,
genesis,* the striking *(schlagen)* of new coin, the coining of a new generation
(Geschlecht), one sex and *one* generation *(Ein Geschlecht)*. True pain then is
the responsiveness of the poet's soul to the holiness of the blue (US, 64/OWL,
183). Those belonging to the new generation do not descend from the old—
they are not the sons of the old—but have an essentially new origin *(Wesensherkunft)*. Their provenance is a new event in the order of *Wesen,* a coming
to presence of a new order of Being, even as the dead soldiers are but the
past, spent order of *Wesen,* the decaying ones whose decay is a matter of
Wesen (ver-wesen: US, 46/OWL, 167). The poet does not poetize the death
of soldiers on the battlefield, or incest, or madness, or solitude, or "the desperation of suicide"—he is infinitely greater than that. The poet poetizes *Seinsverlassenheit,* not the loss of life but the loss of Being, not decaying *(ver-wesend)*
life but the *Un-Wesen* of Being's truth, the withdrawal of Being in the age of
the *Gestell.*

Erörterung and Allegorization

Heidegger's reading of Trakl has a certain craft and undeniable rights of its
own. According to it, everything that occurs in the poetry is to be transferred
to the order of *Denken* and *Wesen,* of *wesentliches Denken.* In my view, this
transference *(meta-phorein)*, which is undertaken in the name of thought's
dialogue with the poet, takes the most traditional form of an allegorical reading.[10] In every image and poetic figure Heidegger hears the sounding of something else *(allos)*, finds a parable of another place *(Ort)* in virtue of which he
is able to submit the poetic discourse to an overpowering code whose axiomatics we have examined in previous chapters. Thus we are told in turn:
"Blueness itself is *(ist)* . . . the holy" (US, 45/OWL, 166); "This animal [the
blue game] . . . is modern man," which is the "rational animal" of metaphysics
(US, 45–46/OWL, 166–67); the madman "is of another mind" (US, 53/OWL,
173); the "unborn one" is the "coming awakening of mankind" (US, 55/
OWL, 175) even as the "decaying generation" is the history of metaphysics
up to the present; the *Abendland* is the occlusion of the First Dawn of Being,
which harbors within it Being's new dawn (US, 79/OWL, 195–96); the unborn
grandsons "are not the unbegotten sons of the sons killed in battle" but the

"coming rebirth of mankind out of earliness" (US, 65, 67/OWL, 184, 185); "pain is the *Riss*" between world and thing (US, 27/PLT, 204–205).

This "is" in every case is the "is" of allegory: this "stands for"; this "takes the place of"; this belongs in another place or site *(Ort)*. The place that is marked off by this powerful code is the topology of Being, the place of the reversal in Being's own truth, for on Heidegger's view Trakl's poetry sings the "destiny" *(Geschick)* of the "casting" *(Schlag)* of the human *"Wesen"* (US, 80/OWL, 196), tracking the back and forth movements between *Wesen* and *Verwesen*.

Such massive allegorizing belongs within the framework of representational thinking, not a calculative representationalism, but a codifying representationalism: this "is" that, i.e., should be allowed to take the place of that; this represents or stands for that. In just this way, the voice of the poet is radically subverted ("deflected") by being systematically translated into the voice of the thought of Being.

Heidegger's *Seinsgeschicklich* hermeneutics is far from absurd. It is not without its defenders, not only among the Heideggerian faithful,[11] but also among literary critics.[12] There is in Trakl a thematics of rebirth, of innocence regained, hope in a "transformation of evil," in something saving beyond all the death and destruction, madness and incest. To be sure, that is hardly the poet's dominant discourse and it subsists in the most profound tension—completely broken by Heidegger's mythologizing—with the thematics of decay and despair.

It is precisely in this allegorizing hermeneutics that one can locate what Foti calls Heidegger's "deflection" of the experience of loss without recompense in the poets he reads. This is carried out by way of a reading that is guided in advance by a phantasmic tale about a gracious turn in Being's journey, a tale that trumps the despair, the disintegration, the decay, the death, that dissipates the pain and transforms all the tormented and suffering figures of the poetry into their opposite by way of a fantastic *Kehre*. Heidegger's allegorization mythologizes a poetry written on the edge of sanity, on the brink of life itself. It Hellenizes a poetry written *de profundis*—which are evidently not bad Latin words for Trakl, who used them once, even though they are not Greek (and do not even translate Greek but Hebrew). It turns a deeply jewgreek poet into a pure Greek; it proceeds by way of excommunication and decontamination.

I do not say that Heidegger's situating of Trakl as a poet of the history of Being, of Being's *Geschick*, is an "illegitimate" *Zwiesprache* between *Denken* and *Dichten*. On the contrary, the very "legitimacy" of this hermeneutics—there is nothing to stop thought's course here, to protect thinking from itself, for it has its own laws—underlines everything that is questionable about *Denken*, about *wesentliches Denken*. For what Heidegger calls thinking has the effect of blunting, attenuating, and anaesthetizing the searing pain which is the situation of this poetry, which is at least one of its sites, allowing Heidegger to transform the tragic site. Heidegger's "location" *(Erörterung)* of the poetic site is a relocation, a massive transportation of the poetry into a mythic space that removes it from the pain in which it is born, turning this pain into Being's own rift. The issue at hand is not whether Heidegger's reading of Trakl is "right," whether we should call the police of truth on Heidegger. The issue is with Heidegger's own text, with the "spirit" of this reading, with the character of essential thinking.

I do not say that the *Erörterung* does not "succeed," but rather that its very success is a scandal. The shock delivered by the incommensurability between Trakl's poetry and the *Erörterung* throws the thinking into question. This complaint cannot be countered by arguing that the objection proceeds from a confusion of levels of discourse, a misunderstanding of an *Erörterung,* which is a thoughtful situating of the poet, not a conventional exegesis. For I am arguing that once you grant thinking the right to conduct its own dialogue with poetry, once you grant it its own space, *then* you discover the scandal. I agree that this reading proceeds as a matter of thought, *eine Sache des Denkens;* but it is against the very character of *Denken* that I am raising an objection. It is the very character of thinking and of its dialogue with the poet that is offensive and insensitive, whereas the poetry is painfully sensitive.

The objection cannot be gainsaid by arguing that Heidegger undertakes a "deconstruction" of the poetry in the name of thought. For whatever this massive allegorization is, it is not deconstruction. There is a limit to what can be called deconstruction. A deconstruction is a contamination, whereas *Erläulterung* and *Erörterung* are decontaminations. Deconstruction does not purify a text or a social practice but it shows how it is soiled by everything else around it, how impure, garbled, interwoven, confused, and miscegenated things are, poems among them. But the work of thought is to purify the poetry of flesh and blood, of everything Jewish or Christian, of everything jewgreek, of whatever is not aboriginally Greek or Hölderlinian. Deconstruction finds the fissures and the rents, whereas the *Erörterung* wants to heal everything over with a wholesome Hölderlinian balm.[13] Deconstruction is not a flight from everthing bloody and unsightly. Heidegger's reading is no deconstruction but a relentless allegorization intent upon finding what incest is an allegory for, since incest certainly cannot "be" incest, not *im Wesen.*

Heidegger "situates" Trakl from the start within the order of "greatness," of great German poets, within what I have called the myth of greatness, which has such a pervasive influence on his texts. But a demythologizing interrogation of Heidegger would raise many questions: Must great poetry always be German if it is not Greek? Is this a matter of fact, or of essence? If German is the only language in which one can think, does it follow that it is the only one in which one can poetize in a manner worthy of thought? Then what about Mallarmé or Joyce? And what about German Jews like Celan and Kafka? What about jewgreek poets?

Trakl is a great German poet who has something to do with Hölderlin—is that too a matter of essential necessity?—and consequently a poet who can be trusted to poetize the only proper subject matter *(Sache)* of poetry, viz., the *Geviert.* Any other kind of poetry is simply not great poetry, maybe not even poetry at all, at best grist for the mill of literary critics who do not think, who at most occupy their time with verse.

Heidegger writes, "Every great poet creates his poetry out of one single poetic statement only" (US, 37/OWL, 160). The *Ort* from which *all* poetry that is *great* poetry arises is *one,* single, unique. But how does Heidegger know this? Has Heidegger read all the great poets and so concluded? Does he read many languages, modern and classical, Western and Eastern (for he insists that poetry cannot be translated)? Or is this a matter of essential intuition, of *wesentliches Denken,* which cuts right through to the *Wesen* of poetry, which authorizes Heidegger to speak on behalf of and about every great poet? If so, then what—in essence—is the difference between a *Wesenanschauung* and *wesentliches Denken?*

Heidegger knows, he assures us, that all of the poems of a great poet say the same thing. There is no doubt; it is not ambiguous. What ambiguity there is, is the ambiguity of great poets, which never degenerates into disseminative dispersal (US, 75/OWL, 192). Great ambiguity is gathered together into a deeper unity by the *logos* that speaks in all the poems of a great poet (US, 75/OWL, 192).

Does it then follow that all great poets say the same thing and that they can be collected together in one great antho-logy of Greco-Germanic poetry? Do all great poets speak a singlemost, proper, primordial *Urwort,* a German *Urwort,* the *Urwort* of *das Heilige,* which means the Greco-Hölderlinian *Geviert?* Is there then but one (Greco-Germanic) language, one (Heideggerian-Hölderlinian) poet, one poem? Are Joyce and Mallarmé not scandals, symptoms of Anglo-Irish and French *Seinsverlassenheit,* more proof that when you begin not only to think but to poetize you can only do so in Greco-German *(Spieg.,* 282)?

But what if we do not think of poems issuing from a common source, gathering themselves together in one great collective *Ge-dicht,* in the *legein* of one massive all-gathering anthology? Imagine them springing up here, there, everywhere, in a kind of multiple genesis and spontaneous combustion. Imagine countless poems, drifting like nomads over new and strange terrains, wandering and adrift, émigrés and wanderers like Abraham or Ishmael, spreading out in innumerable directions, swarming across ever broader surfaces, spreading out and getting lost, breaking up and multiplying themselves, like a viral infection. Suppose not an essentializing anthologizer to gather them together into a unity but a jewgreek cartographer of their heteromorphic and hetero-

logical diversity who announces that there are many poets and poems, too
many to cope with, too many languages and poetic sites, too many to gather
together into one. What if that dispersal is not a loss but rather part of the
very joy that poetry gives? What if the jewgreek myth of Babel is good news
for poetry?

With Lyotard, I confess my incredulity toward a single poetic site and a
single great poetic word and other metanarratives and metamyths. With Lyotard, I prefer an anthology of and about *les juifs*.

According to Heidegger's logic of greatness, a great poet cannot speak about
war. For war is a historical episode, something that belongs to the sequence
of events in which the thoughtless ones live (and sometimes die). It belongs
to a superficial *Geschichte* but not to the essential *Seinsgeschick*. We see at
this point that Heidegger's *Kampf*, his early love of Promethean struggle and
militarism,[14] has been transmuted into a mythic event transpiring in the order
of Being itself, muting the fortunes that befall concrete human agents in history. That muting is signaled in the operation that leads him to separate the
bread and wine from pain, from flesh and blood, to think bread and wine in
terms of sky and earth, to cosmologize them, to phainesthetize them, to anes-
thetize them, while the poet has in mind their fleshly resonances. The extent
to which this mytho-mystification had seized hold of Heidegger is evident
from a ludicrous passage in the *Parmenides* lectures of 1942–43 which, spoken
at a time when the tide of the war was shifting against the Germans, essentializes victory and defeat:

> Therefore we need to know that this historical people, if the word "victory"
> [*Seig*] is appropriate here at all, has already been victorious and is invincible,
> provided it remains the people of poets and thinkers that it is in its essence, and
> as long as it does not fall prey to the terrible—always menacing—deviation from
> and mistaking of its essence. (GA 54, 114/P, 77)

Heidegger consistently situates himself above the level of pain and suffering,
which he has always regarded as an ontico-anthropological phenomenon beneath the dignity of phenomenology or thinking. In the early Freiburg period
pain is always my pain and as such a test of my mettle, something to be
transcended, while the pain of others will make them stronger, provided it
does not kill them. In the 1930s, the ability to transcend pain and to embrace
Kampf is the measure of "this historical people's" greatness. In the later writings, pain is simply allegorized, carried off to a mythic space in which it is
transmuted into an event in Being's divide. Heidegger is consistently scandalized by factical pain, by the body, the flesh, the vital. Onto-theo-logic has
always been scandalized by biology, and Heidegger here repeats a classical
onto-theo-logical gesture.

It follows that war really is infinitely beneath a great poet; great poetry is "infinitely more" than that. So if the poet does seem to say something about pain, suffering, and war, then those who know how to stay resolutely in the element of Being know that these are allegories for episodes in the history of Being, for something happening down deep in the truth of Being and the Being of truth.

The site *(Ort)* of thought, and of the thoughtful dialogue with the poet, is *Wesen* understood verbally, not as *essentia*, as abstract whatness or *quidditas*, which would be a fateful distortion of something primordially Greek. *Essentia*, which belongs to the grossness of medieval Latin, is not nearly fine and essential enough. Understood verbally, *Wesen* means primordial coming-to-presence *(An-wesen)* and passing away *(Ab-wesen)*, trembling momentarily between presence and absence. *Wesen* understood verbally refers to a time long ago when that revealing that brings forth truth into the splendor of radiant appearing also was called *techne* (QCT, 34). Once there was a time of greatness when everything was shining *phainesthai* and beaming beauty, when Greek temples gleamed and sparkled in a Mediterranean sun, uncontaminated by everything ugly and malformed, Jewish and Christian and jewgreek, unstained by the oriental foreignness of Hebrew, by the distortion of the Roman and Latin. Maybe it will come again, if we prepare for it. The possibility is dark and uncertain (SD, 66/TB, 60).

Heidegger takes Trakl to be a great German poet who poetizes in consort with the "holy brother" (see Trakl's *"Helian"*), the poet of the Holy, Hölderlin. As a great poet Trakl is poetizing the *Geviert* (that is a matter of essential necessity). To be sure, Trakl speaks quite a lot about pain and suffering, death and mourning, outlaw and alienation, about a desperate errancy that can never find its way home, can never cross the threshold of pain that divides the cold paths of the stranger from the warmth of hearth and family *(Geschlecht)*. But according to the massive code that Heidegger imposes upon the poet, all this evil and *Unheil,* all this unholy unwholesomeness is but the hail of a new wholeness, of a hale and holy time, in the mode of its withdrawal. The *Unheil* is the *Heilige* in the mode of its hidden withdrawal. It is incumbent upon thinking not to disturb the peace of the poet's song. An *Erörterung* must let the poem sing "from out of its own peace" *(aus seiner eigenen Ruhe)* (US, 39/OWL, 161).

But suppose the place from which the poet sings is a place of war, not of peace? Suppose he does not sing but cry, and of conflict, not of rest? Suppose the question is not whether the thinker disturbs the poet's peace, but whether the thinker pacifies everything disturbing and trembling in the poet? Would that not also constitute an interference?

The "deflection" produced by the *Erörterung* of the poetic experience is essentially an allegorical operation. The result of pressing these Heideggerian texts is to verify a phainesthetics which reaches its sharpest pitch in thinking's hymn to the Greeks as the place where Being makes itself beautiful. Heidegger's phainesthetic thinking is, as Lyotard has argued, peculiarly captive to the categories of beauty and poetic radiance. Essential thinking is devoted to a history of *phainesthai* and thinks everything in its terms. Phainesthetics goes hand in hand with what Lyotard has called a certain Heideggerian "anesthesia," this lack of a "certain" *aesthesis*, or *Empfindung*—we are back again to the forbidden word—which explains thinking's lack of taste. There is a logic of scandal in phainesthetics, a systematic taking offense at what is infinitely beneath the matter of thought, as also of giving scandal, of offensiveness, and insensitivity, which makes light of life and death, of flesh and blood, which subsumes and consumes them in *Licht* and *Lichtung*—which, in short, makes light/*Licht* of evil. That is the scandal of scandals in Heidegger's thought, a point that I pursued in the previous chapter.

Thinking purely in the element of Being means to keep thinking pure—of pain and suffering, of burning flesh and broken jewgreek bodies. Topology is scandalized by biology. The *Erörterung* is always a kind of *Erläuterung*, an attempt to wipe poetry clean of blood and pain. Thinking follows a consistent logic. It is a discourse governed by wholly phainesthetic laws, a discourse that essentializes the most elemental concerns of human life and death. The well-being of everything bodily and vital, of every living thing, animal or human, is thought solely in terms of its ability to serve the needs of a mythic *Geviert*. There is a loss of life, a displacement of the living, in the name of a higher or deeper or more essential concern with the loss of Being's proper *Wesen* and shining *phainesthai*. Thinking seeks to raise itself to so sublime a point as to neutralize the distinction between life and death, to neutralize murder itself.

This logic of "essentialization" *(Verwesentlichung)*, which is a logic of non-contamination, obeys the most profound law of Platonic essentialism: the essence is uncontaminated by that of which it is the essence. The pure flame of this spirit is the spirit of uncontaminated purity. Platonism's most essential spirit returns: the *eidos* of becoming does not become; the form of color is not colored; the form of human beings is nothing human. Just so in Heidegger: the *Wesen* of man is nothing human; the *Wesen* of technology is nothing technological; the *Wesen* of language is nothing linguistic. Heidegger has effectively reconstituted the essential gesture of Platonism, repeated the transcendental/empirical couplet of Kantianism, but this time in the order of *Wesen* understood verbally. He has replicated the distinction between deep Being and empirical instantiation, between the purity of the essence and the "grossness" of the empirical, between the uncontaminated inside and the tainted outside. "*Wesen* understood verbally" continues to obey the logic of essence.

Speaking for myself, I would like to turn the whole of Heidegger's thought around one more time, spinning its *Kehre* on its head, turning it back to the logic of "facticity," to a new version of the now abandoned hermeneutics of facticity. For in virtue of its facticity, human being is always already tainted, always already contaminated, always already weighed down by the gross weight of factical being, which includes pain and suffering in the factical sense. Trakl's poetry is a song of factical grief, the sharp cry of one half born, like Kaspar Hauser. But what remains of pain and evil, incest and alienation, homelessness and grief, once they are carried off by this *Erörterung,* once they are marked by the desire to separate *Wesen* from what it is the essence of, by this logic of noncontamination, of essentialization? Transported to a mythic place that etherealizes the grossness of human flesh and blood, that makes them clear and diaphanous, like the risen body of Christian theology, evil is touched by a spirit which, in thinking it through to its more essential Being, lets it become a cloudy vapor in Being's fabulous story. Essential thinking reduces evil to its essence, distills its vaporous essences, its spirits, its spirit. The spirit returns.[15]

The ironic upshot of a close examination of Heidegger's dialogue with the poets is that this thinker, who perhaps more than anyone else in this century has insisted—rightly in my view—that we listen to the poet and let thinking be disturbed by poetry, has displayed the most systematic refusal to listen to his chosen poets. As Foti tellingly observes, Heidegger's dialogue with the poets is a salient case of what Levinas calls "remaining the same in the midst of the other."[16] He does not listen to anything different from what he is prepared to hear about the Fourfold. It is not that thinking "disturbs" the "peace" of Trakl (US, 39/OWL, 161). On the contrary, it pacifies the disturbance that trembles in Trakl's poetry.[17] Heidegger cannot find the place of the poetry of pain, desperation, dissemination, alienation, and ghastly death, which does not open the difference between world and thing but simply bleeds as an open wound.

Is not Trakl's poetic voice ineradicably Christian and Jewish too, even if it is not only Christian?[18] Is this poetry not deeply jewgreek, and has not Heidegger tried to purify and Hellenize it? For it is not *only,* uniquely, properly, reducibly, identically anything. Its only proper poetic voice is to have many voices, no proper voice. Is not Trakl's poetry haunted by scriptural images of crucified flesh and last suppers? Why must a *denkende Zwiesprache* smash all the Christian images? What does *Denken* fear? Why does it always anathematize what does not belong to the closed hermeneutic circle of *its* exclusive aboriginal community? Why this incessant exorcism and excommunication of whatever is jewgreek, whatever is Jewish or Christian?

Must we not wait for a more poetic and less essentializing dialogue, a more jewgreek and less Hellenizing dialogue with the poet, in order to institute another order of *aesthesis,* over and beyond, in addition to, the phainesthetic order, to lift these bans, to make another *aesthesis*—one not estranged from pain and feeling—a proper matter for thought?

Like Husserl's meant "fire" (*Ideas I,* §89), Heidegger's flame is holographic fire, a fire in brackets, a pure, ghostly fire, *eine Flamme des Denkens, eine gedachte Flamme,* while the poet's fire sears, burns, flares up, is caustic, holocaustic. You can pass your hands through Heidegger's fire as often as you like and you will not feel a thing or smell the horror of burning flesh.[19]

A Concluding Postscript. It cannot be ignored that ever since *Being and Time* Heidegger's aim was to gain a higher or deeper ground than ethics, by which I mean here simply a concern with human well-being, in order to get at something "more originary" *(ursprünglicher)* than ethics, which is what he meant by "originary ethics" *(ursprüngliche Ethik)* (GA 9, 356/BW, 234–35). This he thought to find first in a "fundamental ontology" and then later in the "thought of Being." From an orthodox Heideggerian standpoint, the preceding analysis seems to be beside the point. Is Heidegger to be blamed simply because he wants to conduct his thinking on a level anterior to or more fundamental than ethics, a level that indeed would end up explaining how ethics[20] in the conventional sense is possible in the first place? As I myself argued many years ago, in a spirited defense of Heidegger, "Heidegger inquires into the realm which precedes the ethical and the unethical" but that has nothing to do with "contempt for moral directives."[21] To make ethical complaints about analyses that are not conducted on an ethical plane in the first place appears to miss the whole point of what is being said; it is like complaining that geometry is insensitive to human suffering.

Furthermore, as William Richardson has recently been arguing, if Heidegger does not address the ethical, his concern with *die Irre,* with the errancy of Being itself, with the *lethe* in *a-letheia,* cuts to the core of the issue of "human error" and so also of ethical and political error, not directly, but by exposing the fundamental pull toward evil, error, and ill will, by which human existence is inscribed. Thus Heidegger thinks good and evil, not in the determinate sense, to which metaphysical ethics is accustomed, but in principle, *in radice,* in terms of the roots from which evil springs. The *radix malorum* is not *cupiditas* but *die Irre. Irre* is not evil but it is the condition of possibility of evil.[22]

Reluctant as I am to disagree with such a formidable Heidegger commentator from whom I have learned so much, that sounds to me like a conflation of *Irre* with original sin. But *Irre* is something very Heideggerian-Greek, and it has nothing to do with sin or evil, not even as a condition of possibility. It is a myth of a different sort than the myth of original sin. For *Irre* means the concealment, the forgetfulness that Being is withdrawn, and that is a strictly phainesthetic matter. It has to do with the look which Being has, with *Gestell* and *Geviert,* not with human justice or mercy or love. If mortals slaughtered one another under the sky and on the earth, in the name of the advent of the gods, and all this with handmade swords, then the thought of Being could but smile approvingly. But if universal justice and benignity obtained, that would be of no interest to "thought" unless Being granted itself as *physis* and *aletheia.* Again: If Being gathered itself together in an aboriginal *logos* which assembled men and women in rigid social hierarchies and deprived those on the lower end of the hierarchical scale of the chance to flourish, still all would be well with Being as *logos*. But if in the process of making space for people, things got a little disseminated and Being as *logos* withdrew into the concealment of its concealment, then the thought of Being would wring its hands. Indeed, the loss of *logos*, the occlusion of Being in the epoch of *Subjektität*, seems to go hand in hand with the discovery of political and ethical liberty, with ethical and political emancipation. *Irre* does not lead us into evil but into going along with the occlusion of Being as *physis* and *logos*, and that has at best an indirect and at worst a *downright inverse* relationship to the history of ethico-political emancipation.

Hubert Dreyfus, on the other hand, is closer to the mark when he insists that the clearing and evil are independent of each other, but he would still object that Heidegger's job is to worry about the clearing *(Lichtung)*, not about everything that transpires *in* the clearing, which is where ethico-political questions arise. Somebody after all has to worry about the clearing, and indeed while there are plenty of laborers in the vineyard of ethics, the clearing itself tends to go quite untended, to lie in oblivion.[23]

But I deny the idea that the clearing or *a-letheia* represents a sphere that is *prior* to ethics or more originary than ethics—I would prefer to speak of obligation—that somehow lays down conditions to which ethics must submit. I reject the idea that ethics is not *first*, not originary, not there at the beginning. I deny that the world is constituted in a way that antedates ethics, that there is some kind of pre-ethical space, any pre-ethical *da*, any ontological condition *of* ethics that somehow or another got there before ethics, that managed somehow to get in place before ethics arrived. Ethics is at least as old as Being if Being means clearing.

On the view I am defending ethics is always already in place, is factically there as soon as there is Dasein, as soon as there is a world. Ethics is not something to be fitted into a world that is somehow constituted prior to it. Ethics constitutes the world in the first place; ethics, as Levinas would insist, is "first" philosophy. If you want to think what truly "is" you have to *start* with ethics and obligation, not add it on later. To put it in terms that I would prefer, the space of obligation is opened up by factical life, by the plurality of living bodies, by the commerce and intercourse of bodies with bodies, and above all, in these times, in the times of holocausts and of killing fields, by bodies in pain—but no less by thriving and flourishing bodies, by bodies at play.

On the view I would defend, the body in pain clears the clearing in an originary way, opens up the space in which we dwell from the start, generates the lines of force that are inscribed in human space. There is no more essential pain *(wesentlicher Schmerz)*, no pain which is truly pain *(wahrhaft Schmerz)*, which is not embodied factical pain.[24] Pain opens up the distinction between what is essential and what is not, what matters and what does not. Pain is the threshold that opens up the divide of human space, but this is the kind of pain which cuts flesh or breaks hearts, which divides families or friends or lovers, the pain enforced by disease, separation, or death. There is no more essential pain than these factical pains, and no more essential realm of truth as manifestness within which they are situated. Pain opens up the space within which human lives are conducted, opens up the space of truth, making truth matter, instituting truth as a matter of concern. That is the work not only of pain, but of the whole economy of pain and pleasure, suffering and joy, hostility and hospitality.

Heidegger's *Denkweg* is a sustained lesson in what happens when we try to surmount or transcend a concern with human well-being by reaching out for its transcendental conditions *(Being and Time)* or by stepping back from it in order to find a more originary *topos* (later works). Once we cut the nerve of our obligations to one another, we can never repair it; once we neutralize it we can never reactivate it; once we try to gain the ground of a realm prior to such concern, it will never get back in.

The matter for thought must from the start be a matter of what matters to factical life.

CHAPTER NINE

Heidegger's Gods

FROM DEMYTHOLOGIZING TO REMYTHOLOGIZING

I wish to conclude the analysis of Heidegger's texts by tracing the unfolding of the myth of Being from the standpoint of God and the gods. This allows me the opportunity to tell Heidegger's story one last time and to offer an overview of its entire movement, but this time from a different perspective. The question of the myth of Being, which, as I have been emphasizing, is also the question of the tension between Greek and jewgreek myths, is deeply interwoven with the question of God and the gods, that is, with the movement in Heidegger's thought from a biblical God to the gods gathered in the neomythology of the Fourfold.

From its inception, Heidegger's thought has been bound up with certain religious and theological concerns. One can effectively trace the path of Heidegger's *Denkweg* by following the course of his changing religious views. The myth of Being first takes shape in the 1930s, precisely at the point at which Heidegger moves beyond the God of the Hebrew and Christian scriptures. It appears first in harsh, heroico-mythic tones, in keeping with its Nazi provenance, and then afterwords in the softer mythopoetic tones of the Fourfold, of the kinder, gentler worlding of the world and thinging of the thing. In the 1920s Heidegger took the jewgreek world of biblical Christianity seriously and moved in a demythologizing, ontologizing direction. From the 1930s on, Jews and Christians were shown the door and replaced by a pantheon of "pagan" "gods," pure Greeks, and celebrated in an openly mythologizing thinking, which culminated in the hope that one day one of them would come along and save us.

My claim throughout this study has been that Heidegger's original Freiburg project of an ontological appropriation of the biblical world and of the Aristotelian *polis*, however brilliantly conceived and carried out, was flawed by a fateful, fatal omission, right at the start. I further claim that this omission paved the way for a scandalous neutralization and essentialization of human suffering in the later writings that goes to the heart of the mythopoetics of Being. Heidegger's *Denkweg* traces a path from demythologizing the mythic world of the scriptures to remythologizing the world in the accents of a Greek neomythology. But the movement from demythologizing to remythologizing takes an unfortunate turn, one which silences and excludes a competing biblical myth, what I call in the next chapter the myth of justice, with the result that the "jewgreek," biblical stories of human healing and suffering are displaced by a cosmological myth about Being's shining splendor, by a phainesthetic anesthetics. If the Hebrew and Christian scriptures disenchanted the forest and focused on the question of human suffering, Heidegger remythologized the forest and left human suffering to itself.

Heidegger's Early Theological Writings[1]

The searching historical investigations of Hugo Ott have revealed many of the details of Heidegger's early upbringing and education in a deeply Catholic world. Born in the conservative, Catholic farmlands of southern, central Germany, Heidegger's father was a sexton in St. Martin's Church, which stood across a quaint little courtyard not fifty yards from the Heidegger family house. The Heidegger family was steadfastly loyal to the Church in the controversy that followed the First Vatican Council when "liberal" Catholics rejected the proclamation of papal infallibility. The youthful Heidegger, brilliant and pious, was marked from the start for the Catholic priesthood. Through a series of scholarships funded by the Church, one of which was intended for students seeking to do doctoral work on Thomas Aquinas, the poor but gifted young man was lifted out of these rural farmlands into the eminence of a German university career. Heidegger's earliest publications appeared in 1910– 12 in *Der Akademiker,* an ultraconservative Catholic journal which towed the line of Pope Pius X. There in a series of book reviews the youthful Heidegger, still in his early twenties, spoke out against the danger of "modernism"[2] to the ageless wisdom of the Catholic tradition. Heidegger cites with approval the saying of "the great [Josef von] Görres": "Dig deeper and you will hit upon Catholic ground."[3]

Forced to break off his studies for the Catholic priesthood in 1911 for health reasons, Heidegger turned first to mathematics and the natural sciences and then to philosophy, where he was openly identified with the Catholic confession. His first teaching position was as a temporary substitute in the Chair of Christian Philosophy at Freiburg, which served the philosophical needs of theological students, and his first serious professional disappointment was his failure to secure permanent appointment to that Chair in 1916.[4]

Heidegger's earliest philosophical and theological interests in those days, which culminated in the Scotus book (the habilitation dissertation of 1916), centered on a new and promising appropriation of medieval scholastic philosophy in the light of his research into the foundations of modern logic and Husserl's refutation of psychologism. As a philosopher Heidegger staunchly opposed psychologism—the attempt to found logic and mathematics on the psychological makeup of the human mind—as a form of empiricism and relativism, even as he was opposed theologically to modernism as a form of historical relativism that threatened to undermine ageless theological truth. Heidegger saw a continuity between Husserl's "logical investigations," which put logic and mathematics on the foundation of pure phenomenology, and the Scotistic tradition of "speculative grammar" in the late Middle Ages. According to the Scotist tradition, which was profoundly anti-relativist and anti-psychologistic, the forms of grammar and of language *(modus significandi)* are a function of and reflect pure, universal forms of thought *(modus intelligendi)* which are themselves reflections of being itself *(modus essendi).*[5]

But Heidegger also saw another side to the medieval tradition, let us say its "living" side as opposed to its logical and logocentric side, which is to be found in the religious life that animated what he called, following Dilthey, the medieval "experience of life" *(Lebenserfahrung).* We must understand, Heidegger insisted in the Postscript to his habilitation dissertation, that the abstract and difficult theories of medieval philosophers and theologians proceed from a concrete experience of life, that such theories give conceptual expression to the "soul's relationship to God" just as that is experienced in medieval life. He was already at work in tracing back conceptual philosophical structures to their prephilosophical sources. To gain access to this dimension of medieval life Heidegger says that we must attend in particular to medieval moral theology and medieval mysticism, in particular that of Meister Eckhart (GA 1, 404, 410). For it was the mystical notion that the soul belongs wholly to God, that it is constituted by a kind of transcendence toward God, which we see writ large in the corresponding metaphysico-conceptual notion that the intellect has an inner harmony with and belongingness *(convenientia)* to Being. This notion that thinking "belongs" *(gehört)* to Being is one that Heidegger would always in some way or other maintain as a part of his own later views.

By invoking the living significance of medieval mysticism Heidegger makes his first attempt at a "destruction" of the tradition—which does not mean to level or raze but rather to break through the conceptual surface of traditional metaphysics in order to "retrieve" or recover *(wieder-holen:* GA 1, 509/BT, 437) its living roots and life-giving experiences. This is a gesture that Heidegger would repeat again and again throughout his life, so that the famous "destruction of the history of ontology" in *Being and Time* is always to be understood as a fundamentally "positive" operation, not a negative one (§6).

In 1919, now thirty years of age, and on the occasion of the baptism of his first child, Heidegger broke with the Catholic faith. Writing to Engelbert Krebs, the young priest who had married Martin and Elfride in 1917 and who would have performed the baptism, Heidegger said:

Epistemological insights, extending as far as the theory of historical knowledge, have made the *system* of Catholicism problematic and unacceptable to me—but not Christianity and metaphysics (the latter, to be sure, in a new sense).[6]

This is the first "turn" in Heidegger's thought and its importance cannot be emphasized enough. For with the turn from Catholicism to Protestantism, the philosophical interests of the young thinker shifted correspondingly from the questions of logic to those of history, from pure (Husserlian) phenomenology to the hermeneutics of facticity, and from dogmatic theology to the theology of the New Testament. He took his lead not from scholastic theologians like Aquinas, Scotus, and Suarez but, as we have seen in earlier chapters, from Pascal, Luther, and Kierkegaard, who in turn led him back to Augustine and Paul. Indeed, in 1921 Heidegger went so far as to identify himself to Karl Löwith as a Christian theologian.[7] Inspired by Kierkegaard and Luther, Heidegger undertook to recover the ontological features of authentic scriptural Christianity beneath the conceptual scaffolding of medieval theology,[8] whence the provenance of the hermeneutics of facticity and of the "existential analytic" (GA 1, 97n1/BT, 490n1). The record of those investigations, of Heidegger's youthful theological writings—more open now as the early Freiburg lectures gradually become available in the *Gesamtausgabe*—serves as the point of departure for the present study.

The project that eventually issued in the appearance of *Being and Time* was thoroughly interwoven with these theological questions. It took its origin from a twofold retrieval, of Aristotle on the one hand and of New Testament life on the other. It appears to me that Heidegger thought that these two tasks were one and formed, as I would say, a certain jewgreek unity. He thought that the deconstructive retrieval of the categories of factical life would achieve the same results, whether this was a matter of retrieving Greek or early Christian life, whether one were reading Aristotle's *Nicomachean Ethics* or the New Testament, whether one had in view *polis* or *ekklesia*. For the categories of factical life—the categories of care and existence, of concern and instrumentality, of temporality and historicity—are what they are, wherever they are found. There is a curious kind of ahistoricism in Heidegger at this point, very likely one that was inspired by his attachment to phenomenology as a universal science and to the Husserlian ideal of the common, universal structure of the lifeworld, which is the same no matter where it is realized. The goal of *Being and Time*—a very Husserlian and neo-Kantian goal indeed—was to "formalize" these factical structures, to give them a formal-ontological conceptualization that would be ontologically neutral as to their concrete instantiation. That is what lay behind the famous distinction between the "existential" and the "existentiell," or the "ontological" and the "ontic," which is so central to the existential analytic. Heidegger's aim was to set forth universal a priori structures of existential life, of existing Dasein, without "holding up to Dasein an ideal of existence with any special 'content'" (GA 2, 353/BT, 311), which meant without regard to whether such structures were in actual fact—i.e., as an existentiell matter—Greek or Christian, because they had a kind of jewgreek universality.

Being and Time attempted to keep the existential analytic free of privileging any concrete, factical way to be, like Christian or Greek life. There is no suggestion at this point in Heidegger's writings that Greek existence was any more or less "primordial" than Christian existence, no myth of the Great Greek Beginning. On the contrary, both Greek and Christian alike represented "existentiell ideals" upon which the existential analytic drew in order to bring them to the level of ontological formality.

It was precisely because *Being and Time* was in part the issue of an attempt to formalize the structures of factical Christian life that it was greeted with such enthusiasm by Protestant theologians such as Bultmann (with whom it had in part been worked out during Heidegger's stay at Marburg). When Christian theologians looked into the pages of *Being and Time* they found themselves staring at their own image—formalized, ontologized, or, what amounts to the same thing, "demythologized." What *Being and Time* had discovered, Bultmann said, is the very structure of religious and Christian existence but without the ontico-mythical worldview that was an idiosyncratic feature of first-century cosmologies. The task of demythologizing Christianity for Bultmann came down to isolating the universal-existential structure of religious existence in general. It sorts out existential structures such as care, decision, temporality, and authenticity in the face of death, from cosmological myths about heaven "above," hell "below," and the earth in between, myths about heavenly messengers who shuttle back and forth among these regions. Of the "historical" Jesus himself and what he actually taught, Bultmann said that we know nothing. Of the historical communities that formed shortly after his death and which gave mythological formulation to their collective memories of Jesus we know a great deal and they contain the essence of the Christian message, the saving truth. The task of theology, armed now with the Heideggerian analytic of existence, is to deconstruct and demythologize the canonical Gospels in order to retrieve their *kerygma*, the living-existential Christian message, which was one of existential conversion *(metanoia)*, of becoming authentic in the face of our finitude and guilt, a task which faces every human being.[9]

When Bultmann "applied" *Being and Time* to Christian theology he was "de-formalizing" the existential analytic and articulating it in terms of a historically specific, existentiell ideal, viz., historical Christianity. The reason this deformalization worked so well was that the existential analytic was in the first place and in no small part itself the issue of a formalization of Christian factical life. Bultmann was largely reversing the process that had brought *Being and Time* about in the first place.

Heidegger set forth his views on the relationship between universal phenomenological science and theology in one of his last lectures at Marburg, "Phenomenology and Theology" (1928).[10] Philosophy, as the science of Being itself, differs "absolutely" from theology, which is an "ontic" science of a particular entitative region, not of universal Being. Theology is a "positive" science because it deals with a positive, posited entity (a "positum"), which makes it more like chemistry than philosophy (GA 9, 48–49/PT, 6–7). The positum of Christian theology is "Christianness" (Christlichkeit), by which Heidegger means the factual mode of existing as a believing Christian, of existing in the history that is set into motion by the cross, by the Crucified, by Christ on the cross (GA 9, 53–54/PT, 10). One can see in these formulations the residue of the young Heidegger's interest in Luther's theology of the cross which I discussed above, an interest that was ominously transformed into a *Kampfsphilosophie* in the 1930s.[11] Theology is the work of bringing the existential rebirth that comes by faith to conceptual form. Theology is a science of faith, of existing faith-fully, of existing historically as a Christian. Philosophy does not make faith easier but harder, because it does not give faith a rational grounding but shows rather that such facilitating is exactly what theology cannot do. True faith is hard; everything great is hard.

Theology is founded on faith and faith does not need philosophy; but theology, as a positive science, does need philosophy (GA 9, 61/PT, 17). If the "cross" and "sin" can only be lived in faith, they can only be conceptualized with the help of philosophy. For faith is rebirth from sin, but sin is an ontico-existentiell determination of the ontological structure of guilt, which is worked out in *Being and Time*. The Christian concept of sin depends upon an adequate elucidation of the "pre-Christian" (universal ontological) concept of guilt. This dependence is not a matter of "deducing" sin from guilt, but rather of receiving conceptual help and direction—or rather "codirection" and "correction"—from ontology. The theological concept of sin arises from the experience of faith but it reaches conceptual *form* only with the help of philosophy. None of this denies, Heidegger thinks, the Pauline view of the mortal opposition between faith and philosophy. Indeed, it is this strife, this very foolishness which philosophy and faith seem to be to each other, that keeps each strong (GA 9, 66–67/PT, 20–21). (One sees here very clearly Heidegger's idea of a *Kampfsgemeinschaft*, a community kept strong by the tension of inner contest.) Faith is philosophy's existentiell enemy, but it must contend and consort with the enemy if it wants to assume conceptual theological form.

The National Socialist Years

"Phenomenology and Theology" was Heidegger's farewell to Christian theology as a matter of explicit and personal concern. After he returned to Freiburg as Husserl's successor in 1928 his thought underwent another fundamental shift, a shift which once again reflected and was reflected in a changed theological attitude. This is the beginning of the darkest days of Heidegger's life and work, of the hellish endorsement of National Socialism and his ardent efforts to Nazify the German university. He became, as we saw, an enthusiastic reader of Nietzsche, while Kierkegaard, Luther, Pascal, Augustine, and Aristotle faded into the background. This ominous development in Heidegger's thought, which we examined in more detail above, is intimately related to a changing theology. If he had begun as an ultraconservative Catholic, and if after 1917 he had become deeply involved in a dialogue with liberal Protestant historical theology, he was after 1928 deeply antagonistic to Christianity in general and to the Catholicism of Freiburg in particular, and he gives indications of having become personally atheistic—vis-à-vis the God of Abraham, at least. He became in his personal conduct at Freiburg an aggressive opponent of Christianity. He would not accept as his doctoral students the young Jesuits who came to Freiburg and he treated other Catholic students, such as Max Müller, exceedingly badly. When their dissertations were submitted—under the direction of Martin Honecker, who held the Chair of Christian Philosophy—Heidegger treated them with distance and even disdain on the grounds that they were confessional, not philosophical, works. (After 1945 he claimed them as his students.) When Honecker died unexpectedly in 1941 Heidegger succeeded in having this Chair abolished, the very one to which he himself had aspired a quarter of a century earlier.[12]

His philosophical work, always "methodologically" atheist, lost its ontological neutrality and became openly antagonistic to Christianity. If he thought, prior to 1928, that both Greek and Christian existence, taken in their historical concreteness, exemplified the universal structures of factical existence, his position during the thirties was that Christianity represented a decadent falling away from the primordiality of Greek experience. For the first time, "Greek" means the early Greeks, while, following Nietzsche, Plato and Aristotle represent the beginning of the metaphysical oblivion of Being. The hostility that had now invaded Heidegger's portrait of the relationship between philosophical questioning and Christian faith, and the transition that had taken place from a methodological atheism to a more aggressive atheism, can be seen quite clearly in the following contrast. In 1922 he wrote:

> Questionability is not religious, but rather it may really lead into a situation of religious decision. I do not behave religiously in philosophizing, even if I as a philosopher can be a religious man. "But here is the art": to philosophize and thereby to be genuinely religious, i.e., to take up factically its worldly, historical task in philosophizing, in action and a world of action, not in religious ideology and fantasy.
>
> Philosophy, in its radical self-positing questionability, must be in principle a-theistic. (GA 61, 197)

The art of the believer is to maintain oneself in radical "questionability," i.e., to be able to raise radical questions while at the same time responding to the claim of faith. Philosophical questioning is not and cannot become faith without ceasing to be questioning, but the believer can hold his faith open and keep it free from dogmatic ideology only by exposing it to the difficulty of constant questioning.

But in *An Introduction to Metaphysics* we read:

> Anyone for whom the Bible is divine revelation and truth has the answer to the question "Why are there beings rather than nothing?" even before it is asked. . . . One who holds to such faith can in a way participate in the asking of our question, but he cannot really question without ceasing to be a believer and taking all the consequence of such a step. He will only be able to act "as if". . . . (GA 40, 5/IM, 6–7)

And again, a bit later on in the text, Heidegger assails a work entitled *What is Man?* by the Christian theologian Theodore Haecker, whose recent lecture at Freiburg had been angrily protested by the Nazi students:[13]

> If a man believes the propositions of Catholic dogma, that is his individual concern; we shall not discuss it here. But how can we be expected to take a man seriously who writes "What is Man?" on the cover of his book although he does *not* inquire, because he is *un*willing and *un*able to inquire? . . .
> Why do I speak of such irrelevancies in connection with the exegesis of Parmenides's dictum? In itself this sort of scribbling is unimportant and insignificant. What is not unimportant is the paralysis of all passion for questioning that has long been with us. (GA 40, 151/IM, 142–43)

Prescinding from the fact that Heidegger here attacks Haecker's intellectual integrity, Heidegger now clearly holds that there is an existential (if not a logical) contradiction between real philosophical questioning and religious faith, not a living tension but irresolvable incompatibility. The believer does not have the passion—or the personal honesty—to enter the abyss of the questionability of Being. Where once Heidegger staked out the possibility of a questioning faith, of a believer who exposes himself to the abyss of questionability, here he opposes belief to questioning. In the view that he held in 1935, that also makes the Christian faith a counterrevolutionary force from the standpoint of the National Socialist "renewal." The facade of questioning that the believer puts up will always have a kind of fraudulent "as if" quality. The dishonest labors of Christian writers should not be mentioned in the same breath as the greatness of Greek thinkers like Parmenides.

From the standpoint of a traditional biblical faith, what has transpired in the years intervening between these two texts is that Heidegger's personal standpoint seems to have become unambiguously atheistic. But it would not be quite right so to describe it, for what seems to have transpired is a shift away from a biblical religion to a certain Greek religion. The myth of the Great Beginning among the Greeks, to which the Germans are the sole, appointed, destined heirs, which dwarfs the late Roman and Christian "distortion" of the Greeks, is now securely in place. The Christian—as also the Jewish, for Christianity, while supplying a theology and a politics for antisemitism, remains, however ironically, spiritually Jewish—is a foreign stuff, a Semitic contamination of the Greek and German. Heidegger's opposition of questioning and faith is a political and ideological gesture affirming the unity and the purity of the Greco-German spirit.

It is my contention that everything that transpires on the path of thought, every step along the way, has a religious key. Heidegger now invokes not no God but new gods, new Greek gods in which the energy of the revolution and of thinking are simultaneously concentrated. That passionate seeker after God, Nietzsche, has announced to us the death of God, the withering away and unwinding of the Greco-Christian synthesis (SA, 474). But in the place of the old dead God a new and more radical spirit *(Geist)*, a life-giving and life-sustaining power *(Macht)*, is called for, one which makes an assault on the heavens themselves, one which does battle with Being, *physis, ananke*. Only a god, a Greek god, can save us, and that god's name is Prometheus, the great advocate of men in their struggle with Zeus, who wrests fire from the gods the way we men must wrest truth from concealment. It is the Prometheus of Aeschylus who utters the saving but dangerous word, the word that saves because it is dangerous, around which the *Rektoratsrede* is organized: "*Techne*, however, is far weaker than necessity" (SA, 472). That saying is a call not for surrender but, on the contrary, for constant struggle, for a heroic battle to the end, in which men will prove their eminence among other men by taking on the glorious but finally futile battle with Being. Aeschylus issues a battle call; his Prometheus summons us to battle.

The initial breach with the Christian tradition takes the form of a heroic myth of battle with and among the gods, a battle of men with necessity (Being) itself. The Pauline good fight to keep the faith is displaced with a Promethean battle to wrest Being from semblance and concealment. That heroic task is assigned by destiny, by Necessity itself, to the Germans, who alone are capable of waging battle with Being, that is, of questioning radically and relentlessly, of making the ground quake with the thunder of their questions, of making the earth tremble with the violence of their irruption in the midst of beings, in the midst of Europe, from out of which they will rise up in splendor and majesty.

The first form of the myth of Being was a neomythologizing of Greeks and Germans which went hand in hand with a hellish ideology and purging of the university of dissidence and inconsonance. The myth took the form of purging away the Jewish and Christian from the question of Being, of producing a work of thought that was *Judenrein,* just as the Nazis were doing in the streets and in the public institutions of Germany. Heidegger issues a call for a "spirit" that is at once Greek and German, metaphysical and interrogatory, radical and revolutionary. The myth here is a myth of a monumental age of mighty Greek gods and great Greek questioning uniquely and spiritually allied to a German *Geist.* The text marches in step with the Party's disdain for Christianity, which it raises up a notch to the level of metaphysical questioning and of the place that Being has destined for the Germans. It can never be forgotten that the notion of historical "destiny" first took hold in Heidegger's thinking in the midst of National Socialism, where it signified the destiny of Germany in the history of Being. It cannot be ignored that the construction of this myth depended entirely upon an operation of decontamination, upon the exclusion of the Hebrew and the Christian scriptures from that pure origin and originary purity.

By 1936, as we can see clearly now in the *Beiträge,* the tonality of the neomythology shifted. The bellicose militarism of the Promethean god—he would later on, in a ludicrous attempt to whitewash the past, say he was talking only about a Heraclitean battle (SA, 488–489), the reference to von Clausewitz (SA, 479) being evidently nothing serious—disappeared in favor of a more gentle worlding of the world of the Fourfold, and the tone was one not of *Kampf* but of mystical *Gelassenheit.* That was the Heidegger who burst upon the scene of European philosophy in 1947.

The Later Writings

After the war Heidegger largely succeeded in covering up his past involvement with National Socialism and his past hostility to Christianity. A steady stream of new publications forged the image of the "later" Heidegger, previously known only to the small numbers who were able to follow his lectures during the war years. A new wave of Heideggerianism swept over Continental philosophy, encouraged especially by the enthusiastic reception he received from the French, beginning with the French existentialist "misunderstanding" and continuing today with his appropriation by French postmodernism. The French people—who cannot think in their own language—flocked to his texts to learn to think in German. The 1947 "letter" to the French people (to Jean Beaufret and to the philosophical world) set forth the "humanistic" (i.e., anthropocentric) limits of existentialism and the real demands of the "thought of Being" (GA 9, 326–29/BW, 206-09). It was clear to everyone that Heidegger's thought had taken still another turn.

It is useful from my point of view to think of Heidegger's thought as having passed through three stages, each of which has a significant religious key: (1) the conversion from Catholicism to Protestantism (1917–19), which set the terms for the first Freiburg period and culminated in *Being and Time;* (2) a turn toward an extreme heroic and Nietzschean voluntarism (ca. 1928–29), which culminated in the National Socialist engagement; this is, from the standpoint of a biblical faith, atheistic, but it is more accurately represented as a turn toward a heroic, Promethean neomythological religion of struggle and bombast; (3) the move beyond voluntarism (1936–38) toward the thought of Being, a new mythopoetic meditation upon the Holy and the gods. This later thinking had become radically anti-voluntaristic, anti-Nietzschean, and opened onto a new savoring of the divine, a new mythopoetics of the gods. It construes the metaphysics of the "will to power," the most extreme expression of which is the contemporary technologizing of world and man, as the culmination of this history of oblivion. The task of "thinking" is now identified precisely as not willing, first by willing *not* to will and then by not willing at all (GA 13, 38–39/DT, 59–60). Here willing was taken in a general sense to mean not only choosing and willing in the determinate sense, but all conceptual or "representational" thinking, which goes to the very essence of the Western philosophical and scientific tradition. The heroic accents of the mighty Promethean and Heraclitean "strife" *(Kampf)* between Being and man disappears, and instead of "willing" Heidegger speaks of "letting be," using at this point the word *Gelassenheit,* one of the oldest and most revered parts of the vocabulary of the Rhineland mystics, in particular of Meister Eckhart. Being is not something that human thinking can conceive or "grasp" *(be-greifen, con-capere),* but something which thinking can only be "granted." Thoughts come to us; we do not think them up (GA 13, 78/PLT, 6). Thinking is a gift or a grace, an event that overtakes us, an address that is visited upon us.[14]

Once again a fundamental shift in Heidegger's thinking took place and again with overt religious overtones. The strident antagonist of Christianity during the war years—himself a sometime Protestant and a sometime, very ardent Catholic—had taken on a mystical air. With this latest turn Heidegger was, as he himself said, returning to his theological beginning (US, 96/OWL, 10), at least to one of them, to his youthful interest in medieval mysticism, particularly in Meister Eckhart.[15]

Heidegger's postwar relations with both Catholic and Protestant theologians were dramatically reversed. In the denazification trials held immediately after the war, a besieged Heidegger (he eventually had a minor breakdown) turned first for help from his old friend and counsellor, the then Archbishop of Freiburg, Conrad Gröber, who had gained wide respect for holding his ground against the Nazis during the war (something of which Heidegger hardly approved in those years).

Ever since the 1930s, even during the time when Heidegger was personally hostile to theological students, Heidegger exerted a seminal influence on theologians. A series of Catholic luminaries heard these lectures during the 1930s, a list which, in addition to Max Müller, included Gustav Siewerth, Johannes

Lotz, and above all Karl Rahner, all German Jesuits. Rahner unfolded the problematic of questioning in the direction of a "transcendental Thomism" first marked off by the Belgian Jesuit Joseph Maréchal. Rahner held that questioning, as the radical opening of thinking to Being, represented the dynamism or momentum of the mind toward God. He treated the forehaving of Being by the understanding as a preunderstanding of God inasmuch as God is the Being which is sought in all of our thought and action. In his second major work, *Hearers of the Word,* Rahner appropriated the thematics of speaking and hearing, claiming and being claimed, that Heidegger had begun to enunciate for the first time in the 1930s in connection with his readings of the early Greeks. Rahner put Heidegger's reflections to a theological use which argued that the believer is ontologically disposed to revelation, that there is a kind of ontological structure in Dasein in virtue of which its very Being is to be addressed by Being itself. That ontological structure, worked out in Heidegger's philosophical writings, articulates the condition of possibility of being claimed by the Word itself, which the Father speaks to humankind. Rahner also made significant use of Heidegger's conception of Being-unto-death in a short treatise entitled *The Theology of Death.* Rahner said that he had many good professors *(Schulmeister)* but only one teacher *(Lehrer).*[16]

On the Protestant side, a new wave of post-Bultmannian theologians emerged, led by Heinrich Ott, who showed in effect that the later Heidegger's rejection of humanism opens up new possibilities for theology. Ott confirmed Karl Barth's long-standing objections to Bultmann (and to the Heidegger of *Being and Time*) and showed that Barth's theology of the primacy of God is in fact accommodated by the later Heidegger's turn toward Being. Ott went on to construe the history of salvation as a history of disclosure, on an analogy with Heidegger's history of the disclosure of Being, and to put Heidegger's conception of language as call to use in his interpretation of biblical language. The sentences of the New Testament about the resurrection, for example, are not to be taken as propositional assertions of matters of fact but as a call to a new mode of Being. Ott's work, and the whole impact of the later Heidegger on theological reflection, reached the United States in a volume entitled *The Later Heidegger and Theology.*[17]

Christian theologians have shown a remarkable interest in the later Heidegger's later deeply—albeit generically—religious discourse of giving and receiving, grace and graciousness, saving and danger, address and response, poverty and openness, end-time and new beginning, mystery and withdrawal, and in the thematics of the truly divine God.[18] These theologians have found Heidegger's thought so amenable to theological application only because that thought had drawn in the first place upon theological resources. Heidegger was giving a reading of the early Greeks that it is impossible to believe was not the result of a transference of the categories of Christianity to early Greek texts. The quasi-prophetic call for an "other beginning" resembles a kind of *metanoia* (conversion) and the coming of the kingdom, or even of the Second Coming. The relationship between Being and thinking in Parmenides and Heraclitus is treated in kerygmatic terms, on the view that these early Greeks took Being to be "addressed" to man, that it laid claim to man, and that the Greeks conceived the Being of man in terms of responsiveness and answerability to this claim. Heidegger went on to say that his deeply historical conception of Being, which included even an "eschatological" conception of the "history of Being," was fundamentally Greek in inspiration. But it is clear to everyone but Heidegger's most fanatic disciples that he is clearly Hellenizing and secularizing a fundamentally biblical conception of the history of salvation—a ruse both compounded and betrayed by the radicality with which he tries to exclude the biblical provenance of these operations.

As Kierkegaard had said a century earlier, the discovery of time and history was a Jewish and Christian one[19]—as was, we may add, the whole thematics of speaking and answering, claiming and being claimed. Heidegger had baldly appropriated the *kairological*—the *kairos,* the appointed time, the "moment" *(Augenblick)* of truth and decision in *Being and Time* (§67a)—and kerygmatic conceptions of human existence that he had first learned from biblical Christianity, and gratuitously attributed them to the Greeks, to whom they were quite alien. It was these elements in Heidegger's thought that these Christian theologians found so congenial to their own theological work. That is hardly surprising. When they looked into Heidegger's texts, they beheld their own image.

Heidegger was in the most literal sense building a rival *Heilsgeschichte* to the biblical one that he had discovered in his New Testament studies, a *Heilsgeschichte* that was pure and decontaminated of Jewish and Christian impurities and that was keyed not to the Christian myth but to the myth of Hellas and *Germania*. Having set out to demythologize and raise to the level of a formal ontology the categories of Christian factical life, the "later" Heidegger in fact set about the fabrication of a rival mythology which put father Parmenides and Heraclitus in the place of father Abraham and which made the Germans the people chosen by Being for special favor. Heidegger was not demythologizing the history of salvation and giving it an ontological sense, in the spirit of *Being and Time,* but constructing a rival and competing myth build around the *grand récit* of Being and Germania.

Earth and Flesh: Rival Mythologies

This is by no means to say that in his later writings Heidegger had returned to the faith of his youth. Indeed, the later writings invoke a certain pagan mythic world of mundane gods and divinized cosmic powers. The Marburg project of a fundamental ontology which would lay the ground for an ontic science of faith entirely disappeared in favor of a more radical delimitation of ontological and onto-theo-logical thinking. Where once Bultmann, in the name of fundamental ontology, tried to dispel the heavenly messengers, the angelic powers who shuttle messages back and forth between the heavens and earth, Heidegger bent all his efforts, in a series of mythopoetic essays, to reinstate precisely such a world. What Bultmann called the mythic overlay needing to be demythologized became for Heidegger the experience of the truth of Being, of the worlding of the world and of the truly divine god. To the God of metaphysical theology—the offspring of the unholy wedding of Platonism and Christianity—Heidegger opposed the play of worldly divinities. "Man can neither pray nor sacrifice to this god [of metaphysical theology]. Before the *causa sui* man can neither fall to his knees in awe nor can he play music and dance before this god" (ID, 140/72). In place of the god of metaphysics Heidegger put the truly divine god, the god of song and prayer and praise. The brackets that had earlier been placed around God in the demythologizing project of fundamental ontology in the Marburg period are now lifted. The worlding of the world, the play of the world, now includes an experience of the divine and of gods who show their face in the phenomenal world. If, in virtue of its radical desacralizing *epoché*, phenomenology remained neutral toward God, essential thinking was defined by a certain experience of the Holy and the gods.

The event of Being that holds sway in the contemporary world is the *Ge-Stell*, which is not technology but what essentially comes to pass in technology, the essence *(Wesen)* of technology. The world of tools and technical instruments makes up but technology in its manifestation. Technology in essence is an event in and of Being itself. It is the way Being comes to pass as the challenge issued to man to master the earth. Technological man responds to the challenge and takes up the call by means of a technical-calculative assault upon beings meant to subdue them to human purposes. The world in the *Ge-Stell* is the storehouse of raw material, a stockpile, which submits to the machinations and manipulations of technical man. In and through this *Ge-Stell*—in thinking it through and thinking through it—Heidegger thinks the possibility of turning, a Coming Dawn, a New Day, an Other Beginning, the Dawn of the *Geviert,* the Fourfold, which is a new mythic structure of great poetic power.

The world of the Fourfold means the coming to pass of the heavens, the earth, the gods, and mortals. The "heavens" signifies not the outer space explored by modern technology but the sky which gives the measure of our days and seasons. The "earth" is not the substances studied in geology but the support of our step, the source of our nourishment, and the material womb to which we return at death. "Mortals" are those who live under the heavens and upon the earth. They are the children of the earth, not masters of it, not aeronautical engineers, but men who look meditatively upon the evening sky. They are men of *humus*, humans, in that traditional etymology of the word, born of dust and destined to return to dust. But who are the gods?

> The gods are the beckoning messengers of the godhead. Out of the hidden sway of the gods the god emerges as what he is, which removes him from any comparison with beings that are present. (VA, 177/PLT, 178)

The appearance of the gods is itself made possible only within the dimension of the divine, and the divine is itself made possible only within the dimension of the Holy, and "only from the truth of Being can the essence of the Holy" be thought (GA 9, 351/BW, 230). A "dimension" is that which makes the appearance of a thing possible (and would in the early phenomenological period have been referred to as a horizon). In the present age of the *Ge-Stell* the appearance of the god is prevented by the call to manipulate and enframe the earth. The times have become unholy and the divinity has withdrawn. The gods have flown—"we are too late for the gods" (PLT, 4). But in this "hidden fullness and wealth of what has been" there lies the possibility of a "coming destiny of Being" (VA, 183/PLT, 184), of a New Age, a Coming Dawn, an Other Beginning, a new dispensation of Being and the Holy in which the last god will go passing by (GA 63, 405ff.) and make a new manifestation of the Holy possible.

The most important and salutary aspect of Heidegger's mythopoetizing of the gods is its ecological upshot. Heidegger's later writings provide a powerful neomythology of the earth, around which deep ecologists—who are largely on the political left, today—can draw inspiration. In this age of unrestrained violence toward a delicate ecosystem and the animal world, this age of almost unrestrained destruction of the ozone layer above and the rain forests below, Heidegger's profoundly beautiful and powerful discourses on the "thing," on letting world and earth be, on letting the rose blossom without why, could not be more urgent. The difficulty with Heidegger is that his myth of world and thing, of the Fourfold, his sacralizing of the earth is tied to a geophilosophical myth of Being's history, of its favorite sons and favored languages and chosen lands. At the same time it omits and even preempts the myth of justice, which is another and equiprimordial myth, not a myth of the sacred earth, not a pagan myth of sacred cosmos, but a Hebraic myth of the Holy, of the call of the Other One, of the other person.

That is the Levinasian critique of Heidegger's gods, which turns on distinguishing the immanent "sacred" *(sacré)* from a transcendent and apart "holy" *(saint)*,[20] a distinction that is implicitly at work in my discussion in the preceding chapters of the question of the victim and the fate of flesh in Heidegger's later writings. For the divine does not mean only the Fourfold, but it means the suffering of the least of God's children, the well-being of the poorest and of what the world calls *me onta* (I Cor. 20:28). That of course is not a pagan myth but the myth of Emmanuel, of God standing by us, the myth of biblical justice found in the Hebrew and Christian scriptures. This is the dichotomy between the myth of justice and a cosmic myth, between touching stories about healing a withered hand and feeding the hungry—myths of flesh—and stories of the worlding of the world, myths of earth. The unfortunate, the fateful, the fatal gesture of Heidegger's thinking is its act of decontamination, of excommunication, of the myth of the flesh, of justice, its radical exclusion of everything Jewish and Christian. That is the defining gesture of the myth of the Great Greek Beginning, which first took hold in Heidegger in and with his embrace of National Socialism, whose "proximity" Heidegger never left.[21]

If the young Heidegger understood that faith means *Sorge* but missed the *kardia,* the later Heidegger understood that piety is *Gelassenheit* but he continued to miss the *kardia.* Even after the war had ended, when the suffering of millions was plain to see, Heidegger still had not learned his lesson, still had not learned about pain and misery and destitution. He thought deeply and beautifully about *physis* and *aletheia* but he still omitted *kardia.* The god that emerges in Heidegger's late writing is a profoundly poetic god, a woodland god arising from a poetic experience of the earth as something sacred and deserving of reverence. This is a cosmo-poetic god, not the ethico-religious God of the Hebrew and Christian scriptures, not a God of the suffering, of mercy and justice and flesh laid low. It has nothing to do with the God whom Jesus called *abba* or with biblical works of healing and mercy, with the widow, the orphan, or the stranger. Indeed, Heidegger's later writings are more suggestive of a certain Buddhism, a certain meditative, silent world reverencing, than of Judaism or Christianity and the emancipatory power of biblical justice.[22]

Martin Heidegger died in 1976, in his eighty-sixth year. He was buried in the Catholic churchyard in Messkirch between his mother and his father. At Heidegger's request a Catholic mass was celebrated by Bernard Welte in the church of St. Martin's where Heidegger's father had been sexton, in whose shop in the basement of the church the young Martin had often played as a youngster. Welte, a Freiburg theologian who was also a fellow townsman of Heidegger, delivered the eulogy.[23] Welte said, quite rightly, that Heidegger's thought has shaken this century, that it was a thought that was always seeking, always underway. Welte related this being "on the way" to the Gospel's notion that he who seeks shall find:

"He who seeks"—that could well be the title for all of Heidegger's life and thought. "He who finds"—that could be the secret message of his death.[24]

Heidegger seemed to have come full circle, confirming what he said in *On the Way to Language* that his future lay in his theological beginning (US, 96/ OWL, 10).

We do not know, and it is surely none of our business to know, what lay behind Heidegger's choice of a Catholic burial. We have only texts to read and to think through, and it is clear that in these texts Heidegger's seeking and finding, his path of thought, was defined by a profoundly exclusionary gesture, one which defined the Greek Beginning by excluding the Hebrew and the Christian. The myth of Being, of Hellas and Germania, was made possible by the exclusion of Semitic myth—not only the myths of creation and fall and redemption, but above all by the myth of justice and the stories of suffering and compassion. What Heidegger calls "thinking," what called Heidegger to think, is constituted by this exclusion.

I wish to conclude this study by turning to a thinking which defines itself by its lack of strict borders and firm definition, which constitutes its identity by exposing itself to its other, which attempts to be Greek by exposing itself to what is Jewish, which thinks Being while calling for justice, which takes as its motto that jewgreek is greekjew.

CHAPTER TEN

Hyperbolic Justice

MYTHOLOGIZING DIFFERENTLY WITH DERRIDA AND LEVINAS

I do not take the side of pure demythologizing, which, left to itself, is an operation of pure reason, the work of an *Aufklärer*. In my view, demythologizing inevitably turns out to be a matter of mythologizing differently. However much one demythologizes one is ineluctably drawn into one sort of myth or another. I do not think it possible to make a clean cut with mythologizing, to stand clear of myth, to get to the other side of myth, outside and uncontaminated by myth. The attempt to decontaminate oneself of myth falls prey to the myth of purity and decontamination. It is not a question of getting outside myth but rather of exercising a certain vigilance about the kinds of myth in which one is caught up, which is what it means to be "inside/outside" myth. For there are myths and there are myths, many kinds of myths, too many to master, some salutary and some not, and they do not mean the same thing or reduce to the same deep structure.

To challenge the myth of Being, to call for demythologizing Heidegger, is inevitably to be implicated in another myth, over and beyond Heidegger, the myth of what is otherwise than Being or—since I do not think it is possible to twist free of Being—the myth of being otherwise, which inwardly disrupts and disturbs the myth of Being. I wish to conclude this study with the introduction of another myth, a more Hebraic or jewgreek myth, which I mean to play off and thereby disturb the pure Greek myth, the myth of the purely Greek, that so seized Heidegger's thought. This is a myth of invisibility and impossibility rather than of Being's shining splendor, a myth of contamination and dispersal rather than of native land and language, a myth of Abrahamic wandering rather than of geophilosophical homecoming. I mean the myth of justice, the myth of a care for every hair on our head, of infinite care for the least among us, a myth not of beauty and shining greatness but of the lame and the leper, of the outcast and the orphan, a biblical myth of justice and *kardia,* not of temples gleaming in an Aegean sun, a myth of mercy, not of *moira.* For it is justice that is missing from Being, justice that is mystified and mythologized by Being, justice that is abandoned by Being. It requires a more Hebraic imagination to think—or hear—the call of justice, over and beyond and otherwise than the call of Being.

That more Hebraic operation of mytho-philosophical imagination, that jew-greek imagination which makes no attempt to protect itself from what is Semitic and biblical, which on the contrary nourishes itself from exposure to this "prephilosophical" source,[1] is found today above all in Levinas. Levinas is a great oddity on the contemporary philosophical scene, appearing as a kind of prophet among the postmoderns, a prophetic voice in the midst of Parisian eccentricities. From Levinas the prophetic imagination makes its way, *mutatis mutandis,* into Derrida and Lyotard, where it effects a great divide between postmodern writers, a split between postmodern philosophies of obligation (Levinas, Derrida, Lyotard) and the philosophies of discharge and overflow in Deleuze, Guattari, and Baudrillard.[2] I want at this point to identify this jewgreek imagination, this myth of justice, this prophetic or quasi-prophetic call for justice, for justice as mercy and compassion, issuing in particular from Derrida and Levinas in order precisely to reinstate what has been so radically excluded by the myth of Being. I want in short to show that demythologizing Heidegger is a matter of mythologizing differently.

The Deconstruction of Ethics and Politics

Hannah Arendt has written, from a standpoint which is not precisely deconstruction's but which bears significantly on deconstruction, that political philosophy—to which we can also add ethics or moral philosophy—represents a flight from the complexity and unregulatability of action, of living and acting in the *polis.*[3] For Arendt, political philosophy attempts to escape from what she calls the "frailty of action," by which she means both the unforeseeable initiatives and fresh choices that are made by agents (the "natality" of action) and the unpredictable, uncontrollable outcomes of their actions, the chains of consequences that run beyond the agent's control.[4] Faced with such unforeseeability and uncontrollability, with such unregulated, shall we say such anarchic conditions, political philosophy seeks to impose order, to establish an *archē,* to set up a frame of regularity around the shifting, mobile scene of action, to write a kind of *regulae ad directionem civitatis.*

Political philosophy is an exercise in fashioning or making a city, in building walls around the *polis;* it is, quite literally, statecraft, which means that it is conceived in terms of a kind of *techne,* of making. Political philosophy means to turn out master builders, philosopher-architects. In its earliest, Platonic version, the philosopher-architect keeps an eye on a heavenly pattern, which, being heavenly, is not itself made but serves as the basis for making, which is not an *Abbild* but a *Urbild.* Just so, the archi-constructor must someday be prepared to be called upon to put in time as the philosopher-king, and he (or she—that was Plato's finest hour) says this with great humility. This is not a grab for power; it is even against his—or her—will.[5] This was the first modest proposal put forth by political philosophy. Just as political philosophy would like to be the first among philosophical sciences, the political philosophers would be the first among politicians. First in thought and first in action; *principium principiorum;* first philosophy.

Such a project, objects Arendt, is wrongheaded to the core, a kind of category mistake, for it misconceives *praxis* in terms of *techne* and thereby subjects action to the "metaphysics of making" (GA 24/GP, §§11–12). Political philosophy treats the *polis* as an artifact, as a made object. That makes the state—this is the point that Lacoue-Labarthe pursues—a work of art, perhaps even a *Gesamtkunstwerk,* like a monumental film or building or massive canvas, governed by the laws of *mimesis.*[6] This is to transpose action into the terms of construction, to take acting in technical terms and to submit it to an architectonic. This subjugates the mobility and subtlety of action—the "frailty" of acting—to a master plan, which requires a master name, which authorizes master builders and a whole caste of masters.

Taking our lead from Hannah Arendt we can say that political philosophy—and this goes for ethics as well—"deserves" deconstruction. That means there is a need to loosen the hold of architectonics over action, of *techne* over *praxis,* to slacken the constraints on the mobility of action. Every ethico-political philosophical fabrication is a construct just begging for deconstruction. Law-making and state-crafting are exercises in construction which seek to conceal the unsettling and destabilizing effects of *différance* over which they are stretched as across an abyss. Still, philosophy is inescapable and its desire *(philia)* for the *archē* is (almost) irresistible, (almost) a natural tendency, if there were such a thing. The need for a wall of structure around the frailty of action cannot be simply denied, above all not now, in a world that has grown as dangerous and violent as ours. We are always inside/outside political structures. That is why ethics and political philosophy "deserve" deconstruction in another sense, in the sense that it is worth it. Deconstruction is their just desert, just what ethics and politics deserve. Deconstruction gives ethics and politics justice. We should, out of sheer love for the *polis,* which is our mother, want to deconstruct the constructions of ethico-political philosophers, whose training makes them adepts in wall-building and city planning, in master plans and master names and mastering generally.

The deconstruction of ethics and political philosophy is not bad news for ethics and politics. Ethico-political philosophy is necessary even as it necessarily betrays action; its walls are both unavoidable and dangerous. Deconstruction wants to keep ethico-political philosophy on its feet, if also just slightly off balance. That is the civic duty of deconstruction and the good that it does for the *polis.* Deconstruction is good news for politics and the *polis,* even if the philosopher-kings have an unfortunate propensity to mistreat the bearers of such messages.

The Myth of Justice

In the account of deconstruction that has emerged more and more clearly from Derrida in the last ten years, deconstruction is conceived to inhabit the gap between ethico-political philosophy and the frailty of action. It does not seek to fill this gap but to inhabit it, to move around within it, to operate within the difference. Action belongs in the element of justice. Political philosophy does not ensure justice; it finds justice very elusive. That, I will argue here, is because justice is less an *archē* than an *an-archē,* so that when it concerns justice the philosophers are out of their element. If there were justice, if justice existed, we would not need an *archē.*[7] If justice existed, the political philosophers and politicians would be unemployed or, since unemployment is unjust, employed otherwise. *Polis* and *praxis* would need no walls and statecraft would have withered away. We are tempted to say that justice would be the only rule, except that justice is not a rule or a pattern. Justice is what rules want to have but which they do not possess necessarily, i.e., structurally. Structurally, the "rule" of law and the "reign" of justice are not to be confused. (Does justice "reign"? Or is justice less royal and more democratic? Does it hold sway gently? Or should justice simply flow across the land like water?) Laws should be nourished by justice; laws should yearn for justice; but it is very dangerous to confuse laws with justice. That is why the revisability, appealability, and repealability of law, even the resistance to law, are structurally part of the law and should be built into law. The deconstructibility of laws is part of the structure of the law; it is built right into them. Deconstruction is not bad news but old news. Laws without resistance, undeconstructible laws, represent the nightmare of perfect terror.[8]

Justice eludes law and philosophy, exceeding and transcending them, and often enough even transgresses them. For often enough it is necessary, for the sake of justice, to break the law and even to spend some time in jail, in Birmingham, Alabama, say, or South Africa. Philosophy is the love of the *archē,* the love of law and order, of rules and *regulae.* But justice dwells among the chaos and singularity of action, the idiosyncrasies of human interaction, the unreproducible exchanges between people. If there were justice, that would mean that we would be willing and able to live with the frailty of action and that we would have allowed action to follow its own course.

Ethico-political philosophy needs to be disturbed by justice. That would be good for it, and that is the good that deconstruction wants to do for it. Ethics and political philosophy, like all philosophy generally, need to be disturbed from within, in their most interior recesses, by their other, which is justice. That is because philosophy conducts its business in the element of the universal, in the sphere of principles, *archai,* of rules, or of maxims that it wants to make into rules. But justice is "older" than that, older than all rules. Justice belongs to a time immemorial, to a past that has never been present and that has taken hold of us without our consent.

The time of justice is not the time of a golden age, of a Great First Beginning, Greek or otherwise. To instantiate this time in some concrete historical moment, to point to some golden age of past actuality—even if the past is radicalized and essentialized from *Vergangenheit* to *Gewesenheit*—is precisely to degrade this time and to give it a mythic status in just the sense of myth we now seek to avoid. For to instantiate a mythic structure, to say it is actualized here or there, in some place or people, some language or age, is to institute privileged times and privileged places, to authorize hierarchization and elitist rank-orderings among existing beings. Justice cannot be localized, pinned down to a place or a time. The myth of justice does not take the form of a geophilosophical myth precisely because it is a myth of what is owed to the homeless and the uprooted. The condition of possibility of a salutary myth, which is also its condition of its impossibility, is that it is not actual. Justice does not belong to a time that can be recalled, recollected, interiorized, repeated,[9] to a time that was or has been all along, but to time immemorial, a time unremembered, to unrememberable time, an impossible time that never was actual even as it calls out incessantly for actualization. Or to a place, to some land or soil, some nation or fatherland.

That brings it in sharp contrast to Heidegger's mythologizing operation, which, as we have seen, consists precisely in locating the mythic space in actuality, giving it a historical name, attaching it to "this people" (two of them, actually). The whole idea behind the myth of justice is to avoid playing favorites, which is why the myth of justice is betrayed by locating a chosen people (the Jews), or the people of God (the Christians), as if some people were and some people were not God's, as if God prefers Jews to Egyptians, Christians to Jews, Europeans to non-Westerners, and so on. The whole idea behind justice is not to exclude anyone from the kingdom, which means the kingdom is nowhere in particular.

We belong to the time and place of justice, the no-time and no-place of justice, more deeply than we can say. We have always already been delivered over to the time of justice, to the immemorial claim of justice; we have always belonged to the place that is nowhere to be found. The claim of justice has been imposed upon us from of old. We were never consulted about it, never asked for our consent; there is no manager with whom we can register a complaint.[10] The claim of justice does not wait for us to consent or legitimate it; it is older, more primeval than us, even if it does not exist, or only barely exists, or has not quite managed to exist. It belongs to a past that was never present and to a future that will never be present, to a place that is nowhere to be found.

Justice does not exist, has never existed, will never exist. It is not an actuality, past, present, or future. Justice has no Being or, since we cannot twist free of Being into some sphere that has purified itself of Being, has at most a being-otherwise. That means that justice is a myth, that it belongs to a mythic past and an equally mythic future, that it is a thing in and of mythic time and mythic space, that it is the stuff of a mythic desire, not the myth of a privileged time and place, which enforces inequality, but the myth of no time and no place.[11]

In saying justice is a myth I am not saying that justice is a *"fiction"* in the sense of Lacoue-Labarthe, a mimetic myth, a myth of imitating and making, a *fictus,* a work of formative, plastic art. The myth of justice is not the myth of an ideal pattern, a heavenly archetype. It is a myth of another sort, a way of mythologizing differently, one that I am groping here to identify, a myth of a nonmimetic, nonrepresentational sort, a myth that has to do not with making but with action, not a mytho-technics but a mytho-praxis.[12] The myth of justice is not a myth of an ideal form or perfect model which we strive haltingly to imitate here on earth. As it is not a myth of a beautiful form so it is not a myth of a First Beginning whose shining splendor we long to see return. It is the myth of what is unrepresentable, invisible, inactual, impossible—and it is more likely to consort with what is ugly than beautiful, forgotten than remembered, dishonored than honored, excluded than included. The thought of justice is not a thought but a deed. The thought of justice is not an *Andenken,* a recollective retrieve, but a command to make something actual. Justice is not to be recalled but invented in the moment, which is but a small break or crevice in the textuality of everyday life. If justice is a kind of repetition, it is a repetition forwards, a repetition that produces what it repeats, that makes something new, here and now, wherever it is possible, without *Seinsgeschicklich* pretensions.

But what sort of myth is that?

A myth *(mythos)* is, at the least, a story, a memorable story. But the myth of justice is a tale we tell about something that belongs to time immemorial and an unheard-of place. The myth of justice is not a story about Being's comings and goings but about particular men and women. When it comes to justice, the best thing to do is to tell a story about a man or a woman who effects justice, or who suffers for it, or who presumes to run roughshod over it, and to let it go at that. It is less a question of having a theory of justice than a good story. Such stories make their point although they fall short of philosophy's love of the *logos,* of *theoria,* its desire for the *archē.*[13] Philosophy dwells in the element of universals, of *archai,* of *principia,* while the stories of justice have to do with particular men and women—like Antigone or Abraham—whose life and works bring us up short and give us pause, descending upon us with a shock.

The stories of justice have to do with the radically singular. Radical singularity, of course, is, strictly speaking, not quite possible; it is impossible to address the singular in an absolutely singular way. Storytelling, like every form of discursivity, slips back inevitably, structurally, into the element of the universal, of the iterable and repeatable. But always in such a way as to remind us all the more persistently of the singular, to point us all the more forcefully to the radically singular. Stories about justice cling persistently to the singular, even as they slip inevitably into the universal. Antigone is not just some particular sister, but something like "the" sister, a mythic sister, a sister in mythic space, in just the same way that Abraham and Isaac are not just a particular father and son. So the myth of justice tosses back and forth between universality and singularity, occupying that impossible space between the clarity of the universal and the density of the individual. The myth of justice is inevitably affected by a *logos,* inevitably mythological and logomythical. That is the best it can do. It cannot do otherwise.

The stories of justice are stories about something (im)possible, about an ancient desire, an immemorial demand. We must have justice even though justice is nowhere to be found. Justice must be possible; it is what we desire, even though justice everywhere eludes us. We must have justice now, even though justice is always deferred.

What is justice? But how can we even ask a question of the form "what is," which is philosophy's most classical gesture, which is a classically Greek thing to do? Would it not be better to ask "how to be just?" or "how does justice happen?" Would it be better not to interrogate justice at all, but rather to let ourselves be interrogated by it? What sort of myth is this? What sort of impossible desire is it that we have, or that has us? What do we desire when we desire justice or when justice is desired of us? Of what do we dream when we dream about justice? What is it that does not exist, has never existed, is nowhere to be found, even as it belongs to an immemorial past? What is this that solicits us when we are solicited by justice?

Derrida's Scandal: The Undeconstructibility of Justice

The work that Derrida has more and more been doing in recent years, his work on law and friendship and justice, has ineluctably drawn him into this mythic space and mythic time. That is how I read the utterly startling statement he has made about what he dares to call the "undeconstructibility of justice." This unflagging adversary of the dream of perfect presence who terrifies Allan Bloom and William Bennett, who has given his critics the impression that he is out to destroy the temple and the prophets, turns out to be a bit of a mythmaker. He has had a dream, more like Martin Luther King's than like Descartes's, for it is not a question of getting purely and simply outside dreaming, but of the sort of dreams one has. He has confounded not only his critics but his friends, Franco-American academics everywhere who pride themselves on their resistance to the lure of Being-in-itself and on their tough-minded immunity to dreaming. Here is Derrida's hard saying:

> Justice in itself, if such a thing exists, outside or beyond law, is not deconstructible. No more than deconstruction, if such a thing exists. Deconstruction is justice.[14]

Undeconstructible justice? What can that be if not an ageless truth, an unshakeable foundation, a *fundamentum inconcussum* lying beneath the surface of deconstruction? It is not as if Derrida does not know what he is doing, as if he does not realize the scandal he is causing his friends and how many academic gowns will be rent by the saying:

> If I were to say that I know nothing more just than what I today call deconstruction (nothing more just, I'm not saying nothing more legal or more legitimate), I know that I wouldn't fail to surprise or shock not only the determined adversaries of said deconstruction or what they imagine under this name but also the very people who pass for or take themselves to be its partisans or practitioners (FL, 957).

So he says he will not say it, but of course it is too late; it has already slipped out.

This is a text that will repay a closer look. Derrida is distinguishing between "law" (*droit; also loi*) and justice. Laws, he says, are essentially deconstructible, and this because they have been constructed in the first place. The possibility of deconstruction is "built into" laws: laws are "drawn up," "made," "written": they do not fall from the sky but are woven from the fabric of *écriture*. But the deconstructibility of laws is not "bad news," Derrida adds, because it is the only way for politics and the *polis* to make historical progress. That is where deconstruction comes in:

> But the paradox that I'd like to submit for discussion is the following: it is this deconstructible structure of law [*droit*], or if you prefer of justice as *droit*, that also ensures the possibility of deconstruction. (FL, 945)

The deconstructibility of law is the enabling legislation of deconstruction; it gives deconstruction its charter, charges it with a task. But that is (literally) only half the paradox. For Derrida likewise insists that the undeconstructibility of justice—this is the scandal—is likewise a condition of deconstruction, also part of its enabling charter. Deconstruction is possible only insofar as justice is undeconstructible, for justice is what deconstruction aims at, what it is about, what it *is*. There are thus two conditions for deconstruction:

1. The deconstructibility of law (for example) or of legitimacy makes deconstruction possible. 2. The undeconstructibility of justice also makes deconstruction

possible, indeed is inseparable from it. 3. The result: deconstruction takes place
in the interval that separates the undeconstructibility of justice from the deconstructibility of law (authority, legitimacy, and so on). (FL, 945)

Deconstruction moves back and forth, traverses the terrain, explores the
territory, between undeconstructible justice and deconstructible law, looking
for the cracks and crevices in the wall of the law through which the flowers
of justice have begun to grow. The aim of deconstructing the law is not to
level the law, to bring down the wall—because it is the strong arm of the law
that holds oppressive, unjust forces in place—but to give the law flexibility
and "give." To deconstruct something is not to wreck it but to rewrite it,
reformulate it, redo it, remake it; better still, it deconstructs itself, auto-decon-
structively (FL, 981). Deconstruction thus is essentially positive, an affirmation
of everything that we want to dig out from under the constructions under
which it labors, in order to prevent the distinction between justice and law
from becoming hard and fast.[15]
The interval between undeconstructible justice and deconstructible law is
the distance between the singular—which is somehow beyond or in excess of
the law—and the universal. Justice concerns the call of the "singular," i.e.,
the demand of the singular, of the other one:

> . . . justice always addresses itself to singularity, to the singularity of the other,
> despite or even because it pretends to universality. (FL, 955)

The law can never do that, because, as Levinas points out, and Derrida on
this point is repeating Levinas (FL, 949), the law concerns the "third" one.
Justice is what I owe you, in your singularity. It is the responsibility I have to
the demands you place upon me with the full force of the singular demand
which you, in your unique and unreproducible individuality, have always already put upon me. The demands of justice issue neither from a Platonic Good
nor from a Kantian Ideal, but from this singular one, here, now, who lays
claim to me—in all the singularity and idiosyncrasy of his/her singularity. The
singular one lies on the margins of language and iterability, both possible and
impossible. The formal structure of the myth of justice is this structure of
im/possibility, of what cannot be said even as it must be said. *Individuum
ineffabile est.*
One can see the biblical or prophetic provenance of this "model" by consid-
ering how perfectly it is exemplified by a biblical story like the account of
Jesus healing the man with the withered hand on the Sabboth (Mark 3:1–6).
The man with the withered hand is the singularity who demands justice; the
Sabboth is the Law, the universal, which is structurally blind to singulars,
while the Pharisees are the keepers of the Law. The story opens the eyes of
the reader to the call of singularity, i.e., justice, and allows us to see that

justice is a matter of singularity not universality, of *kardia* not law-keeping. Making the blind to see is not only a biblical miracle-story; it is an emblem of the very operation of story telling about justice; the mythic operation itself, justice itself.

But the law is necessary. That is because there is a third person, besides you, so that you cannot claim everything from me, your singularity cannot become exclusive; it forces me to distribute my responsibility among many who cannot be named by name; the law wants to be impartial. The law arises, on this Derridean-Levinasian account, not only in order to restrain injustice, but in order to restrain justice, so that justice will not be spent entirely in one place. So the law is formulated as a universal—that is what the law is, what it means to be—and thus it necessarily, structurally, loses sight of the singular. Law belongs in the element of calculation (FL, 947). We must calculate a law carefully and precisely—the I.R.S. code is a good example of a law, even if it is not an example of a good law (unless you are wealthy)—in order to allow it to take account of as many cases as possible, in order to ensure a certain proportion between the law and the individual cases. But if we were, *per impossibile,* to write a perfect set of laws, that would look like a map so detailed as to be the same size as the region it is mapping.

The task of deconstruction is to keep the singular one in view, to keep traversing the space between the universal and the singular, between the law and justice, between the calculable and the incalculable, to keep the lines of communication open between them. The law lives on credit: it promises to take justice into account, and laws are only as good as they are able to deliver on their promises. But the authority of the law is borrowed from the authority of the singular one who calls to us from beyond the law and in the name of whom we have erected the law. The task of deconstruction is to hear that call and in so doing to suspend the credit of the law, to suspend its authority, and thereby to risk an *epochē,* or even a teleological suspension, that fills us with anxiety:

> This moment of suspense, this period of epochē, without which, in fact, deconstruction is not possible, is always full of anxiety, but who pretends to be just by economizing with anxiety? And this anxiety-ridden moment of suspense—which is also the interval or space in which transformations, indeed juridico-political revolutions take place—cannot be motivated. . . except in the demand for an increase in or supplement to justice, and so in the experience of an inadequation or an incalculable disproportion. (FL, 955–57)

Deconstruction holds the law up for scrutiny, lets it waver in instability. For Derrida, conduct must be both regulated—we always already act within a tradition of laws—and unregulated—we want always to be responsive to the singular one who calls from beyond the law, whom the law misses. But trying to keep one's balance on such shifting terrain leads to aporias, Derrida says, at least three of them.

Let us call the first the aporia of *phronesis:* mere conformity to a law does not ensure justice. Rather, the law requires a "fresh judgment," a judgment which "conserve[s] the law and also destroy[s] it or suspend[s] it long enough to have to reinvent it in each case" (FL, 961). Otherwise the judge is a calculating machine. What is to be done cannot simply be calculated—it must be judged. Furthermore, a just decision, which is never a merely programmed, calculated application of a rule, is always made in the element of undecidability, must always pass "through the ordeal of the undecidable," in which our respect for the universal trembles before "the unique singularity of the unsubsumable example" (FL, 963). Every decision worthy of the name, every decision which "cuts," which must give itself up to the "impossible decision," is haunted by the ghost, by the aporia of undecidability. Finally, one must decide; one cannot deliberate forever. Justice cannot wait for all the results to come in. We are pressed by the urgency of the moment of decision, precipitated into action. "The instant of decision is a madness, says Kierkegaard," delivered over to "acting in the night of non-knowledge and non-rule" (FL, 967), always implicated in the "irruptive violence" that cuts off deliberation and acts in a moment of "precipitate urgency" (FL, 988) (the aporia of decision).

The mention of Kierkegaard here is telling. The whole analysis of undeconstructible law sounds like a citation of *Fear and Trembling,* a repetition of distinctly Kierkegaardian motifs. For it was Johannes de Silentio who made the universality of the law tremble—in the name of the story of Abraham, a very old Jewish story about the absolute incommensurability of the existing individual. Derrida's analysis takes the form of a discussion of three problemata (aporias) that surround the decision in which the singular one exceeds the universal. It describes a moment of "anxiety-ridden suspension." It thematizes the decisive "cut" (of Abraham) which passes through the "ordeal" (the proper category for Abraham and Job, whom God was testing) of undecidability and which is exposed to fear and trembling. It invokes the madness of an infinite economy which confounds the stockbrokers of the finite.[16]

There are very prophetico-mythic voices in Derrida's remarkable essay on the force of law: that of Kierkegaard and Abraham, not to mention the (silent) voice of Johannes de Silentio, who suffers from the disadvantage that he does not exist, which is not necessarily a disadvantage if justice is a myth. It may even be a clue to the nature of the myth of justice. Maybe even a decisive one. Perhaps there are other prophets haunting this text on mystical forces.

Hyperbolic Justice

We are inching closer to the meaning of the myth of justice. But to get any further we must clear our heads and raise tough questions. For, given the presuppositions of deconstruction, we need to ask what undeconstructible justice can possibly *be* or *not be* or *be otherwise than*. How can justice happen? Is it happening? Is not the myth of justice an undisguised metaphysical postulate, one that threatens at every point to adorn itself with capital letters, to become an *archē*? What is the Being of undeconstructible justice, or its being-otherwise, if it indeed exists? Or should we follow Levinas and say that it is altogether beyond Being, otherwise than Being? In short, what has Derrida wrought? Has he gone mad (over justice)?

Unless he has simply lost his senses, Derrida cannot mean that justice in itself, were there such a thing, is a kind of Platonic *agathon*, an absolute being-in-itself *(Ansichsein)*, a subsistent absolute against which all sensible, particular actions and transactions should be measured. That would be precisely, paradigmatically, what Derrida once called the metaphysics of presence, the very exemplar of metaphysics in its most uncritical and innocent form, the form of pure and perfect presence, which likewise formed the basis of the whole mimetic myth of the state.

Nor can he mean that the undeconstructibility of justice represents an Idea in the Kantian sense, a regulative Ideal that monitors the empirical search for justice, a transcendence effected by letting reason roam beyond its proper limits (FL, 965–67). For that is more of the same thing, more philosophical idealism, even if the Idea has ceased to be a subsistent entity and has become instead an inexistent ought.

It is no less believable that such justice has the status of an absolute, categorical command, of Kant's famous "categorical imperative." For Kant's imperative is the issue of pure reason, of reason which has made a "clean cut"[17] with every empirical and pathological impulse, and it issues not in the ineffability of singularity but absolute universalizability. But undeconstructible justice concerns the singular, and it is full of *pathos* and very empirical.

Nor can he mean that "justice," the sign that includes both the signifier and the signified, unlike every other signifier, stands outside the economy of *différance*, that the name of justice is not an effect of *différance*, and so is not implicated in its opposite, injustice and inequality. He cannot mean that "justice" always produces justice, that there is a "justice" which is never unjust, that innocent blood has never been spilled in the name of justice. Surely the name of justice is no more or less venerable than that of God or truth or peace or freedom, in whose name the most unspeakable atrocities are committed with unfailing regularity.

The one comparison that Derrida allows (aside from Kierkegaard) is to Levinas, and even this is to be held at a distance (FL, 959, 969). Responsibility in Levinas's sense is the claim of the absolute Other, the singular one who, meeting us face to face, places us in a situation of absolute responsibility, or better, who awakens us to the fact that we have never *not* been placed in such a situation—that it belongs to our oldest *Befindlichkeit*. For Levinas, it is not politics that is first philosophy but ethics; politics, on the other hand, is war. That is not a deconstruction of politics, I think, but a riding roughshod over it that will not do because it does not take into account the fact that we are always inside/outside political totalities.[18] If we are to understand what truly is and is truly, Levinas says—if we are to be up to the oldest task of metaphysics, if we wish to reach what we have called from of old "first philosophy"—then we must acknowledge the ethical. We must grant that the ethical comes first, that it does not float skittishly outside reality like a deontological "value" or "ought" outside the "is" and that it is not something merely "ontic" that must wait for ontology to clear its way and make it possible. The ethical is there from the start and does not require either ontological preparation (the Heidegger of *Being and Time*) or a deontological foundation (value theory, criticized by Heidegger). The ethical does not wait and does not need to have a space prepared for it.

The ethical comes first, comes at us and toward us, like a kind of *physis* and *An-wesen,* which rises up and surges toward us, concerning us and laying claim to us. But it comes toward us by confronting us frontally and unequivocally, face to face, which is not *physis* at all, but something more. That is what Levinas calls the metaphysical: *meta,* because it is more than *physis,* infinitely more, because its claim exceeds and excels *physis,* because, in surging up and coming toward us, it lays claim to us absolutely, in a way that is denied to *physis.* For *physis* is finite, is not transcendent, does not truly exceed us, *is* not fully, infinitely excellent. *Physis* is still visible, phenomenal being. *Physis* for Levinas can be seen and secured, owned and eaten, apportioned and appropriated. *Physis* cannot resist us, cannot withdraw into the secrecy of its hidden recess, cannot command us to stop the assault, to halt the aggression. For Levinas, *physis* is not the Overwhelming, as it is for Heidegger in *An Introduction to Metaphysics,* but rather lies helpless before us, vulnerable, visible, edible. But the other person exceeds our grasp, resists our assaults, commands us to stop. The other person exceeds the visible world, exceeds *physis,* is more than and beyond *physis.* The other person introduces us to metaphysics, leads us into it, shocks us out of our self-enclosed immanence with a command that issues from a sphere beyond *physis,* beyond Being, if Being means *physis.*

The question is, can this be the status enjoyed by "undeconstructible" justice? I would say most assuredly not, and for the following reason. For Levinas, the commanding claim of the Other who comes from beyond is nothing visible, for it cannot have to do with the paganism, the *sacré,*[19] of earth and sky. The Other is not a part of a pagan myth. It is neither on the earth nor under the sky; it is otherwise than earth and sky, otherwise than *physis.* So we are not to think that it is beyond Being in the manner of something merely normative, a mere value that has been superadded to facts and that somehow fails to be *(sein)* even as it has normative validity *(gelten).* It is not beyond

Being because it is less than Being but rather because it is *more* than Being, because it exceeds Being. It is beyond Being because it *is* so radically, so absolutely, so fully, that it cannot be contained by Being (so long as Being means *physis*). That is why it is preeminently and paradigmatically metaphysical. Would it not be an ironic outcome for Derrida, for deconstruction, to eventuate in the affirmation of what is eminently and preeminently metaphysical?

This Levinasian gesture is not without philosophical precedent; indeed, it is an old and venerable operation of a certain traditional philosophy: "When I said that God was not a Being and was above Being," Meister Eckhart said, "I did not thereby contest his Being, but on the contrary attributed to him a *more elevated Being*."[20] That, I would say, *pace* Levinas, is the Levinasian gesture, the lever that operates both *Totality and Infinity* and *Otherwise than Being or Beyond Essence*. Against Levinas, against Levinas's deepest desire, against the desire of Levinas, at the risk of heresy and of being shown the talmudic door, I would say it is impossible for what is otherwise-than-Being to avoid being-otherwise.[21] To say the Other comes to us from on high, in a way that is higher and more eminent than Being *(physis)*, is to attribute to the Other a higher being, a being higher. Across the curved space that the Other traverses there stretches the *via eminentiorae*, the path of excess, i.e., of eminence beyond negation, of supereminence and transcendence, as a certain *hyperphysis* or *hyperousia*. The gesture is completely classical: the Other is a phenomenal face *(via affirmationis)*; but this is to be denied, for the Other is more than that, more than a visible phenomenon, more than being *(via negationis)*; the Other commands from on high in a way that is beyond Being as phenomenality *(via eminentiorae)*.

That is why undeconstructible justice in Derrida cannot be assimilated to Levinas's infinity, which, if it is neither Platonic, Cartesian, nor Kantian, is rather more Neoplatonic, like the One beyond *nous*, like an inexhaustible Neoplatonic infinity. That is also why I do not think that Derrida can quite believe Levinas, why he must hold him at a distance, why he cannot accept the infinity of Levinas (although he perhaps would like to and is willing at least to offer Levinas as a point of comparison). For if it is neither a Platonic Good nor a Neoplatonic One, neither a Cartesian infinity nor a Kantian noumenon, there is just no accounting for Levinas's infinity.

There is no accounting—unless one were willing to say that it is hyperbole, that this discourse on excess is an excessive, emphatic discourse, meant to emphasize the special valorizing of the Other, that Levinas's discourse on infinity is to be deconstructed down to an infinite discourse, to a hyperbolic infinity, which is what Derrida seems to say. All of this interrogation of the law, he says, arises because deconstruction "hyperbolically raises the stakes of exacting justice"; far from showing indifference to justice, deconstruction is a hyperbolically sensitive to justice (FL, 955).

I propose to locate what Derrida does not hesitate to call deconstruction's "infinite demand for justice" (FL, 955) in a grammatical operation, a rhetorical trope, a work of grammar and linguistic invention, which arise by way of a response to the demands that are placed upon us by the singularity of the Other. Infinity for Derrida is not symbolic but hyperbolic infinity, as opposed to Levinas, for whom it is expressly something metaphysical and even theological, something ethico-theo-logical. The Levinasian gesture that requires deconstruction, even demythologization, is to reify this infinity, to make it a metaphysical being—which Levinas then cannot call Being and will not call a mere fiction. The Levinasian gesture is like the Heideggerian to just this extent: that it attributes actuality or reality to what it valorizes, that it claims this infinity is real, *ad literam, ad infinitum.* But in Derrida, the quasi infinity of undeconstructible justice is neither Being nor otherwise than Being; the excess is not the excess of being but the excess of a linguistic performance, an excess within the operations made possible and impossible by *différance,* in response to the singularity lying on the edge of *différance.* In Derrida, infinity means a hyperbolic responsiveness and responsibility, a hyperbolic sensitivity.

I will defend this interpretation of undeconstructible justice by offering a historical anecdote and analogy. When Meister Eckhart, who was called on the carpet by the Roman Curia for saying that God is beyond Being and a pure Nothing, and for saying that God and the soul were not merely united but one, when the boldness of his language seemed to lead him into heresy, he responded by saying that such language is "an emphatic expression *(emphatice),* commending God's goodness and love."[22] Such excessive language, such a language of excessive unity and *apophasis,* is in fact a language of *emphasis,* an affirmation to an extreme of God's care for the soul. In the case of Derrida the hyperbolic extreme is not a metaphysical extreme (Levinas) nor the extreme of mysticism and negative theology (Meister Eckhart). It is rather an extreme of responsibility, of responsiveness and sensitivity to the demands of singularity, which, being neither effable nor ineffable, lies on the extreme limits of language. I will not say that this is the extreme of ethics, since ethics aims at principles and universality, but rather the extreme of something otherwise than ethics, let us say the extreme of responsibility and obligation to singularity (for obligation is something that ethics contains without being able to contain).[23] What is at work in the texts of Derrida is an affirmation of the singular one, an *affirmatio ad infinitum,* without limit, for the only limit of responsibility to the other one is other responsibilities, responsibilities to still others.

This affirmation of and response to singularity is directed toward whoever bears a proper name. The myth of undeconstructible justice is a myth of proper names. The question of the im/possibility of proper names is the subject of an old argument conducted for many years in Derrida's texts. The name of justice is not the name of propriety and appropriation itself, of *Ereignis,* not the name of Being's appropriating event, but the myth of the smallest singularities. This is not a myth of the massive movement of *aletheia* across the epochs, of the Great Greek Beginning and of the possibility of an Other Beginning, but the myth of the smallest hair on your head, of the least among us. This is not a myth of Being but of being otherwise, of justice.

That, I think, is the use Derrida makes of Levinas, what becomes of Levinasian justice in Derrida, how Levinas becomes Derrida. The work of Levinas comes over us today like the voice of a Jewish prophet, like the cry of Amos demanding that justice flow over the land like water, like a prophet among the postmodernists, inspiring a prophetic postmodernism. We are awed, shocked, even scandalized by the sublimity, by the excess, of what Levinas demands, which is clearly too much. Who can endure these hard words? What Levinas asks is not possible. But that is no objection, for the most interesting things are often impossible and learning to think what is impossible is a salutary exercise, a way to give philosophy life while leaving what is possible to the other disciplines. It is even perhaps a little mad, exorbitant, off its axis, part of an irrational economy of excess, of the expenditure of self without demanding a return. It is even violent—toward oneself: one is held hostage, one allows oneself to suffer deprivations and outrages that one would protest if it befell the Other.

I would say that what we find in Levinas is prophetic hyperbole. If it is taken seriously, held to the canons of philosophical discursivity, it cannot be believed or defended and it lapses at strategic points into the most classical Neoplatonic metaphysics and negative theology.[24] So it is a mistake to take Levinas on his own terms, in the way that Levinas himself demands—metaphysically—for then Levinas is vulnerable to all of the criticisms that beset metaphysics, for this is metaphysics indeed, a metaphysics of the Good not the true, a metaphysical ethics, not a deontology, but metaphysics still. In my view, Derrida hears instead a prophetic voice, one that soars and sears with prophetic hyperbole, one that tells unbelievable stories.

We do not believe the stories the prophets tell, and it is a degradation and a distortion of mytho-prophetic discourse to treat it as if it were a record of eyewitnessed events, to measure it in terms of truth taken as *adequatio*. We are rather to be instructed otherwise by their impossible tales, which have to do always with justice—which is, I have been arguing im/possible. These stories belong to the myth of justice. The prophets use their stories to make impossible, mad demands on everyone, especially themselves. The voice of the prophet interrupts the self-assured voices of the powerful, of the *archē*, the princes of this world, bringing them up short, calling them to account for themselves. That is why the prophets had a habit of getting themselves killed, a most serious occupational hazard. They were perhaps a little mad, mad for justice, mad about injustice, and maybe, just a little, plain mad.

But then is Derrida's undeconstructible justice prophetic justice? Is Derrida the latest in a long line of Jewish prophets? That would be mad, excessive, too much, too scandalous, too emphatic, an overemphasis, and he has warned us against such exaggerations (FL, 965–96). I do not want to risk saying anything that mad lest I too be mistaken for the follower of a prophet and risk incurring a prophetic fate for which I have no taste. ("I do not know the man.") But I would say what Derrida has said, that this discourse on undeconstructible justice is "not far away" from prophetic discourse,[25] though it has no strings attached to God or to divine revelation and still less to any institutional religion. Derrida would certainly demythologize any such myth, especially insofar as it functions to warrant powerful institutions which punish dissent, which reduce not to mystical silence but to silence plain and simple, to silencing the opposition. But he does so, in my opinion, in the name of another, perhaps postreligious myth and of prophesying differently. For I would say the discourse on undeconstructible justice has the ring of prophetic justice, that it traffics with prophetic myth, that this is its *glas*.[26] This is not, *stricto sensu,* prophetic religion or prophetic hyperbole but a kind of deconstructive hyperbole cut to fit the needs of obligation, which for Derrida always has to do with singularity.

I would say that at the point Derrida begins to speak of undeconstructible justice he is reproducing, in terms of obligation, his discourse on singularity and the proper name. The whole thing has the ring *(glas)* of *Glas.* From its opening passages, which are already a repetition, the citations of the opening passage of Hegel's *Phenomenology of Spirit* and Genet's "What Remains of a Rembrandt," *Glas* is implicated in im/possibility, in the impossible movement between the singular and the universal. *Glas* has chosen to slip and slide on the treacherous terrain that stretches between the unrepeatable, incommunicable being of the individual and the system of universals or repeatability, which communicates across many particulars. The singular is from the start im/possible, a failed project, deferred:

> what, after all, of the remain(s), today, for us, here, now, of a Hegel? (*Glas,* 1a)

The aim of the language of immediacy is the absolutely singular: what is immediately present, here and now. Here: without spatial difference (displacement); now: without temporal difference (deferral). The immediate without mediation, without difference, without *différance.* For justice is demanded here and now; it cannot pass over the individual for the sake of the universal; it cannot be deferred. But that is a dream, the dream of being without *différance,* of laying aside difference, of unveiling Being in its naked beauty, its immediate Being. That is a pure myth, the myth of pure immediacy. For we are always already too late for such unveilings. As soon as language has arrived on the scene the singular has already fled, already slipped out the back door. The singular one is gone, *vorbei,* passed on, past, absolutely past. The time of justice and the time of singularity are the same. Like justice, singularity belongs to a past that was never present to begin with. The absolutely singular one is not a past presence but absolutely past; not a future presence, but absolutely unforeseeable, unforegraspable, unforehaveable. The immediacy of the singular is blocked off by the massive mediation of "here" and "now," which are linguistic operations whose intervention has made the singular an im/possible dream, both possible and impossible. "Here, now" are in uncontrollable slippage; they are always different. No two heres ever occupy the same place; no two nows are ever simultaneous. It is never now twice even though it is always now. The individual is always already in flight. The singular always already steals away, is always stolen, like the watches that Genet lightly lifts from our pockets. The lure of singularity is a useless passion. "Here" and "now" are universalizing operations and cannot reach the particular.

In other words, the absolute propriety of the proper name is blocked off by the very structure of the name as a repeatable, coded signifier. An absolutely proper name would not be intelligible as a name or legible as a signature; we would be unable to recognize its letters or its phonemes, would have no idea what language it belonged to, or even that it was language, much less a name. In order to be understood a proper name must, in principle, be able to belong to other individuals and so it must, in principle, bear within itself a structural impropriety. There is no such thing as an absolutely rigid signifier. It is only the pragmatics of context that fixes the proper name in place long enough for it to achieve success.

Yet, on the other hand, the Hegelian attempt to lift up singularity into the life of the universal is likewise a failure and an impossibility. If absolute singularity is an impossible dream, a universal that has raised up and assimilated what is essential in the singular, the universalizing-uplifting operation of speculative thought *(auf-heben)*, is no less impossible. The universal is insistently haunted by the ghost of its other. To put it in the language of *Glas*, the smooth glide of the eagle's flight is disrupted by the alien power of singularity. Its operation of universal assimilation is frustrated by irreducible singulars, the fragments and remains which it is always already unable to sweep up, the leftovers and residue that slip through the teeth of the Hegelian machine. The motto that Johannes Climacus set at the beginning of *Concluding Unscientific Postscript to the "Philosophical Fragments"* could serve no less well as an epigram to Column A of *Glas*: "But really, Socrates, what do you think this all amounts to? It is really scrapings and parings of systematic thought, as I said a while ago, divided into bits" (*Hippias Major*, 304a). The whole of Column A of *Glas*, no less than Kierkegaard's *Postscript*, can be read as a commentary on and a confirmation of this text. The universal never quite fits, can never quite be fitted into the concrete. The individual situation is always more complicated and it is never possible to anticipate, to have in advance, the idiosyncrasies of the particular, never possible to prepare the universal for the disruptiveness of the singular. The universal cannot fold its eagle wings around the individual and lift it up to its heavenly home, cannot enfold the manifold of intuition, cannot embrace, circumscribe, encompass the singular. The universalizing *glas*-machine won't work. It gets jammed, clogged, every time we press it against the surface of the singular; it cannot digest these particulars, cannot make its gears mesh on the terrain of singularity. It always leaves something behind, a remnant, a residue, an undigestible fragment that will not yield its materiality to this powerful spirit. The singular resists. The gears of the system are jammed by the glue of the singular, by singular glue, gluey singles. The lure of the concrete universal is likewise a failed project.

So then we are tossed back and forth between two impossibilities: the failed universal and the impossible singular, which both belong to the same system. For it is only in virtue of having a language at all, a set of coded repeatable traces, a network of universals, that it is possible to pick out the singular, to sound their names, to summon them up, to call upon them, to call their *glas*. Language is nothing but a system of universals, of iterable signifiers, even as a truly concrete universal is an impossible dream. The singular always steals away even as the concrete universal always leaves something singular out. Pure singularity and a perfectly concrete universality: two impossibilities, two unerectable columns, belonging to the same (non)system. That is the "argument" of *Glas*.

This necessary but impossible singularity is what interests *Glas*, which is punctuated with figures of singularity. In the one column, Abraham, Jesus, Antigone: all of whom take the side of singularity against the universal. Abraham, the fearsome father of faith, the father of fear and trembling, who breaches the universal in the name of the existing individual, who ruptures everything *heimlich*, everything that ties him to home; Jesus, who takes the side of withered hands and lepers against the Law; Antigone, the absolutely unique sister who takes her stand on behalf of the corpse of an irreplaceable brother, who sides with nighttime singularity against the daylight law of the polis and the father. Column A is a column of prophets and religious madness summoned up to torment the System *(sa)*! In the other column, the exceptional fags with names like nuns. We cannot say their names, cannot call them up, cannot give them a family name, cannot enter them on a register or a roll call—not without killing them. If we ever call their name, class, *Gattung, Geschlecht,* they are dead men, and the fate of these undecidables is decided (*Glas,* 86b). They are classic *(glas)* exceptions. We do not know their proper names. How shall we call them? What shall we call them? How will they answer? How will they know their name when they hear it? How will they answer our call? What bell will call them to order, line them up in an order of rank?

In *Glas* proper names are necessary, for only the individual exists and it is the call of singularity to which we must continually respond; and impossible, for they are possible only in virtue of the iterability of the codes to which they belong. But proper names are also dangerous, for to have someone's name is to have a means of surveillance, a way of tracing and tracking and monitoring and ultimately of punishing individuals. Once the law learns the names of Genet's transvestites, they are dead men.

Glas traverses the terrain between the failed universal and the inaccessible singular, swings across the abyss that opens up between the impossible universal and the singular that steals away. It moves within the space of two impossibles and that twofold impossibility constitutes the condition of its possibility. This abyss is likewise the interval between law and justice. The discourse on justice is isomorphic (iso-*a*morphic) with the discourse on singularity and the proper name. They trade in the same impossibilities, the same amorphousness; they dream the same dreams, awaken to the same realities, traffic with the same myths.

What then is absolute singularity for Derrida? It is an impossible project, a failed operation of *différance* which produces the effect of singularity while at the same time prohibiting it. But singularity is a special effect, charged with a particular energy, arising from an operation of hypervalorization, of hyperbolic valorization, induced in us by a hypersensitivity, a hyperresponsiveness and responsibility. For the *call* of singularity is the call of justice, the call of alterity, the demand for justice by the other. Proper names are not only ways of calling others but ways of being called by others and responding to what calls for recognition, what calls for justice. The law must blind itself to proper names. The law *(droit)* must be written without proper names, whereas justice must always come as a response to proper names.

That explains the prophetic tone, or the quasi-prophetic tone that Derrida sometimes adopts. (Derrida has many tones, many voices, many languages, which is not a matter of being undisciplined but of having many disciplines.) It has nothing to do with God, about whom Derrida writes only infrequently, or institutional religion, in which he shows no interest whatsoever. It has no backups from "on high." Derrida's quasi-prophetic tone is "not far away" from prophetic exasperation and exaggeration, from prophetic hyperbole, from the prophetic demand for justice "here, now," for this one, for this broken body or ruined life, without waiting, without delay, without deferral. Justice is called for here and now, even as the law soars with serene ease in the element of the universal and, spreading its eagle wings, swings over earthbound singulars.

The undeconstructibility of justice is implicated with the impossibility of singularity; it is a function of it. Justice in itself, if there is such a thing: that is a hyperbolic demand for justice for this one, here and now. The myth of justice is a hyperbolic myth and it turns on a hyperbolic, not a true, infinity. Unlike Levinas, it has no divine backup, no veritable Infinity, Platonic or Neoplatonic, Cartesian or Kantian, Jewish or Christian, that leaves its trace in the visible world. Deconstruction lacks Levinasian assurances, Levinasian depth, and it traffics in a more uncertain, more finite world. This is not divine hyperbole or prophetic religion. The point of deconstructive hyperbole is not ethico-religious but ethico-political. It has not written off politics as war or made war on politics; it means merely to deconstruct politics.[27] It is not God that commands but the singularity of the situated Other who always slips away. If the other commands without a divine backup, then so be it. The call that issues from the Other is not a categorical command cutting through the film of appearances and putting us in contact with the noumenal world. The call is what it is, an appeal without infinite resources, without absolute foundation, without authorizing credentials issued by the *mundus intelligibilis*. The call of undeconstructible justice is the call for immediate justice, without delay or deferral, justice for this singular one here. It calls for justice, for what it cannot say, for what it is impossible to say, for what eludes saying, for what saying causes to slip away. It is a hyperbolic demand, for it demands what is im/possible and is responsive to impossible demands.

The myth of justice is to be traced to a hyperbolic operation that attaches infinite worth to the singular, that valorizes and hypervalorizes singularity. But this hypervalorization issues not from subjective valuing—for it has nothing to do with value-theory—but from the depths of responsiveness and responsibility.

That is a biblical, a jewgreek operation, the operation of valorizing every hair on our head, and it issues in a biblical, or jewgreek conception of justice. On such a view justice is what befits the singular one, in particular, the least among us; that is a biblical justice, which means as much mercy and compassion as justice. If the rule of law connotes justice to us, that is because of our philosophical tendency to identify justice with the universal. But the paradigm of biblical justice, of jewgreek justice, is a paradigm of singularity where justice means what is owed to each and every one of us, even and above all the least and most humble. In the jewgreek paradigm, the power of justice is the power of powerlessness, and the rule of justice is the rule that holds sway just on behalf of those who have no power, who are overpowered by the powers of this world. It is that atypical and anomic law of justice, as opposed to the philosophical conception of justice as universality, that inspires the works of Derrida and Lyotard; and this jewgreek justice is the trace that has been left in their work by Levinas.

The Im/possible

The oldest desire of philosophy is for the *archē*. But the desire for justice is an-archic, for it has to do with the im/possible singular. But this is not simply anarchic (even as it is not simply impossible), a simple anarchy that inverts and reverses the *archē*. Deconstruction is always the deconstruction of such simplicity. Justice is the desire to respond to the anarchic, to the singularity that eludes or is beaten down by principles. The desire for justice, of the absolutely singular, is an impossible desire that courts ineffability. As soon as we open our mouths it is already too late. The singular has withdrawn, is deferred, put off, always and already. So justice has no choice except to adopt the prophetico-mythic mode, which means to call for justice, and to tell stories. Justice calls from an impossible place and it calls for something impossible, something we cannot say, something we can only broach by way of impossible stories.

Do we call for justice or does justice call for itself? Who can say? In either case, justice is called for. What is the call of justice? What does it say? The call says "Come!" That is all. The call is indefinite, because justice is indefinite, and that is because of the indefiniteness and frailty of action. Justice does not call for a plan, even though plans are called for. It only calls for justice. Plans are drawn up; plans are constructions. The call for plans is the call upon which deconstruction insistently intervenes in order to keep the plans just, in order to keep the plans pliable. The role of deconstruction is to expose all such constructions to their own deconstructibility.

Far from building from a plan, the projection of justice is utterly without a plan, utterly devoid of patterns, heavenly or earthly. The myth of justice is not a mimetic myth, and it does not enjoin the imitation of heavenly exemplars or making copies in the earth of heavenly models. The projection of justice has to do with action, not making. It is a projection upon the possible, not a remodeling of the world according to a model or *archē*.

Justice is unforeseeable, so the mytho-prophetic tone in deconstruction has nothing whatever to do with telling the future. (See FL, 969–71)

Justice is unrepresentable, unmakable, unmodelable. It is not a matter of executing a plan, reproducing a design. It has nothing to do with mimetics. We do not know what we want when we want justice, because it has to do with singularities and has no "what," even though justice is *what* we want.

Justice, come!

That is a quasi-prophetic call, a call from nowhere, a call to nowhere, a call for no-thing, a mythic call from time immemorial toward an unforeseeable future. The call of justice cultivates the possible as possible (GA 2, 347/BT, 305–306). The myth of justice is the myth of time immemorial and of an unforeseeable *avenir*.[28] It calls from a past that was never present toward a future that is open and indeterminate, which is only "to come." The formal structure of this myth has been delineated quite insightfully by Heidegger in *Being and Time,* for whom the call comes from beyond and says nothing and for whom the *Zukunft* is what is coming, what is only to come. In *Being and Time,* being-toward-the-future is a matter of holding oneself open to an indefinite, open-ended future, not the calculated expectation of a more or less foreseeable future actuality. I locate the fateful, fatal failure of Heidegger in his having contracted the indeterminate structure of the call of what is "only coming" into the determinateness of a historical actuality. The fatally mythologizing gesture of Heidegger was to instantiate the future as the future of the Germans or of the West and to have determined the future as the repetition of a pure and primordially Greek Beginning, of something local and geo-loco-philosophical.

In so doing, the utopic myth of justice becomes the myth of the topology of Being and the topology of Being becomes the geography of Being, the geopolitics of Being, geophilosophy. The thought of Being, instead of remaining in the sphere of the possible as possible, finds a home in actuality, settling into a native land and speaking a native language. Demythologizing Heidegger on my accounting amounts to holding Heidegger's hand to the fire of *Being and Time,* to the indeterminate structure of the call of conscience and to the indefinite indeterminateness of the future, to the possible as possible, which is also the im/possible.

The future toward which justice calls, what is called for by justice, is not definite, not a future-actuality, which would reduce it to a matter of prediction and of working toward a preset goal, of reaching a mark which we set for ourselves, an articulated telos toward which we need only strain our wills (although that is hard enough). The call of/for justice, of/for mercy and compassion, maintains itself resolutely in the sphere of the possible, of radical openness and flexibility, which is to inhabit a mythic space. It is not a call for chaos but a call to stay open to the frailty and fragility of the future, to refuse to be taken in by the prestige of accumulated actuality.

Hyperbolic-prophetic justice does not mean to foretell the future, as if we were predicting an earthquake. The call of hyperbolic justice is a wail, a call for mercy and compassion, a cry against injustice. We do not know what we want. We cannot lay it out, because it depends upon the contingencies of the situation, the idiosyncrasies of the details, the multiple frailties of action.

Justice is im/possible. A myth. A story we tell about the fate of singulars. Hyperbolic justice is neither legal nor philosophical justice, both of which desire the *archē,* both of which can subsist only in the element of the universal. Still it must inform politico-philosophical justice, waxing the strings of the law lest they be drawn into too tight a knot. Hyperbolic justice is an-archic. It calls from beyond the universal, from the abyss of singularity. It calls upon us, calling for a response, calling upon our most secret responsiveness and responsibility.

What does the call say? Who calls? Who is being called upon? What is being called for?

Abyssus abyssum invocat.

CHAPTER ELEVEN

Conclusion

HEIDEGGER AND THE JEWGREEKS

Over and against Heidegger's myth of purity and monogenesis I have, at the end of this study, placed the work of Derrida, for whom "[m]onogenealogy is always a mystification. . . ."[1] Far from turning on the myth of the pure origin, Derrida's work—this is also true of Lyotard, another virtuoso of plurality—is entirely and, one might be tempted to say, systematically on the side of contamination, impurity, derivativeness, non-originariness, undecidability, marginalization, polygenesis, miscegenation. Derrida consistently—by which I mean strategically[2]—takes the side of whatever is left out or drops to the bottom in the various orders of rank that issue from Greco-German philosophizing—from Hegel, Heidegger, and Nietzsche in particular, however much attached he is to their philosophizing. The expression "jewgreek," as I am using it here, tries to capture the miscegenation of what is never purely Greek or Jewish, German or French or American. It embraces *"les juifs"* of Lyotard, the differends who are always left out, silenced, or victimized by their difference. That is the point in the work of Derrida and Lyotard at which they both make contact with Levinas, who is the most deeply biblical philosopher, the most deeply philosophical talmudist, the most jewgreek/greekjew thinker this century has produced.

Whatever debt Derrida owes to Heidegger—and this debt is considerable and it is not wise to understate it—on this point at least, of jewgreek contamination and miscegenation, "deconstruction" and the "thought of Being" could not be more deeply at odds. It is not too much to say that the whole point—the stylus tip, not the gathering *logos*—of deconstruction is to argue against the possibility of making clean distinctions, of establishing rigid borders and neat margins. Such borders invite and authorize policing by the keepers of the law, the guardians at the door—be they the doors of the university, policing the "disciplines," or the doors of nations and states, policing races, classes, languages, and peoples (whether the latter are taken biologistically or spiritually). The point of *différance* is to show the uncontainable proliferation, the uncontrollable dissemination, and the hopeless contamination of these zones of mythical purity, and thereby to make plain the violence of a pure Greek Beginning, the violence of a pure German repetition, the violence of purity itself, be it a pure beginning or a pure ending or a pure path.

That is why Derrida—like Levinas and Lyotard but most decidedly unlike Heidegger—is a philosopher of concrete obligation and factical responsibility, of responding not to the call of Being but to the call of the concrete singularity of the one in need, to the "widow, orphan, and stranger," a biblical discourse that Levinas has injected into poststructuralist thought. "Not Being, but one being, one time," Lyotard says.[3] That is also why Derrida is singularly resistant to what Lyotard calls Heidegger's "geophilosophy," which makes a fetish of native land and mother tongue instead of heeding the dispossessed, the homeless, the émigré, the Abrahamic, those whose native tongues are suppressed, instead of celebrating multilingual and multicultural multiplication.[4] To the monogenealogical Heideggerian myth of the spiritual kinship of Hellas and Germania, I have opposed, in the name of Derrida, a counter-myth, the jewgreek myth of Babel,[5] the jewgreek story of confusion and multiplication effected by God, who would, in that case, have found it handier to have a theory of *différance* than of the unitary site of thinking and poetizing. Responsibility in Derrida—following Levinas—is a jewgreek conception of the concern with the least among us, with the outcast and the foreigner, the oppressed and the dispossessed.

I have also found it pertinent to point out above the alliance of Derrida with certain Kierkegaardian themes: of the existing individual, of the particularity that exceeds universality, of the singular moment and the time of decision, of everything in Kierkegaard that constitutes the "religious" sphere over and above the sphere of ethical rationality. The right comparison of Derrida to Kierkegaard is not, as Derrida's critics imagine, to the Kierkegaardian aesthete who indulges himself in the "play of signifiers," as if undecidability meant evading the principle of contradiction by avoiding choice, which is the aesthetic principle advocated in the papers of "A" in *Either/Or*, Volume I. The right comparison of deconstruction with Kierkegaard is to the religious sphere, to the "Ultimatum" at the end of Volume II, where the obscure country parson puts sanctimonious Judge Wilhelm on the spot, exposing the limits of ethical rationalism and of the Judge's ethical braggadocio and moral athleticism.[6]

The *re-ligare* in Derrida, who is not a religious thinker, the *re-ligare* in Kierkegaard and Levinas, who certainly are, is the *ob-ligare,* the bond of responsibility to the singularity of the "wholly Other," the bond of the one-on-one of the self to the Other. In this sense, in the sense of this religion, Heidegger is not religious, not with the religiousness of this religion. It is true that the bond of thinking to the call of Being in Heidegger is structurally a bond of responsiveness and responsibility, even to what is called "wholly Other." It is also true that this bond of belongingness bears the detectable mark, *sous rature,* of having been drawn from biblical sources. Even so, it is a bond that has been utterly purified of its biblical content and made over into a matter of responding to a shining *phainesthai* and an anonymous *physis,* a bond in which the grief or well-being of living beings is simply not a matter for thought.

What is missing from Heidegger, what Heidegger always missed and excluded, what he never managed to think or come to grips with, is the jewgreek economy that runs through Kierkegaard, Levinas, Derrida, and Lyotard, the outlines of which I will briefly sketch here by way of a conclusion to this study of Heidegger's thought.

I will not call this jewgreek economy "ethics," because in a more precise sense it stands *against* ethics. I say this because ethics is Greek and because jewgreek thinking does not presume to appropriate such a congratulatory term for itself, because it wants to make self-approval and self-assurance tremble,[7] because it is more like the parson from the Jutland heaths than like Judge Wilhelm, because it wants to avoid the pride of ethics. It does not pretend to a metaphysics of morals and it does not invoke universal, rational or natural laws to justify, legitimate, and stabilize judgment. On the contrary, it exposes itself to the fragility of action (Arendt), to the frailty of judgment, to the anxiety of decision (Kierkegaard) in the midst of undecidability (Derrida), to a judgment which Lyotard says is "without criteria."[8] Lyotard is not endorsing wild caprice with this remark but pointing rather to the fact, a certain quasi-Aristotelian fact, well recognized in post-Kuhnian philosophy of science. In difficult cases the criteria are not much help and they are more easily formulated after the fact, after the decision, when they are no help at all, when we all have the advantage of seeing how things actually turned out.[9] If this jewgreek responsiveness and responsibility are not entirely unresponsive to the "universal" and "natural," they are more deeply interested in becoming responsible *for* the universals of philosophy (DPR, 9). Jewgreek thinking watches very closely to see what philosophy abolishes as irrational, unnatural, and particularist in virtue of the intimidating power and prestige of reason, nature, universality, and humanity.[10]

I will not call this jewgreek economy an economy of dialogue, which is a paradigm that has dominated philosophy from Plato to Buber and Gadamer. The jewgreek "other" is not quite up to being a dialogue partner, if only because she may have been deprived of speech or an idiom, may have been silenced and rendered unable to register a complaint or state her case. The jewgreek other is not quite up to the speed of Rorty's conversation of mankind and may even be a little illiterate. She may be done in by being drawn into such a conversation, which is what happens again and again to native populations when they are led to negotiate with the powerful visitors from afar who have come to live in their home. The other in this jewgreek economy comes toward us not as a conversational counterpart but as a claim *(Anspruch).* She does not appear across the plane of a conversation, on a more or less level surface, in a more or less homogeneous space. She comes to us from on high, and this just because she has been laid low, in a space that is curved against her, unequal, unfair, where her voice is excluded, distorted, silenced. That is why, in this jewgreek economy, which is slightly mad and excessive, a strategic reversal is effected in her favor, curving that space in the other's favor. The other comes to me with the power of a claim, with the force of a disruption whose otherness I cannot appropriate or assimilate.

In this jewgreek economy, language does not have a single site and does not say a self-same single *Urwort,* but it is drawn into multiplicity and Babelian confusion. Language arises from plurality, from the differences between us, so that to hear someone else is always to be instructed, that is, to be overtaken by something that is not our own, to effect that transcendence in which something other comes to me from without—rather than being recollected or recalled.[11] The idea is not to let all these discourses be gathered in the self-same site of a single *logos.* That would extinguish particularity and eventually silence everyone. The idea is, beyond merely keeping the lines of communication open, to invent new, startling, and barely communicable communications, for there can be no end to the novelty and otherness that arise when people get together. Instead of looking for ways to be gathered into agreement, Levinas prefers to let speakers be *kath auto.* That is why it is an essentially Levinasian—and Babelian—idea for Lyotard to suggest the priority of *dissensus* over consensus, which is to prefer innovation to reproduction, to resist mightily being gathered into the unity of an all-gathering *legein.*

For the jewgreeks, plurality is a positive feature, belonging to a positive plenitude, which Levinas describes as "anti-Parmenidean." Parmenides set the stage for onto-theo-logic by so privileging unity, by so identifying being with unity, that multiplicity and diversity have been suspect ever since. Plurality is not a fall from unity, a decline, a loss, nor even sheer numerical multiplicity. Plurality is the excess of the being of the other over and above my own projections.[12] Plurality is a creationist idea which sees multiplicity in terms of fertility, superabundance, overflow, the emergence of difference and the novel, and not in the Platonic and Neoplatonic categories of participation, analogy, and emanation.[13]

The jewgreek is not other than philosophy, not simply other, because we—who are "we"?—are all Greek, always and already Greek, and philosophical conceptuality is—for those of us who have been enculturated in the Euroworld—an inescapable given. But by putting the question of the other *to* philosophy, jewgreek thinking in fact raises the question of the other *of* philosophy. The jewgreek experience of the other, the passionate intensity of a jewgreek poetics or quasi-ethics of mercy and *kardia,* irrupts in the center of philosophy and disrupts its project of comprehension. That rupturing of philosophy, Derrida says, is what interests him most about Levinas and functioned as a "model" for his own attempt to delimit and deconstruct the metaphysics of presence.[14]

The jewgreek discourse on the widow, the orphan, and the stranger sounds odd to our philosophical ear just because it is picking up on something "other" than Heidegger's pure Greek, something other than pure philosophy. The oddity and impurity of the jewgreek is its focus on what has been "excluded," its hyperbolic sensitivity to the claim of the other, its demand for justice for the least among us, for the despised, the different, the dispossessed, and the helpless.

The historical sources of the jewgreek tradition are clearly biblical. Nietzsche was absolutely right to despise socialism and the call for justice for the wretched of the earth as a thinly disguised Christianity, which he denounced as slave morals. His theological insight is unmatched by the churches that sit down to table with the powers that be. The jewgreek economy draws upon the prophetic conception of justice in the Hebrew scriptures and the gospel of *kardia* in the Christian scriptures. In Levinas, the biblical source operates in a conscious and explicit manner. In Derrida it is not anything he has tried to monitor or sustain:[15]

> Though I was born a Jew, I do not work or think within a living Jewish tradition. So that if there is a Judaic dimension to my. thinking which may from time to time have spoken in or through me, this has never assumed the form of an explicit fidelity or debt to that culture.

Whether Christian or Jew, no reader of so-called postmodern literature—of Derrida or Lyotard or Foucault, e.g.—can fail to be impressed by its biblical cast of characters—the AIDS-afflicted/leper, the mad (possessed), the lame and ill, the law-breakers, the marginalized, the lost sheep. As such this "postmodern" discourse is not a new but an old story, belonging to an old jewgreek economy. It belongs to the oldest of the old, not to old Greeks, not to old father Parmenides or to snobby old Heraclitus, who loved the order of rank, but to old Abraham. It is a child of father Abraham, the father of us all, not just of father Parmenides. It also wants to know who our mothers are.

By systematically purifying the path of thought of every such jewgreek contaminant, by purging it of whatever is not primordially and phantasmatically early Greek, by acknowledging only one father, Heidegger paid a high price. These jewgreek figures, these disfigured figures, these figures of dismemberment and misery, have never figured in the thought of Being.[16] Never the matter of the question of Being, they have always remained out of the question—never questioned, never thought, never remembered, the matter of the most unsettling oblivion. They have never mattered to the matter of thought.

That is not a simple gap or an omission on Heidegger's part, something he "forgot"—he had too many reminders—but on the contrary something systematically neutralized by essentializing thinking. The task of essentializing thinking is defined by this essential exclusion. The absence of the jewgreek proceeded from a radical act of exclusion demanded by the thought of Being, by the demand to stay purely in the element of what Heidegger calls Being, by the essence and the purity of that thought, by the myth of the pure Origin, by the mythical purity of the aboriginal Beginning. It is not an omission that can be remedied with a little supplement that fills in the missing part. The thought of Being is inwardly defined and constituted by the exclusion. How would one "include" the jewgreek in the *Andenken* of what is purely Greek? How would one add a little supplement to the Thought of Being, to the effect that one must also not forget what is Otherwise than Being?

How to demythologize Heidegger? Would that not involve starting all over again, going back to where he himself started, to the prephilosophical sources from which he hoped to give philosophy a new start, and to try it again—this time with heart?

What would the hermeneutics of facticity look like if it started out all over again and began with the obligation that descends upon us from on high, from those who are laid low, if such obligation were one of its categories or anticategories, if it included everything that Heidegger sought to exclude?

Who is Heidegger demythologized, made to answer to another responsibility?[17] Would that not be another Heidegger, a Heidegger against Heidegger, a Heidegger who represents all that Heidegger fought against?

NOTES

Introduction

1. I say too unguarded, but I do not say absolutely unguarded. *The Mystical Element in Heidegger's Thought* (Athens: Ohio University Press, 1977; 2nd. rev. ed., New York: Fordham University Press, 1986), chapter 5, raises a series of critical questions about the status of ethics and rationality in the later Heidegger. *Heidegger and Aquinas: An Essay on Overcoming Metaphysics* (New York: Fordham University Press, 1982), which is written primarily, but not exclusively, from Heidegger's standpoint, seeks to find in Aquinas a point of extrication from Heidegger's delimitation of onto-theo-logic; see chapter 9.

2. See below, chapter 1.

3. See *Radical Hermeneutics: Repetition, Deconstruction, and the Hermeneutic Project* (Bloomington: Indiana University Press, 1987), chapters 6–7.

4. The work of Victor Farias is now available in a revised edition in English: *Heidegger and Nazism*, ed. Joseph Margolis and Tom Rockmore, trans. Paul Burrell, Dominic DiBernardi, Gabriel R. Ricci (Philadelphia: Temple University Press, 1989); Hugo Ott, *Martin Heidegger: Unterwegs zu seiner Biographie* (Frankfurt and New York: Campus Verlag, 1988). For one short, scintillating, incisive, sizzling summary of the whole story, see Thomas Sheehan's now famous review "Heidegger and the Nazis," *The New York Review of Books* (June 16, 1988): 38–47. Sheehan concludes this piece by saying—at exactly the same time my "Demythologizing Heidegger" was appearing—that the way to deal with the issue is "not to stop reading Heidegger but to start demythologizing him." See also his latest statement, which keeps up the heat: Thomas Sheehan, "A Normal Nazi," *The New York Review of Books* (January 14, 1993): 30–35, and the subsequent controversy with Derrida in the next few issues.

5. Both works are now available in English: Philippe Lacoue-Labarthe, *Heidegger, Art and Politics*, trans. Chris Turner (Oxford: Blackwell, 1990); Jean-François Lyotard, *Heidegger and "the jews,"* trans. Andreas Michel and Mark Roberts (Minneapolis: University of Minnesota Press, 1990).

6. See below, chapter 7.

7. On this view, e.g., feminists can best make their way not only by demythologizing patriarchal myths but also by inventing a new, empowering mythology of the maternal and feminine and—beyond that—of the androgynous and the hermaphroditic. In speaking of the need to mythologize differently, I am departing from Lyotard's notion that mythic thinking is essentially geophilosophical, essentially aligned with a sacred earth and fatherland. To the myth of the sacred earth, I oppose the myth of the holy, of the Other who calls from on high. See Lyotard, *Heidegger and "the jews,"* p. 80.

8. See John van Buren's *The Young Heidegger*, forthcoming from Indiana University Press; Theodore Kisiel, *The Genesis of Heidegger's Being and Time* (Berkeley: University of California Press, 1993); and Kisiel and van Buren's co-edited volume, forthcoming from SUNY Press: *Re-interpreting Heidegger: Essays in His Early Thought*.

9. Lacoue-Labarthe has brilliantly developed the relation of the Nazi myth and the *Seinsgeschicklich* myth in *Heidegger, Art and Politics*. See also Philippe Lacoue-Labarthe and Jean-Luc Nancy, "The Nazi Myth," *Critical Inquiry*, 16 (1990): 291–

312; Jean-Luc Nancy, *The Inoperative Community*, trans. C. Fynsk (Minneapolis: University of Minnesota Press, 1991), chapter 2.

10. Jacques Derrida, *The Other Heading: Reflections on Today's Europe,* trans. Pascale-Anne Brault and Michael B. Naas (Bloomington: Indiana University Press, 1992), pp. 11–12.

11. "Aber dies 'nur' ist Alles, das Eine, Einzige." SG, 188.

12. I do not concede Hölderlin to Heidegger; I do not concede Heidegger's Hölderlin, which seems to me likewise to require demythologizing; see Veronique Foti, *Heidegger and the Poets: Poiesis, Sophia, Techne* (Atlantic Highlands: Humanities Press, 1991), chapter 4.

13. As opposed, for example, to the utterly personal attack on Paul de Man by David Lehman in "Paul de Man: The Plot Thickens," *The New York Times Book Review* (May 24, 1992), in which we are told that de Man abandoned his wife and children. That, if it is true, is highly deplorable but not relevant, for example, to understanding *Allegories of Reading* or (another important target) Derrida's *Of Grammatology.* The highly personal character of the attack that Farias makes on Heidegger tends only to undermine what is of factual worth in Farias's book; without Hugo Ott's more judicious work, the serious matters raised by Farias would have been dismissed as an attempted lynching.

14. Otto Pöggeler, *Martin Heidegger's Path of Thinking,* trans. Dan Magurshak and Sigmund Barber (Atlantic Highlands: Humanities Press, 1987), p. 272.

15. See the Foreword that Heidegger added in 1961 to his *Nietzsche* (Pfullingen: Neske, 1961), vol. I, p. 9. Engl. trans. *Nietzsche,* vol. I, *The Will to Power as Art,* trans. David Krell (New York: Harper & Row, 1979), p. xv.

16. For example, see the absurd mystification of the war in the 1942–43 course on Parmenides (GA 54, 113–114/P, 77).

17. See below, chapter 6.

18. The task is not only to disrupt the Greek with the Jew, but also to disrupt Heidegger's Greeks with *other* Greeks, with Antigone and Oedipus, with torn flesh and gouged eyes, with unburied brothers and sisters buried alive, scenes that are entirely missing from Heidegger's mythologization of the Greeks—a point I pursue more fully elsewhere (see below, n. 22).

19. Jacques Derrida, *Writing and Difference,* trans. Alan Bass (Chicago: University of Chicago Press, 1978), p. 153: "Are we Jews? Are we Greeks? We live in the difference between the Jew and the Greek. . . . 'Jewgreek is greekjew. Extremes meet.'"

20. For a brilliant commentary on this text in a work criticizing Heidegger—and Derrida—from a "jewgreek" point of view, see Jean-Luc Marion, *God Without Being,* trans. Thomas Carlson (Chicago: University of Chicago, 1991), pp. 83–107.

21. In writing "jewgreek" I am not saying only Jewish and Greek and nothing else, nothing Christian, Roman, Islamic, etc. On the contrary, I am speaking on behalf of miscegenation, polygenesis, and heteromorphic pluralism. For a useful delimitation of "Jewgreek is Greekjew," see Adriaan Peperzak, *To the Other* (West Lafayette: Purdue University Press, 1993), pp. 8–10.

22. *Against Ethics: Contributions to a Poetics of Obligation with Constant Reference to Deconstruction* (Bloomington: Indiana University Press, 1993). The two books could be conceived as a single project on "Obligation": Part One: *Against Heidegger* (and for a certain ethics); Part Two, *Against Ethics* (and for obligation).

1. *Aletheia* and the Myth of Being

1. Tom Rockmore, *On Heidegger's Nazism and Philosophy* (Berkeley: University of California Press, 1992); Richard Wolin, *The Politics of Being* (New York: Columbia University Press, 1990).

2. See Wolin, *The Politics of Being,* chapter 2.

3. Furthermore, after an ultraconservative Catholic upbringing as a vigorous opponent of "modernism" (historical relativism) in theology, by 1914 Heidegger advocated a return to and a renewal of medieval logic by way of the advances of modern Husserlian and transcendental logic; see my *Heidegger and Aquinas,* chapter 1; Kisiel, *The Genesis,* pp. 72–75.

4. See chapters 2 and 3, below.

5. One might say that in the 1930s he brought his metaphysical orientation in line with his social and political agenda, instead of the other way around. One can certainly imagine alternate political futures for *Being and Time,* say, of the sort given to it by Sartre.

6. In "The Anaximander Fragment" this expression signifies the decline of modernity, while in the Marburg period latecomers have the advantage.

7. Franz Brentano, *Von der mannigfachen Bedeutung des Seienden nach Aristoteles* (Freiburg: Herder, 1962); photographical reproduction: Hildesheim: Olms Verlag, 1960.

8. The notion of being forsaken by Being, on analogy with being forsaken by God *(Gottverlassenheit),* is prominent in the *Beiträge* (GA 65), which are contemporaneous with GA 45.

9. One can see how this "giving" or "granting" is the "letting be" in the later writings that replaces transcendental letting be, as a transcendental condition of possibility, which is the model of the early writings.

10. See the famous essay *"Différance"* in *Margins of Philosophy,* trans. Alan Bass (Chicago: University Press, 1982), pp. 3, 7.

11. For a careful accounting of this debate, see Robert Bernasconi, *The Question of Language in Heidegger's History of Being* (New York: Humanities Press, 1985), chapter 2. For more on the etymological issue, see Alexander Mourelatos, *The Route of Parmenides* (New Haven: Yale University Press, 1970), pp. 63–67.

12. The definitive case for this complaint against Heidegger's reading of the poets is to be found in Veronique Foti, *Heidegger and the Poets.* For a critique of pure Greek temples over and against Jewish temples, see Caputo, *Against Ethics,* chapter 8, discourse No. 4, "Temples," pp. 150–66.

13. This privileging of the Brentano book is the official story of the authorized biography put out by Heidegger, which is in no small part intended to erase the place played by the crucial first Freiburg lectures (1919–1923), which I will discuss below.

14. For more on this Derridean construal of Heidegger, see my *Radical Hermeneutics,* chapters 6 and 7.

15. Rockmore, who finds nothing redeeming at all in Heidegger, does not believe this either; see *Heidegger's Nazism,* pp. 204–43.

16. According to Heinrich Wiegand Petzet, *Auf Einem Stern Zugehen: Begegnungen und Gespräche mit Martin Heidegger (1929–76)* (Frankfurt: Societäts-Verlag, 1983), p. 143, Heidegger was a great admirer of Cézanne.

17. Richard Rorty, "Taking Philosophy Seriously," *The New Republic,* 11 (April 1988): 31–34.

2. Heidegger's *Kampf*

1. Pöggeler thinks Heidegger tends to undergo a radical transformation "about every five years"; *Martin Heidegger's Path of Thinking,* p. 280.

2. These words are chosen intentionally. They mark off different points on Heidegger's path: "life": the problematics of the hermeneutics of facticity (1919–1923); "existence": the existential analytic of *Being and Time;* "history": the political turn of the 1930s. There is another renewal, with which I am not concerned here, which has come

fully into view as a result of the researches of Hugo Ott: the call for a radically Catholic renewal, the ultraconservative Catholicism (1910–1912) that warns against the relativist and "modernist" threat to Catholicism and calls for a radical repetition of the oldest truth of the Catholic faith. See Hugo Ott, *Martin Heidegger: Unterwegs zu seiner Biographie*, pp. 45–66. Cf. my *Heidegger and Aquinas*, chapter 1; Kisiel, *The Genesis*, ch. 2.

3. The first commentators to draw attention to Heidegger's interest in the New Testament experience of life were Otto Pöggeler, *Martin Heidegger's Path of Thinking*, pp. 24–31; and Thomas Sheehan, "Heidegger's 'Introduction to the Phenomenology of Religion, 1921–22,'" *The Personalist*, 60 (1979), 312–24. Above all, Kisiel, *The Genesis*, has recently given us an impressive and painstakingly precise picture of the pre–*Sein und Zeit* period. I also want to emphasize the importance of the recent work of John van Buren, who has massively documented and incisively interpreted these early lectures in *The Young Heidegger*, forthcoming from Indiana University Press.

4. The notion of a "formal indication" in these lectures is quite important and has been carefully developed in the work of Kisiel and van Buren (above, n. 3).

5. See George Stack, *Kierkegaard's Existential Ethics* (University Park: University of Alabama Press, 1977), pp. 133–37.

6. See, e.g., E. P. Sanders, *Jesus and Judaism* (Philadelphia: Fortress Press, 1985); and more recently John P. Meier, *A Marginal Jew: Rethinking the Historical Jesus* (New York: Doubleday, 1991).

7. Søren Kierkegaard, *Philosophical Fragments*, trans. H. Hong and E. Hong (Princeton: Princeton University Press, 1985), pp. 107–108.

8. See the "Interlude" on *kinesis* in *Philosophical Fragments*, pp. 72–88.

9. This is the argument of *Repetition*, trans. H. Hong and E. Hong (Princeton: Princeton University Press, 1983). See my *Radical Hermeneutics*, chapter 1.

10. *Repetition*, p. 309.

11. Otto Pöggeler claims that this chaos had a deep influence on Heidegger; see *Heidegger's Path of Thinking*, pp. 273ff., and "Heidegger's Politische Selbstverständnis," in *Heidegger und die Praktische Philosophie*, eds. A. Gethmann-Siefert and O. Pöggeler (Frankfurt: Suhrkamp, 1988), pp. 20ff. See Wolin, pp. 69–75.

12. Winfried Franzen, "Die Sehnsucht nach Härte und Schwere," in *Heidegger und die Praktische Philosophie*, pp. 78–92. In fact, Heidegger at one point says that the existential analytic *does* proceed from a definite factical ideal (GA 2, 411/BT, 358).

13. On the place of Jünger in Heidegger's thought in the 1930s, see Michael E. Zimmerman, *Heidegger's Confrontation with Modernity: Technology, Politics, and Art* (Bloomington: Indiana University Press, 1990), pp. 66ff. On the thematics of danger in Heidegger and Jünger, see Franzen, "Die Sehnsucht nach Härte und Schwere"; Nicholas Tertullian, "The History of Being and Political Revolution: Reflections on a Posthumous Work of Heidegger," in *The Heidegger Case: On Philosophy and Politics*, eds. Tom Rockmore and Joseph Margolis, pp. 217–18; Hans Peter Söder, "National Socialism in the History of Being: A Discussion of Some Aspects of the Recent 'L'Affaire Heidegger,'" *Philosophy Today*, 33 (1989), 109–20.

14. For a careful and thoughtful textual account of *Kampf* in Heidegger's thought, see Gregory Friel, "Heidegger's *Polemos*," *Journal of Philosophical Research*, 16 (1991): 145–95. Friel, who makes a sustained effort to cast Heidegger's ideas in the best light, sees *Kampf* and *Auseinandersetzung* as Heidegger's attempt to form a positive conception of "community," viz., as a creative tension among competing, self-asserting identities. Thus, instead of a universal community (the League of Nations, e.g.) Heidegger advocated vigorous national communities in healthy strife (a more Nietzschean model). Friel is not uncritical: "Would a good little war here and there

... be too high a price to pay in the wager to find a crossing-over to the other beginning ... ?" (p. 184). Friel is chiding postmodernists who advocate "difference" by pointing out that Heidegger's nationalism is such a philosophy of difference, i.e., of the right to the German difference (or the French, American, etc.). But of course postmodernism wants to make the very idea of "the German" (or "the French," etc.) tremble and to see in that nationalist right to be different a right to excommunicate and purify whatever is not the same (i.e., German or French, etc.). Postmodern difference is not nationalist difference but a multicultural, multilingual, multivaluing, miscegenated polymorphism; it makes the idea of a self-affirming identity tremble. Heidegger's *Volk* is anything but a postmodern philosophy of difference. Furthermore, and this is important, in its Levinasian version, postmodernism does not conceive the relationship with the other in terms of strife, but in terms of obligation, of the claim laid by the other on the same.

15. Theodore Kisiel, "Heidegger's Apology," *Graduate Faculty Philosophy Journal,* 14–15 (1991–1992): 363–404.

16. See Peter Gay, *Weimar Culture: The Insider and Outsider* (New York: Harper Torchbooks, 1968).

17. See below, chapters 7 and 8.

18. Ernst Jünger, *Werke,* B. 5, *Essays I* (Stuttgart: Klett Verlag, n.d.), p. 151. See also *"Kampf als inneres Erlebnis,"* pp. 11ff. Heidegger writes: "Tell me what you think about translation and I will tell you who you are." *Gesamtausgabe,* B. 53, *Hölderlins Hymne "Der Ister"* (Frankfurt: Klostermann, 1984), p. 74.

19. Friedrich Nietzsche, *Ecce Homo,* trans. R. J. Hollingdale (New York: Penguin Books, 1979), p. 41.

20. Jean-François Lyotard, *Heidegger and "the jews,"* p. 3.

3. *Sorge* and *Kardia*

1. See Theodore Kisiel, *The Genesis of Heidegger's Being and Time,* pp. 38–59.

2. See John van Buren, "The Young Heidegger," *Philosophy Today,* 33 (1989): 99–108; and "The Young Heidegger and Phenomenology," *Man and World,* 23 (1990): 239–72.

3. Kierkegaard, *Philosophical Fragments,* pp. 107–108; *Repetition,* pp. 131–33. For a fuller analysis of this conception of repetition, see my *Radical Hermeneutics,* chapter 1.

4. The commentary on this text is to be found in the forthcoming GA 60: *Augustinus und der Neuplatonismus.*

5. Alasdair MacIntyre, *After Virtue: A Study in Moral Theory* (Notre Dame: University of Notre Dame Press, 1981), pp. 169–74.

6. 1 Cor. 1:26–29. See the illuminating exegesis of this text in Jean-Luc Marion, *God Without Being,* pp. 83–101.

7. See Derrida's interesting note on Nietzsche in EO, 23–24, note.

8. It should not be lost sight of that the root of *phronesis* is *phren,* the heart, midriff, or diaphragm, which in Homer was taken to be the seat of the soul, of both feeling and thinking. But Plato and Aristotle follow a Pythagorean tradition, which located the seat of thought in the brain; for them the word *phronesis* had a more noetic force. Heidegger gave passing notice to Aristotelian *synesis* (understanding what someone else says), which he evidently translated as *Rücksicht* ("considerateness") and *syngnome* (forgiveness: *Nichomachean Ethics,* VI, 11), which he translated as *"Nachsicht"* ("forbearance"); see GA 2, 164/BT, 159. But even these Aristotelian virtues were directed at a closed circle of equals and were nothing like the radical biblical virtues of serving the outcast and lowliest.

9. *Summa Theologica*, I–II, Q. 65.

10. "Dasein in Heidegger is never hungry." Emmanuel Levinas, *Totality and Infinity*, trans. A. Lingis (Pittsburgh: Duquesne University Press, 1969), p. 134.

11. See Sander Gilman, *Disease and Representation: Images of Illness from Madness to AIDS* (Ithaca: Cornell University Press, 1988). I have examined the question of the "flesh," of its corruptibility and vulnerability, in *Against Ethics*, chapter 9.

12. Elaine Scarry, *The Body in Pain: The Making and Unmaking of the World* (Oxford: Oxford University Press, 1985). See especially Scarry's treatment of torture.

13. Frederick Nietzsche, *Ecce Homo*, p. 41.

14. See above, n. 2.

15. On the Trakl reading, see below, chapter 7; on essentialization, see below, chapter 6; on the "scandals," see below, chapter 8.

16. There are clear links between my interpretation of the history of Being and what Derrida calls spirit in OS. See my references to OS below, in chapters 6 and 8, and in chapter 9, "The Nazi Years."

17. See *Fear and Trembling*, p. 7. I have organized a good deal of *Against Ethics*—which amounts to a kind of postmodern restaging of *Fear and Trembling*—around this text, which seems to me to say in a word what is needed today to begin to respond to the phantasmic conception of the "history of Being," the phantasmic counterpart to the "history of the Spirit."

4. Heidegger's Responsibility

1. As opposed to the valorization of chance, contingency, and event-fulness in thinkers like Rorty, Lyotard, and Derrida.

2. Heidegger's view is like the Hegelian idea that a purely formal *Moralität* must become a substantive *Sittlichkeit*. Wolin's demand for "criteria" (*The Politics of Being*, pp. 46–53) here is a bit of misbegotten Habermasianism, for all the reasons given by hermeneutics—stemming from the paradigm of *phronesis* which lies behind *Being and Time* and confirmed by the post-Kuhnian delimitation of criteriology—that can be laid against criteriological thinking; see above, chapter 3, on *phronesis* and *kardia;* and *Radical Hermeneutics*, chapter 8.

3. This is explained very carefully by Friel, "Heidegger's *Polemos*."

4. Ott, *Martin Heidegger: Unterwegs zu seiner Biographie*, 171–72: Heidegger made a "spectacular display" of entering the Party on May 1, 1933.

5. Karl Löwith, *Mein Leben in Deutschland vor und nach 1933* (Stuttgart: Metzler, 1986), p. 57; Eng. trans. "My Last Meeting with Heidegger in Rome, 1936," trans. Richard Wolin, *New German Critique*, No. 45 (Fall 1988), pp. 115–16.

6. See Heidegger's letter "An das Akademische Rektorat der Albert Ludwig Universität," in Karl Moehling, *Martin Heidegger and the Nazi Party: An Examination* (Ann Arbor: University Microfilms, 1972), p. 265.

7. For a Derridean critique of this sort of hermeneutics, see my *Radical Hermeneutics*, chapters 6 and 7.

8. One saving feature of the later writings, even if it does represent a reincarnation of the German-Japanese axis of World War II, is the dialogue with the Japanese and the affinity of German with a non-European language suggested there (US, 85ff./ OWL, 1ff.)

9. I say "supposed to be" because I questioned above to what extent it creeps back into the idea of "ownmost possibility."

10. See below, chapter 6.

11. On "To Lead the Leader," see Wolin, *The Politics of Being*, chapter 3.

12. So the rectorial address both is and is not humanistic (= subjectivistic). It is

humanistic/subjectivist in virtue of its massive voluntarism; but it begins the overcoming of humanism inasmuch as it thinks of willing as responding to something more than human, to a fate or call, which calls for a response. See the debate between Luc Ferry and Alain Renaut, *Heidegger and Modernity,* trans. Franklin Philip (Chicago: University of Chicago Press, 1990), pp. 2–6, and Derrida, OS, 66 and Lacoue-Labarthe, *Heidegger, Art and Politics,* p. 95. Ferry and Renaut, and with them Tom Rockmore, *On Heidegger's Nazism and Philosophy,* pp. 278–79, confuse the issue by taking humanism to mean something like humanitarianism instead of voluntaristic subjectivism, which is its Heideggerian sense.

13. Hugo Ott recounts the military-style camp Heidegger ran at Todtnauberg to inaugurate the academic year in October 1933, which included a footmarch from Freiburg to Todtnauberg (no small distance); see Ott, *Martin Heidegger,* pp. 214–223.

14. See GA 53, 68: "We today [1942] know that the Anglo-Saxon world of Americanism is resolved to annihilate Europe, and that means the homeland and the beginning of the West. The incipient is indestructible. The entrance of America into this planetary war is not the entrance into history but rather is already the last American act of American lack of history and self-destruction." See also GA 51, 84, 92.

15. On the *Beiträge* and Nazism, see Rockmore, *On Heidegger's Nazism and Philosophy,* pp. 176–203; Nicolas Tertulian, "The History of Being and Political Revolution: Reflections on a Posthumous Work," in *The Heidegger Case: On Philosophy and Politics,* eds. Tom Rockmore and Joseph Margolis, pp. 208–227.

16. In the famous *Der Spiegel* interview [1966] he is at a loss to offer any political advice at all. See *Spieg.,* pp. 278–81.

17. See my *The Mystical Element in Heidegger's Thought,* chapter 2.

18. Allan Bloom, *The Closing of the American Mind* (New York: Simon & Schuster, 1987), pp. 217ff.

19. It has been a mark of Derrida's treatment of responsibility to differentiate the multiple senses of "responsibility"—from Levinas to the Heidegger of the 1930s. See DPR and PF. I have defended this Derridean approach to responsibility, particularly as regards SG, in my "Beyond Aestheticism: Derrida's Responsible Anarchy," *Research in Phenomenology,* 18 (1988): 59–73, which is organized around DPR.

20. Still, even on this more generous construal the whole discussion remains attached to "geophilosophy," a philosophy of the native land, which leaves out the homeless and the émigré. See Lyotard, *Heidegger and "the jews,"* pp. 91–94.

21. Here is the sense in which we can understand the maxim "Tell me what you think of translation and I will tell you who you are." Cf. GA 53, 76; and Derrida, OS, 4–5.

5. Heidegger's Revolution

1. This is a constant theme in Hugo Ott, but see especially pp. 164–65, 190–91.

2. Heidegger resigned the rectorship in April 1934, but Ott thinks that the Party had already made up its mind on Heidegger by December 1933 and that Heidegger had by then already determined to resign the rectorate (pp. 229–30). It did not take long for Heidegger to discover that he was going nowhere in the Party (Ott, p. 240).

3. The notorious declaration of Nov. 3, 1933—"Let not propositions and 'ideas' be the rules of your Being. The *Führer* alone is the present and future German reality and its law." (*New German Critique,* No. 45 [Fall 1988], p. 102)—may have been a warning not to heed Party ideologues, but only the Führer, whose true leadership Heidegger feared, was being subverted.

4. I take this text to be a reference to Max Schmeling (b. 1905), the world heavyweight boxing champion from 1930 to 1932, who had become a symbol of "Aryan

superiority" by handing the black American prizefighter Joe Louis (1914–1981) his first defeat, in a 12-round knock-out fight in 1936 (only to be knocked out by Louis in a 1938 rematch). Heidegger seems to take the popular preoccupation with the Louis-Schmeling rivalry to be a deplorable confusion of what Heraclitus meant by *polemos* and hence of the essence of the *Kampf.*

5. Heidegger evidently said "Party" not "movement." See Harmut Buchner, "Fragmentarisches," in *Erinnerung an Martin Heidegger,* ed. Günther Neske (Pfullingen: Neske, 1977), p. 49; and Thomas Sheehan, "Heidegger and the Nazis," *The New York Review of Books* (June 16, 1988), pp. 42–43.

6. Heidegger had a constant interest in the university from the first Freiburg period to the 1928 Antrittsrede to the Rectoratsrede; see above, chapters 2 and 3; Kisiel, *The Genesis,* pp. 63–69.

7. Farias, *Heidegger and Nazism,* p. 165.

8. Farias, p. 187.

9. Farias, p. 204. See also Ott, pp. 191, 243.

10. The sentences in square brackets in IM were added in 1953 and generally show the movement beyond the voluntarism of the 1930s.

11. Manheim's translation erases the occurrences of *Erleichterung* and *Erschwerung* in these two paragraphs.

12. Milan Kundera, *The Unbearable Lightness of Being,* trans. M. H. Heim (New York: Harper & Row, 1984). See Winfried Franzen, "Die Sehnsucht nach Härte und Schwere," in *Heidegger und praktische Philosophie,* eds. Otto Pöggeler and A. Gethmann-Siefert, pp. 78–92.

13. Farias (pp. 220–21) tries to argue that Heidegger was not criticizing racism or biologism but trying to found biological racism on the notion of spirit. That seems to me contrived and merely polemical.

14. Jacques Le Rider, "Le dossier d'un nazi 'ordinaire,'" *Le Monde* (October 13–19, 1988), p. 12; cf. Ott, p. 254, n. 174.

15. See Martin Bernal's controversial *Black Athena: The Afroasiatic Roots of Classical Civilization,* Vol. I: *The Fabrication of Greece, 1785–1985* (New Brunswick: Rutgers University Press, 1987); Vol. II: *The Archeological and Documentary Evidence* (New Brunswick: Rutgers University Press, 1991).

16. See Derrida's treatment of the Kierkegaardian "moment" in DPR.

17. See below, chapter 6, "Heidegger's Essentialism."

18. Ott, pp. 156–57, 279.

6. Heidegger's Essentialism

1. I am translating *Wesen* as "Essential Being" instead of as "coming to presence," not in order to diminish the verbal sense of the word, which I do not deny, but in order to retain its connection with the classical concept of essence, which I wish to assert. Veronique Foti's convention, *essence,* tries to capture at once both the verbal sense *(esse)* and the classical term; see her *Heidegger and the Poets,* p. xix *et passim.* For more on *esse* and *essentia,* see my *Heidegger and Aquinas,* p. 106.

2. *Spieg.,* 282. Who were these French? Were they speaking French or German at the time? Can the poverty of French be expressed in the French tongue, or does this confession also require the use of German? Can any of this be discussed in English? Could Farias express the poverty of Spanish in Spanish? See Derrida, OS, 68–70.

3. Jacques Derrida, "On Reading Heidegger," *Research in Phenomenology,* 17 (1987), 172–73 and 180–81.

4. In "Work and *Weltanschauung:* The Heidegger Controversy from a German Perspective," in *Heidegger: A Critical Reader,* eds. Hubert Dreyfus and Harrison Hall

(Oxford: Basil Blackwell, 1992), pp. 186–208, a trenchant and uncompromising critique of Heidegger which also served as the introduction to the German edition of Farias, Jürgen Habermas quite rightly criticizes what he calls "abstraction via essentialization" (198–201), a mystification of concrete historical actuality in favor of an essential truth known only to an elite thinker.

5. "Die Metaphysik stellt zwar das Seiende in seinem Sein vor und denkt so auch das Sein des Seienden."

6. "Aber sie denkt nicht das Sein als solches, denkt nicht den Unterscheid beider." "Being itself" is omitted from the translation in BW.

7. That the logic of facticity strains against the "purity" of Being and sees to it that the ontological is always contaminated by the ontic shows up in Heidegger's own text in the discussion of "metontology" in Martin Heidegger, *The Metaphysical Foundations of Logic,* trans. Michael Heim (Bloomington: Indiana University Press, 1984), pp. 156–59.

8. "Die Metaphysik fragt nicht nach der Wahrheit des Seins selbst."

9. "Sie fragt nicht daher auch nie, in welcher Weise das Wesen des Menschen zur Wahrheit des Seins gehört."

10. "Der Leib des Menschen ist etwas wesentliches anderes als tierisches Organismus."

11. See chapter 3.

12. Frank Capuzzi, the English translator, translates *abgründig* as "appalling," as if it scares and sickens us.

13. "World-poor" is a motif in GA 29/30, §§45–63, where Heidegger gives his most extended treatment of the body.

14. Jacques Derrida, "*Geschlecht* II: Heidegger's Hand," *Deconstruction and Philosophy,* ed. John Sallis (Chicago: University of Chicago Press, 1987), p. 174.

15. For a delimitation of Heidegger's reading of Rilke, see Foti, *Heidegger and the Poets,* pp. 30–43.

16. See the remarkable investigations of Elaine Scarry, *The Body in Pain: The Making and Unmaking of the World.*

7. Heidegger's Scandal

1. Jacques Maritain, "St. Augustine and St. Thomas Aquinas," in *Augustine: His Age, Life and Thought* (New York: Meridian Books, 1957), pp. 199–223.

2. Habermas, "Work and *Weltanschauung*," p. 197.

3. Pöggeler, *Heidegger's Path of Thinking,* p. 272.

4. Lyotard, *The Differend,* pp. xi *et passim.*

5. Heidegger wrote to Erhart Kästner, "Wer das Denken nicht angreifen kann, greift den Denkenden an." Cited by Philippe Lacoue-Labarthe, *Heidegger, Art and Politics,* trans. Chris Turner (Oxford: Blackwell, 1990), p. 15, n. 4. For more on Kästner, see Heinrich Petzet, *Auf einen Stern Zugehen* (Frankfurt: Societäts-Verlag, 1983), pp. 110–114.

6. Hans A. Fisher-Barnicol, "Spiegelungen-Vermittlungen," in *Erinnerung an Martin Heidegger,* ed. G. Neske (Pfullingen: Neske, 1977), pp. 95–96. This anecdote is also recorded by Farias, p. 289.

7. *Poems of Paul Celan,* trans. Michael Hamburger (New York: Persea, 1988), p. 293.

8. I use the translation of Thomas Sheehan in "Heidegger and the Nazis," *The New York Review of Books* (June 16, 1988), pp. 41–43. Sheehan is translating the German as it appears in Wolfgang Schirmacher, *Technik und Gelassenheit* (Freiburg: Alber, 1983), p. 25, who himself cites p. 25 of a typescript of the lecture. The first

part of the sentence also appears in "The Question Concerning Technology" (BW, 296). The attempt to determine the "essence" of technology in terms of the *Gestell* is the context of Heidegger's remark. The German is as follows: "Ackerbau ist jetzt motorisierte Ernährungsindustrie, im Wesen das Selbe wie die Fabrikation von Leichen in Gaskammern und Vernichtungslagern, das Selbe wie die Blockade und Aushungerung von Ländern, das Selbe wie die Fabrikation von Wasserstoffbomben."

9. Sheehan, p. 41.

10. Philippe Lacoue-Labarthe, *Heidegger, Art and Politics*, p. 34.

11. Habermas rightly complains that, from the standpoint of this abstraction by essentialization, "everything becomes one and the same"—communism, fascism, and democracy; exterminating Jews and expelling East Germans; exterminating Jews and running tractors. "Work and *Weltanschauung*," p. 201.

12. See above, chapter 4, concluding section.

13. See above, chapter 6, "Heidegger's Essentialism."

14. Lyotard, *Heidegger and "the jews,"* pp. 40–41, 79–80. For a commentary in a similar vein, see Richard Bernstein, *The New Constellation: The Ethical-Political Horizons of Modernity/Postmodernity* (Cambridge: MIT Press, 1992), chapter 7, "Heidegger's Silence?: *Ethos* and Technology."

15. See Heidegger's reading of *dike* and *adikia* in "The Anaximander Fragment" in GA 5, 354–361/EGT, 41–47.

16. Guilt and conscience were essential features of the analytic of Dasein; but they have disappeared from the history of Being (or been transmuted into responding to Being's call); see above, chapter 4.

17. Jean-François Lyotard, *The Differend*, Nos. 9–27. *The Differend* can be read as a book about Auschwitz, which is mentioned in every chapter and is the subject of the central chapter, "The Result."

18. Faurrison, cited by Pierre Vida-Naquet, "A Paper Eichmann," trans. M. Jolas, *Democracy* I (1981), 2: 81; this is itself cited by Lyotard, *The Differend*, No. 2.

19. What follows is a paraphrase of Amos 5:18–24, one of the most important texts in the prophetic literature on justice, which is what I call here the myth of justice as opposed to the myth of Being (see also Isaiah 1:10–17). This prophetic voice is today the voice of liberation theology, which constitutes the Christian churches' finest hour in this century, their most biblical moment, the essential—if I may use this word—gesture of religion.

20. See my *Radical Hermeneutics*, pp. 266–67.

21. My thanks to Andrew McKenna for his help in rethinking these final paragraphs, which differ from the original version.

8. Heidegger's Poets

1. This thesis has been defended with great acumen and sensitivity by Gerald Bruns, *Heidegger's Estrangements* (New Haven: Yale University Press, 1989). Bruns's book is best read as a second or demythologizing reading of Heidegger, a reading that holds Heidegger's hands to the fire of poetry in a way of which Heidegger himself is incapable—a reading from which, I might say, Heidegger himself is "estranged." Bruns has written the sort of book about Heidegger's poets that one would write who reads beyond the difficulties of Heidegger's essentializing, mythologizing, allegorizing tendencies.

2. Veronique Foti, *Heidegger and the Poets*, p. xix.

3. Foti, p. xix.

4. Of course we know how steadfastly this mythologizing thinking avoids pathos. In *The Truth in Painting*, trans. G. Bennington (Chicago: University of Chicago Press,

1987), Derrida quite rightly describes the account of the shoes in the van Gogh painting as "a moment of pathetic collapse, derisory, and symptomatic, significant" (262); he refers to it as a "ridiculous and lamentable" passage and speaks of the "heaviness of the pathos" (292); a "pathetic tirade" (320). For an equally lamentable text, see "Warum Bleiben Wir in der Provinz?" in GA 13, 9–14.

5. I have discussed these matters above, chapter 7.

6. A Derridian formulation. Throughout *Of Spirit,* Derrida is asking about the "return" of the *revenant,* i.e., the recurrence of *Geist* after it has been put in scare quotes in *Being and Time* (like *Wesen*), another essence/spirit.

7. In fact, of course, far from being a cause for celebration, the sight of the wounded, dying soldiers actually precipitated the poet's suicide. We know that this poem was composed on the front when Trakl had volunteered to serve in the Austro-Serbian war and was assigned to work in a field hospital unit. At the battle of Grodek, in 1914, he was faced with caring for ninety seriously wounded casualties, for which he had neither adequate professional preparation nor the drugs. As Frank Graziano writes: "At one point the moans and the agony cries of the injured soldiers were shattered by a gunshot; one suffering patient had committed suicide. Having run to attend to this death, Trakl was repulsed and overwhelmed by fragments of the patient's brain sticking to the wall. He ran from the barn in which the hospital was housed in order to escape this horror, but outside yet another nightmare awaited him: the limp bodies of hanged partisans were swinging in the trees" (*Georg Trakl: A Profile,* ed. F. Graziano [Durango, Colorado: Logbridge-Rhodes, 1983], p. 15). Shortly afterwards, having attempted suicide unsuccessfully, Trakl was hospitalized, where he died a short time later from a self-administered overdose of cocaine. For more on Trakl, see Herbert Lindenberger, *Georg Trakl,* Twayne World Authors Series (New York: Twayne, 1971).

8. Jacob Wassermann, *Caspar Hauser,* trans. Caroline Newton (New York: Carroll & Graf, 1985).

9. Antigone herself is never mentioned in *An Introduction to Metaphysics;* it is as if the title of the play is written in such large letters across the play that Heidegger never notices the woman. When she is discussed later, in GA 53, 127ff. (*"Das Wesen des Antigone"*), she is drawn into the violence of *deinon* celebrated in IM.

10. On Heidegger as allegorist, see Bruns, pp. 68–69.

11. For faithful reproductions of Heidegger's view of pain in the Trakl essays see Parvis Emad, "Heidegger on Pain: Focussing on a Recurring Theme of His Thought," *Zeitschrift für Philosophische Forschung,* 36 (1982), 345–60; and Orville Clark, "Heidegger and the Mystery of Pain," *Man and World,* 10 (1977): 334–50.

12. Heidegger's views are defended on a literary-historical basis by Richard Detsch, *Georg Trakl's Poetry: Towards a Union of Opposites* (University Park: Pennsylvania State University Press, 1983). His most strident critic is W. H. Rey, "Heidegger-Trakl: Einstimmiges Zwiegespräch," *Deutsche Vierteljahresschrift,* 30 (1956), 89–136.

13. Neither do I concede Hölderlin to Heidegger. As Foti (*Heidegger and the Poets,* chapter 4) shows, Hölderlin is also cleaned up to meet the needs of essential thinking.

14. See chapter 2, above.

15. I am applying here to Heidegger both the logic and the rhetoric of *revenant* in Derrida's *Of Spirit;* see OS, 83ff.

16. Foti, p. xx. For an excellent account of the distance between Trakl and Heidegger's *Erörterung* see Foti, 13ff. and also her earlier "The Path of the Stranger: Heidegger's Interpretation of Trakl," *Review of Existential Psychology & Psychiatry,* 17 (1986), 223–33.

17. In chapter 2, "Heidegger's *Kampf,*" I argued that Heidegger celebrated milita-

rism, the danger and the struggle; now I argue that he mystifies it. Either way, he consistently deflects violence and destruction.

18. The debate about the Christian character of Trakl's poetry, which raged in the 1950s, was set off by Eduard Lachmann, *Kreuz und Abend,* Trakl Studien I (Salzburg: Müller, 1954), who was challenged by Walter Killy. See *Euphorion,* 52 (1958), 397–413, for an exchange between the two.

19. The Holocaust is a fundamental concern of the poetry of Celan, which also belongs to Heidegger's silence.

20. In *Against Ethics,* pp. 1–19 *et passim,* I express my reservations about the word "ethics," about what Derrida calls its complacency, hypocrisy, and self-assurance. For present purposes, and by way of not letting things get any more complicated than need be, I use the word "ethics" to mean a concern with human well-being. See Derrida, "Passions: 'An Oblique Offering," *Derrida: A Critical Reader,* ed. David Wood (Oxford: Blackwell, 1992), pp. 14–15.

21. "Heidegger's Original Ethics," *The New Scholasticism,* 45 (1971), 127–38 (p. 133).

22. See William Richardson, "Heidegger's Truth and Politics," in *Spirit and Danger,* eds. Charles Scott, Arleen Dallery, and Holley Roberts (Albany: SUNY Press, 1992), pp. 11–24; in this piece Richardson argues that Heidegger "skidded" into Nazism because he was "seduced" (p. 17) by *die Irre;* he asks, "But how could it have been otherwise?" (p. 18). Are we to believe that *die Irre* made him do it?

23. Dreyfus made this observation in the discussion following the presentation of this paper at the Spindel Conference, Memphis State University, 1989.

24. I am not saying that you cannot make pain a metaphor for something else. I am just saying that one has to judge whether that makes for a more interesting case, and I am sounding an alarm about thinking suffering away.

9. Heidegger's Gods

1. I borrow this expression from Gadamer, who is himself adapting it from Nohl's edition of Hegel's "Early Theological Writings." Gadamer used it to introduce Heidegger's 1922 Aristotle lecture, which appeared in *Dilthey-Jahrbuch,* 6 (1989): 228–69.

2. A late nineteenth-century movement emphasizing the historical limits of dogmatic formulations which was condemned by the Vatican as a form of relativism. Graduates of pontifical universities have for many years taken an "oath against modernism."

3. See "Martin Heidegger's Contributions to *Der Akademiker,*" with a preface by Hugo Ott, trans. John Protevi in *Graduate Faculty New School Journal,* 14–15 (1990–91): 481–519; see pp. 492–493.

4. Ott, *Martin Heidegger: Unterwegs zu seiner Biographie,* pp. 44–104; the Görres citation: p. 64; the grant to study Thomism: 79; passed over for Chair: 91–92. For more on Heidegger's early Catholicism, see my *Heidegger and Aquinas: An Essay on Overcoming Metaphysics,* chapter 1; and especially Kisiel, *The Genesis,* chapter 2.

5. The habilitation dissertation is found in GA I. It has not been translated. I have discussed it in some detail in "Phenomenology, Mysticism, and the *Grammatica Speculativa,*" *Journal of the British Society for Phenomenology,* 5 (1974), 101–17. See also Roderick Stewart, "Signification and Radical Subjectivity in Heidegger's 'Habilitationsschrift',"' *Man and World,* 12 (1979), 360–68; and Kisiel, *The Genesis,* pp. 25–38.

6. This letter can be found in *Heidegger and Aquinas,* p. 60; cf. 56.

7. Karl Löwith, "The Political Implications of Heidegger's Existentialism," *New German Critique,* 45 (1988), 121–22. For a commentary see Theodore Kisiel, "War der frühe Heidegger tatsächlich ein 'christlicher Theologe'?" *Philosophie und Poesie:*

Otto Pöggeler zum 60. Geburtstag, ed. Annemarie Gethmann-Siefert (Berlin: Frommann-Holzboog, 1988), 59–75. The letter itself can be found in D. Paperfuss and O. Pöggeler, eds. *Zur philosophischen Aktualität Heideggers,* B. 2: *Im Gespräch der Zeit* (Frankfurt: Klostermann, 1990).

8. In addition to chapters 2 and 3, above, see Otto Pöggeler, *Heidegger's Path of Thinking,* pp. 24–32, and "Being as Appropriation," *Philosophy Today,* 19 (1975), pp. 156–58.

9. See *Kerygma and Myth* (New York: Harper & Row, 1961). On Heidegger and Bultmann, see John Macquarrie, *An Existentialist Theology: A Comparison of Heidegger and Bultmann* (New York: Harper Torchbooks, 1965); Hans Georg Gadamer, "Martin Heidegger and Marburg Theology," in *Philosophical Hermeneutics,* trans. D. Linge (Berkeley: University of California Press, 1976), 198–212.

10. "Phenomenology and Theology" in Martin Heidegger, *The Piety of Thinking,* trans. J. Hart and J. Maraldo (Bloomington: Indiana University Press, 1976), pp. 3–22. The German text is in GA 9.

11. See above, chapters 2 and 3; on Luther, see Alister E. McGrath, *Luther's Theology of the Cross: Martin Luther's Theological Breakthrough* (Oxford: Blackwell, 1985).

12. For Heidegger's hostility to Christianity during these years see Ott, pp. 259–67; and Tertulian, "The History of Being and Political Revolution," p. 218: "It is the fury against Christianity that is striking in the Heideggerian discourse of this period." See also Hugo Ott, "Heidegger's 'Mentality of Disunity.'" in *The Heidegger Case,* pp. 93–113.

13. Ott, *Martin Heidegger,* pp. 255–59.

14. Caputo, *The Mystical Element in Heidegger's Thought,* pp. 137–39.

15. He had announced a lecture course on medieval mysticism for 1919 but the preparations for the course were apparently interrupted by the First World War and the course was never given. Käte Oltmanns, a Heidegger student in the late 1920s, published a book on Eckhart in 1935, which had been a dissertation done under Heidegger's direction; see Käte Oltmanns, *Meister Eckhart,* 2nd. ed. (Frankfurt: Klostermann, 1957). For a full account of these matters see my *The Mystical Element in Heidegger's Thought* and Kisiel, *The Genesis,* pp. 108–12.

16. *Martin Heidegger in Gespräch,* ed. R. Wisser (Freiburg: Alber, 1970), pp. 48–49; see Rahner's doctoral dissertation *Spirit in the World,* trans. William Dych (New York: Herder & Herder, 1968); *Hearers of the Word* (New York: Seabury Press, 1969); *On the Theology of Death* (New York: Seabury Press, 1971). Rahner also discussed *Being and Time* in "The Concept of Existential Philosophy in Heidegger," trans. A. Tallon, *Philosophy Today,* 13 (1969), 126–37. On Heidegger and Rahner, see Thomas Sheehan, *Rahner: The Philosophical Foundations* (Athens: Ohio University Press, 1985) and my "Heidegger and Aquinas: Deconstructing the Rahnerian Bridge," *Philosophy and Theology* (1990), disk supplement. For a discussion of Heidegger and Lotz, Siewerth, and Müller, see my *Heidegger and Aquinas,* chapter 7. A good account of the later Heidegger and Catholic theology can be found in Richard Schaeffler, *Frömmigkeit des Denkens: Martin Heidegger und die Katholische Theologie* (Darmstadt, 1978). See also *Heidegger et la question de dieu,* eds. R. Kearney and Joseph O'Leary (Paris, 1980). The best recent work by a Catholic theologian with a distinctly Heideggerian inspiration is Joseph O'Leary, *Questioning Back: The Overcoming of Metaphysics in Christian Tradition* (Minneapolis: Winston Press, 1985).

17. Heinrich Ott, *Denken und Sein: Der Weg Martin Heideggers und der Weg der Theologie* (Zollikon: 1959); *The Later Heidegger and Theology,* eds. J. Robinson and J. Cobb (New York: Harper & Row, 1963). See also Heinrich Ott, "The Hermeneutic

and Personal Structure of Language," in *On Heidegger and Language,* ed. Joseph Kocklemans (Evanston: Northwestern University Press, 1972); *Theology and Preaching,* trans. Harold Knight (London: Lutterworth Press, 1965).

18. See the dialogue between Heidegger and the theologians constructed by Derrida in OS, 110–113, in which Derrida has the theologians assure Heidegger, "You say the most radical things that can be said when one is a Christian today." That is because Heidegger has lifted this discourse from Christianity.

19. Søren Kierkegaard, *The Concept of Anxiety,* trans. Reidar Thomte (Princeton: Princeton University Press, 1980), pp. 89–90.

20. See Emmanuel Levinas, *Nine Talmudic Readings,* trans. Annette Aronowicz (Bloomington: Indiana University Press, 1990), pp. 91ff.

21. Pöggeler, *Heidegger's Path of Thought,* p. 272.

22. There is a vast literature on Heidegger and Eastern religion. The best single volume is *Heidegger and Asian Thought,* ed. Graham Parkes (Honolulu: University of Hawaii Press, 1987). See also my *The Mystical Element,* pp. 203–17.

23. Welte had taken up Heidegger's work in a forceful and interesting way on the Catholic side by extending Heidegger's view that the illusion of human mastery overshadows the appearance of God. Welte also wrote sensitively about Heidegger, Meister Eckhart, and Thomas Aquinas. See Bernard Welte, "The Question of God in the Thought of Heidegger," *Philosophy Today,* 25 (1982), 85–100; "La Métaphysique de Saint Thomas d'Aquin et la pensée de l'histoire de l'être de Heidegger," *Revue des Sciences Philosophiques et Théologiques,* 50 (1966), 601–14.

24. "Seeking and Finding: The Speech at Heidegger's Burial," in *Heidegger: The Man and the Thinker,* ed. Thomas Sheehan (Chicago: Precedent Publishing, 1981), pp. 73–75. See also Sheehan's useful biographical piece on Heidegger's early years in this same volume (3–19).

10. Hyperbolic Justice

1. That, of course, was the idea behind Heidegger's first Freiburg lectures on the hermeneutics of facticity.

2. I have developed this divide in *Against Ethics,* chapter 3, as has Edith Wyschogrod in *Saints and Postmodernism,* pp. 191, 223, 229.

3. Hannah Arendt, *The Human Condition* (Chicago: University of Chicago Press, 1956), p. 222; cf. pp. 220–230 and 192–197.

4. Not to mention the abyss within the agent, the destabilization of agency by everything that decenters the subject.

5. The analogy of Heidegger and Plato is tempting.

6. Philippe Lacoue-Labarthe, *Heidegger, Art and Politics,* pp. 61–70, 93–98.

7. One problem with Richard Wolin's *The Politics of Being: The Political Thought of Martin Heidegger* is his failure to see—induced by a preoccupation with Habermas, which invariably blinds one to what is going on in postmodern writing—that such "anarchy" is not reducible to Carl Schmitt's authoritarianism, to a right-wing call for a suspension of universal law in the name of a powerful leader. He misses the biblically inspired left-wing anarchy, deriving from Levinas and Derrida, which leaves law in place while calling for justice for everyone the law grinds under. See Wolin, pp. 28–35, 53–66.

8. On the notion of terror as the reduction of an opponent, as utter elimination from a game, see Jean François Lyotard, *Just Gaming,* trans. Wlad Godzich (Minneapolis: University of Minnesota Press, 1985), pp. 67–68, 99–100; on the "victim" as one whose capacity for dissent or for registering dissent is eliminated, see *The Differend,* pp. 9–14.

9. This is neither Plato's *anamnesis*, nor Hegel's *Erinnerung*, nor Heidegger's *Wiederholung*.

10. These are the terms in which Constantin Constantius complains about having been thrown into actuality without having been consulted; see Kierkegaard, *Repetition*, pp. 200–201.

11. Because it is the myth of every time and place, of everything that has a proper name and has a date; see Lyotard, *The Differend*, No. 179.

12. I will not say it is more a Jewish myth than a Greek myth but more a jewgreek myth than a pure Greek myth. That is why Lacoue-Labarthe is mistaken to agree with Blanchot that, because they reject idols, "the Jews embody the rejection of myths." (Lacoue-Labarthe, *Heidegger, Art and Politics*, p. 96). As the authors of one of the world's great bodies of literature, they had a powerful mythic imagination, albeit one which refused to express itself in graven images. Their mythic imagination had nothing to do with the "fiction" of politics in Lacoue-Labarthe's sense but with a myth of another sort, a myth of justice and the law. On the Jewish imagination, see Elaine Scarry, *The Body in Pain*, pp. 60ff., and Richard Kearney, *The Wake of Imagination* (London: Hutchinson, 1988), pp. 37–78.

13. Edith Wyschogrod makes this point very well in *Saints and Postmodernism: Revisioning Moral Philosophy*, pp. 1–31.

14. I am not saying that Derrida subscribes to a myth of origins, and still less that he subscribes to Benjamin's "mythic violence"—discussed by Derrida in the second half of "The Force of Law"—which he thinks communicates with aestheticizing, mimetic myth (cf. FL, 1041). The myth of undeconstructible justice is a myth of quite a different sort, as I hope to show here.

15. In the second half of "The Force of Law," Derrida discusses Walter Benjamin's claim that the law is inherently violent, both in its original founding and in the way it sustains itself in existence, that occasionally its naked violence is exposed, and that parliamentary systems are naive to think otherwise. See Walter Benjamin, "The Critique of Violence," in *Reflections*, ed. Peter Demetz (New York: Schocken Books, 1978), pp. 277–300. Benjamin is pushing the "constructed" character of the law to an anarchistic extreme rejected by Derrida, who is set not on the destruction but on the deconstruction of the law (cf. FL, 1044–45) and who wants to keep up the communication between justice and the law. Dominic Capra seems to think that Derrida is inadvertently implicated in just such a violent view of law in "Violence, Justice and the Force of Law," in *Cardozo Law Review*, 11 (1990), 1065–78; see Drucilla Cornell's rebuttal of that point of view in "The Violence of Masquerade," *Cardozo Law Review*, 1047–64.

16. This is no place to recount the essentials of *Fear and Trembling*. Apart from the famous account of the decision made in the dark night of faith, I draw the attention of the reader to the recurrent economic images in this text in which de Silentio accuses Christendom of looking for a bargain in matters of faith (getting it *aufgehoben* in speculative thought) and of trying, to use Derrida's felicitous expression, to "economize on anxiety." Like the merchants in Holland who threw their spices into the sea to drive up the price, de Silentio wants to drive up the price of faith. See *Fear and Trembling* in *"Repetition" and "Fear and Trembling,"* pp. 5, 27, 121. Just so, deconstruction wants to drive up the price of a just decision. In "Donner la mort," in *L'éthique du don: Jacques Derrida et la pensée du don* (Paris: Métailié, 1992), pp. 11–108, a work published after the completion of this study, Derrida confirms my hunch about Kierkegaard by presenting an interesting and substantive discussion of *Fear and Trembling* on the suspension of universality in the name of singularity; Derrida also brings Levinas's views closer to Kierkegaard's.

17. Derrida is critical of Kant's desire for a clean cut (the regionalizing, border-patrolling character of the three critiques) in *Truth in Painting*, trans. Geoff Bennington and Ian McLeod (Chicago: University of Chicago Press, 1987), pp. 83ff. In the "Afterword," trans. Sam Weber, to *Limited, Inc.* (Evanston: Northwestern University Press, 1988), pp. 152–53, Derrida does speak of an "unconditional appeal," explicitly mentioning Kant, but he means by that nothing noumenal, no traditional "philosopheme," nothing "simply present . . . outside of all context"—but the constant claim of the moment of non-closure, of the one who interrupts the operation of totalization.

18. On the inadequacy of Levinas as a political thinker, see "Ethics and Politics" in *The Levinas Reader,* ed. Sean Hand (Oxford: Blackwell, 1989), pp. 289–97, in which Levinas has not quite reconciled himself to the thought that the Palestinians represent the "other" who call upon the Israelis, who demand their affirmation; he thinks instead that it is a good idea to keep an army on hand for self-defense.

19. Levinas distinguishes biblical holiness (*saint,* apartness, transcendence) from Heideggerian paganism (*sacré,* immanence) in *Nine Talmudic Readings,* pp. 140–141 and 91ff. *et passim.*

20. This text of Meister Eckhart is cited by Derrida in his famous "Violence and Metaphysics" article on Levinas in *Writing and Difference,* trans. Alan Bass (Chicago: University of Chicago Press, 1978), p. 146. The point of this remark, Derrida rightly points out, is to affirm the Being of an infinite existent. For a fuller treatment of Derrida and negative theology, see my "Mysticism and Transgression: Derrida and Meister Eckhart," *Continental Philosophy,* II (1989), 24–41.

21. Levinas tries to take precautions against just such a claim at the beginning of *Otherwise than Being or Beyond Essence,* trans. Alphonso Lingis (The Hague: Martinus Nijhoff, 1981), pp. 3–4.

22. For a fuller account, see *The Mystical Element in Heidegger's Thought,* p. 125. Meister Eckhart and I are taken to task for this recourse to emphatic language by Alasdair MacIntrye, *Three Rival Versions of Moral Enquiry: Encyclopedia, Genealogy and Tradition* (Notre Dame: University of Notre Dame Press, 1990), pp. 167–69. In *Otherwise than Being,* pp. 183–84, Levinas claims that his own analysis proceeds by way of "hyperbole," by which he means the surpassing excellence of transcendence and exteriority. He does not mean an operation of *différance,* as I do.

23. This is the point of my *Against Ethics;* see pp. 1–5.

24. The argument Derrida mounts against negative theology in his debate with Jean-Luc Marion applies in its essentials to Levinas. See "How to Avoid Speaking: Denials," in *Languages of the Unsayable,* ed. S. Budick and W. Iser (New York: Columbia University Press, 1990), 3–70.

25. In an interview with Richard Kearney, Derrida says, "It is possible to see deconstruction as being produced in a space where the prophets are not far away." See Richard Kearney, *Dialogues with Contemporary Continental Thinkers* (Manchester: Manchester University Press, 1984), p. 119.

26. Neither should it be confused with Benjamin's "divine justice," which for Derrida opens up the possibility of seeing the Holocaust as an expiation demanded by a just and angry God (FL, 1044–45). Seyla Benhabib suggests that Derrida and Levinas are taking up in their own way a "negative utopianism," the utopia of what can never be represented or named, the gesture of an unnameable hope, which is more biblical than Greek, and which is first found in Adorno and Benjamin; see Benhabib's "Critical Theory and Postmodernism," *Cardozo Law Review,* 11 (1990), 1446–47, n. 27. That is an interesting suggestion.

27. For further evidence, if such is still needed, of the concrete political engagement of deconstruction, see the recent, extensive (663 pages) collection of Derrida's work

on the university and educational politics entitled *Du droit à la philosophie* (Paris: Galilée, 1990).

28. Because Levinas thinks that myth is always a myth of Being, that it is always on this side of Being, he calls for the "demythization of the myths." *Otherwise than Being,* p. 180. In my view, the saying of a signification on the other side of the said, of absolute proximity and of passivity, is not only a "demythization" (or demythologization) of the myth of the sacred earth, but also the constitution of another myth, a prophetic and hyperbolic myth of responsibility and of what is otherwise than being.

11. Conclusion

1. Derrida, *The Other Heading,* pp. 110–11.

2. This is not a purely formalistic strategy taken without regard to the merits of the case. Derrida does not side with homicidal rapists if they happen to be out of favor. The "marginalized" are always victims, not producers of victims.

3. Lyotard, *The Differend,* No. 113, p. 70.

4. Lyotard, *Heidegger and "the jews,"* pp. 91–94.

5. Derrida, "Des Tours de Babel," trans. Joseph F. Graham in *Difference in Translation,* ed. Joseph F. Graham (Ithaca: Cornell University Press, 1985), pp. 165ff.

6. I have developed this argument in "Beyond Aestheticism: Derrida's Responsible Anarchy," *Research in Phenomenology,* 18 (1988): 59–73, small parts of which I am including in the present chapter with the kind permission of Humanities Press. I am gratified to report that in "Donner la mort" Derrida has recently and definitively settled the hash of those critics who think that deconstruction is an aestheticism rather than something "ethico-religious"; see above, ch. 10, n.16.

7. See Derrida, "Passions: 'An Oblique Offering,'" trans. David Wood, in *Derrida: A Critical Reader,* ed. David Wood (Oxford: Blackwell, 1992), pp. 13–15.

8. Jean François Lyotard, *Just Gaming,* trans. Wlad Godzich (Minneapolis: University of Minnesota Press, 1985), pp. 14–16.

9. See my discussion of scientific rationality from a poststructuralist position in *Radical Hermeneutics,* pp. 214–22.

10. Lyotard has recently spoken on behalf of the "inhuman," given that the effect of speaking in the name of humanism is to abolish difference, experimentation, heterogeneity, and dissent. See "About the Human" in *The Inhuman: Reflections on Time,* trans. Geoffrey Bennington and Rachel Bowlby (Stanford: Stanford University Press, 1991), pp. 1–7. Speaking in another idiom but to the same point—viz., that inhumanity is insensitivity to alterity—Levinas says that the truth of "modern anti-humanism" is its displacement of exaggerated views of the subject. "Humanism has to be denounced," Levinas says, "only because it is not sufficiently human." *Otherwise than Being,* pp. 127–128.

11. See Kierkegaard, *Philosophical Fragments,* pp. 23–37: if the disciple is in the untruth, then one must be given the truth by a teacher; one cannot recollect it.

12. See also Hannah Arendt's notion of "natality" in *The Human Condition,* pp. 177–78.

13. Levinas, *Totality and Infinity,* p. 80.

14. See Kearney, *Dialogues with Contemporary Continental Thinkers,* p. 107.

15. *Dialogues with Contemporary Thinkers,* p. 107.

16. See chapter 9 of *Against Ethics.*

17. I spoke above of another, more "critical" thinking of the *Es gibt,* as opposed to a "memorializing" thinking (chapter 1); of another responsibility (chapter 4); of making the privilege granted to Greeks and Germans by the question of Being tremble in questionability (chapter 5).

INDEX

Abraham, 7, 51, 62, 161, 175, 181, 191, 192, 210, 213
Adorno, Theodor, 131
Aeschylus, 87, 97, 117, 177
Aletheia, 2, 16, 19–29, 33, 70, 122, 129, 166, 167, 184; as correctness, 18–21, 24; in Plato, 23–25
Allegory, 158–60, 162–63
Amos, 3, 146, 201
Anaximander, 5, 19, 22, 26, 30, 31
Angelus Silesius, 29
Animals, 120, 122–27, 158
Antigone of Sophocles, 111–13, 117, 191, 192, 204, 225n9
Apartness, 155–58
Aquinas, Thomas, 64, 120, 170, 172
Arendt, Hannah, 41, 64, 187, 188
Aristotle, 4, 5, 6, 10, 13, 17, 18, 19, 20, 22, 24, 25, 32, 41, 44, 45, 50, 51, 52, 55, 56, 57, 58, 61, 62, 63, 64, 67, 72, 74, 75, 117, 118, 120, 169, 172, 175, 211
Atheism, 43, 175–76
Augustine, 51, 61, 131, 132, 172, 175
Austen, Jane, 63

Barth, Karl, 180
Baudrillard, Jean, 187
Being and Time, 9–16, 75–82, 172–73
Bennett, William, 192
Bloom, Allan, 63, 93, 192
Brentano, Franz, 16
Buber, Martin, 211
Bultmann, Rudolph, 3, 10, 132, 173, 180, 182

Call, 75, 78–79, 81–82, 83, 84, 88, 93–94, 99, 137–38, 143, 147, 186, 204, 206, 207, 208, 210
Catholicism, Roman, 170–72, 175, 176, 179–80, 184–85, 217n3, 217–18n2, 227n15, 228n23
Celan, Paul, 132, 148, 161
Cézanne, Paul, 35
Clausewitz, Karl von, 90, 178
Climacus, Johannes, 51, 62, 203
Conscience, 75–78, 99
Constantius, Constantine, 51, 62
Critical history, 29–33, 36, 37

Danger, 53–54, 55, 56, 72, 88–89, 111, 117, 225–26n17

Deconstruction, 2, 3, 7, 11, 21, 61, 62, 93, 98, 106, 131, 160, 187–89, 192–93, 199, 206–07, 209, 210, 213
Deleuze, Gilles, 187
Demythologizing, 3, 5, 7–8, 9, 29, 38, 59, 83, 91, 92, 95, 115, 131, 186, 200, 202, 208, 214, 231n28; Heidegger's thought as a form of, 10, 169–70, 173, 181
Derrida, Jacques, 1, 2, 3, 6, 7, 8, 23, 25, 57, 59, 84, 93, 99, 103, 119, 120, 122, 124, 128, 154, 187, 189, 192, 193, 194, 195, 196, 197, 199, 200, 201, 205, 206, 209, 210, 211, 212, 213
Descartes, René, 11, 13, 71, 120, 126, 192, 199, 205
De Silentio, Johannes, 74, 196
Destruction of the history of ontology, 10–11, 13, 17, 171
Différance, 23, 25, 126, 187, 197, 200, 202, 205, 209, 210
Difficulty, 40–41, 46–47, 52, 55–56, 58, 62, 68, 71, 74, 90, 106–07, 174
Dike, 31, 144
Dilthey, Wilhelm, 44, 171
Dreyfus, Hubert, 167
Duns Scotus, 61, 170, 171, 172
Dwelling, 136–39

Ecology, 183
Ereignis, 16, 22, 30–31, 35, 37, 91, 200
Essentialization, 6, 73, 74, 78–79, 80–81, 85, 116, 118–30, 131, 139, 157, 161, 162, 164, 165, 190, 214, 224n11; *see also* Wesen
Ethics, 166–68, 187–89, 198, 200, 206, 211, 212, 216n22, 226n20
Evil, 154, 156, 157, 158, 159, 164, 165, 166

Factical life, 44–50, 55, 56, 60, 65–69, 73, 74, 79, 85, 121, 130, 164–65, 167–68, 172; *see also* Hermeneutics of facticity
Facticity. *See* Factical life
Faith, 174–76
Farias, Victor, 2, 105, 114
Faurrison, Robert, 145
Feeling, 68–72, 129, 149–50, 164
Fichte, Johann Gottlieb, 84
Fiction, 191, 229n12
First Beginning, 1, 4, 18, 19, 27, 28, 36, 73, 74, 87, 91, 93, 95–96, 102, 108, 109–10,

115, 144, 173, 182, 184, 190, 191, 201, 208, 213–14, 221n14
Fischer-Barnicol, Hans A., 132
Flesh, 57–58, 65–72, 162, 183
Fóti, Véronique, 148, 159, 165
Foucault, Michel, 35, 213
Fourfold, the, 182–83
Francis, Saint, 123
Franzen, Winfried, 53

Gadamer, Hans-Georg, 41, 64, 99, 211
Galileo, 32
Gelassenheit, 29, 36, 112, 118, 146, 178, 179
Genet, Jean, 202, 205
Gestell, 35, 56, 120, 133, 135, 155, 158, 166, 182–83
God, 76, 79, 93, 99–100, 119, 169–80, 182, 183–84, 197, 200, 202, 205
Gods, the, 182–83
Görres, Josef von, 170
Great Beginning. *See* First Beginning
Great Greek Beginning. *See* First Beginning
Gröber, Conrad, 179
Guattari, Felix, 187

Habermas, Jürgen, 102
Haecker, Theodor, 176
Heart, 59, 60ff. *See also Kardia*
Hegel, G. W. F., 51, 62, 120, 202, 203, 209
Heidegger, Elfride, 171
Heraclitus, 5, 40, 90, 108, 109, 110, 117, 136, 178, 179, 181, 213
Hermeneutics: radical, 98; postmodern, 100; allegorizing, 159–60
Hermeneutics of facticity, 3, 6, 41, 50–52, 56, 58, 59, 63, 67, 73–74, 85, 118, 119, 131, 164, 172
Historicality, 80–82, 83
Hofstadter, Albert, 136
Hölderlin, Friedrich, 5, 28, 29, 34, 55, 56, 72, 83, 111, 119, 144, 148, 160, 161, 163
Holocaust, the, 131, 132, 134, 142, 148
Homer, 23
Honecker, Martin, 175
Husserl, Edmund, 25, 26, 29, 44, 49, 50, 52, 67, 72, 84, 121, 165, 170, 171, 172, 175

Isaac, 192
Ishmael, 161

Jaensch, Walter, 105, 110
Jewgreek, 6–7, 41–42, 50, 130, 159, 160–61, 163, 165, 169–70, 206, 209–14, 216n21
Job, 196
Joyce, James, 6, 7, 29
Jünger, Ernst, 5, 52, 55, 58, 72, 111
Justice, 31, 37–38, 74, 116, 128–29, 144, 146, 166, 184, 186, 188, 189–208. *See also* Myth: of justice

Kafka, Franz, 161
Kampf, 6, 39–59, 60, 72, 82, 90, 109–12, 162, 174, 178, 179, 218–19n14
Kant, Immanuel, 10, 11, 13, 14, 17, 86, 98, 120, 172, 194, 197, 199, 205
Kardia, 6, 5, 60–74, 124, 184, 195, 212, 213
Kaspar Hauser, 156–57
Kierkegaard, Søren, 5, 6, 12, 17, 42, 45, 47, 48, 51, 56, 57, 61, 65, 72, 75, 116, 172, 175, 181, 196, 197, 203, 210, 211
King, Martin Luther, 192
Kisiel, Theodore, 3, 56, 61
Krebs, Engelbert, 171
Krieck, Ernst, 105
Kuhn, Thomas, 32, 211
Kundera, Milan, 107

Lacoue-Labarthe, Philippe, 2, 133, 149, 188, 191
Law, 189–90, 193–96, 205, 206, 211, 229n15
Leibniz, 92
Levinas, Emmanuel, 2, 3, 7, 8, 59, 74, 99, 116, 129, 165, 167, 187, 194, 195, 197, 198, 199, 200, 201, 202, 205, 206, 209, 210, 211, 212, 213
Lotz, Johannes, 179–80
Löwith, Karl, 56, 83, 172
Luther, Martin, 6, 51, 57, 61, 172, 174, 175
Lyotard, Jean-François, 2, 3, 7, 8, 58, 59, 131, 143, 144, 145, 152, 162, 187, 206, 209, 210, 211, 212, 213

MacIntyre, Alasdair, 63
Mallarmé, Stéphane, 29
Margolis, Joseph, 2
Maritain, Jacques, 131
Marx, Karl, 108
Meaning, of Being, 10–11, 14–16, 30
Meister Eckhart, 29, 36, 199, 200
Merleau-Ponty, Maurice, 65, 126
Metaphysics, 120–22, 198–99, 201
Mimesis, 188, 191, 197, 207
Modernity, 9–10, 17, 34, 93
Mörike, Eduard, 148
Müller, Max, 175, 179
Myth: of Being, 2–3, 4, 5, 6, 9, 16–17, 37–38, 39, 59, 74, 75, 82, 91, 101, 133, 169, 177, 185, 186–87, 213–14, 231n28; of the Great Beginning: *see* First Beginning; of justice, 2–3, 6–7, 116, 183–84, 185, 186–87, 189–208, 229n12
Mythologizing, 1, 9, 21, 28, 29, 82–83, 95, 100, 121–22, 148–49, 159, 169–70, 181, 186–87, 190, 191, 208, 215n7, 216n18, 229n12, 231n28

National Socialism, 2, 4, 5, 40–41, 82–90, 91–92, 101–17, 131, 174–78, 179

New Testament, 4, 6, 41, 45, 50–52, 55, 57, 58, 61, 62–64, 74, 118, 172, 181, 213
Nietzsche, Friedrich, 1, 5, 42, 44, 52, 58, 64, 72, 93, 101, 108, 120, 127, 128, 175, 177, 179, 209, 213

Oedipus, 111
Ott, Heinrich, 180
Ott, Hugo, 2, 105, 114
Ousia, 12–13, 120

Pain, 57–58, 67, 68, 70, 120, 127–29, 137, 149–55, 159–60, 162–63, 165, 167–68, 226n24
Parmenides, 5, 162, 181, 211, 213
Pascal, 45, 51, 52, 61, 172, 175
Paul, 51, 52, 55, 56, 61, 63, 172, 174, 177
Phainesthai, 22, 25, 29, 63, 70, 142, 145, 152, 157, 164, 211
Phainesthetics, 142–44, 145, 146, 152, 154, 162, 163–66, 170, 211
Philosophy, 42, 48–50, 57, 59, 61, 72, 103–07, 212–13
Phronesis, 50, 62–65, 196, 219n8, 220n2
Physis, 111, 112, 113, 166–67, 184, 198–99
Plato, 10, 13, 16, 17, 18, 19, 20, 22, 23, 24, 25, 36, 40, 43, 51, 69, 120, 139, 155, 164, 175, 182, 188, 194, 197, 199, 201, 205, 211, 212
Poetry, 148–49, 152, 159–66, 224n1
Poets, 109–10, 119, 143, 146, 152, 158, 159, 161–66, 224n1
Pöggeler, Otto, 5
Polyneices, 157
Postmodernism, 106, 187, 201, 213, 218–19n14, 228n7
Prometheus, 87, 88, 90, 162, 177, 178, 179
Proper names, 200–05
Prophetic, the, 2–3, 6, 59, 187, 194, 196, 201–02, 204, 207, 213, 224n19, 230n25
Protestantism, 172–73, 175, 179, 180
Pythagoras, 28, 46

Questionability, 48–49, 88–89, 114, 117, 175–76
Questioning, 42, 88, 96, 101–10, 114–17

Rahner, Karl, 180
Reason, principle of, 92–100

Religious, the, 210–11, 229n16, 231n6
Rembrandt, 202
Revolutionary: Heidegger as, 39–40, 52, 58, 61, 67, 89, 90, 101–17; National Socialist: *see* National Socialism
Richardson, William, 166
Rickert, Heinrich, 43
Rilke, Rainer Marie, 127, 148
Rockmore, Tom, 2
Rorty, Richard, 37, 211

Sarah, 7
Scarry, Elaine, 149
Schelling, F. W. J., 154
Schmeling, Max, 102, 108, 111
Schopenhauer, Arthur, 42
Sheehan, Thomas, 132
Siewerth, Gustav, 179
Singularity, 189, 191–92, 194–96, 197, 200–08, 210
Socrates, 43, 56, 62, 203
Sophocles, 40, 97, 102, 108, 111, 117
Suarez, Francisco, 172

Technology, 132–36, 140–41
Thales, 36
Trakl, Georg, 73, 127, 148, 151, 152, 154, 155, 157, 158, 159, 160, 161, 163, 164, 165
Truth, as *aletheia*. *See aletheia*, as correctness

University, the, 41–44, 52, 56, 72, 82–90, 94, 99, 103

Values, 102, 113, 198, 206
Van Buren, John, 3, 51, 57, 61, 72
Victim, the, 131, 133, 138, 139, 143, 144, 145, 146–47, 183, 228n8, 231n2

Wasserman, Jacob, 156
Weber, Max
Welte, Bernard, 184
Wesen, 6, 26, 51, 84–90, 107, 116, 118, 119, 122, 123, 129, 130, 131, 133, 135, 137, 139, 140, 145, 147, 149, 153, 158, 163, 164, 165, 182, 222n1. *See also* Essentialization
Whitman, Walt, 35
Wilhelm, Judge, 210, 211

JOHN D. CAPUTO is David R. Cook Professor of Philosophy at Villanova University. His publications include *Against Ethics: Contributions to a Poetics of Obligation with Constant Reference to Deconstruction; Radical Hermeneutics: Repetition, Deconstruction, and the Hermeneutic Project; The Mystical Element in Heidegger's Thought;* and *Heidegger and Aquinas: An Essay on Overcoming Metaphysics.*

CPSIA information can be obtained at www.ICGtesting.com
Printed in the USA
BVOW11s0608070415

395039BV00010B/21/P

9 780253 208385